THE UNABASHED SELF-PROMOTER'S GUIDE

WHAT EVERY MAN, WOMEN, CHILD AND ORGANIZATION IN AMERICA NEEDS TO KNOW ABOUT GETTING AHEAD BY EXPLOITING THE MEDIA

BY
DR. JEFFREY L. LANT

THE UNABASHED SELF-PROMOTER'S GUIDE

WHAT EVERY MAN, WOMAN, CHILD AND ORGANIZATION IN AMERICA NEEDS TO KNOW ABOUT GETTING AHEAD BY EXPLOITING THE MEDIA

For Kevin and Shelby, my siblings
in rivalry and revelry.

© Copyright, 1983, Jeffrey Lant Associates, Inc.
ISBN 0-940374-06-4

Reproduction of any portion of this book is permitted for individual use if credit is given to Dr. Jeffrey Lant and Jeffrey Lant Associates, Inc. Systematic or multiple reproduction or distribution of any part of this book or inclusion of items in publications for sale is permitted only with prior written permission.

Acknowledgements: The author wishes to thank Dr. Simone Brenner for assistance during the preparation of the manuscript, Ed Golden of *The Associated Press*, and, as always, John Hamwey who provided his usual competent technical help.

TABLE OF CONTENTS

INTRODUCTION, WHY I WROTE THIS BOOK

This is my fifth book. I have some very pointed reasons for having written it, which I would like to share.

The Poverty of Existing Material

There are, to be sure, books about public relations. Over the last several months I have immersed myself in them with growing fury. They usually focus on a few of the basics, usually on how to write media releases (which most of their authors persist in erroneously calling press releases). Their significant features are:

- a style so boring, sluggish and unappealing that any literate reader could be forgiven for directed derision
- content infuriatingly superficial and unspecific
- a glaring lack of proficiency by the writers about the techniques they are advancing despite the grandiose pretensions of a phrase like "twenty five years as a public relations professional."

Writers write books for many reasons. One of mine was to rage against the prevailing mediocrity of the current literature. You are paying a considerable amount of money for this book; I haven't slept in hotel rooms across America for years and lived a crazy quilt existence to give my media advice away, and I offer no apologies for the handsome profit I am now reaping. But you can at least rest assured you are getting immediately usable information, not pap.

Debunking A Myth

I have also written this book to begin the long process of debunking one of the media's most sacred shibboleths, the myth of its objectivity. In the early spring of 1983 NBC's Tom Brocaw, he of the sybilant esses and irredemably boyish demeanor, outraged significant sections of the media community by giving an interview to **Mother Jones** magazine, a publication which takes suspender-popping pride in rather inconsequential journalistic achievements. Brocaw's interview was, in fact, the slapdash jeremiad of a dressed-up trust-fund hippy: he didn't like Ronald Reagan much, he thought him a poor administrator, he had some better ideas about how the world could be run more humanistically, more communally, and a niagara of comparably ill-advised drivel. Even his mentor Mary McGrory, never known for mincing words, dismissed it out of hand.

What outraged the news media, however, was not the sentiments (which I suspect are widely shared) but the fact that a dragoman of the news should so far forget himself in public as to allow people to suspect he even had views instead of just an empty, if comely, head. Outrageous.

The media want us to believe that they are the repositories of truth and untarnished equity. All other institutions, the theory goes, are frail, human, fraught with personalities, replete with backbiting and pettiness, hypocritical. Not so the media.

Bit by bit the media has been knocking off its institutional adversaries. It is symbolic, to say nothing more, that Woodward and Bernstein, having done their damnedest on the presidency, should have next cast a spotlight on the Supreme Court in a book which has many of the justices looking like creatures come uncertainly from beneath great rocks.

The Great Myth of Journalism is that the press, electronic or print, offers authenticated gospel, received wisdom, unquestioned truth — in a detached fashion beyond criticism.

That is why there is such wailing from within journalistic ranks whenever there is a challenge to this myth.

The Janet Cooke case is a sterling example. This, you will remember, involved an enterprising little lady from the **Washington Post** who lied her way to a Pulitzer Prize stubbornly maintaining that her composite story on infantile drug addiction was in fact one actual case. Anyone not familiar with the Great Myth would have had a good deal of difficulty comprehending just why so much space was devoted to what was essentially a trivial event: a young woman, consumed with a very understandable desire to succeed, lied *con brio* and was caught. Challenged by her superiors, she took the usual way out — and lied some more.

In fact, however, Cooke had all-too-unwittingly threatened the Great Myth, that journalists are dispensers of received truth and can do no wrong. It was very important that she be cast out of the order with every possible malediction so that that order could continue with its role as handler and provider of sacred writ, the new American clerisy, to borrow a phrase from Coleridge.

I have for long found it distressing — if entirely understandable — that this order, which prides itself upon its omnipresence and its determination to know all (and to tell it, too) should be so very, very careful to avoid looking at its own machinery and activities in the same way. There is a very palpable reluctance about doing so.

But with ruling classes it has been ever thus. Mediaeval priests who were incautious enough to scrutinize their own order may receive a good press from latter-day historians but they had, on the whole, a very hot and miserable time in their own day. So it would be for any journalist daring to look too closely at the foibles and practices of his colleagues.

The inevitable result of this general lack of internal scrutiny has come to insure a very privileged position for the media, for remember that they have now succeeded to much of the public trust once reposed collectively in the presidency, the Congress, the Supreme Court, captains of industry and other now tarnished or even toppled titans. The inevitable result is that media people have gathered onto themselves the usual attributes of any ruling class. All too often you will find them, therefore:

- rude
- brusque
- impatient
- arrogant
- elitist
- surly
- abrupt

They manage your time to suit their needs; you, to them, are nothing more than a commodity.

It needs hardly be said that they do not, amongst each other, evince these same distasteful traits. As in all aristocracies, once an individual has passed the difficult portal of entry they become warm, open, sincere, even playful. Within the fraternity the boys and girls of the media are charming creatures.

Recently in reading Kenneth Rose's biography of Lord Curzon, once Viceroy of India and Foreign Secretary in the waning days of the British imperium, I was reminded of this seeming dichotomy. Notoriously stiffnecked in public, Curzon was within his selected circle (called "The Souls") boyishly engaging. He was even known to play lawn tennis in the buff — if his partners all had blood as blue as his own. So it is with many, many media people — and the more prestigious their outlet, the more likely they are to offer the stark contrast between formal hauteur and informal whiffenpoofery.

This is also true, to some extent, if you have once been accepted by the media. I suspect, though it is only a suspicion, that most media personalities and journalists harbor deep-seated insecurities about themselves and their work. They realize their own inadequacies to be the purveyors of truth. They have no outside body of dogma, no Code Journalistique to reinforce their positions; (perhaps we have this to look forward to). They are not well paid (except at the upper reaches), and in a society which is obsessed with ready cash, most journalists are comparatively impecunious and hence abashed.

Today's journalists are like the parvenu down the ages. Insecure themselves, ill prepared to cope with the often awesome power they inevitably have, unaccepted by other powers within the land by whom they (rightly) feel exploited, journalists react according to the time-honored formula of the arriviste: acting with a callous inconsideration, disdain, and manners so appalling they would be the first to complain — vociferously — if they were applied to themselves.

All those who have confronted the media as unknowns have probably experienced this Dark Side of the Force, unless they have been willing to adopt that extremely successful ploy to help deal with the problem. That is, The Ingénue.

The ingénue can be a man or woman. An ingénue is a bright-eyed innocent whose very behavior implicitly confirms the power and authority of the idol. "I am small and meek," the ingénue seems to say, "You are big and strong. You can help me. Please do not let me appeal to you in vain." Such an appeal can work, very very well. This is why many, many successful self-promoters have had a start as the ingénue. Remember the film "All About Eve." As this classic shows in melodramatic detail, the ingénue need not *be* innocent, dewey-eyed or at sea, he must simply appear to be so. All ruling classes are vulnerable to the calculating ingénue, and journalists are no different. Journalists can, in fact, be beguiled by anyone who confirms the public impression they have of themselves as powerful people. An illuminating incident at the Washington Gridiron Club is a good example of what I mean.

Throughout the winter of 1982-83 Ronald Reagan's press flagged. He was widely portrayed as a master rhetorician but a slothful administrator, more interested in lazy vacations than the taffy pull of presidential politics and policy making. Many commentators confidently predicted an early retirement. Then came the Gridiron dinner at which the president, outfitted in serape and sombrero, poked fun at himself in a series of light-hearted satiric verses sung to the tune of "Mañana."

The panjandrums of the press went berserk with joyous celebration. The President of the United States had come to pay tribute to the assembled mandarins in their holy of holies. A spate of wildly enthusiastic articles followed which, when coupled with the first trickle of beneficial economic news, made the president into the darling of the media who had previously dismissed him. Nothing really had changed except that the overweening press, with its cosmic and sensitive ego, had had itself stroked and was willing to repay the presidential obeisance with what it can best give: an avalanche of good press.

Master Media Manipulators

Because he is willing to pay court to the press in just such a fashion, Ronald Reagan is very likely to be perceived as a master politician, to the fury of his opponents who fume and sputter at the apostasy of the media.

But in fact, as thoughtful media commentators are well aware, the media can be gulled and exploited by the crafty as easily as child's play. John F. Kennedy and Henry Kissinger are two examples who readily spring to mind. They, of course, had to spare what the parvenu power brokers dramatically lack: glamor and legitimacy and the pretense of real news. At that potent level it is, of course, most easy to manipulate the media. Kennedy and Kissinger did so with an artful mastery. Had Richard Nixon been less consumed with jealousy about JFK and had mimicked that which was most successful about the unsuccessful Kennedy presidency — his press relations — there would have been no national crucible of Watergate.

Very, very few of us will ever play the media game at that exalted level. However, wherever we play it, we must recognize several salient facts:

- The media constitutes the new American power élite. Reputations are made and broken, fortunes created and multiplied through the media. It is, of course, possible to succeed without the media, and it is possible to fail with their support, but these will increasingly be exceptions. Most individuals wishing to achieve success in this country will need to exploit the media to reach their goal.
- The media sees itself as the purveyor of absolute truth, the standard of right, the new clerisy. This makes them vulnerable to the unabashed self-promoter who has simply to confirm the media's validity and then go to work.
- The media personnel, for all their façade of objectivity, are no more objective than the rest of us. They are constantly advancing the interests of their friends and punishing their enemies by using the powers that are available to them. Remember your Lord Acton, "Power corrupts; absolute power corrupts absolutely." All media personnel have power; some few have absolute power. All are capable of using this power in subjective ways. This book is about how to get them to use it on your behalf and make you in the process more well known, richer, more respected — an individual of perceived importance and worth.

Instruction

Next, I have written this book so that any reasonably intelligent individual can take advantage of the bounteous media possibilities which are available. Reasonable intelligence and unstinting determination are, alas!, necessary. If you lack either, I suggest you give this book to a better audience.

It has pained me to be privy to many, seemingly interminable, discussions with professionals of every description who bewail either their lack of professional recognition, an underpopulated client list, or a pervasive feeling that they are not "reaching their potential" (that odious phrase). Yet these otherwise intelligent people have no media plan, do not appear regularly in the media, have no idea how media personnel should be dealt with, how materials can be gathered and shaped, and on and on.

This book is for them — and for you. Henceforth I shall never again be witness to such a wailing session. In the pages which follow are suggestions, plenty of them, which will help insure success. Let us all give short shrift to those who, for whatever reason, senselessly eschew this counsel. They deserve to fail and deserve to be avoided.

Money

Finally, I have written this book to make money. I make no apology for this. All my books make money. That's as it should be. They are very, very good. I would offer you nothing less — for my sake as much as yours.

Unlike many of my *soi-disant* "self-help," "how to" colleagues, I have lived every suggestion I make. I am very happy to share with you exactly what worked — and why —, and what didn't. If I protect you from the mistakes which I have so creatively made, I have succeeded in my task. And if you pay me handsomely to preserve yourself from ignominies, you should be grateful to me. As I'm sure you will be when you have finished this volume — and begun to use it, as you should, time and again, to insure your fame and fortune.

Hail to thee, bright-shining, transcendent, unabashed self-promoter!

Jeffrey Lant
Cambridge, Massachusetts
September, 1983

CHAPTER 1

TECHNICAL & MENTAL PREREQUISITES FOR THE UNABASHED SELF-PROMOTER

Technical Prerequisites

Success is always the result of technical competence and mental preparedness. Of these proper mental conditioning is by far the more important. Nonetheless those who fail to achieve technical competence, however mentally prepared, obstruct their way to success, perhaps forever. This book as a whole is designed to give you, the unabashed self-promoter, the techniques which will insure success in dealing with the media. However your ability to implement these techniques depends ultimately on your developing basic research skills, a solid English prose style, the ability to make a cogent oral presentation, and upon your capacity to manage your time. This book cannot give you all the information you need on these important topics, but I thought a few words on each would be pertinent.

Basic Research Skills

Every unabashed self-promoter is in the information processing business. We must become adept at finding the information we need — for the articles by us and our speeches, workshops and seminars. This is why, in Chapter 3, I have supplied a goodly number of bibliographical works and reference guides. There is scarcely a day of my life that I do not have the need to use such materials. You'll need them, too.

If you have not previously had occasion to do any research and are not familiar with basic research techniques, at the very least call your local library and ask for a familiarization tour, particularly of its reference collection. Learn, too, what periodicals the library subscribes to and whether it receives periodicals in your field which excerpt the current literature.

People consistently ask me whether my training as an historian has assisted me in my current work. Of course it did! I spent many years in some of the world's premier research libraries ferreting out often arcane information. I learned how to find what existed and what I needed. This was, of course, a substantial investment of time — but it pays off now.

While you need not undertake such a lengthy apprenticeship, remember that your success as an unabashed self-promoter depends in part on your ability to spot trends, quickly gather information about them, and then package what you have found in a format easily accessible to both readers and listeners. For the first and second of these imperatives, basic research skills are necessary.

A Solid English Prose Style

Once you have gathered the material you need, you must place it in a usable format. This book will be of the utmost value to you in suggesting the formats you must master and in advising you on how to arrange your information. This volume is packed with samples of recommended formats and gives specific information about each.

Even so, many readers will fail to produce the written materials they need to succeed as an unabashed self-promoter and their dreams of exploiting the media will evaporate.

Why?

Most Americans are poor writers. Many articles, of course, focus on the appalling writing skills of young people. These are shameful even at the best schools and colleges. (I should perhaps say that I once taught expository writing to freshmen at Harvard.) The fact is, however, that their parents are scarcely better off. When they decide, therefore, to exploit the media, they have problems.

Let me say as strongly as I can: while the great English stylists will always be few in number, it is open to all of us to produce solid, workmanlike prose. Like anything else the achievement of this objective comes through practice.

I can attest that many of you who know the value of exploiting the media and who earnestly want to succeed will still have trouble producing the written materials you need, despite the fact that this book provides you with all the basic samples and specific information on how to produce them.

I have had occasion over the last several months to work with a fairly young consultant (not yet 30) on a series of projects. His practice grows in a desultory fashion, and he has not the resources for a paid advertising campaign. Exploiting the media, as he is well aware, constitutes his best hope to achieve his objectives and build his firm, and his ability to exploit the media depends on his ability to produce the wide varity of written documents presented in this book. He knows all this.

And yet because writing has never been easy for him (and perhaps because he foolishly believes in that snare, inspiration), he avoids the task — and so produces nothing. Worse, he will not take the steps that will deal with his problem.

What are these steps?

Good writers practice. I write every day, every day. I write in my office; I write on airplanes; I write in the backs of taxis. I am totally disciplined. To give you but two examples of what I mean and of the standard you need to attain, consider the following:

When I was writing my first book, ***Insubstantial Pageant,*** I came down with a charateristic bout of bronchitis. I decided this would be a good time to test my discipline. I was at the time writing 1000 words a day. Each morning I dragged myself out of bed to write through the sweat, the chills, the fever. And each day when I had reached my quota I stopped — even though I might be in the middle of a sentence — with a note to myself on what to take up next. I never missed a day or fell behind my schedule.

One more example. I was writing one day in Chicago's O'Hare Airport, a notoriously distracting place. A young mother was burping her baby over her shoulder (and over mine as it turned out). One solid maternal tap produced a cascade by baby of his lunch down my back. I jumped up, brushed off the worst débris, washed off the rest — and went back to work.

Keep these examples in mind.

If you have trouble with writing, take the necessary steps to help yourself:

- Buy a good book with the information you need on developing a good prose style. JLA Publications offers one of these books, and you will find it on our order form in the back of this volume.
- Take a writing course. Put yourself into a situation where you are forced to write regularly. Use as your assignments producing the different formats in this book.
- Force yourself to produce a number of words each day. A good assignment for beginners is 250 words per day, one typed page double spaced.
- Don't give up. I think my young friend has decided he is incapable of writing decent prose. He has therefore imposed failure on himself despite his rhetorical flourishes to the contrary. Don't you do the same. People defeat themselves. No one was born being a good writer. Take heart from Winston Churchill's example. As a schoolboy he was thought so ill-prepared in English prose that he was forced to repeat it. Yet this man, adjudged by his masters to be little short of a dunce, produced some of the most brilliant English prose since Shakespeare. Follow his example.

Cogent Oral Presentations

Like good writing skills, good speaking skills do not come as standard equipment with the beast. They must be learned. In this regard, please keep in mind that your career as an unabashed self-promoter will necessarily be abbreviated if you do not develop such skills, for they are of the utmost importance during a radio or television show, in a seminar or workshop, or on the lecture circuit.

There is no absence of literature on the job of how to turn you into a contemporary Demosthenes. In fact the quantity is staggering as even a cursory glimpse at **Books In Print** affirms. This is scarcely surprising given the sheer number of presentations made each day, the ill-preparedness and anxiety of those making these presentations, and the fact that our school systems continue to graduate students without giving them adequate instruction in public speaking. Unfortunately the quality of much of what is available on this important subject is most disappointing.

Over the next year I intend to do something about this problem both in articles, training sessions, and very likely in a new book. However, until this project is more advanced, I suggest you do the following:

- Enroll in a public speaking course or in Toastmasters International (See Chapter 17). Good speakers, like good writers, are practiced speakers. Your goal is to stand before an audience with just a few notes in hand (and a polished epigram or two in reserve) and to hold it transfixed. Begin to achieve this goal today.
- Practice at home on your family. Good speakers play with works and ideas, trying them out. They build their best presentations bit by bit from their everyday conversations. I myself carry a notebook with me everywhere, and if I happen upon a good phrase or idea during a conversation, I jot it down for future use. Do the same.

Note: If you have young children, spare them the anxieties about public speaking which you may feel by starting them early in addressing groups. Children need to be shown that speaking before others is natural and exciting, not the cause of fear. Help them today, so that they may have greater opportunities tomorrow.

Time Management

The greatest problem the advanced unabashed self-promoter faces is time management. No wonder. As you become adept at the techniques discussed in the following pages, you will find yourself with more and still more opportunities, more than you can reasonably exploit. How, then to deal with this situation?

First, learn to structure your time for success. Most people pass time. The unabashed self-promoter cannot afford to be so lax. You must structure your time so that, whatever your investment, a success results.

I have, for instance, set as my personal objective having at least one mention in the media each day: an article by or about me, a radio or television show, an announcement about a new product, service, or achievement, &c. I consistently meet this goal.

I attribute the regular realization of this goal to several factors not the least of which is dogged perserverence and the ability to manage my time to produce a desired result. This book will assist you in identifying and creating self-promotional opportunities, but you must make a commitment to yourself to work at the process of self-promotion each day, to give yourself the time you need both to perfect your methods and execute them.

I say this from the depths of my experience: if you can only spend a half hour each day on self-promotion, so be it. But make this time count. Do not undertake so considerable a project that you cannot make it successful and hence become despairing. Structure your project to your available time and then work at it consistently, day by day, until you achieve the success you want.

Time management is synonomous with success management. Those who cannot manage their time cannot achieve maximum success. Know, then, that as an unabashed self-promoter there are many things that you have to do and that most of these proceed simultaneously:

- develop your image
- research media outlets
- create and maintain your self-promotion network
- find and use information
- produce articles by and about you
- handle media interviews
- create books by and about you
- speak in seminars, workshops and lectures

The life of the unabashed self-promoter is necessarily a balancing act: while you are lecturing on a given subject, you must be developing your information sources for your next talk presentation. While you are promoting your current book, you had best be developing your next. While you are looking for a publisher for the last article by you, you are researching information sources for material for your next. This never stops.

After a time the seasoned unabashed self-promoter becomes adept at dividing his life between prospecting, production, and promotion. If you are not so adept just now, spend a little time each day on each necessary area. Don't just do one or the other, or the system you are trying to establish will never run smoothly, will never be synchronized.

The ability to operate such a synchronized system differentiates the unsophisticated self-promoter from his seasoned colleague. The former most often works only sequentially, developing an idea, then producing the appropriate product, undertaking the marketing, then delivering the product. The latter not only works sequentially but also has tasks in all areas simultaneously so as to maintain the full functioning of the self-promotional system. This is true even if the self-promoter can only put a very little time into each separate activity.

Remember: the unabashed self-promoter is marked by his ability, in the face of severely limited time, to pursue success in each of the several critical areas of prospecting, production, and promotion. Because all these areas are essential to any self-promotional effort, the art of time management for the unabashed self-promoter lies in dividing the available time so that each regularly produces the necessary result and so insures the smooth, consistent operation of the entire system.

Beyond Technical Competence

Research skills, a solid English prose style, good oral delivery, and time management — all these are technical skills which can be taught and learned. Rather different are the mental prerequisites needed by the unabashed self-promoter. These prerequisites, beginning with a sense of entitlement, are ethereal; for all that they are often quite aggressive and thrusting, they approach the spiritual. How and where they are developed continues to be the subject of debate, but it is clear to me that they are what truly distinguishes the successful self-promoter from all the common run of mankind.

Entitlement

The unabashed self-promoter feels entitled to the exposure, the good press, the sparkling superlatives, the plethora of promotional paragraphs. Without exception every unabashed self-promoter I have ever known has felt this way rather than cringingly grateful for any condescending consideration. And for good reason, too.

First, we are providing a service, both to the media and to those who gain access to our material. All unabashed self-promoters, all, are service providers; we make the lives of media personnel and their public easier. Never forget this.

Insensitive, untutored media personnel will feel, and sometimes the more boorish will say, that they are doing us a favor to promote us. That is not true. In the intensely symbiotic relationship we have with the media, each serves the interests of the other.

All unabashed self-promoters of worth possess information, a product or service, which will enrich the lives of large numbers of individuals. These individuals are entitled to the information we have, the media has an obligation to publicize it, and we, unabashed self-promoters, have a responsibility to insure the widest possible dissemination of information about our beneficial product or service. We also have a responsibility to build our own reputations so that we can gain even more media access and so help still more people.

The unabashed self-promoter who has followed the techniques recommended in this book is entitled to be heard. He is a person of worth and consequence with an important social mission — not least helping the media do the best job they can.

Unfortunately at the beginning of your self-promotional career very few people may believe in you and your mission. It is at this intensely difficult time that you need to draw from your inner strength and evidence a series of crucial traits which will sustain you until such time as an apathetic, antipathetic world shows its first faint signs of welcome and support.

Sustaining Qualities Of The Unabashed Self-Promoter

At this moment make a vow to yourself, to yourself and to no one else. With this vow guarantee yourself that you will not be merely technically competent but also mentally prepared for the necessarily difficult instructory stage of unabashed self-promotion. And that you will give yourself what you need to succeed:

- self-motivation
- self-love
- determination
- enthusiasm

If you do not now feel these traits, vow that you will give them to yourself. They come from within; they are self-generated, not conferred by others. If you wait for someone else to affirm that you have them, you will waste a lifetime. Instead, confer them on yourself. The capacity for these traits is within all people. Alas! Only a few work assiduously to develop them.

Be one of these few.

I am continually asked as I travel the nation when one assumes the outlook of a winner, when and under what circumstances one says, "I now love myself. I now feel motivated to succeed. I now have both the determination and enthusiasm I need to succeed."

When?

Before you have success. Before you are celebrated by the media. While your cash reserves are low. While you are still working on the development of your image and perfecting your writing style. In short, before you have anything on which to base your decision except for that unfathomable gleam of inner direction, *that* is the moment to assume the outlook of a winner and a winner's commitment, dedication, and happy certainty about the inevitability of the desired outcome. And that moment is now.

A contemporary Diogenes, I search the world for those individuals who have not only made the commitment to themselves to become technically competent but also have vowed to achieve success and who in the early difficult period of their drive sustain themselves out of their own deep inner-personal resources. If you are this person, there is no end to what you can attain, and you will make the best use of this book.

Additional Traits Of The Unabashed Self-Promoter

The unabashed self-promoter is a visionary. And all visionaries build not just for today but for the many days ahead.

Building a national reputation, becoming the elusive household name, developing and disseminating your beneficial message, all take time. And though your ultimate goal may never change, your methods and intermediate objectives will change over time and as circumstances alter. Be prepared for this.

The unabashed self-promoter is distinguished by two more important traits in addition to those mentioned above. While never losing sight of our goal, we are receptive to new ideas and use them to leverage the result we seek, and we are never satisfied with merely short term success. We want to achieve a sequence of short-term successes to insure the realization of our long-term goal.

The Lifestyle Of The Unabashed Self-Promoter

The unabashed self-promoter is a wonderful creation. You are reading this book either because you already know yourself to be wonderful, or because you wish to learn how to. You've come to the right place.

You must know, however, that the bulk of mankind is neither wonderful nor striving to become so. Most people lead lives that are distastefully Hobbesian, "nasty, brutish, and short." Worse, they prefer this unappealing condition.

The unabashed self-promoter does not.

This makes us, gentle reader, decidedly different. And the more successful we become as unabashed self-promoters, the more different we will be. And the more most people will work, however subtly, to pull us back into their mundane orbits.

As an unabashed self-promoter you have a mission, and it is not one most people have or can even understand. You mission is total self-realization.

In pursuit of this goal you will work hard, travel long distances, keep long hours, baffle your more slothful friends and associates, and draw deep from a stamina which is replenished less from your body than your mind. Success, which you will first reckon in terms of how many column inches you have garnered, how many hours of airtime, you will ultimately measure in terms of movement to complete self-realization, a goal not shared by most people, their rhetoric notwithstanding.

The bulk of this book concentrates on process information, how to master a necessary series of steps which assure your ability to exploit the media and disseminate your message to the farthest extent.

This is the shortest chapter of the book. Yet, as I have written before, it is perhaps the most important. Come back to it to refresh your spirit and renew your vow to succeed, especially at such times as you feel depleted and if you are finding an admittedly challenging cause exceptionally trying and debilitating.

We are all, alas!, only human. We will, therefore, give way to depression, frustration, and uncertainty. Do not, however, give way to them for long. They are part of the human condition, but they are the lesser part. Instead, do the following:

- Renew your commitment to success by rereading this chapter.
- Structure some success, however small, as soon as possible so that your sequence of success is again functioning.
- Go back to the business of disseminating your message, spreading information about you, your product, or service.

- **Do something to increase your look of success. As the unabashed self-promoter knows better than most, success breeds success. To look successful is to induce others to believe you are successful, and hence worthy of still more success.**

Turn the page and begin to build a Quintessential American Success Image, but never forget the true source of your success: your own heart and mind.

CHAPTER 2

FASHIONING A QUINTESSENTIAL AMERICAN SUCCESS IMAGE

Every one has an image, that is to say some leading idea of oneself as perceived by others. Most often this image is casual, not deliberate, and arises from accident and neglect. If considered at all, it is considered sporatically and superficially. It is, therefore, unsatisfactory and incomplete.

The matter of image cannot be so handled by the unabashed self-promoter. You necessarily have a vital interest in projecting for the media a thorough, considered, deliberate image, an idea of stark, compelling simplicity, necessarily evanescent, but capable of being comprehended in an instant and designed to appeal to the largest number of people.

An image is not comprehensive. It is not capable of embracing the totality of your complicated being. It is not designed to do so. A good image is an appealing intrusion into the lives of others. It is a look which snags the attention of another individual and produces the desire on his part to act as you suggest he should. The best images, the most effective, compelling, persuasive, are necessarily simple. Their considerable motivating power lies in this simplicity.

As you develop your image you must keep in mind the following critical facts:

- Subtlety is beyond the power of the public. When dealing with the public, you must always present yourself in the least complicated fashion and with no more than one leading idea. To do more is to risk accomplishing nothing.
- Likewise, the media cannot comprehend complexity. Thus all those dealing with the media must present themselves in the most simple, uncomplicated, direct fashion possible. In the media all ideas, all images are weakened if they deviate from the necessary standard of profound simplicity.
- You cannot afford either to worry or despair about the fact that your image is not the whole you. It never can be, never will be.

An image is a considered statement by you which summarizes in an intense, powerful thrust not so much who you are but who your followers, your constituency, your buying public wants you to be. An image is the bridge which links you with their hopes, dreams, and aspirations. It presents, palpably, a substantial, vivid representation of who they themselves want to be.

Your image, while simple, is powerful because it ignites in your audience a chain reaction connecting you to their deepest, most satisfying desires, the more desirable because for most continually, tantalizingly beyond realization.

The Inadequacy Of The Current Image Literature

Just how to create such an image has not been much discussed. In fact, the literature which currently exists on the subject is severely one dimensional and is of almost no utility to large numbers of success seekers.

A book like John Malloy's **Dress For Success** epitomizes what is good and not good about the current crop of material. Malloy's book, like every other current volume on imaging, directs its attention solely to the corporate sphere, particularly to the ranks of Fortune 500 companies. Here, Malloy suggests, success may be achieved through the careful choosing and calculated wearing of certain suits of certain colors and select shirts with sets of sequenced stripes. No doubt he is right — as far as he goes.

The fact of the matter, however, is that America is rich with success images and the Corporate Clone image advanced by Malloy is only one of dozens of possibilities. While it is perfectly acceptable for any author to select his own topic, no reader should suppose that the suggestions made by Malloy and his image counterparts are universal or apply outside his selected milieu.

Moreover, the universe where Malloy and his colleagues direct their attention is a relatively stagnant place. Recent studies of American employment patterns demonstrate conclusively that the major economic growth in this country will not take place within this sector, that indeed additional employment there will be negligible and that opportunities for general advancement will be more and more difficult to achieve.

This situation has, of course, produced anxiety within those employed in this sector. And it is upon this anxiety that Malloy and his peers have so adeptly preyed. Malloy's book is in fact a White Knight volume (see Chapter 7), for having sparked anxiety in his readers he then proceeds to offer the solutions to their problems and to make certain that you know his consulting firm is available on an individual basis to help you directly implement his advice. Very clever, of course, but you need not feel the slightest compunction about ignoring the advice in all those many situations where it does not apply.

Hitherto, as I can testify from sustained attempts to locate literature and information, those writing on the subject of image have focused on a small, if important, slice of American life and have produced advice which is not applicable to most people and does not take into account the dozens of success images which necessarily have highly differentiated and distinct sumptuary requirements from those current in the corporate world. It is now time to broaden the discussion considerably and so both free most Americans from the need to follow advice which does not in fact assist them and inspire them with the possibility of formulating a more authentic, compelling image of their own.

Quintessential American Success Images

What follows is not a comprehensive list of Quintessential American Success Images. As I attempted to formulate such a list, it ran on for column after column without a sign of being complete. Instead what follows is a representative selection of these images.

Some have deep historical roots; some are distinctive to the present. Most are capable of being assumed by both sexes. Some as yet are not. Whenever possible I have attempted to suggest a contemporary figure who represents and epitomizes the image.

Please note: no one can be all these images, although I will later suggest that cross-fertilization of images is a good thing and ought to be considered whenever possible. Moreover, in no case is the representative of the image encompassed by it. The representatives, however, probably don't worry about this fact; if they do, it is on their way to the bank.

I have two purposes in including this information:

- To isolate the current writers of image literature and to put their contributions to the field in perspective. What they have done is interesting and even important within a certain part of

American life, but it is by no means definitive; slavishly followed by most of us, it would produce unhappy results.

- To suggest to the unabashed self-promoter the range of successful image possibilities and to spur your creativity both in adopting and developing those I have suggested and the many which I have not.

The All-American Mother

Mom lies at the root of many of our fantasies and insecurities, and the All-American Mother image takes full advantage of this fact. The growth of the women's movement in the 1960s and 1970s may, for a time, have obscured the deep power of the All-American Mother image in our national life but recent events have again underscored its importance.

Phyllis Schlafly is a good contemporary example of an individual who has benefitted from this image. She, a most aggressive, determined person, succeeded against great odds in stopping the Equal Rights Amendment which stood on the verge of enactment. Under this image, of course, any woman is allowed to be as aggressive as necessary in defense of her nest and family. With this image, then, female aggression, otherwise so often inappropriate, is seen as entirely admirable, even heroic. This image, therefore, remains the single most powerful any woman can adopt, and one of the most compelling in the image hierarchy.

The Underdog

Americans like underdogs. As a nation we have taken the myth of David and Goliath very much to heart, always on the side of David.

A shrewd self-promoter lacking resources will always play on our national predilection for the underdog, the little guy, even when he is anything but. One very good example of this kind of thinking has come out of the early revelations about the now-celebrated briefing book which some Carter operative leaked to the Reagan camp during the last presidential election.

Jimmy Carter was advised in this book to play against candidate Reagan the beleaguered underdog. When you consider that Carter at the time was the incumbent President of the United States, you will realize that this image is one of perception, not reality. Particularly to self-promoters just starting out, The Underdog remains an image of wonderful possibilities.

The Devil-May-Care Adventurer

We are in a regimented world working by rules we didn't set, regulations we did not formulate. Bowed down with the burden of responsibility and lacking the means of escape, we delight at the idea of those individuals who, with a light heart and sureness of touch, can break away to happiness and prosperity.

Traditionally these adventurers have been men, but there is absolutely no reason why more women cannot rise to this very attractive image. For this image a sense of humor is required and an aura of gallantry. The World War I flying aces would be good people to study in formulating this image.

The Side Kick

An important (if little considered) success image in this country is The Side Kick. This individual personifies loyalty, empathy, and other directedness. So often uncelebrated, The Sick Kick is in fact a Quintessential American Success Image. So many Americans feel that the stuff of heroics is beyond them, but most of us have no trouble feeling capable of being a side kick — Alice B. Toklas to a Gertrude Stein, Annie Sullivan to a Helen Keller, Tonto to a Lone Ranger. Side kicks are indispensible to heroes and as such have a Quintessential American Success Image all their own.

The Frontiersman

Americans have long been enamored of the hardy individual breaking new ground. Our literature and myths are full of such people. Now that our geographical territory has been explored and we have no new territorial frontiers, the image is more important than ever as a vital link to our past.

The Frontiersman is one of our most cherished national images, and a wise self-promoter will define what he does in terms of the frontier he is breaking. John F. Kennedy did just that and in the ringing rhetoric which was his most masterful accomplishment brought in "The New Frontier" in 1961. It was a very shrewd move for a man from the effete eastern seaboard and was designed to mitigate any charge of parochialism and to link him to an historic national image.

The Accessible Expert

This is very much a contemporary success image borne of the growing specialization of knowledge and a prevalent fear rightly felt by most people that general understanding is beyond them.

In an age of information this image is a most popular one. It can be assumed by both men and women and is designed to show at once not only that you, the unabashed self-promoter, are in fact expert in your field but also that you are accessible to the average individual and will make the information you wield accessible, too. Dr. Timothy Johnson in medicine, Dr. Jean Mayer in nutrition, Neal Chayet in the law are all examples of such individuals. It is an image which no information-based self-promoter can dismiss without considering.

The Entrepreneur

Americans are do-ers. We are always and forever in search of the better mousetrap. We honor the individual who develops it and enrich him beyond the dreams of avarice. Collectively we remember that we were, not so long ago, a complete wilderness and that we have become great and rich because of the continuing inventiveness, drive, and determination of our entrepreneurs.

As I write, we have again, after a lapse of several years, reentered a period when The Entrepreneur is a valued image. Images, like all other currencies, rise and fall in value, and that of The Entrepreneur, in the wake of renewed interest in the private sector, is transcendent.

An unabashed self-promoter can link himself to a powerful image by defining his work in terms of enterprise and himself as an individual with a social mission: to enrich not just himself but others. Traditionally, of course, The Entrepreneur image has been for males alone, but this is no longer true. A shrewd female self-promoter can make very good use of this image, which, as far as women are concerned, is still relatively infrequently done.

The Blithe Eunuch

Is this a Quintessential American Success Image?

Very much so. Consider, for example, Richard Simmons who came out of nowhere and is now a multi-millionaire media celebrity.

The Blithe Eunuch image can be assumed only by a male who is regarded as suitably unthreatening to spend time with women while their men folk are away from home. He amuses them and makes them both more alluring to their men physically (exercise) and more domestically productive (cookery, house keeping, &c.) He operates in the contemporary version of the harem.

The entirely nonthreatening male is allowed tremendous latitude with the women — physical displays of affection, touching, kissing &c. — because, in the last resort, he is incapable of any more sustained, threatening activity.

Richard Simmons, of course, is ideal for this role. Very much The Blithe Eunuch, he is the safest of safe companions to America's menless females — and as such he has become celebrated and rich.

The Victim

The Victim may seem another unlikely Quintessential American Success Image, but consider: it has already made millionaires of both Meryl Streep and Richard Gere to name but two contemporary exemplars.

Take Streep, for example. She performs for us a pivotal role: she offers fulfillment for her lover/antagonist through sex heavily intermixed with violence. Streep's profound appeal lies in the fact that she is forever at the mercy of her lovers who know that they may cherish or maim her as they wish. They, of course, can scarcely believe their good fortune and so behave accordingly — in the most bestial and abominable ways. The Victim responds with unstinting love, bewildered of course (in part by the pain, in part through incomprehension at what has caused it), but does not withhold continuing affection. What could be better?

Richard Gere is the male equivalent. His success lies well beyond his sexuality, well beyond a developed body which is by no means exceptional. It lies in a mixture of sexuality with vulnerability. He is a victim, and every woman knows it — well before men catch on to the fact.

Gere's success lies in the fact that women as much as men crave a victim, someone who may at first seem dangerous but who cannot hurt them nearly as much as they can hurt him. For, of course, in the long run Gere is eminently disposable, not worth a second thought to those with the attenuated contemporary conscience. His ability to project this image, it needs hardly be said, has made him a very wealthy, sought-after man.

The Little Man's Friend

Many self-promoters wanting to get ahead have a critical choice to make. All wanting to be wealthy, of course, the choice is whether they will be perceived as serving the rich or the poor. Ronald Reagan, a poor boy, made the entirely characteristic decision to serve the well-heeled; John F. Kennedy, a rich man's son, made the equally characteristic decision to be perceived as the champion of the dispossessed. In point of fact, these were almost tactical decisions, a question of which means were most expeditious to achieve the same result, the American presidency.

The Little Man's Friend is a very powerful, traditional Quintessential American Success Image. Politicians have always benefitted from assuming this image. Right now it is in an ebb period, and hence may be worth capturing by some unabashed self-promoter. The last generally perceived champion of this group was Robert Kennedy, although others have since tried. I think this image is ripe for exploitation.

The In-Command Technocrat

This is another success image for our times. It can be assumed by both men and women and has the added advantage that it can be used to good effect by someone who lacks a sense of humor. A technocrat is a master of process; it is his responsibility simply to make things work. He needs to project an image of intelligence, control, and certainty. Iciness and the lack of certain human qualities are not necessarily hurtful in the propagation of this image, very much a development of our technical times.

If Your Image Is Not On This List

Most people who read this book will find one or more of the foregoing images to be apposite. Some of you, however, will find nothing suitable. If this is so, consider the following as you craft your own Quintessential American Success Image.

It is clear that the most powerful success images serve the needs of others; they are empathetic, not selfish. If they use authoritarian methods, they do so as a means of assisting to deliver a generally-beneficial result.

No Quintessential American Success Image is perceived as selfish. This is one trait which cannot be allowed. All unabashed self-promoters work on their own behalf, of course; you cannot, however, afford to assume an image which bluntly proclaims this fact.

Quintessential American Success images are directed on the whole to the improvement of the world. Such an image means being challenged by difficulties not embittered by them, means taking problems in stride and not complaining about them.

Quintessential American Success images always have a vision of a better way. Whatever personal foibles those who have such images possess, they are always rendered unimportant by their good hearts. Those with a Quintessential American Success Image are smart enough to assist, not just impress.

Whenever possible such images should be rounded off with a gallant spirit and with joy. We are a people prepared to forgive much if only we can see evidence of gallantry and joyful empathy and spirit. Make sure that you season your success image with these necessary ingredients.

The Author's Image: The All-American Whiz Kid

The greatest success images transform possible negatives into perceived advantages. The wise self-promoter will look at himself objectively and will take account not merely of his evident strengths but his all-too-evident weaknesses.

Yet be very clear about these weaknesses. Properly handled, they can become the most useful possible props to a Quintessential American Success Image. There is no mystery about this.

All people have weaknesses, all. Most give in to them and let their weaknesses dictate an incomplete, unsatisfactory life. Yet at some level all these people know that it is not their handicap which is to blame but an essential frailty and failure of spirit. When some special soul appears equally handicapped in fact but gifted with the determination to be unbowed by this disability, our hearts go out; we admire this individual the more because of his evident difficulties. Thus in the long run these handicaps have a very real value in shaping a Quintessential American Success Image.

Handicaps, of course, are often circumstantial. They are not always the same in all times and places. Here are some of mine:

- At age 36, I still have many days when I resemble an adolescent.
- I talk very quickly, often in bursts of machine gun rhetoric.
- I feel uncomfortable in a suit or anything resembling standard business clothing.
- I do not drive.

My problem was to find or fashion a Quintessential American Success Image which would turn these possible drawbacks into perceived strengths, part of an image of authenticity and appeal. The All-American Whiz Kid is the result.

Whiz kids need not dress, need not drive, need not wear a watch, carry a briefcase, or, importantly, look sagely distinguished. Moreover the fact that I talk fast, often very fast, became a positive benefit; it's the way adolescents talk when they are excited about somethng. The enthusiasm and excitement which I have at my command are two of my most admirable traits and have been much commented upon.

Quintessential American Success images are not just composed of positive traits; they are composed of potentially perceived negatives which, because of the image, are transformed into positive benefits.

Reviewing and assessing these potentially negative traits is of very real value to the unabashed self-promoter. Aspects of your life which you may hitherto have found unappealing can now be regarded more philosophically, more favorably as promoting the image which insures your success. It is no wonder that a fully functioning, seasoned self-promoter is among the most self-accepting of people. He has seen himself, warts and all, and upon finding that the warts are indeed beneficial has come to love them as an essential part of what makes him successful, attractive. This is no mean achievement in itself.

In achieving this satisfactory result it may be that you will have to draw from other Quintessential American Success images through cross-fertilization.

The Cross-Fertilization Of Images

In addition to the potential liabilities cited above, I also have these possible problems:

- I live in Cambridge, Massachusetts.
- I was educated at Harvard and Oxford.

Each of these facts could, in selected situations, be detrimental to my success if not properly handled and dealt with. To neutralize if not transform them to positive benefits, I use other Quintessential American Success images as any unabashed self-promoter must do to become the most universally acceptable successful symbol.

Transforming Yourself Into A Universal

For better or worse, mere location can be both as an asset and a drawback to your success. Cambridge clearly suggests intellect, scholarship, research. It also conjures up Harvard, privilege, élitism, arrogance. While most successful Easterners, being part of this network, are not bothered by this suggestion, those elsewhere often are to the chagrin of the unabashed self-promoter with products and services to sell. Cross-fertilizing your image can mitigate this problem.

To deal with the whole issue of Harvard and the East, which do not always sit well elsewhere, I have cross-fertilized my All-American Whiz Kid image with The Frontiersman, a very potent success image. My line is this: while the old frontier was geographic, the new one is informational and technical. I am a pioneer working on this frontier.

This line has not only been very popular with the media who like the idea of the pioneer from Harvard Square, but with people beyond the Mississippi who can with the assistance of this image, overcome any possible aversion to my clipped accent and button-down shirts.

In other circumstances I make use of the In-Command Technocrat, Accessible Expert, and Entrepreneur success images. One or more of these has been pivotal in building and maintaining my consulting, publishing, and lecturing enterprises. Indeed, the fact that you regarded me as one or more of these things probably influenced your decision to buy this book.

Maintaining Multiple Images

As you see, I have no problem maintaining either wholly or in part at least 5 significant images. Here they are:

- All-American Whiz Kid
- Accessible Expert
- In-Command Technocrat
- Entrepreneur
- Frontiersman

There is no necessary incompatibility about maintaining more than one image nor should you hesitate to do so both to neutralize any negative points, insure that you are getting full credit for all your positive aspects, and make yourself into the most universal figure possible.

I make use of one or more of these images as necessary or any combination therefore. I am under no illusion that these Quintessential American Success images encompass my being. They don't. But they provide the media with the hooks they need about me to make sense of the information I give them, and they provide my public with a neat impression, an image which induces my chosen constituencies to act as I want them to act. Thus these images do all that they are capable of doing.

Supply People With The Image Hook They Need

Once you have picked an image and begun to develop it, don't fail to tell the individuals with whom you come in contact about it, particularly media people. The grand thing about an image is that you can by supplying it to your audience trigger a train of response.

Thus when I call myself a Frontiersman in a media interview, I can predict the response. This word, this image conjures up a whole train of related words and ideas: resolute, hardy, daring, adventurous, bold, &c. &c. — all words which the media source supplies as a result of my directing him with the word "frontiersman." It is very, very neat.

The careful selection of an appropriate image is imperative to the unabashed self-promoter. Once it has been selected you have a considerable influence on all subsequent media notwithstanding factual evidence which runs directly against the success image you are promoting.

Consider, for example, the debate in 1968 about the "new Nixon," warm, empathetic, humane. The man himself and his advisers carefully selected this image because they knew he needed it, and both the press and public bought it despite a lifetime of evidence to the contrary. This is how powerful the whole matter of image can be.

Never, never fail to inform media people — or anyone else, for that matter — what your image is if they have not figured it out for themselves. If you have come to embody your image, of course, to look right, talk right, and act right these hints will be infrequent, and yet, to insure that the point is made, you should never hesitate to make it and make it again if you need to.

A Word About Quintessential American Failure Images

Just as there are Quintessential American Success images, so, too, are there Failure images. Such images insure the failure of those who project them whatever admirable traits they happen to have secondarily. What needs to be kept in mind, however, is that all of our national failure images can be overcome by adopting a more powerful Quintessential American Success Image.

Here are a few Quintessential American Failure images:

The Uriah Heep (Self-Righteous, Morally Superior)

If you remember your Dickens you recall that Uriah Heep was an unctuous character forever proclaiming to his betters his humility while at the same time focusing his rage on those he considered menial. His chief trait was rubbing his hands together in a gesture which might equally signal rapaciousness or humble pie. Jimmy Carter was perceived as such a man, and his presidency was, as a result, a fiasco.

Americans have a pronounced dislike for humbug — or the whiff of the sanctimonious. Unabashed self-promoters should do everything in their power to avoid this taint.

In Carter's case, his Quintessential American Failure Image could be transformed into a Quintessential American Success Image by adopting the Spiritual Voyageur/Missionary Image. As you will remember, Carter often said that he would like to end his life as a Baptist overseas missionary. By adopting the Spiritual Voyageur Image, exemplified by such celebrities as Albert Schweitzer and Mother Theresa, Carter can overcome a generally-perceived weakness and transform it into a source of strength and regeneration.

The Cry Baby

Americans have a profound and sensible aversion to cry babies and tale bearers. Alex Haig, during his ill-fated stint as Secretary of State, should have known this and behaved accordingly. Cry babies are weak, selfish people, critical, mean-spirited, petulant and nagging — all traits we as a people disdain. Unfortunately Haig had them all and with his Cry Baby Image was doomed for an abbreviated career in the Cabinet.

Haig can, however, redeem himself by assuming any one of a number of success images including: The Man of Steel, The Staunch Anti-Communist, or The Patriot, all of which take into account his military background and his conservative politics. Haig can be redeemed, but he must first dissipate our lingering suspicion that taking umbrage is what he does best.

The Sneak

Sneaks make the rest of us feel positively unclean, even though we may enjoy the information we hear or sympathize with the need to make it public. I recall Daniel Ellsberg, for instance, who publicized the Pentagon Papers. Ellsberg's redeeming image was The Patriot. Properly handled this trumps The Sneak. Unfortunately so powerful is our national aversion to The Sneak (and so poorly did the timorous Ellsberg handle his defense) that the man seems forever tainted, dismissed by some as an odious sneak, by others as an insufficient patriot.

Traits of Quintessential American Failure Images

The Quintessential American Failure Image is the opposite of the Quintessential American Success Image. Those with such images are regarded as self-centered, selfish, and uncaring. They are not perceived as fighting against the world's wrongs to improve things for everyone but as complaining about the inadequacies which bother them.

They often perceive themselves as victims or at least allow us to so perceive them. They seem to be dark, furtive, subterranean characters and are without the apparent openness which distinguishes the success images.

There is no joy emanating from failure images. They cannot generate the excitement it takes to lead people, so, instead, they are reduced to bullying. They rule by fear and force rather than by the promise of love and acceptance.

Those with a Quintessential American Failure Image are perceived to be alone or to exist within a protective group. They are said to lack the "common touch." They seem to be confused or confounded by the range of human emotions. They compel us to do things "for our own good" rather than inspiring us to choose a course which is in our best interest.

They are not the kind of people we invite home to dinner.

The Redeemed Sinner

It should be clear to you that both success and failure images have their hierarchies and that those who have been brushed by a Quintessential American Failure Image need to develop their most powerful success image and so redeem themselves.

Perhaps the most powerful redemptory image and one of the most powerful of all the Quintessential American Success images is The Redeemed Sinner. Keep it in mind, particuilarly if you, as an unabashed self-promoter, do something particularly egregious and need to lie low for a while.

To use this image properly, you need to sin mightily and then, thrusting yourself into the swiftly-flowing waters of the American evangelical tradition, repent mightily, too.

Sin big, go to ground, see the light, be reconfirmed as a success seeker with the mantle of The Redeemed Sinner.

Hey, Look Me Over! Are You Ready To Go Public?

Once having made an image selection, you must now make sure that it is thorough going, that there are no obvious incompatibilities in your image, and that you will project a strong, coherent idea of authenticity. To do so you must be unified in mien, milieu, and message.

Mien

Think through the appropriate bearing and manner for your chosen image. Are they coherent? The fact that I wear no socks all summer and appear wherever I go in khaki pants and lacoste shirts is entirely appropriate given my image. They are not right for everyone. Remember: an image has everything to do with how your constituency wants to see you. To insure that your mien is satisfactory and persuasive look to the group you are trying to influence. If they are happy with what you are doing, you are correct.

Milieu

You must construct your habitat so that it is in conformity with your image and strengthens it. In the beginning when your resources are their most slender, this will be more difficult than later. In the beginning of your self-promotional career, therefore, plan to have as many of your interviews as possible away from your usual locale. However, as you write your basic media materials (see Chapter 8), accentuate the positive. Bring into the article about you those personal details which will reinforce in the reader's mind the image you are projecting and fostering.

Message

This is the most important point of all. Your mesage must be absolutely consistent with your image. Moreover, your diction and delivery must also reinforce this image so that the final result is strong, unified, consistent, convincing.

A Lifetime's Work

To achieve this mastery of your image(s) is a lifetime's work, not least because images, like the humans who shape them, change and develop over time.

It takes time to select an appropriate image and make it your own, time to come to know what this image allows and disallows, time to shape an appropriate, reinforcing milieu, time to hone your message and to learn just how to deliver it for maximum effect. Time, that is, and determination.

Your goal as an image maker is clear: you aim to create a concept that at once realizes the dreams and aspirations of your selected constituency and so motivates them to act as you wish and simultaneously builds on your best points and transforms your weakest into perceived attributes.

This is no easy task, and it is one which is quite beyond most people.

It cannot, however, be beyond you, the unabashed self-promoter, for consider: its successful realization will provide the media with the necessary hook they need on which to hang their coverage of you and gives your public an inspiring model they themselves can emulate if only they have the good sense to follow your message or buy your product or service. Which if you have constructed your image properly, they will.

CHAPTER 3

INFORMATION SOURCES FOR THE UNABASHED SELF-PROMOTER

Introduction

This chapter contains information on information sources: where to find what you need to know about newspapers, magazines, television, radio, newsletters, and other prime targets for the unabashed self-promoter. Every one of us must become an expert on where to find information we need. The unabashed self-promoter is necessarily adept at information processing: he knows how to find what he needs and how to use it once he's found it.

In considering the information in this chapter, keep in mind the following points:

- What follows is broad, but it is not definitive. I have added only those publications which I feel are of the most value to you. If you know of other publications which you have found helpful, please let me know. I'll add them to future editions of this book.
- Information sources age quickly. Indeed they are out-of-date at the very moment of publication. If you are sending a general mailing of media materials, this fact may be of less importance. If, however, you are contacting a single media source and individual, call to get the most current information. It is most embarrassing to be told that the person you have written to left his job two years ago.
- Libraries don't seem to have many of these publications. A survey of the major Boston libraries revealed that the standard library public relations collection is both tiny and severely dated. Thus, you must consider beginning your own publicity library. However, be advised that many of the publications which follow are quite expensive. Thus see about getting your local library to order the basics. Since library acquisitions is not likely to want to order many publications for you alone, get a friend or two with similar interests to request volumes, too. Also, consider forming an informal public relations consortium with these friends and having each purchase publications which all can share.
- Before you do buy, however, ask for a sample copy of newsletters, magazines, or at the very least for a descriptive brochure. There is no sense in getting something which does not meet your needs.
- Once you have the publications, read and re-read them. The more familiar you are with the range of media sources and the kinds of opportunities which are available, the more ideas you'll have about how to take advantage of them.
- Don't let the immensity of possibilities overwhelm you. I find the sheer number of possibilities an unending challenge. My goal is to be featured by each. So should yours be.
- As your materials age, consider donating them to a local nonprofit organization. You will get a credit for doing so based on the still useful life of the product and this credit, applied against your taxable income, will diminish the cost of your next purchase. Remember: *all* such purchases are legitimate business expenses.

Note: The author wishes to thank that indefatigable and most knowledgeable source on the media Richard Weiner for his assistance in recommending and discovering key sources. Readers wishing additional source information or more detailed information on selected sources following are encouraged to purchase Weiner's thorough volume, **Professional's Guide To Public Relations Services,** 888 Seventh Ave., New York, New York 10019. This and the Gebbie **All-In-One Directory** (below) are 'musts' for your public relations library.

Directories And Information Sources Of Prime Interest

1) **All-In-One Directory**
Gebbie Press, Inc.
Box 1000
New Paltz, New York 12561 Phone: (914) 255-7560

Includes basic information about daily newspapers, weekly newspapers, radio stations, television stations, general consumer magazines, professional business publications, trade magazines, farm publications, Black press, and news syndicates. Price $50, payment with order. $58, billed.

2) **Ayer Directory of Publications**
Ayer Press
One Bala Avenue
Bala Cynwyd, PA 19004 Phone: (215) 664-6205

Covers over 21,000 magazines and newspapers nationally. Lists newspaper feature editors; agricultural, college, foreign language, Jewish, Black, fraternal, religious, and trade publications; general magazines and newspapers. $79 plus $2.50 shipping.

Also, **Ayer Public Relations & Publicity Stylebook.** List of feature editors of newspapers with circulation of 100,000 and over. $12.95 plus $1.50 shipping.

3) **Bacon's Publicity Checker**
Bacon's Publishing Company
332 S. Michigan Avenue
Chicago, IL 60604 Phone:(312) 922-2400

Covers trade and consumer magazines, daily newspapers, and over 8000 weekly newspapers in the United States and Canada. Lists types of publicity material used. Arranged in two volumes. Price $110 plus $2.80 shipping including supplements.

4) **Editor & Publisher International Year Book**
Editor & Publisher Company
575 Lexington Avenue
New York, New York 10022 Phone: (212) 752-7050

Daily and Sunday newspapers in the United States and Canada; weekly newspapers; foreign daily newspapers; special service newspapers; newspaper syndicates; news services; foreign language and Black newspapers in the United States; clipping bureaus; house organs. Price $40.00

5) **Literary Market Place**
R.R. Bowker Company
1180 Avenue of the Americas
New York, New York Phone: (212) 764-5144

Information on over 1400 book publishers in the United States issuing three or more books during the preceeding year plus book printers, binders, selected syndicates, newspapers, periodicals and radio and

TV programs that use book reviews or news. $35 plus $2 shipping. Send orders to: R.R. Bowker Company, Box 1807, Ann Arbor, MI 48106
(Phone: 313-761-4700)

6) **Publisher's Weekly**
1180 Avenue of the Americas
New York, New York 10036 (212) 764-3368

Most anything you wanted to know about the publishing industry. This is the one publication the people in the business are sure to read. $33

7) **Standard Periodical Directory**
Oxbridge Communications, Inc.
183 Madison Avenue, room 1108
New York, New York 10016 (212) 689-8524

Includes information on over 70,000 magazines, journals, newsletters, directories, house organs, association pubications, &c. in the United States and Canada. Price $160, payment with order. $163 billed.

8) **Ulrich's International Periodicals Directory**
R.R. Bowker Company
1180 Avenue of the Americas
New York, New York 10028 (212) 764-5100

65,000 current periodicals published throughout the world classified by subject. $78. Send orders to R.R. Bowker Company (see #5 *supra.*)

9) **U.S. Publicity Directory**
John Wiley & Co.
605 Third Avenue
New York, New York 10016

Five volumes on newspapers, magazines, radio and television, business and finance, and communications services. $65 for any one volume; $185 for the series.

10) **Working Press Of The Nation**
National Reserch Bureau
310 S. Michigan Avenue, suite 1150
Chicago, IL 60604 (312) 663-5580

In separate volumes covers syndicates and over 6,000 daily and weekly newspapers, over 8000 radio and television stations, nearly 5000 magazines, also includes feature writers and photographers and internal house organs. Price, Set $241 or each of the five volumes. $111 each.

11) **Writer's Digest**
9933 Alliance Road
Cincinnati, OH 45242

Gives information about different newspaper and magazine markets, concentrates on a particular market in each issue. $7.95 subscription.

NEWSPAPER DIRECTORIES

1) **College Student Press in America**
Oxbridge Communications, Inc.
183 Madison Avenue
New York, New York 10016

Lists over 5,500 newspapers, yearbooks and magazines published by students on about 2,500 campuses. $35.

2) **Editor & Publisher Annual Directory of Syndicated Services Issue**
Editor & Publisher Company
575 Lexington Avenue
New York, New York Phone: (212) 752-7050

Syndicates serving newspapers in the United States and abroad with news, columns, features, comic strips, and editorial cartoons. $50.

3) **Family Page Directory**
Public Relations Plus, Inc.
Box 327
Washington Depot, CT 06794 Phone: (203) 868-0200

550 newspapers with family-interest pages or sections. $45.

4) **Free Circulation Community Papers Media Guide**
National Association of Advertising Publishers
313 Price Place
Madison, WI 53705 Phone: (608) 233-5306

Gives information on free circulation newspapers, shopping guides, and private distribution systems. $21.50.

5) **Media Guide International: Newspapers and News Magazines**
Directories International, Inc.
150 Fifth Avenue
New York, New York 10011 Phone: (212) 807-1660

Newspapers and news magazines, international, national and regional in scope, from 111 countries including the U.S. $85

6) **National Directory of Weekly Newspapers**
National Newspaper Association
1627 K Street, N.W., Suite 400
Washington, D.C. 20006
Phone: (202) 466-7200

7,800 listings including name of newspaper, address, county, type of area, circulation, &c. $35.

7) **News Bureaus In The U.S.**
Public Relations Publishing Company, Inc.
888 Seventh Avenue
New York, New York 10106
Phone: (212) 582-7373

Over 500 news bureaus operated by 200 major newspapers, magazines, business publications, wire services, and syndicates. Includes state capitals, suburban and regional bureaus, bureaus in Washington, D.C., and all bureaus nationwide of The Associated Press, United Press International, &c. $25.

8) **Newspaper Guild — Address List Of Local Officers**
Newspaper Guild
1125 15th Street, N.W.
Washington, D.C.
Phone: (202) 296-2990

85 local and district councils of The Newspaper Guild. Free

9) **Suburban Newspapers Of America — Membership Directory**
Suburban Newspapers of America
111 E. Wacker Drive, suite 600
Chicago, IL 60601
Phone: (312) 644-6610

Includes publication name, publishing company name, address, phone, names of key newspaper personnel and principal communities served. $10.

10) **Syndicated Columnists Directory**
Public Relations Publishing Company
888 Seventh Avenue
New York, New York 10106
Phone: (212) 582-7373

Lists over 800 major syndicated newspaper columnists. $30.

MAGAZINE DIRECTORIES

1) **Advertisers Guide to Scholarly Periodicals**
American University Press Services, Inc.
One Park Avenue
New York, New York 10016
Phone: (212) 889-3510

Describes about 2,500 periodicals in 45 categories. Data includes book reviewer's name and address (often different from publication address). $50.

2) **Catalog Of Literary Magazines**
Coordinating Council of Literary Magazines
1133 Broadway
New York, New York 10010 Phone: (212) 675-8605

Several hundred magazines whose principal content is fiction, poetry, &c. $3.50

3) **Directory Of Small Magazine/Press Editors and Publishers**
Dustbooks
Box 100
Paradise, CA 95969

About 3,500 publishers and editors. $10.95 plus $1.25 shipping.

4) **Folio Magazine — Folio 400 Issue**
Folio Magazine Publishing Corporation
125 Elm Street
New Canaan, CT 06840 Phone: (203) 972-0761

List of leading American magazines ranked according to circulation. $15.

Also, Folio Magazine's Magazine Watch Section. New general interest, special interest, professional, trade and technical publications. $4. per copy.

5) **Free Magazines For Libraries**
McFarland & Company, Inc.
Box 611
Jefferson, NC 28640 Phone: (919) 246-4460

Over 400 periodicals published by firms, universities, and associations available free to libraries. $17.95 plus $1.25 shipping.

6) **Magazine Industry Market Place**
R.R. Bowker Company
1180 Avenue of the Americas
New York, New York 10036 Phone: (212) 764-5144

About 5,400 periodicals and their publishers. $39.95. Send orders to: R.R. Bowker Company, Box 1807, Ann Arbor, MI 48106.

7) **Media Guide International: Consumer Magazines**
Directories International, Inc.
150 Fifth Avenue
New York, New York 10011 Phone: (212) 807-1660

Magazines published by airlines, hotels and motels, and travel organizations as well as art magazines. $30.

8) **Media Personnel Directory**
Gale Research Company
Book Tower
Detroit, MI 48226 — Phone: (313) 961-2242

Editors, publishers, columnists, art directors, book reviewers, foreign and domestic correspondents, and bureau chiefs on staffs of 700 magazines and periodicals in the United States. $50.

TELEVISION DIRECTORIES

1) **Cable Services Report: Local Programming**
National Cable Television Association
1724 Massachusetts Avenue, N.W.
Washington, D.C. 20036 — Phone: (202) 775-3550

Over 800 cable television systems. $10.

2) **Directory Of Rights And Permissions Officers**
Association of Media Producers
1101 Connecticut Avenue, suite 700
Washington, D.C. 20036 — Phone: (202) 296-4710

Personnel at member television networks, distributors of programs, some Public Broadcasting System stations, and nonprofit television agencies to contact for permission to use copyrighted materials. Free. Send SASE.

3) **International Television Almanac**
Quigley Publishing Company
159 West 53 Street
New York, New York 10019 — Phone: (212) 247-3100

Includes biographies of celebrities, motion picture information, and information about TV personnel. $33. The Quigley Publishing Company also issues a Motion Picture Product Digest which is also $33 per copy. The two publications can be purchased together for $50.

4) **Television Contacts**
Larimi Communications Associates, Ltd.
151 East 50 Street
New York, New York 10022 — Phone: (212) 935-9262

Covers about 900 television stations, networks and syndicates interested in guests or outside scripts. $117 including monthly updates.

5) **Television Factbook**
Television Digest, Inc.
1836 Jefferson Place, N.W.
Washington, D.C. 20036 — Phone: (202) 872-9200

Commercial and noncommercial television stations and networks worldwide. $165.

6) **Television Index, Inc.**
Jerry Leichter, Editor
150 Fifth Avenue
New York, New York 10011
Phone: (212) 924-0320

Weekly reports cover network television programming, major independent television production, sponsors, productions news and performance records. $175 annually. Also, Mr. Leichter publishes Media News Keys, four pages weekly dealing with network, local radio and television programs. $70.

7) **TV News**
Larimi Communications
151 East 50 Street
New York, New York 10022
Phone: (212) 935-9262

About 750 local television news departments and about 150 national and regional network news programs and their staffs are covered. $70.

8) **TV Publicity Outlets Nationwide**
Public Relations Plus, Inc.
Box 327
Washington Depot, CT 06794
Phone: (203) 868-0200

Deals with over 2500 local and network television programs which use outside guests, film, or script. $89.50 per year.

9) **Who's Who In Cable Communications**
Communications Marketing, Inc.
2326 Tampa Avenue
El Cajon, Ca 92020
Phone: (619) 461-7891

Lists over 1,400 cable and pay television executives. $59.95 plus $3.50 shipping.

RADIO DIRECTORIES

1) **National Radio Publicity Directory**
Peter Glenn Publications, Ltd.
17 East 48 Street
New York, New York 10017
Phone: (212) 688-7940

Covers over 3,500 network, syndicated and local talk shows in the nation's 200 major markets and over 4,500 local and college radio stations. $85.

2) **Radio Contacts**
Larimi Communications Associates, Ltd.
151 East 50 Street
New York, New York 10022
Phone: (212) 935-9262

3,000 local, syndicated and network radio programs interested in guests or outside scripts or information. $126 per year including book and monthly updates.

3) **Radio Programming Profile**
BF/Communication Services, Inc.
7 Cathy Court
Glen Head, New York 11545 Phone: (516) 676-7070

3,000 AM and FM radio stations in top 200 markets with basic format information. In two volumes. $181.

4) **Traveling With A Radio**
Donnelly & Sons Publishing Company
Box 7880
Colorado Springs, CO 80933 Phone: (303) 473-5107

Deals with over 8000 AM and FM radio stations in the United States. $6.

TELEVISION AND RADIO DIRECTORIES

1) **Broadcasting/Cablecasting Yearbook**
Broadcasting Publications, Inc.
1735 DeSales Street, N.W.
Washington, D.C. 20036 Phone: (202) 638-1022

All television and radio stations and cable television systems in the United States and Canada. $65.

2) **International Radio And Television Society — Roster Yearbook**
International Radio and Television Society
420 Lexington Avenue
New York, New York 10170 Phone: (212) 867-6650

Over 1,300 people professionally involved in television or radio or connected to them through publishing, business, or teaching. Available to members only.

3) **North American Radio, TV Station Guide**
Howard W. Sams & Company, Inc.
4300 W. 62 Street
Indianapolis, IN 46206 Phone: (317) 298-5400

Covers over 12,500 AM, FM and television stations currently in operation in United States, Canada, Cuba, Mexico and West Indies. $7.95

4) **People In Public Telecommunications**
National Association of Educational Broadcasters
1346 Connecticut Avenue, N.W.
Washington, D.C. 20036 Phone: (202) 785-1100

Covers 500 public television and over 3,000 individuals in public/educational broadcasting. Includes national telecommunication agencies with staff listings. $10.

5) **Radio-Television News Directors Association-Directory**
Radio-Television News Directors Association
1735 DeSales Street, N.W.
Washington, D.C. 20036 Phone: (202) 737-8657

Lists over 2000 individuals including those in Canada. Available to members only.

6) **Radio-TV Contact Service**
Media News Keys
150 Fifth Avenue
New York, New York 10011 Phone: (212) 924-0320

Radio and television programs (both local and network) which use guests and originate in New York City area. $85.

7) **Talk Show Directory For Radio And Television**
National Research Bureau, Inc., Division
Automated Marketing Systems, Inc.
310 S. Michigan Avenue
Chicago, IL 60604 Phone: (312) 663-5580

Interview, panel, call-in, and other types of radio and television talk shows from over 8,300 stations nationwide. $105.

NEWSLETTER INFORMATION

1) **National Directory Of Newsletters And Reporting Services**
Gale Research Company
Book Tower
Detroit, MI 48226 Phone: (313) 961-2242

Periodicals of a newsletter format issued on a regular basis by both commercial and noncommercial publishers. Entries include newsletter title, name and address of publisher, phone, name of editor, brief description of newsletter's title, name and address of publisher, phone, name of editor, brief description of newsletter's scope and purpose. $85 for four-issue set.

2) **Newsletter Yearbook /Directory**
Newsletter Clearinghouse
44 West Market Street
Rhinebeck, New York 12572 Phone: (914) 876-2081

Covers about 2,400 newsletters available by subscription. $35.

3) **Oxbridge Directory Of Newsletters**
Oxbridge Communications, Inc.
183 Madison Avenue, room 1108
New York, New York 10016 Phone: (212) 689-8524

Deals with over 8,000 newsletters in the U.S. and Canada. $45 plus $3 shipping.

PHOTOGRAPH INFORMATION

1) **Directory Of Professional Photography**
   Professional Photographers of America
   1090 Executive Way
   Des Plaines, IL 60018 Phone: (312) 299-8161

Over 15,000 portrait, commercial and industrial photographers who are members of the PPA; also includes guide to photographic equipment and supply manufacturers and distributors. $12.50

2) **Photoletter**
   Photosearch International
   Osceola, WI 54020 Phone: (715) 248-3800

Magazine and book publishers currently soliciting photographs for publication. $60 per year.

3) **Where And How To Sell Your Photographs**
   Amphoto, Division BPI
   1515 Broadway
   New York, New York 10036

About 300 book and magazine publishers and other markets for photographs $9.95

AUDIO VISUAL AND FILM INFORMATION

1) **Back Stage Film/Tape/Syndication Directory**
   Back Stage Publications, Inc.
   330 West 42 Street
   New York, New York 10038 Phone: (212) 581-1080

Over 3,500 producers and service firms involved in the nontheatrical and industrial film and videotape industries plus ad agencies and TV stations. $15.00 on payment with order.

2) **Hope Reports Perspective**
   919 S. Winston Road
   Rochester, New York 14618 Phone: (716) 458-4250

Specializes in the audiovisual industry, designed for producers, distributors or users of filmstrips, motion pictures, tapes or other AV materials. $30.

STATE, REGIONAL, CITY MEDIA DIRECTORIES

— California

1) **California Media**
Box 327
Washington Depot, CT 06754 Phone: (203) 868-0200

Detailed listing of personnel at daily and weekly newspapers, radio and television stations. $49.50

2) **Hollywood Reporter Studio Blu-Book**
Hollywood Reporter, Inc.
6715 Sunset Boulevard
Hollywood, CA 90028 Phone (213) 464-7411

Motion picture studios and producing companies, firms serving the industry, casting agencies, national theater circuits and theaters in the Los Angeles area, network television companies, production companies and distributors, Los Angeles television stations, phonograph record companies and independent producers, recording and sound studios, music publishers, network broadcasting companies, and Los Angeles radio stations. $25.

3) **KNX (CBS) Radio**
6121 Sunset Boulevard
Hollywood, CA 90028

Free directory of media and advertising agencies in Los Angeles area.

4) **Southern California Media Directory**
Publicity Club of Los Angeles
1258 N. Highland Avenue
Los Angeles, CA 90038 Phone: (213) 469-5066

1,000 newspapers, magazines, radio and TV stations and other media in 8 county southern California area. $55.

— District of Columbia

1) **Hudson's Washington News Media Contacts Directory**
2626 Pennsylvania Avenue, N.W.
Washington, D.C. 20037

Includes information about more than 4,000 publications, bureaus, correspondents, editors and free-lance writers. $60 including revisions.

2) **Washington Information Directory**
Congressional Quarterly, Inc.
1414 22 St., N.W.
Washington, D.C. 20037 Phone: (202) 887-8500

More than 5,000 information sources in Congress, the Executive Branch, private associations, and the media.

3) **Washington Journalism Review**
2233 Wisconsin Avenue, N.W.
Washington, D.C. 20007 Phone: (202) 333-6800

Orientation is to Washington-based media, including also national publications and bureaus. $16 per year.

— Georgia

1) **Atlanta's PR/News World**
Southeastern Press Relations Newswire
161 Peachtree Street
Atlanta, GA 30303
Larry Keller, Editor Phone: (404) 523-2515

Four-page newsletter published sporatically with news and comments about media in southeast, particularly Atlanta. Free

2) **Atlanta Publicity Outlets And Media Directory**
Box 54105
Atlanta, GA 30308

Has over 500 media listings in 15-county Atlanta area. $49.50

— Illinois

1) **Chicago Publicity Club**
Suite 110, 1441 Shermer Road
Northbrook, IL 60062

Lists personnel at Chicago daily newspapers, wire services, radio and TV stations, magazines, community and suburban newspapers, freelance writers, professional reference sources and suppliers. $25.

2) **Publicity In Chicago**
Chicago Convention Bureau, Inc.
332 S. Michigan Avenue
Chicago, IL 60604

Free 30-page guide including listing of department editors and other personnel at Chicago dailies, radio and TV stations as well as local bureaus of wire services, syndicates, magazines, newspapers and newsreels.

3) **Midwest Media**
Midwest Newsclip, Inc.
360 N. Michigan Avenue
Chicago, IL 60601

Annual directory of radio and TV stations, daily and weekly newspapers in Illinois. $45.

— Massachusetts

1) **Greater Boston Media Directory**
Media Directories Division
New England Newsclip
5 Auburn Street
Framingham, MA 02107 Phone: (617) 879-4660

Lists newspapers, radio stations, televisions and cable TV systems, periodicals, college publications and media-related organizations in the Greater Boston area. $17.50 This company also publishes the **New England Media Directory** with similar information about Connecticut, Maine, New Hampshire, Rhode Island, Vermont and Massachusetts ($49) and the **New England Talk Show Directory** for radio and television stations. ($30)

— Michigan

1) **Southeastern Michigan News Media Directory**
c/o Greater Detroit Area Hospital Council
Seth Lampe
1900 Book Building
Detroit, MI 48226

Information on Greater Detroit media. $2.

— Minnesota

1) **Media Information Systems Corporation**
1536 S. Oberlin Circle
Fridley, MN 55432

Provides comprehensive publicity mailing to media, publishes general directories and provides other services for Minnesota. Books include **The Minnesota Publicity Handbook** ($89), **Minnesota News Media Contacts** ($69) and **The Twin Cities Publicity Handbook** ($59)

— New York

1) **New York Publicity Outlets**
Public Relations Plus, Inc.
Box 327
Washington Depot, CT 06794 Phone: (203) 868-0200

Consumer media in metropolitan New York area including over 100 radio and TV stations, about 200 radio and TV interview shows and about 500 daily and weekly newspapers. $55.

2) **Talknews**
213 East Broadway
New York, New York 10002

Comments about New York talk radio programs. $3.60.

— Pennsylvania

1) **Burrelle's Pennsylvania Media Directory**
Div. of Burrelle Press Clipping Service
75 East Northfield Road
Livingston, NJ 07039 Phone: (201) 992-7070

Newspapers, periodicals, college publications, house organs, radio and television systems, advertising representatives. $38.

2) **Philadelphia Publicity Guide**
Fund-Raising Institute
Box 365
Amber, PA 19002

Over 510 local publications and stations. $23.

— Regional Directories and Information Sources

1) **Burrelle's Media Directories**
Burrelle's Press Clipping Bureau
75 East Northfield Road
Livingston, New Jersey 07039 Phone: 1-800-631-1160

Burrelle's and its affiliated companies publish the **New York State Media Directory** ($20, personnel of over 700 daily and weekly newspapers, 200 college publications and over 175 periodicals, plus all radio and TV stations), the **New Jersey Media Directory,** and the **New England Media Directory.** Burrelle's also publishes specialized media directories in seven categories: Blacks, European-ethnics, Hispanics, Jews, Senior citizens, Women, Young Adults and activists.

2) **Finderbinder**
4141 Fairmont Avenue
San Diego, CA 92105 Phone: (714) 284-1145

Finderbinder is a group of public relations agencies licensed to produce local media directories in their areas. There are currently about 20 directories at about $40 each. Cities or areas include: Arizona, Denver, Milwaukee, Cleveland, Dallas, Houston, Oklahoma City, Pittsburgh, Portland, St. Louis, and Seattle.

3) **Television/Radio Age — Ten City Directory**
Television Editorial Corporation
1270 Avenue of the Americas
New York, New York 10020 Phone: (212) 757-8400

4,000 commercial radio and television stations, trade publications, networks for New York, Chicago, Los Angeles, San Francisco, Detroit, Atlanta, Dallas-Fort Worth, St. Louis, Philadelphia, and Minneapolis-St. Paul. $5.

ALTERNATIVE, BLACK, HISPANIC, WOMEN MEDIA SOURCES

— Alternative

1) **Alternative Press Directory**
Alternative Press Syndicate
Box 1347
Ansonia Station
New York, New York 10023 Phone: (212) 974-1990

2) **Citizens Media Directory**
National Citizens Committee for Broadcasting
Box 12038
Washington, D.C. 20005 Phone: (202) 462-2520

400 national and local media reform groups, public access centers, community radio stations, alternative news services, film and video producers. $3.50

3) **Directory of Intercultural Education Newsletters**
Information Consulting Associates
303 West Pleasantview Avenue
Hackensack, NJ 07601

Over 125 newsletters concerned with bi- and inter-cultural education at all levels. $10.

— Minority

1) **Directory of Minority Media**
San Francisco Redevelopment Agency
Box 646
San Francisco, CA 94104 Phone: (415) 771-8800

More than 60 radio stations, television stations, and publications oriented to Asian Americans, Blacks, Native Americans, and Spanish-speaking Americans in northern California. Free.

2) **Minority/Ethnic Media Guide**
Directories International, Inc.
150 Fifth Avenue
New York, New York 10011 Phone: (212) 807-1660

Over 800 newspapers, magazines and 420 TV and radio stations with special appeal to specific ethnic and minority groups including Spanish-speaking Americans, Asian Americans, handicapped, gays, the elderly, American Indian, Irish, Polish, &c. $75.

3) **Black Press Periodical Directory**
Black Newspaper Clipping Bureau, Inc.
68 East 121 St.
New York, New York 10037 Phone: (212) 281-6000

Newspapers, magazines, newsletters, radio stations, and news services in the U.S. which are Black owned or oriented. $40.

4) **Nationwide Black Radio Directory**
CDE
Box 41551
Atlanta, Ga 30331

About 500 Black-owned radio stations, broadcasting firms, music organizations, &c. $20.

— Women

1) **Guide To Women's Publishing**
Dustbooks
Box 100
Paradise, CA 95969

More than 100 women's journals and newspapers, agencies distributing women's publications and women's presses. $12.50

— Children

1) **Children's Media Market Place**
Neal-Schuman Publishers, Inc.
23 Cornelia Street
New York, New York 10014 Phone: (212) 473-5170

Covers publishes, audiovisual producers, wholesalers, distributors, bookstores, book clubs, associations and organizations concerned with children's media, radio and television broadcasters with children's programming. $24.95

2) **Getting Your Child Into TV Commercials**
Pilot Books
347 Fifth Avenue
New York, New York 10016 Phone: (212) 685-0736

List of children's agents franchised by Screen Actors Guild. $2.95

RELIGIOUS MEDIA

— General

1) **Annual Directory Of Religious Broadcasting**
National Religious Broadcasters
38 Speedwell Avenue
Morristown, New Jersey 07960 Phone: (201) 575-4000

Over 3,000 radio stations, radio programs, television stations, program producers, book publishers, and recording companies. $25.

2) **Oxbridge Directory Of Religious Periodicals**
Oxbridge Communications, Inc.
183 Madison Avenue
New York, New York 10016 Phone: (212) 689-8524

Over 3,000 religious periodicals, directories, educational materials published in the United States and Canada. $25.

— Born-Again Christian

1) **Born-Again Christian Catalog**
M. Evans and Company, Inc.
216 East 49 Street
New York, New York 10017 Phone: (212) 688-2810

Radio and television broadcasting for fundamentalist evangelical Christians. $6.95

— Catholic

1) **Catholic Press Directory**
Catholic Press Association
119 N. Park Avenue
Rockville Center, New York 11570

Annual guide to all recognized Catholic publications in U.S., Canada, and the Caribbean. $10.

— Jewish

1) **American Jewish Press Association — Roster Of Members**
c/o Pittsburgh Jewish Chronicle
315 S. Bellefield Avenue
Pittsburgh, PA 15213 Phone: (412) 687-1000

Over 70 privately-owned and federation-owned Jewish newspapers in the U.S. and Canada. Available to members only.

2) **Anglo-Jewish Media List**

R.K. Communications
98-15 65th Road
Rego Park, New York 11374 Phone: (212) 275-2546

Over 330 Jewish news services, news weeklies, biweeklies, monthlies, national publications, house organs and specialized journals. $38.

3) **Jewish Press In America**
60 East 42 Street
New York, New York 10017

Names of editors, editorial requirements, provides information on publicity and photo needs and special feature issues published by about 120 publications in 65 cities. $10.

POLITICALLY-CONSERVATIVE MEDIA SOURCES

1) **AIM Report**
Accuracy In Media, Inc.
777 14th Street, N.W.
Washington, D.C. 20005

Conservative orientation. Monitors primarily the eastern press. $15.

2) **Family And Freedom Digest**
Family & Freedom Foundation
100 Brooks Avenue
Rochester, New York 14619

Covers about 90 conservative educational and political organizations; another 30 organizations and 20 periodicals are listed. $12.

MEDIA SOURCES OF PRIMARY INTEREST TO BUSINESS AND SPECIFIC INDUSTRIES

1) **Business Wire Newsletter**
   235 Montgomery Street
   San Francisco, CA 94104

Business Wire is a private teletype service with offices in San Francisco, Los Angeles, Seattle, and Boston. Circulation is limited to members. It includes media personnel changes, also candid comments about the problems of publishers, broadcasters, and publicists.

2) **The Corporate Communications Report**
   112 East 31 Street
   New York, New York 10016

Bimonthly newsletter most useful to accountants, lawyers, and financial specialists working with large publicly-owned companies. $65.

3) **The Design And Building Industry's Publicity Directory**
   c/o MRH Associates
   Box 11316
   Newington, CT 06111

Lists consumer magazines and trade journals using news, feature stories about development, planning, design and construction firms.

4) **editors newsletter**
   Box 774
   New York, New York 10010

Monthly compilation of news and comments about trends and techniques of interest to business communicators. Greatest use to house organ editors.

5) **Health Media Buyer's Guide**
   Nautillus Publishing Corp.
   Box 4790
   Stamford, CT 06907

Primarily for advertisers in the health field, this three-volume loose-leaf publication includes data about 1,600 national, state, and local medical and other health publications. $90.

6) **Internal Publications Directory**
   National Research Bureau, Inc.
   104 S. Michigan Avenue
   Chicago, IL 60603

One and only source of detailed information about internal and external house organs of more than 3,500 U.S. and Canadian companies, government agencies, clubs, and other groups. $64.

7) **Media Guide International: Business/Professional Publications**
Directories International, Inc.
150 Fifth Avenue
New York, New York 10011 Phone: (212) 807-1660

7,100 business and professional publications in 106 countries. $75.

8) **Speed Sport Public Relations Newsletter**
Ernie Saxton & Associates
Box 795
Langhorne, PA 19047

Monthly publication for motor sports promoters.

9) **Travel News And Publicity Directory**
Discover America Travel Organizations, Inc.
1899 L Street, N.W.
Washington, D.C. 20036

Lists over 1,000 travel writers, media and source in the U.S. and elsewhere. $25.

INFORMATION SOURCES ON ASSOCIATIONS

1) **Encyclopedia Of Associations**
Gale Research Company
Book Tower
Detroit, MI 48226 Phone: (313) 961-2242

Information on over 16,000 active organizations divided into 17 categories. $150.

2) **National Trade And Professional Associations Of The U.S.**
Columbia Books, Inc.
777 14th Street, N.W., suite 236
Washington, D.C. 20005 Phone: (202) 737-3777

Over 6,000 associations are dealt with. $35

INFORMATION ON WHERE TO FIND INFORMATION

1) **Information Industry Market Place**
R.R. Bowker Company
1180 Avenue of the Americas
New York, New York 10036 Phone: (212) 764-5100

About 2,500 firms and individuals who produce information products or who service the information industry. $37.50. Also publishes the **American Library Directory** listing all U.S. libraries.

2) **Information Sources: The IIA Membership Directory**
Information Industry Association
316 Pennsylvania Avenue, S.E., suite 400
Washington, D.C. 20003 Phone: (301) 654-4150

Over 130 companies producing information products. $25.

3) **Names and Numbers: A Journalist's Guide To The Most Needed Information Sources And Contacts**
John Wiley & Sons, Inc.
605 Third Avenue
New York, New York 10158 Phone: (212) 850-6418

20,000 information sources and contacts including: airports, toll-free telephone numbers, railroads, hotels and motels, prominent Americans, special interest groups, institutions, colleges, government agencies, sports leagues, information and research services, associations and societies, television and radio stations, publishers, &c. $35.95 Send orders to: John Wiley & Sons, One Wiley Dr., Somerset, NJ 08873. (201-459-4400)

4) **Sources: A Guide To Print And Nonprint Materials Available From Organs, Industry, Government Agencies, And Specialized Publishers**
Neal-Schuman Publishers, Inc.
23 Cornelia Street
New York, New York 10014 Phone: (212) 473-5170

About 2,000 sources for materials which publishers feel "escape the traditional bibliographic net" including books, periodicals, filmstrips, cassettes, posters, games, &c. $70

THEORETICAL AND PRACTICAL INFORMATION ON THE PUBLIC RELATIONS BUSINESS

1) **Channels**
Public Relations Society of America
845 Third Avenue
New York, New York 10022

Oldest newsletter in the public relations field. Monthly mix of news and features on nonprofit agency public relations, management, and fund raising. $24.

2) **Columbia Journalism Review**
700 Journalism Building
Columbia University
New York, New York 10027

Bimonthly. Aims to stimulate enhanced journalistic professionalism. $14.

3) **The Gallagher Report**
230 Park Avenue
New York, New York 10017

Confidential letter to marketing, sales, advertising, and media executives. Comments about media and advertisers, particularly in magazines. $96.

4) **Impact**
203 N. Wabash Avenue
Chicago, IL 60601

Monthly newsletter on trends, techniques, issues and tools for communicators. $18.

5) **Jack O'Dwyer's Newsletter**
271 Madison Avenue
New York, New York 10016

Covers New York public relations agencies. Publishes two directories, too: one on public relations agencies, the other about public relations departments of companies.

6) **Journal Of Communication**
Annenberg School of Communication
University of Pennsylvania
3620 Walnut Street
Philadelphia, PA 19103

Quarterly publication for those involved in the theory, research, policy, and practice of communication. $15.

7) **Media Industry Newsletter**
150 East 52 Street
New York, New York 10022

News, features, research reports, predictions, candid opinions about publishers and broadcasters. Primarily of interest to advertising, marketing, and media people. $58.

8) **PR Aids' Party Line**
PR Aids, Inc.
330 West 34 Street
New York, New York

Current placement opportunities in all media. This is the insider's tip sheet. $90.

9) **pr reporter**
PR Publishing Company, Inc.
Box 600
Exeter, New Jersey 03833

News of personnel, accounts, and activities in public relations. $80.

10) **Public Relations Journal**
Public Relations Society of America
845 Third Avenue
New York, New York 10022

Only monthly magazine in public relations field. Free to PRSA members; others $9.50.

11) **Public Relations News**
127 East 80 Street
New York, New York 10021

Weekly newsletter with news and comments about public relations events, accounts, and people. Also has weekly case study dealing with recent campaign, project, or special event. $147.75.

12) **Public Relations Quarterly**
44 West Market Street
Rhinebeck, New York 12572

Concentrates on the theory and practice of public relations. $12.

13) **Public Relations Review**
College of Journalism
University of Maryland
College Park, MD 20742

Bridge between public relations and social and behavioral science. $10.

14) **The Quill**
35 East Wacker Drive
Chicago, IL 60601

Published by Sigma Delta Chi society of professional journalists with news of the members and articles about the print media. $10.

15) **The Ragan Report**
Lawrence Ragan Communications, Inc.
407 S. Dearborn Street
Chicago, IL 60605

Deals with both news and public affairs issues. $50.

16) **Social Science Monitor**
Communication Research Associates, Inc.
7338 Baltimore Blvd.
College Park, MD 20740

Translates the social and behavioral sciences for use by public relations, advertising, and marketing people. $64.

ADVERTISING INFORMATION SOURCES

1) **Advertising Age**
740 N. Rush Street
Chicago, IL 60611

Gives detailed consideration to information of interest to advertisers and advertising agencies. $40.

2) **Media Guide International**
Directories International, Inc.
1718 Sherman Avenue
Evanston, IL 60201

Comprehensive package of advertising reference materials about international markets. Currently publishes six directories: **Newspapers And News Magazines** ($55), **Airline/Inflight And Travel Publications** ($25), 4 volumes dealing with 44 subject categories in business and the professions. ($198 for the four).

3) **Standard Rate & Data Service, Inc.**
5201 Old Orchard Road
Skokie, IL 60077
Phone: (312) 470-3100

Publishes the following volumes of interest to advertisers:

- **Community Publication Rates & Data.** Non-daily newspapers and shopping guides. $20.
- **Consumer Magazine And Farm Publication Rates & Data.** About 1,200 consumer and 200 farm periodicals; international consumer magazines. $126.
- **Network Rates & Data.** Radio and television networks, their owned stations, and affiliated stations. $23 plus $2 shipping.
- **Newspaper Rates & Data.** More than 1,600 newspaper and newspaper groups including newspaper-distributed magazines, nationally and locally edited comics, religious newspapers, Black newspapers, and specialized newspapers. $42.
- **Spot Radio Rates & Data.** Over 4,300 AM stations and over 2,11 FM stations. $28.00
- **Spot Radio Small Markets Edition.** Radio stations in markets of 25,000 or less. $45 plus $2 shipping.
- **Spot Television Rates & Data.** All television stations and regional networks and groups. $125 plus $5 shipping.

MISCELLANEOUS: A FEW FINAL INFORMATION SOURCES

1) **The Editorial Eye**
Editorial Experts, Inc.
5905 Pratt Street
Alexandria, VA 22310

Informal tips, tests, listings, other material for editors and other communicators including typists and word processors. $45.

2) **Models Guide**
Leo Shull Publications
134 West 44 Street
New York, New York 10036

Model agencies, photographers, TV commercial producers and other companies using models in New York City area. $6.85.

3) **Military Publications**
Richard Weiner, Inc.
888 Seventh Avenue
New York, New York 10019

The only book which provides circulation, advertising rates and other data about government and civilian newspapers and magazines for U.S. military personnel and their families. $15.

CHAPTER 4

PRODUCING THE STANDARD MEDIA KIT

The unabashed self-promoter, before he even considers approaching media sources, must have produced all the written materials he needs. Actually approaching media sources should be mechanical; the real thought and preparation all occur in advance of contact, particularly in drafting and assembling the materials of your Standard Media Kit.

What You Need

What you need, of course, depends on what you are trying to accomplish and who you'll be dealing with. The following, however, is a list of virtually every kind of written document you will need in dealing with the media:

- notice of event or media conference ("The Tip Sheet")
- media advisory
- standard media release
- biograpical documents
- fact sheet
- chronology
- position paper
- list of contacts
- prepared statement
- media schedule
- clip sheet
- previous media contacts
- photographs
- public service/calendar announcement

Notice Of Media Event Or Media Conference: "The Tip Sheet"

The Tip Sheet gives an assignment editor advance information about what is taking place, when, and who to contact for further or follow-up information. One excellent format for the Tip Sheet is this one:

Contact: Name ______________________________

Company ______________________________

Address ______________________________

Telephone Number (business) ______________________________

(after business hours) ______________________________

FOR IMMEDIATE RELEASE

SUMMARY HEADLINE

Event: ______________________________

Date/Time: ______________________________

Location: ______________________________

(Directions if difficult to find) ______________________________

Background information: ______________________________

The Tip Sheet should be typewritten and offset print or photocopied on your official stationery. If you seriously want media people to attend your event, you must follow it up with a telephone call.

Notification Of Media Conference Or Event

A variation on the Tip Sheet is used when notifying the media about a forthcoming media conference or event in which you'd like them to participate. This form is necessarily sparse on details. It tells the media that an event is about to take place, when and where it will occur, the general thrust of what will be said or will happen. But it does not supply detail. This detail will be provided at the event itself, and you do not want to announce it in advance or your event will loose some of its impact.

This notification needs to be sent about a week in advance of the event. Make follow-up telephone calls as soon as possible, in practice about 2 to 4 days before the event is scheduled.

Notification Of Media Conference: Format

Day & Date: ______________________________

Time: ______________________________

Place: ______________________________

Contact: Name, Title ______________________________

Telephone: (business) ______________________________

(after business hours) ______________________________

SUMMARY HEADLINE

Information to be included

Name of group sponsoring media conference or event: ______________________________

Purpose of conference or event: ______________________________

Reiteration of information about where and when event will take place: ______________________________

Names of other organizations affected by event (if you are co-sponsoring, list these; if your media conference has been arranged to advance or counter criticisms about organizations and individuals, list these): ______________________________

This notification should be printed on your stationery and mailed one week before the scheduled event.

Media Advisory

The media advisory is a more elaborate form of the Tip Sheet and media notification. Essentially it gives the flavor of the event which is about to take place. It indicates to the media what the story is and why it is worth covering. It is the skeleton for the story which you hope and expect the media to publish or broadcast. Here's what you need to include:

Name of event: ______________________________

Day /date: ______________________________

Time: ______________________________

Place: ______________________________

Contact person: Name, title ______________________________

Business telephone: ______________ ______________

After business hours telephone: ______________________________

SUMMARY HEADLINE

First paragraph: Repeat information summarized above. Who is participating (complete name of individual or organization). What is the event, when is it taking place, where is it taking place, what time is it taking place.

Second paragraph: Background information about event. What are the reasons why people will be interested in this event? Is it unique? Different? Timely? Give specific reason for public (and media) interest. These constitute the hooks on which the media will hang their stories.

Third paragraph: Give background information about the event or individual to establish a context for the reader. This is necessary background information. This paragraph includes the most important background information about the organization sponsoring the event, the event itself, or the individuals who have organized the event or who are being featured in it. What do people most want to know?

Fourth paragraph. This paragraph adds important information about the organization, event or individual which is not, however, of the same weight and significance as that in paragraph three but which you would like to be used, if possible.

Fifth paragraph. This paragraph adds additional background information which is less important than the material appearing in paragraphs three and four.

Sixth paragraph. Advises reader who to call to set up interviews, get further background information, photographs, &c.

Addendum: It is a wise idea to alert the media, particularly when you are traveling, just when you will be available for interviews and media engagements. Be flexible. Media people work around the clock; the unabashed self-promoter must do the same. Do not just include times between 9 and 5. If you are available in the evening, say so.

This document should be typewritten or typeset on your stationery and photocopied. While this media advisory may be generally distributed, if you are serious about any particular media target, you will need to follow it up with a telephone call. (See samples, page 295).

Standard Media Release

Most people know that in approaching the media they will need a Standard Media Release. All too often, however, novice self-promoters are inclined to rest their case exclusively on such a release; once written it is simply mailed away and never followed up. Note: A good media release can rarely help you. Media people expect them. You therefore get no credit for doing it well. On the other hand, a bad release can hurt you, often fatally. It indicates that you are, at best, an unsophisticated amateur, hence not particularly worthy of notice. The unabashed self-promoter knows that media he is serious about reaching need a good, detailed media release and one or more follow-up calls. A media release on its own, however good, is seldom sufficient, particularly at the beginning of your career.

The key to a good media release is that it should read *exactly* as the story you want. It should include every fact, every description, every quotation just as you'd like a reporter writing about you to write it. The closer your release is to an actual story the more likely it is to be used. Here's what you should include:

Contact: Name, title ______________________________

Company/Organization: ______________________________

Address: ______________________________

Telephone number (business): ______________________________

Telephone number (after business hours): ______________________________

Release Date ______________
(usually "For Immediate Release"
or for specific date)

SUMMARY HEADLINE ______________________________
(typed in caps, gives
leading facts about story)

Dateline: City of origin ______________________________

Body of Release

Paragraph 1: Include complete name of featured individual or organization. Provide specific information on who they are, what the event is, where and when it will take place. This paragraph should include the 5 W information: who, what, where, when and why.

Paragraph 2: If you are targeting this release to a specific media source (the most likely way to have it used), introduce the name of that publication into this paragraph. this indicates to the source that you are providing them with an exclusive.

The name of your featured individual or organization must appear in this paragraph. Modify it with a significant fact which will underscore its importance. Next include a quotation from the chief individual associated with this project. This quotation should be directed to the most significant readers of the article. All articles have many types of readers. The unabashed self-promoter keeps in mind only those who can do him the most good: his immediate client prospects. The quotations in paragraph two should be directed to these prospects. It should hook their interest and compel them to pay further, closer attention.

Paragraph 3: This paragraph gives additional significant information about the individual, organization or event being featured. It should add a further noteworthy fact about the featured item and another pithy quotation. If this release focuses on one individual, then this quotation should come from that individual; if an organization is being featured, it is perfectly acceptable, even desirable, to quote a second individual.

Do not forget to add personal touches to this release. Remember: whenever possible, you are writing the exact article a reporter would write, not just including factual material. In this regard, it is desirable to add descriptive information about the featured individuals.

Paragraph 4: Adds further, though less important, information of interest to the targeted population. Again, the name of any individual appearing in this paragraph should be modified with a significnt fact that makes this individual more substantial to the reader or which adds to his credibility. Also, add another quotation.

Further paragraphs: These indicate to the reader what you want him to do as a result of learning about your story. Include all necessary follow-up information: how much does your product, service, event, &c cost? How can the reader get involved? Who does he call? When? Where? Look at this paragraph as a specific free ad and write it accordingly. Unlike advertising, however, leave out the hype; what media people want is the facts, just the facts.

The media release can be typewritten and offset print on your stationery. It can be sent out as part of a general mailing or targeted. It is my firm belief (which will be stressed throughout this book) that targeted releases work best. Write your release with a particular media source in mind and follow-up accordingly. Keep in mind, however, that as your career as an unabashed self-promoter progresses there will be times when you will simply want to send out an untargeted release. This is quite alright, so long as you remember that the releases most likely to be used will be those followed up personally by you.

More Tips About The Standard Media Release

- Keep it short. 500 words, two typewritten pages, with 250 words per page double spaced, should be quite sufficient for any media release.
- Write it like a story. Don't just supply facts and expect the media source to edit and rewrite for you. Your copy should bear as near a resemblance to an actual printed story as possible, quotes and all. Don't forget this. Particularly with the weeklies, newspapers and other publications are understaffed and are most happy to use your material *exactly as is* so long as it conforms to their editorial requirements. It is your job to see that it does.
- Use only one side of the page. In this book, we use both sides of the page to produce the samples. In real life, however, only use one side of the page. If your release extends over two pages, at the bottom of the second page add the word "more" and continue at the top of the second page. Repeat your headline in caps and write "page 2 of 2" (or three, or, God forbid!, four, &c.) Once you have finished, simply type the word "end" in the middle of the page under your last sentence. Some people use the number "30" which is archaic journalistic jargon. I have,

however, always found this affected. "End" does quite nicely, thank you. If you have more than 1 page, simply staple them together.

- Double space your copy. All copy should be typed and double spaced. If you are a particularly unsophisticated writer, triple space. This allows an indulgent editor to write the sentence the way it should have been written in the first place. Such editors are, however, exceedingly rare.

In spacing your copy on a page, always conclude with a complete paragraph. If this leaves an inch or two of white space at the bottom of the page, so be it.

- Take care of your diction and tone. Because you are writing a news or feature story which may be printed just as it is, give careful consideration to diction and tone. Use fact and examples; back up any speculation opinion with a quotation which can be attributed. Be wary of adjectives, adverbs, and the exclamation point. These belong to advertisers who have paid for the privilege of making liberal use of them.

Never forget, of course, that you are promoting, too, but that you are doing so under the protective mantle of accessible expert, public servant, knowledgeable citizen knowing something others wish or have to know, too. Crisp, clean, fast-moving, fact-filled prose is the best way to get your message across.

Biographical Information

Media people need biographical background information about individuals being featured in your standard media releases, media conferences, events, &c. There are two basic biographical formats.

Standard Biographical Narrative

In about 200-250 words, provide the following information in narrative form:

Paragraph 1: Introduction

- name of subject
- business affiliation
- title
- years with company or organization
- type of organization if not apparent

Paragraph 2: Vocational Background

- previous positions held indicating progress to present eminence
- professional awards
- distinctive, pace-setting ideas
- professional associations
- include any information which indicates to the reader that subject is important in his profession

Paragraph 3: Information Indicating General Worth

- education
- community, civic, social, fraternal, &c. associations including offices held
- publications written
- all facts which indicate substance, weight, importance of subject

Paragraph 4: Personal Information

- age
- marital status
- children
- hobbies

This information should be photocopied on office stationery and headed with the name of the subject. At the top left corner of the page the following information should also appear:

"For further information contact:

- Name of subject:
- Company or organization:
- Complete address:
- Telephone (business):
- Telephone (after business hours):

Biographical Feature Story

A Biographical Feature Story is a profile of you, written by you to influence what a media source might write or broadcast about you. It is you, the unabashed self-promoter, as you desire your media, your public to see you. This piece should be between 250-400 words in length. Any longer and you might as well begin the autobiography you're destined to write.

Unlike the biographical narrative, which is a source for media, the biographical feature stands alone as a story. It must therefore be interesting, provide significant, appealing background information, quotations by you, a real feel for who you are. It goes much, much farther than the preceeding biographical narrative in establishing a sense of the person you are, a person who compels our interest and attention.

Paragraph 1. The Hook. Just like a fishing hook, this paragraph must capture the reader's attention. You need to stand forth from the first minute as refreshing, different, uncommon, interesting, significant, important, unique, likable. Nothing less will do. Answer the question: "Why would anyone want to spend time with me?" And you're on your way.

Paragraph 2. Support Data. Begin to develop yourself as a personality. The first paragraph includes many, perhaps most of the 5 W's: who, what, where, when, why. The remainder of the article continues to develop the last of these. While it is quite acceptable to include quotations in the first paragraph, it is mandatory that they be used in the second and subsequent paragraphs. These help establish a sense of conversing with the reader. Don't hesitate to give a sense of the utterly characteristic, engaging you. Bring in your working milieu, characteristic gestures, clothing, ways of acting. Again, the reader wants to see you "as you really are." What you produce, of course, is entirely controlled, but it must seem natural, uncontrived. This is the art of the unabashed self-promoter.

Paragraph 3. Bring in facts of weight and substance which establish you as a figure of significance. While you want your readers, potential clients, to know that you are human ("Oh, shucks, I'm just like you!"), you also want them to be quite clear that you are a master of your trade, technically competent, a pace-setter, forerunner of a future that we must all live with.

Paragraph 4: Paragraphs hereafter should mix human detail with evidence of further technical competence and professional accomplishments. If you just add one fact demonstrating technical competence onto another demontrating technical competence, you run the very real risk of losing your audience. "How can I ever be as good, as thorough, as well prepared, as expert as he is?" Once having decided they can't be, you will lose them. Instead, bring forward one human facet with each one or two evidences of professional competence. Add a mildly self-deprecating quotation (I have no fear you will overdo it), a joke, yet more evidence of the "real" unaffected person beneath. In American politics I call this process the "Log Cabin Syndrome." It is the intense desire of men born with silver spoons to convey the impression that if they did indeed learn to eat with such an exalted implement it was purely because the itinerant peddler who supplied all the humble family's humble wants mistakenly left it behind one day.

Subsequent paragraphs. You may want to include as many as 4-6 paragraphs in your biographical feature depending on the number of things you have done in your life which you wish your public to know about. These paragraphs should present a judicious mixture of hard fact, personal information and pithy quotations which give further evidence of who you really are.

Final paragraph. Inevitably the biographical feature concentrates on work activities. As an unabashed self-promoter and entrepreneur in good standing, work may in fact be your chief hobby. Don't say so. Americans tend not to like workaholics; they make the common run of our countrymen feel inadequate, slothful. Which, of course, they are.

So invent a hobby. Start working out in a gym, reading to inner-city youth, anything so that you can end your biographical narrative with a bit of protective froth. Dogs and children ordinarily lend just the right note of empathetic bonhomie.

Like all other documents in this chapter, this one should be typewritten and photocopied or offset print on your official stationery. You will want to make good use of it not only with print media sources but with those in broadcast media, too, who will probably just read chunks of it over the air. The closer it reads to an actual article, the more likely they are to do so. Toastmasters will also use it in introducting you before their organizations. (See samples, page 298.)

Fact Sheet

As surely must be clear by now, the more work you do for any media source, the more they are likely to use the story that you have prepared for them. Working under tight deadlinies, chronically understaffed, no more curious or dedicated than the rest of us, media people will quite happily use your material until such time as you demonstrate that you are ill-prepared, inaccurate or so nakedly partisan as to be untrustworthy. This is why you must work to maintain your credibility.

The Fact Sheet is a simple document. In concise, no-nonsense form it lists critical factual information that a media source will need as background to a story in which you are involved. This document, often called a "Backgrounder," may include any kind of factual information: statistics, charts, graphs, &c, but it always includes their source.

Thus in addition to the usual follow-up information in the top left hand corner of the pages (name of organization, address, telephone numbers and contact person), don't forget to give a complete biographical citation for locating the facts used, even if it is a document which you yourself have written or published. (See samples, page 301.)

Chronology

As we all know, certain problems can take years to resolve. Oftentimes the background to problems becomes fuzzier and fuzzier as events progress. The Chronology helps clear things up.

Like the fact sheet, the chronology is a very crisp, fast-moving document. Its tone is factual, and you should give the source for your information, especially if it is likely to be in dispute.

Chronologies, of course, usually pertain to the development of issues; you may, however, adapt this and use it as a way of presenting personal facts about yourself as a sort of concise, fact-filled narrative résumé.

Again, do not neglect to include the organization name, address, telephone number and contact person. Chronologies are most helpful at a media conference or in situations where, as the sentinel for the interests of your client prospects, you are trying to establish a case on their behalf. (See samples, page 302.)

The Position Paper

While the chronology is a list of facts, a statement of what has already happened, the Position Paper is an advocacy document suggesting what you, your company or organization think should happen next. It is an interesting commentary on our times that while most political candidates and many not-for-profit advocacy organizations are adept at drawing up and issuing position papers, American corporations are not.

The background to a position paper will not necessarily be a concise document. The reports of presidential commissions, for instance, often run to hundreds of pages. However, a true position paper, to be released to the media, should be no more than 500 words long. While it should always indicate by a full bibliographical citation on what it is based and where further information is available, the position paper itself must summarize its major suggestions and recommendations and, in 50-100 words, the leading arguments for them. It is also helpful if the corresponding arguments of opponents are cited here and your counter-arguments given. (See samples, page 303.)

List of Contacts

You can further influence how the media handles your case, if you provide journalists with a list of other individuals to contact. If you are smart, these will only be people known personally to you or who are sure to share your sentiments. Before adding their names to a Contact List, ask their permission to do so; don't hesitate to send them all the materials you are distributing to the media. You want to minimize the chance that any of your arguments and information will be contradicted by another source.

A list of contacts should include:

- name of contact
- organization
- title
- address
- telephone number
- an indication of why you suggested this person (has written a book, testified before the legislature, been an officer in a relevant trade organization, &c.)

Don't bother to give more than 6 such contacts. Even in major stories, media people rarely quote or otherwise cite more than this number.

Prepared Statement

A Prepared Statement is most often used at a media conference. It should be typed, double spaced on organization letterhead. In the upper left hand corner, the name of the speaker should be given, his position or affiliation, and his age. A contact telephone number for both speaker and organization should also be added for the sake of convenient follow-up.

This statement should be as short as possible without unnecessarily distorting your case by dropping critical facts. Remember, however, with the media, shorter is always better. Whether your prepared statement is 5 minutes long or 25 minutes will probably not matter, especially as far as the broadcast media are concerned. You will discover that your brilliant prepared statement has been transformed into a 15-second quotation.

Why bother to provide a prepared statement then? Remember the example of the Emperor Augustus and his wife, Livia. Livia was a notorious termagent, so dangerous that she may, in the end, have poisoned her husband. The emperor adopted the necessary expedient of speaking to her only with a prepared text, "so that I should say neither too much nor too little."

A prepared statement gives you the necessary control when issuing your information, particularly at a media conference when you are most likely to use this format. At such occasions you may find that you are nervous and so misspeak yourself. The prepared statement is there to indicate to the media precisely what you meant to say. (See samples, page 303.)

Media Schedule

A Media Schedule should be drawn up when a series of related events will occur on a single day or over a brief period of time. This schedule should be printed on your stationery. It should include a headline or name for the series of events, the name of the organization sponsoring them, address, telephone, and contact person. It is most desirable that all information about the events be dispensed from a single individual. A headline in bold face print should list the day or days of the events.

All events should be listed on one page. Listings should include:

- the time of the event
- the day, if all are not being held on one day
- place
- directions to place, if difficult to find
- a synopsis of what will happen
- names and titles of people involved
- an individual contact person for this event, if different from the name listed at the top of the page.

If you have released a tentative schedule of events early in your planning, make sure that you follow this up with the final version. Clearly mark this document "Final," especially if any significant changes have been made.

Clip Sheet

As I shall stress throughout this book, you need to photocopy articles by and about you and have them available for other media sources. You should photocopy them on your stationery with:

- the name of the publication
- the date the article appeared

The only time I advise against sharing clips (or leave behinds, as I usually call them) is with competing media. Thus it would not be a good idea to share a story about yourself with a reporter from a competing metropolitan daily, although it would be very much in your interest to distribute it to other media sources.

Previous Media Contacts

A clip sheet only pertains to print media. The equivalent for electronic media is a list of all those shows and stations on which you have previously appeared. On a piece of your stationery list:

- the name of the program
- the call letters of the station
- the city and state
- the date the program was broadcast (use the taping date if the broadcast date is not known)
- the name of the host
- the name of the producer

Public Service/Calendar Announcement

If you are sponsoring an event of some sort, a fair, a march, a fund raising dinner dance, &c., don't forget to draw up a Public Service or Calendar Announcement. Ordinarily the media will not use such information if you are for-profit, but there are many exceptions to this rule.

Public service announcements are designed for broadcast media; calendar announcements are their print equivalents. In general these announcements should not exceed 50 words in length. The public service announcement when read should take exactly 30 seconds. A public service or calendar announcement should be typed, double spaced on your stationery, photocopied and should include:

Name of Organization: ______________________________ Release Date ____________
Address: ____
Telephone number: ______________________________________
Contact person: ____
Telephone number (if different) ___________________________

HEADLINE SUITABLE TO BE READ ON THE AIR OR PRINTED IN CALENDAR ANNOUNCEMENT

The text in 50 words covering:

- who
- what
- where
- when
- why
- price of admission
- telephone number or other pertinent follow-up information

Note: If this is a public service announcement, type the word "Announcer" in caps just before the text. If you have written this announcement properly, the announcer can read from your text directly.

Different stations and publications have widely different policies regarding the use of public service and calendar announcements. It is alway best to check with the source. In general, however, these announcements should be sent two weeks in advance of the event. Direct them to "Public Service Director" (for radio and television) or "Calendar Editor" for print sources.

Photographs

Calendar announcements should often be accompanied by a photograph, especially if the event you are promoting lends itself to pictures. As you will see from Chapter 11, every unabashed self-promoter needs to make good use of photographs. Suffice it to say here that there are two good sizes for photographs, 5" x 7" and 8" x 10". Your photographs should be black and white; horizontal shots are more popular than vertical ones.

On the back of *each* photograph you send, place a sticker. This sticker should:

- identify the subject
- include the complete names of those pictured
- give complete details of an event
- give follow-up information including the name of a contact person and a telephone number.

Do not write this information on the back of the photograph and do not type it. It will show. Stickers are best.

One final word on photographs: Do not expect them to be returned. They won't be. Keep your originals safely at home.

TIPS ON PRODUCING, USING AND PACKAGING YOUR STANDARD MEDIA MATERIALS

Follow-Up Information

I have consistently stressed throughout this chapter that every document produced by you for distribution to the media needs your name, address and telephone number on it. I'll stress this point again now. It is amazing to me how many self-promoters produce materials for distribution without this information, but I see examples constantly. Material without follow-up information is useless, absolutely useless, and nothing should be sent to the media from your office without it.

The Look Of Your Documents

All documents should be typed, double spaced on your stationery. When dealing with the media, you should never attempt to squeeze every word possible on a page; err on the side of wide borders. Conclude each page with a complete paragraph; start subsequent pages with a new paragraph. All copy should look clean and neat. You are asking for something of great value, namely broadcast time and print space; at least have the good sense to appear to deserve it.

The Tone Of Your Documents

Keep your documents brisk, authoritative, fact-filled and professional. In some of your documents (as for instance your biographical feature), personal details are not only advisable but necessary; most often, however, media people simply want the facts, ma'am, just the facts.

When You Need What: The Basic Media Kit

When you begin your career as an unabashed self-promoter, you probably won't need to produce each document presented in this chapter. For you, a basic media kit will do. It should include:

- media advisory
- standard media release
- biographical information
- fact sheet
- clip sheet
- list of previous media contacts
- photographs

The other materials you can produce as necessary.

Packaging

I myself have not, as a matter of course, resorted to pretty packaging for my documents. The documents speak for themselves. I simply enclose them in a regular business envelope, or where they are the more numerous, into a manila envelope and send them on their way. The exception is at media conferences.

At a media conference, you will ordinarily have several documents to distribute. To insure that each member of the media has a complete set of everything being distributed, place the documents, at the very least, in manila folders. Although this is not often done, I have found it helpful to include a Face Sheet listing each document which is enclosed in the packet. This spares needless aggravation on the part of media personnel, who otherwise may wonder whether they have everything they ought.

Final Words About The Standard Media Kit.

It is a sad fact of the unabashed self-promoter's curious life that he will gain no credit with the media for producing documents and materials which are all that they should be: clear, concise, well-written, factually accurate, substantial, informative, even interesting. All this is expected. If you expect compliments from this source on your hard work, you may expect to be disappointed.

On the other hand, if your media materials fall short of this exacting standard, it will tell against you. Inevitably. As you, the unabashed self-promoter must forever keep in mind, you are in a race with hundreds of thousands of organizations and even more individuals for the limited available print space, the limited air time.

Offering the media what they want, doing their work for them, offering what you have in a way that media can most easily use with fewest changes — all this will make you, your message, your product and service, welcome.

Otherwise, beware: There is more than enough suitable material to choose from in this country and as the message and techniques of this book are circulated, there will be far more.

CHAPTER 5

CREATING AND MAINTAINING YOUR SELF-PROMOTION NETWORK

Everyone knows it's not what you know, but who. But how do you get connected? That's always been the problem, and that's where networking comes in.

Networking is a trendy word and is today much bandied about. Several books have been written about the subject in an attempt to provide the key to connecting. I have, however, found these books inadequate not least because they do not tell you who you really ought to be meeting and fail to provide a simple, thorough system for getting to them. This chapter ought to correct matters. I use networking daily, and I am always staggered both by how effortless it can be and how dramatically efficacious.

What Is Networking?

Networking is a process for moving you to your destination by taking advantage of people with valuable connections and turning them into success connectors for you. Networking is an action process. It can be successful only if there is movement, only if you succeed in reaching your objective: motivating an individual capable of helping you to do so.

I have identified three major networks. This chapter concentrates on one only, The Self-Promotion Network. You should know what the others are, however, and should implement them using the methods of this chapter.

The Mandarin Network

The inspiration for this network came from my ongoing interest in the world's aristocrats and my continuing desire to divest myself of life's nagging inessentials. The mandarins of ancient China seemed to be an apt illustration for what I had in mind. They grew their fingernails to outrageous lengths to indicate to an overburdened world that they did not work. My work has as its ultimate objective reestablishing this congenial universe in my own life. This means concentrating on that which will insure such a result and stripping away — with pressing single-mindedness — all that detracts from it. Thus mandarins need service providers.

In my life I concentrate on just two things, two inter-related objectives: making money and raising an apathetic public's consciousness about my exploits. All other things, all, are superfluous. I have thus brought in others who can take care of them.

I have, for instance, an accountant, a bookkeeper, a graphic designer, a typesetter, several sets of printers, a houseboy, two lawyers, and on and on. They free me to do what I do best — and to march inexorably towards my objectives. I do not cut grass, do grocery shopping, wash laundry, file papers, drive a car, or do any of the other inconsequential, draining activities which devastate lives. You should not do them either.

It is not difficult to recruit people for the Mandarin Network. They are, after all, paid, but you use your network to insure compatibility between the people who are serving you and your own lifestyle. My accountant recruited my bookkeeper. A consulting colleague recruited my driver who in turn recruited my houseboy. You get the picture. I rely on people already in the Mandarin Network not just to provide me with a good service but to identify those who can provide other services that I need in ways which are compatible with my general lifestyle and my continuing need for quality.

Everyone who expects to succeed needs a Mandarin Network.

The Next Check Network

The independent contractor, service provider is dependent both on identifying and motivating clients and customers to buy his product or service. The Next Check Network can help. For each product or service you offer there is a group of individuals who constitute your prime buyers. Networking can help connect you with them.

Here are some of the divisions of my Next Check Network:

- Nonprofit Technical Assistance Supergroup. The prime targets here in order of their importance to me are:
  - executive directors of nonprofit organizations
  - chairmen of nonprofit boards of directors
  - other directors

- JLA Publications (which brings you this book)
  - business book buyers of national book store chains
  - book club buyers
  - managers of local book stores

- JLA Mobile University (which brings you workshops and seminars)
  - deans and directors of university continuing education programs
  - presidents of colleges and universities
  - trustees of universities

First, note that in the Next Check Network your preferred targets may actually be of lower status than your secondary targets: in my Mobile University, for instance, I am more interested in directors of continuing education programs than I am in college presidents. The key is: Who can authorize payment of my next check?

Also, note that each network has a finite, though always fluid, membership, often quite small and manageable despite the fact that it may be national. There are, in fact, only about 2800 deans and directors of college continuing education programs in the country. This is typical of the small, self-contained universe in which networking works so well.

The Self-Promotion Network

The purpose of this network, as its name suggests, is to connect you to individuals who can directly or indirectly assist you with your self-promotion. Here are some targets:

- editors of local newspapers
- proprietors of newsletters
- radio talk show hosts
- nationally syndicated columnists

The key is to get access to them. There are only two ways: through networking and by making direct contact.

Finding Networking Contacts

Contacts which can be of use to you are everywhere. Everywhere. That is why the unabashed self-promoter is never off duty. He can meet a critical contact anytime, any place. I get them from:

- professional groups
- clients
- alumni organizations
- friends who have been covered by media sources
- individuals casually encountered while traveling

And, of course, I get them from media people themselves.

Handling The Networking Conversation

I have two objectives when I begin a conversation with anyone no matter how casual or insouciant I seem: to make the appropriate impression and to find out whether the person I am speaking to either has direct or indirect relevance to any of my networks. I approach the realization of these objectives with absolute determination.

Making The Appropriate Impression

I have never liked the expression "making an impression" on someone. It is imprecise. The phrase should be "to make an appropriate impression." In this game, I am a past master.

The key for a self-promoter seeking to play the impression game is to realize how very well prepared he is for it. First, he must take stock of his protean identities. The unabashed self-promoter has many. Here are some of mine:

- English monarchic historian
- author
- media personality
- columnist
- lecturer
- publisher
- corporate president
- consultant
- world traveler
- poet
- art collector
- businessman

The totality of these roles is, who can deny?, most impressive. The problem is: There are very, very few people who have glimpsed them all, and these are mostly people I have given up impressing: family and friends who believe the printed nonsense of Kahlil Gibran. I must captivate the rest of the world using much less than full power.

The key to a successful networking conversation is to give the person you are trying to motivate to work on your behalf the right piece of impressing biography. The more roles you have, the better you can do so.

I begin each networking conversation with an imaginary questionnaire in mind and attempt to complete as much as I can during the time we have together, be it only five concentrated minutes.

Each person's questionnaire will necessarily be different because the networker ordinarily seeks to discover information in this order: Next Check Network, Self-Promotion Network, Mandarin Network.

Here's what my mental questionnaire might look like if written:

- name of contact
- company affiliation
- position
- duties
- years of employment
- company publications
- Has contact ever written for same? Been featured in same?
- Does he know editor?
- professional organizations
- publications of same
- Has contact ever written for same? Been featured by same?
- education
- highest degree
- institution
- involvement with alumni organization
- nonprofit connections
  - school
  - religious
  - community organizations

This kind of information is ridiculously easy to get. It is a truism, of course, that people love to talk about themselves. I can testify to its constant accuracy.

The networking conversation is based on this fact, but this conversation has its own peculiar rhythm.

- Even if I do not begin the conversation, I take charge of it as soon as possible, *not*, however, by talking about myself (I don't learn what I need to know that way), but by directing a steady stream of questions to my contact.
- I gage how much time we are likely to have together and allot my question period accordingly. I act as if this will be the only time in my life we shall be together — all too often I'm right as I meet thousands of new people every year. Thus my mission must be entirely accomplished in the time we have, however brief it is.
- Having considered how much time we have, I make a decision of when I shall enter the conversation. I must find out first whether this person is or has a connection I want. I must then impress him sufficiently so that he will want to use it on my behalf, pressing me to accept it without my having asked. I must do this all in the allotted time which is often very, very brief.

After I have begun the contact talking about himself, providing me with more and still more information, I must decide when I wish to substantially enter the conversation:that is enter with a piece of impressing information.

This depends on two factors: the amount of time available and whether I have a sure feel for that which will impress and interest my contact. Based on what your contact is telling you, what you yourself perceive, the circumstances under which you met, &c., you have got to make an initial decision about what you've got that will sufficiently impress your listener. This is the art of networking.

I know, for instance, that the average businessman will not be impressed by my admirable book on the court of Queen Victoria, but my Dun & Bradstreet rating will alert him to the fact that I am an individual of consequence worthy of a second look. By the same token, the elderly lady I sat next to on a plane one day was enchanted by my stories of Windsor Castle and my book on Harvard. This was the right aspect of my life to draw upon. She reciprocated by telling me she was the trustee of a Florida university. Of course . . .

What you are trying to establish during whatever time you have is that you are special — to the person you are talking to. A stick of gum might do it for the pesky five year old beside you on a train (whose otherwise elusive mother is on the board of a major nonprofit organization). You have to make the decision about what will work, what will captivate your audience. Once you have done so, the next thing to do is to fix the initial impression. There is where your leave behinds come in very handy.

I do not own an attaché case (whiz kids can do without), but I do carry a flight bag wherever I go. In it, I keep a wide assortment of materials which can be used to reinforce the impression I have now launched, namely that I am a notable creature. Occasionally, of course, serendipity comes to my assistance. One day while traveling from San Francisco to Los Angeles, my seatmate was carrying the latest copy of *Business Week*. I asked if I might just look at it briefly. As I well knew, there was a piece on me in the magazine.

He, the flight personnel and indeed the entire section of the airplane, ultimately discovered this fact and, with great diffidence and many expressions of humility, I acceded to the general demand for information about the book which was featured in the article. It does not always happen this way, but you may savor it to the full when it does.

Instead, plan to carry with you not just business cards (which everyone carries) but a whole range of supporting materials which reinforce the point that you are memorable. I carry:

- leave behinds about my books
- media releases
- articles by me
- articles about me
- order blanks (if you've made a suitable impression, you'll need these!)

It is important that the transfer of this material be handled carefully lest you dispel the image you have now begun to craft. Make it appear that giving it to your contact is a courtesy on your part, that you are meeting the contact's need. This is very easy to do if you have handled your part of the conversation properly. Remember: You have already established a sequence of courtesies. You have politely asked after the contact's life and interests, followed with appropriate information about yourself, and have never ostensibly dominated the conversation (while at all times subtly leading it). It follows, therefore, that passing on material about yourself and what you do should be perceived as yet another courtesy.

No matter how brief your encounter with a contact, it can be worthwhile to you and the pursuit of your objectives if you have left the impression that you are an individual of significance — and empathy.

If you have succeeded in portraying yourself this way, your contact will want to help you. Indeed, there is something deep within our national character and essential to it which motivates Americans to want to help others. I see this constantly. This is a fact of the utmost importance to the unabashed self-promoter.

If I have directed the conversation properly, I shall be the beneficiary of this generosity. Nowadays I expect to be. If I am talking about nonprofit concerns, lo and behold! my contact will talk about his and will — spontaneously — offer the names of organizations with which he is connected — and exactly how. I am merely being gracious to accept this information — and to follow it up. And this is the point. The unabashed self-promoter — always assertive — need not be perceived as anything other than considerate and empathetic. That is the delight, the magic of networking. I maneuver you into giving me information I need while appearing to be interested in your concerns; I then accept your generous offer to make use of this information on my behalf — to oblige you. Very, very neat.

The Pyramid Of Contacts

So now you've got your contact. You have discovered, as I discover constantly, that your client's cousin is a reporter for the local newspaper, that the taxi driver you have just met works part-time as a technician at the all news radio station, that the ambassador you are going to the theatre with has a sister who is vice president of the **Washington Post**. I have invented none of these examples. Each has happened to me within the last year, along with dozens more.

The Pyramid of Contacts allows you to plot your next steps, quickly, efficiently. Here's what it looks like:

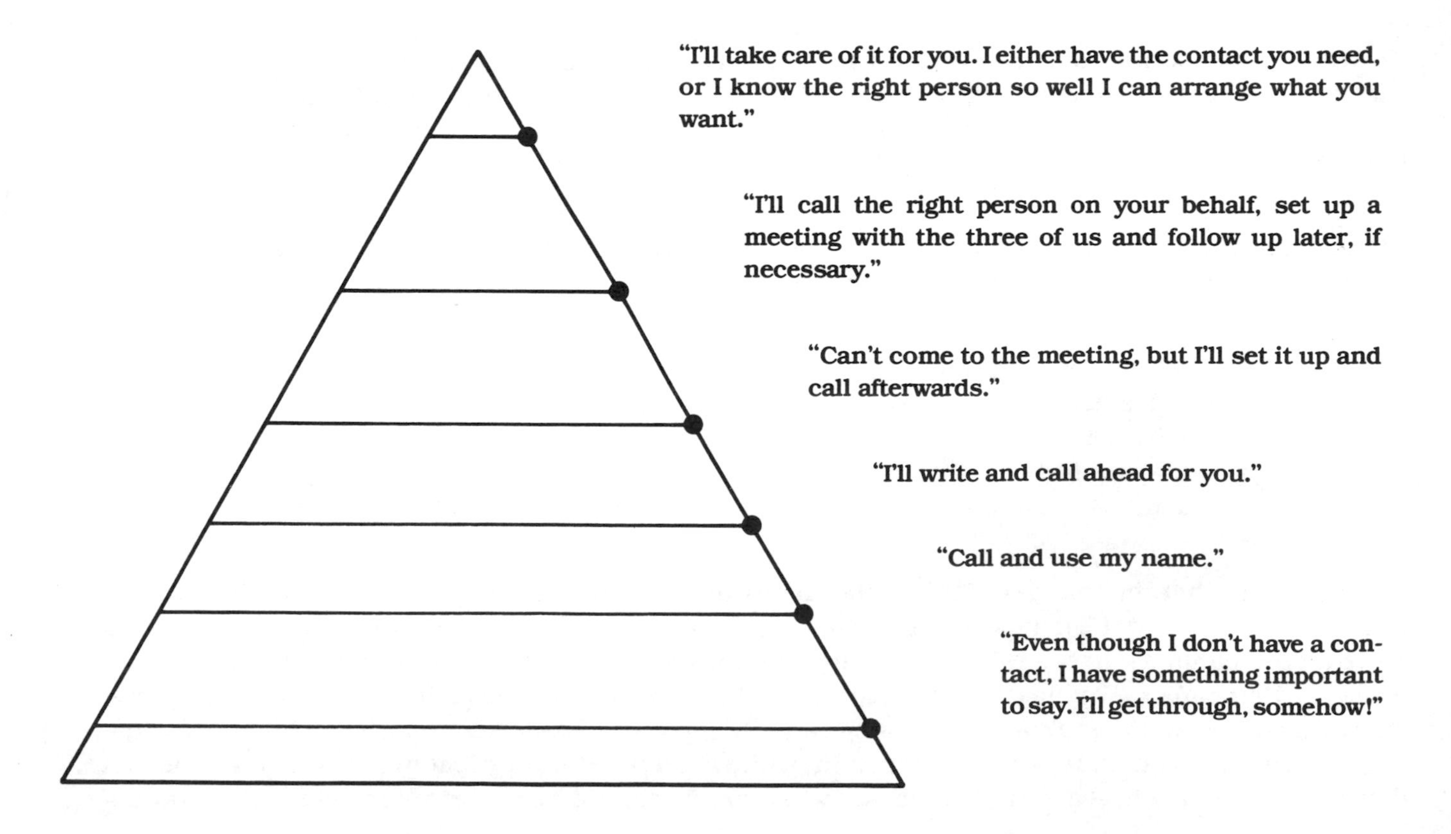

Indirect Contacts

Let us say that the person you have spoken to is associated with a college and you have, through further questions, discovered that this college has a campus radio station. A college radio station can be a good self-promotional target, either if you are a novice self-promoter seeking experience in the medium or it is a substantial station within your marketing area (as such stations can often be.) Now what?

It is your responsibility to follow up the lead once you know about it, whether or not you have received it from the contact spontaneously, or whether you have actually asked for it: "I wonder whether you know anyone at the station?" It surely goes without saying that if the lead you want is not presented to you, you will request it.

Never expect the person who has the connection to take the next step. From time to time, of course, we are all blessed with someone who not only has a connection but actually follows through on it for us — without being asked. But this is rare.

The unabashed self-promoter understands that people generally mean well but that they ordinarily are casual about delivery. This is the way of the world and is not particularly distressing to the seasoned self-promoter who knows that if he wants something to happen he better work at it himself.

Here is the right way to follow-up with an individual who is not himself the direct target — that is to say the person who has the connecting lead but is unable to personally deliver the objective:

- Whenever possible leave supporting materials with the contact and ask him to pass them along to the decision maker.
- If you want to follow up this lead now, do so immediately. Send an immediate follow-up letter (see samples, page 308) with a complete packet of supporting materials. Again request that your contact either mail it to the decision maker or personally drop it off, if possible.
- Keep the Pyramid of Contacts in mind at all times. What you want is for the person with the contact to confer on you automatic acceptance with the target by doing as much as possible on your behalf: establishing you as a person of worth and consequence, getting you past the obstructionist secretary to direct contact with the decision maker, in all ways making it easier for what you as the unabased self-promoter really want to do — forego the bothersome business of establishing your credibility and proving yourself and instead walking directly into a one-to-one relationship with the decision maker and an enhanced likelihood of the coverage you want. If you are not able to motivate your contact to do more than say, "Call and use my name," or another of the less-useful alternatives, then you know your initial conversation — or indeed your entire relationship — is not a very important one to the contact. Work on refining your approach. People will give most generously to those who are capable of helping them in return. If you get responses from your contact which are towards the bottom of the Pyramid, it simply means you have failed in your bid to be perceived as an interesting, vital, important individual who may, at some point, offer the contact assistance in return.

Having written this, I trust it goes without saying that if this is the best you can do (perhaps because the person, not uncommonly, has over-stated to you the strength of his connection and really can do no more), move ahead into the opening. The unabashed self-promoter early learns that many crumbs a gourmet meal make.

- If your contact can be persuaded to send a letter of introduction on your behalf, make sure he sends you a copy. If you don't get it within 10 business days after the initial conversation (or a follow-up reminder call), call again. Give your contact every reasonable opportunity to work on your behalf. But be resigned to the fact that you will probably need to be gently persistent.

I use my calendar as a tickler system. I note on any given date not only which calls I am supposed to make but also the calls that are supposed to be made on my behalf. I am then reminded to check with my contact and see whether they actually have been.

When you are beginning your career as an unabashed self-promoter, most of the leads you will get will be indirect, thereby necessitating a tickler system. As you do more and still more self-promotion your contacts, drawn from media personnel themselves, will be more direct. Nonetheless, even though I have now done hundreds of interviews, I network on every occasion. It is, in fact, a game — but like all other aspects of unabashed self-promotion the prizes are substantial.

Direct Leads: Parallel Networking

The best direct leads usually come from media people themselves. This is the case because the most easy direct networking for any given profession always takes place within that profession. In this connection I remember the anecdote repeated to me by a client who had asked her uncle, the president of a large bank, whether he knew any other bank presidents. "All I know," he bristled, "is other bank presidents." And that was that. So it is with media people. Media people, card carrying mandarins all, are especially clannish because (in part) people are constantly stalking them to get coverage. Like any élite group, they thus fall back on themselves, feeling less vulnerable to unabashed solicitation if they are amongst each other. Media people work with, consort with and often live with other media people, for with their own kind they have lives approaching normalcy. The unabashed self-promoter can make good use of this fact through Parallel Networking, using people at the top of the Self-Promotion Network to connect him to other people similarly placed.

Parallel Networking works like a charm. One day I was on a radio station in Braddock, Pennsylvania (you see, I do go everywhere). During the course of my live radio interview, the host said, "I hear you are a champion networker. Can you tell us how it works." "Better yet," I replied, "I'll show you." I told the audience that in under 5 minutes I would get 5 media leads which would be of very real worth in my Self-Promotion Network. The host looked doubtful.

"Is this your first job in the media?", I asked.
"No," she said. "I also have worked at (and she named two radio stations.)" I wrote the call letters and the cities down.
"Did you part on good terms?" (Clearly an attempt to establish the value of the contact.)
"Oh, yes!," she ejaculated. But then again, we were on the air. What else could she say?
"What's the name of the local newspaper?"
She told me.
"Do you know anyone on the staff?"
"The Editor has been a guest on this show."
I noted his name.
"Do you date anyone in the media?"
"My boyfriend is program director of (the local rock station)."
I noted my fourth contact.
"Does this station use syndicated news and features?"
"Yes. (Name of Company) provides them."
"Could you get me an introduction there?"

This interchange proceeded at a very fast clip because in point of fact all I needed to discover to begin matters was whether my contact had other contacts useful to me. My good interview (not to mention my bravura display of networking technique) was no doubt sufficient to convince her: that I was not going to be an embarrassment, that she could safely pass me along, and that I was someone useful for her to know. And so it proved.

You handle networking with media people the same way as with anyone else. It just happens, however, that when you are networking with decision makers your payoff is ordinarily quicker and more substantial. Again, of course, the key is follow-up. It is your responsibility to take the information given, prioritize it, and act on the most important items. But what about a situation like that of Braddock where, as is so often the case, I was in town just to do one broadcast and then move on, perhaps never to return. Did I just demonstrate my networking skills and discard the information. Absolutely not!

I might indeed return, or one of my colleagues might pass through, glad to be put under an obligation to me in return for effortless media exposure. No, this information — even if never put to my direct use — has a definite value. How then to store it?

Preserving Networking Information

The networking information you gather is valuable and needs to be saved for future reference. First, never trust your memory. I have an excellent memory. But I would never rely on it for something as important as networking information. As I have indicated elsewhere in this book, I always have with me, whether in the office or on the road, a spiral bound note book. Even in the midst of a "personal" conversation, I am very likely to pull out this book and jot notes to myself, not just about what you are saying, either, but about other ideas which your conversation may be inspiring. The best organized and most effective individuals live by lists, and the unabashed self-promoter is no exception.

It should go without saying, but doesn't, that when you are given a complicated name, you should not only ask for the spelling but also the pronunciation. Write down the phonetics in your note book.

When you get back to your office you have several alternatives:

- Simply photocopy the notes of your trip and file them under the city or geographic area to which they pertain. Thus notes from my Braddock networking would be filed under Pennsylvania unless other states and cities are also involved, as will very often be the case given the peregrinations of media personnel.

- Make sure you review your note book regularly. Every couple of months I read through past "editions" of my note book. I follow up on pending odds and ends, place courtesy calls, and drop notes to my contacts. I often annotate entries in these notebooks with additional personal information about the media people I have met and also a sentence about how they treated me. Anything, in short, which will ease my next contact or that by a colleague I want to help. If I am doing media in states which maintain specific media directories (see Chapter 3), I will often place some of these notes right in the text for easy reference.

- I have not until now mentioned business cards. Clearly they are helpful in networking, but as you see my techniques extend far beyond merely collecting a card or — far worse — merely handing out your own. I do as a matter of course ask people for cards, and I suggest annotating the reverse of the card so that it shows:

- where you met
- the date you met
- subjects discussed
- networking leads

I confess I have no elaborate means of dealing with these cards, in part because I ordinarily have the same information elsewhere where I do make systematic use of it. To each his own. I have seen very elaborate card filing mechanisms. The important thing is that no scrap of this information gets lost, since it is both valuable and continually reusable. Networks properly taken care of grow exponentially. Here are some tips on how to maintain yours, particularly your Self-Promotion Network.

Maintaining Your Self-Promotion Network

I spend a lot of time cultivating media people and transforming them from contacts into something more. Every unabashed self-promoter needs to do the same. What is the nature of this "something more"? Acquaintances, I think, more often than friends, something offering the promise of mutual respect, civility, and a good working relationship. This to me is quite sufficient. I want to be admitted to collegial status, not necessarily become a bosom buddy and pal. I have several means of reaching this result.

First, I entertain regularly. How I entertain will be explored in more detail in Chapter 20 for like Louis XIV I never give my more substantial entertainments without a correspondingly substantial self-promotional purpose.

Nonetheless I long ago learned that media people, particularly in print media, seem to be perpetually starved and in need of a drink. Furthermore, many of them are lonely and always enjoy warm festive events in which they can participate, not just cover.

Perhaps a word about the loneliness. Not only do many media people work strange hours, many more of them (not just younger ones, either), move, often with the speed of light, from job to job. Radio stations alter their formats overnight. Television stations drop programs. Newspapers change owners or — these days — simply go out of business. Thus media people always retain a nomadic aspect, nowhere more apparent perhaps than among the "boys in the bus," the journalists who remain rootless during the ever-longer duration of presidential campaigns. They are, perhaps, the most celebrated nomads, but they are not — by a long shot — the only ones.

The unabashed self-promoter can use this nomadic element to his benefit. Media people new in town have been grateful to be invited by me for drinks, dinner, the grander staged parties. They know they will be well received, and they're glad for the human contact. In this spirit I have set up dates for media people, kept the scotch flowing as they poured out their lives and loves, and given them introductions to friends in the new cities where their nomadic lives take them. I have done everything, in fact, but go to sports events, for though I am entirely unabashed even I have my limits. The murderous glint in my eye in the sixth inning of a seemingly-interminable, unremittingly tiresome event makes me, I'm afraid, a less than appealing companion at the ball park.

In the same way I am profligate of notes congratulating my media acquaintances on their professional prizes and on a story which may otherwise go unnoticed, but which I, because of my knowledge, know they are proud of. And, when the station format changes, when the television show is cancelled, when they find themselves out of work, I send the appropriate condolence. Media people, like weeds, will pop up next season, and I want to be remembered. I am.

As one reporter from the **Boston Globe** told me last year, "I know you're exploiting me, but you do it so well, I do what you want, and I won't complain." I take that for a compliment. Others, less well versed in the fine art of getting ahead, might not.

Objections to Networking

Despite the very real advantages to networking, there are those who criticize it for the following reasons:

- "Aren't you using people?"

Yes, networkers are using people. Whether they acknowledge as much or not, they operate on the belief that some people are more worth knowing — for them — than others. There's nothing wrong with this. Moreover, it is in fact necessary for people in the Self-Promotion Network to be used — or else their egos suffer. Powerful people, as media people are, need to have this sense of themselves reinforced at regular intervals. The unabashed self-promoter can help do this. It is important to remember that although media people are powerful, they are also very, very insecure. Media exists — and profits — because of advertising. However eminent the journalist, he is infinitely less important to the owners than the people who produce advertising revenues. Journalists — however exalted — are expendable as the irregularity of their employment testifies. Moreover, despite their evident power, which continues only as long as their employment, they are not high wage earners. Thus, they do not have the means to live up to their pretensions. Media people thus live in a situation of continual anxiety, whether explicit or implicit. They have intermittent power but no authority. They have job-related status, but no money. They are perceived as important by the public, but they are regarded as expendable and of secondary consequence to the media owners.

No wonder they need us unabashed self-promoters, who not only make their jobs easier because of the material we give them, but always reinforce in the minds of media personnel the comforting picture of their power, importance, human and professional consequence. Who could resist this siren song?

And, of course, they don't, no matter how gruff and resistant to it they may at first appear. It goes without saying that unceasing cultivation, good humor, and dogged persistence succeed in charming all but the most hard-bitten cynics. And even these, in their hearts, can hardly avoid feeling complimented.

- "Since I don't know the person well, I don't see how I can ask for a favor."

Anyone having considered this chapter will dismiss this objection out of hand as unworthy of further notice. People assist all networkers, the unabashed self-promoter among them, for many reasons, not the least of which is that they feel pleased and honored to do so. Who am I to deny anyone that pleasure?

- "I don't want to ask for a favor, because I'm afraid I'll be asked for one back."

This is most curious reasoning, especially if you gain an actual benefit and only fear some future request for reciprocity. I am always, always willing to bet that I shall be more organized, more persistent, more thorough about seeing a contact through than other people who request me to help them. I know myself.

The correct posture for the unabashed self-promoter is this: to indicate by mien and implication rather than by declaration that he is willing to be of comparable assistance when the time comes and to rely upon your contact's sloth, disorganization, lack of ambition and disinclination to trouble you to save you from further effort.

If, however, they ask, you can calibrate what you are willing to do precisely based on the value of the contact they gave you and the overall value of the relationship. Remember the Pyramid of Contacts. When you are networking, move the person with the contact up the pyramid until he says, "I'll take care of it for you" — and is pursued until he does it. While being networked, push the person making the request down the pyramid. Most people requesting a favor are too timorous to say, "Call and use my name," just won't do.

Using The Direct Approach

Though I use networking every day of my life, though I am persistent about gathering contacts, completing leads and maintaining connections, though I have in fact a staggering array of contacts for each of my networks, there are still many situations where I have an objective to reach but where I do not have a connection and cannot wait for one to materialize.

The remainder of this book presumes that you will work assiduously to gain and cultivate connections and that you will use them when you can. It also presumes that the lack of a connection will not deter you from proceeding once you have determined that you have marketable material and have identified the right media people to offer it to. The unabashed self-promoter is both familiar with and uses the appropriate technique — be it networking or salesmanship.

If you are forced to use the latter, however, as you undoubtedly will be, realize this: identifying the right source, working to establish the link, giving a compelling media performance either in print or electronically is a significant investment. The contact you have made, like the material you have developed, pays off only from repeated use. Thus, once you have the media contact, use it — to connect you to other media contacts and to capitalize the investment you have already made.

CHAPTER 6

HOW AND WHERE TO GATHER INFORMATION

In the years to come more and still more of us will become information managers. As a result every unabashed self-promoter must become adept at knowing where to look for information, how to get it, and how to use it.

The 'research' that we do is less original (in the sense of creating information) than knowing where to look for information. In fact, the unabashed self-promoter has very limited time available for Pure Research. You must be able, instead, to find out what research others have done which bears on your own interests and make use of it for your own self-promotional purposes.

Specialized Newsletters

To this end, specialized newsletters are the unabashed self-promoter's best friend. There are approximately 75,000 of these newsletters, just exactly how many no one knows because so many of them are decidedly ephemeral. The best source for information about 8,000 of them is:

Oxbridge Directory of Newsletters
Oxbridge Communications
183 Madison Avenue
New York, New York 10016
(212) 689-8524

(Note: Oxbridge also publishes other specialized publications directories, see Chapter 3.)

There is really only one purpose for a newsletter: to disseminate important developments in any field with the utmost celerity. Such information may involve government regulations, pending legislation, trade and professional organization policy, publication of new books, movements of personnel, available grants and contracts, &c.

The information in a specialized newsletter is a godsend to the unabashed self-promoter. You can learn:

- what important matters are pending
- who has information about them
- what the public ramifications of policies may be
- when decisions are likely to be reached
- where groups are lining up on an issue.

Newsletters are chocked full of this kind of material.

The problem for a self-promoter is how to decide whether an issue mentioned in a newsletter is worth any further time and attention. Is it, in short, a suitable vehicle for unabashed self-promotion?

The answer lies in the proper consideration and evaluation of the following points:

- The issue bears directly on the interests of the people you would like to be known by, that is people who are in a position to buy you, your services and products. The unabashed self-promoter need not have any interest in the subject himself; he must discern, however, that it is of considerable concern to any possible clients.

- If this has been satisfactorily established, the next question to be answered is: Who has information on this subject who will hand it over to me, the self-promoter, to use as I see fit? This is a pivotal consideration.

  The unabashed self-promoter needs at all times to have a clear sense about what kinds of people under what circumstances will provide necessary material to him, so that he does not have to commit his own time and resources to gathering it.

- Is the subject such that it is likely to break into the general media quickly? That is, will the self-promoter find himself competing in short order against full-time print and electronic media journalists, and so very likely loose control of the issue?

- Is there a suitable media source available to the self-promoter so that once he has received the necessary material and molded it in a suitable fashion for dissemination there is a place that will very likely print or broadcast it?

- Is the material capable of multiple use? That is, once the unabashed self-promoter has spent the time to collect the material, understand it, and disseminate it, can he re-use it for further advantage?

The Sample article (page 313) from the **Boston Globe** of May, 1981 shows how the unabashed self-promoter can use this process to his advantage.

The article concerns one aspect of President Reagan's Economic Recovery Act of 1981, namely credit for charitable contributions made by taxpayers using the short tax form. I originally became aware of this through a specialized newsletter. This newsletter provided:

- essential background information
- reasons why this legislation was of interest to nonprofit organizations
- prospects for passage (bleak)
- principal backers

The topic met all my essential criteria for commitment of time and effort.

- Importance of subject to my clients. At a time of decreasing federal and state expenditures, my clients feel hard-pressed for funds and maintain a strenuous interest in any subject which promises to augment their resources. This tax initiative does just that. Because the subject bears upon the interests of my clients and client prospects and is capable of motivating them, it is a suitable promotional vehicle for me. In fact promoting this issue places me in a decidedly advantageous position *vis á* vis my clients, namely as their humane, solicitous problem solver, very much on the *qui vivre* regarding their interests. This is a superb position to be in.

- Information easily accessible. The unabashed self-promoter is not a slothful creature. That much should be perfectly clear already. But he is not inclined to do one iota of needless or unnecessary work. He is, in fact, quite prepared to use the work of others to advance his interests, such as, for example, using the work done by knowledgeable individuals.

The self-promoter regards research information as a necessary tool of his trade and is grateful to (even dependant on) whoever provides him with this material. He realizes that government agencies and institutions are a fertile source of useful material.

In this case, the newsletter indicated the chief sponsors of the legislation, that is the people who (either directly or through their staffs) need to be convinced to assist you.

This isn't hard.

In this instance, I called the office of the chief congressional sponsor and asked for the name of the legislative assistant responsible for monitoring this issue for the congressman. Each essential issue in which the congressman is involved (often as a co-sponsor, *always* as a chief supporter and promoter of the legislation) is assigned to a staff aide who:

- does background research
- keeps abreast of breaking developments affecting the legislation
- briefs his congressional employer on what he knows
- helps build internal congressional support and external support from interested individuals and organizations and the media.

This staff aide welcomes your interest in his project and will assist you in your self-interested designs so long as he can justify the expenditure of time and money as being in his own ultimate interests (e.g. sustaining his own good image with the congressman and insuring his own job security by securing that of his employer.)

The best approach is a letter (see samples, page 310) outlining:

- your interest in the particular issue
- a word about your credentials to deal with this issue
- your plans to be of assistance
- your need for specific assistance from the congressional office.

If you have written this letter in a suitable fashion (that is, the congressional staffer upon concluding it has a clear idea as to why helping you is in *his* best interest), the kind of response you desire will be immediate and effusive.

Within 3 to 4 days of my first contact with the congressional office I had all the information I needed and much, much more. Here's what you are likely to get and should, in fact, request:

- background fact sheet: essential information about the issue in hard-fact format
- list of congressional co-sponsors (you are particularly interested in those from your home state.)
- legislative testimony

- press clippings of previous articles on the subject
- insertions from **The Congressional Record**
- detailed research information.

In actual fact, you will probably have far more than you need.

What Next?

Even before contacting the congressional office you should begin thinking about how you will use the information once you've received it, the format in which you will use it, and where you intend to broadcast or publish it. Other chapters will deal with your approach to the media. Suffice it to say that at this point you need to consider whether:

- an advance ("query") letter is necessary to interest a media source in your topic (see samples, page 332)
- time pressures necessitate a cold telephone call to the media
- you should simply go ahead and write the piece and submit it, hoping for the best.

My rules of thumb are:

- If the subject is timely, there is some danger of the general media picking up the issue and the format you are using (say, an op-ed column) does not consume a great amount of your time, submit the copy cold. A good article ultimately speaks for itself. Under these circumstances, you might want to alert an appropriate editor to the fact that you are mailing in a piece. A simple telephone call will do.
- If you have previously published or broadcast on radio or television, call your contact to discuss your desire to submit material. What you are looking for in this case is availability of time or space. If the individual has previously used your material, you have presumably developed some reputation as a useful source. The issue in this case is not whether you can do the piece, but whether once completed it can be used owing to other commitments, breaking news, &c.
- Send a query letter if and only if you are convinced your subject is not in danger of being poached by someone else (particularly a professional journalist) either because you are the world's reigning authority or there is no danger of events overtaking it. In this way query letters are most appropriate for highly-specialized trade and technical publications and for feature pieces.

In the case of my **Boston Globe** column, it was highly unlikely that my issue would be stolen by the general media. First, the media was concentrating on major tax matters and on what really interested them: the battle between a conservative president and a newly-defensive Democratic House leadership. My issue was significant, but it did not begin to offer the drama of the larger issues. Besides, it was not, strickly speaking, a new issue having been brought unsuccessfully before the Congress before. Finally, the congressional monitor filled me in on what was happening with the issue, and whether anyone else *in my area* was likely to be writing about it. (No, no one was, hence his enthusiastic interest in me.)

Finding The Suitable Media Source

The unabashed self-promoter not only developes a sixth sense (as any prospecter) for when he has discovered something valuable but comes to have a feel for what kind of media vehicle would be most interested in what he's got.

We are not born with this skill. Unabashed self-promoters develop it. Our understanding of this critical process marks us as the consummate public relations professional who focuses his attention for maximum results with minimum expenditure of time and money.

As an unabashed self-promoter you must come to know media intimately. It is not necessary, mind you, that you know about every media outlet in the nation, only that you come to know well those media outlets which are capable of producing material by and about you, your message, products, and services.

Each of these outlets, as it clear from Chapter 12, has its own distinctive personality, its own interests, its own approach *and* its own list of subjects and angles which are entirely without interest. It is your responsibility to know these.

What the unabashed self-promoter does, however, is to play with his material to see which slant is most appropriate for the media source he is approaching. The most appropriate approach has everything to do with what the source sees as its mission and its audience and how your material and your angle square with them.

At all times, the unabashed self-promoter wants to direct his attention first to the largest print and broadcast media which will be interested in his material, his format and slant. I firmly believe that given world enough and time the unabashed self-promoter can have virtually anything printed by or about him. Getting your material published, however, should not be your sole or even your most significant objective. No. Getting known to the largest number of *suitable* readers and listeners should be. "Suitable" means those who will respond to your message and buy your products and services.

In this instance, the **Boston Globe**, New England's largest daily newspaper, was the right place to look, for it has access to the largest number of suitable readers.

What did I take into account before approaching them? Why, that is, did I think this place, perhaps the most competitive outlet in New England would, in fact, be the easiest?

- The **Globe**, like all daily newspapers, wants its stories to be universal. The more the story applies to the interests of its 1,200,000 readers, the better. Taxes is one such issue. In this case, the issue potentially involved all those using the short tax form, an enormous number.
- It piggybacked on the most significant then-current news item, the Reagan tax package. While media has a decidedly short attention span and is notoriously capricious, when it gives its attention to a subject it often does so in a very concentrated way. That is why in general interest publications you will often find clusters of articles on aspects of the same subject.
- While the issue was universal, there was a local angle. Boston prides itself (without much reason, I confess) not just on being a cultural mecca but on its creativity in developing means to sustain its necessarily nonprofit institutions. The legislation in question was a new, innovative approach to doing so.
- Clearly, however, the legislation had to be enacted, and this meant gaining the support of some hitherto reluctant or apathetic local congressmen. This column acted in typical **Globe** fashion as a goad. The **Globe**, like many substantial media sources (remember the media, the new clerisy) prides itself on its ability to discern a necessary reform and prod rather less farsighted lawmakers into acting on it. This column in its role as enlightened advocate fell in with the habitual mildly reforming attitude of the newspaper.
- Finally, there was specific follow-up possible. Enlightened advocates like their followers to do something — today — to make things better. Often the nature of news and features makes such follow-up unlikely or impossible. But in this case here was an opportunity for readers to help themselves.

Let me assure you that when I came to decide to approach the **Globe**, I did not write down these points and weigh them before acting. As with any seasoned professional, my analysis was quick, nonverbal, passing for the instinctive. The day will come when it is the same for those of you who practice these techniques, too. Until it does, however, sit down with your yellow pad and write the reasons why you think any given media outlet — print or electronic — will be interested in what you've got. Once they are written, don't forget to share them with the target.

Format

The format in which you choose to present your material will influence whether it is used. You must first be aware of the different alternatives and then develop a feeling for which of them is appropriate for this self-promotional project. The **Boston Globe** could have printed several kinds of articles on my subject:

- news
- news-feature
- interview
- column

Unfortunately, not all were right for me in this instance.

This first of these three alternatives wouldn't do because I was not involved in:

- researching the legislation
- drafting the legislation
- introducing the legislation, &c.

Since I was not a principal in this legislation I did not have news standing in the issue.

Now, to be sure, I could have gotten it, if I'd wanted to.

Let's say, for instance, that I set up a local organization called "Citizens For More Tax Deductions" and was assisting organize my state on behalf of this measure. Then I would have had news value.

Frankly, the unabashed self-promoter must be wary of creating this kind of organization, however. If it is ersatz, the merest shell of an organization, this could hurt you if it became known. If, however, you are taking the time to build an organization, this activity could deflect you from your important self-promotional purposes. On the other hand, such an organization could be most useful and entirely appropriate in promoting your message, your services and your products. But you must be very hard headed in evaluating whether the commitment of your time is warranted in terms of possible return.

In my case, it was not necessary to form a local chapter of an organization or a free-standing group because my objectives were entirely realized through the publication of the column (called an Op-Ed piece, because it is opposite the editorial page). What were these objectives:

- Enhanced perception as a leader. I always like my clients and client prospects to perceive me, not as a salesman, but as a leader on behalf of their interests. I am always alert to the preservation, protection and augmentation of my clients' interests. This column is the equivalent of a neon light saying, "JLA Never Sleeps!"

- Creation of an Alternative Credential. Mandarins do not carry resumes. They possess alternative credentials which underscore their standing in their field. This column is such a credential.
- Creation of a suitable leave behind. The goal of the unabashed self-promoter is to create a piece which it is in the interests of other organizations and individuals, preferably client prospects, to distribute on his behalf. In this case, this piece was brought to the attention of numerous organizations possessing newsletters and other publications for reprinting. In addition, these organizations can distribute my leave-behinds to rally opinion behind a piece of legislation of value to them.
- Reprinting in **The Congressional Record.** All pieces dealing with national issues or significant regional issues should be reprinted in **The Congressional Record.** In this case, since it is to the interest of the congressman sponsoring the legislation to draw maximum attention to his issue, he will put your article in this important source. When you create your leave behinds, you may use the insert from **The Congressional Record** rather than the publication to increase the perception of your article as a public service piece.
- Creation of a speech topic. Articles in publications should assist the advancement of your speaking career. (See Chapter 17.)
- Creation of a suitable lever for entré into television and radio. This article says very clearly that you are an expert, a knowledgeable individual and source of information on an important public topic. As such the electronic media should be interested in you. (See Chapter 13.)
- Payment. Yes, you actually get paid for many of these pieces, particularly major magazines and newspapers. I was paid for the **Globe** sample article.

All of the above are the predictable outcomes.

What also happened, though not predictable, is frequent: within a couple of days after publication of my **Globe** Op-Ed piece. I received an invitation from an agency of the U.S. government to speak at a conference they were sponsoring on alternative funding mechanisms for nonprofit organizations. As an expert in the field, my presence was eagerly requested. Was I available?

Was I ever!

At the invitation of the United States government, I was about to be put in the most enviable of positions for the unabashed self-promoter with a product or service to sell: as a paid speaker and acknowledged expert to potential clients of my firm. In other words, the government was actually making my marketing efforts profitable! Yes, I was certainly available.

Other Sources Of Free Information

To the continuing delight of any unabashed self-promoter, there are thousands upon thousands of organizations and individuals continually working to provide critical information — for us! What are some of them?

- trade and professional associations
- unions
- legislative committees
- specialized interest groups
- state and federal offices
- presidential commissions

Each of these sources is constantly producing valuable information, publishing it, making it readily available — to us! — at minimal or no cost. The key is to remain abreast of what is happening and to develop your sensitivity for the issues which are of the most concern to your client prospects which you can most easily exploit for your own benefit.

Never fear that there will be too little information for you to use. The problem the seasoned self-promoter faces is that there is far too much. In its way, of course, this is a rather comforting problem as it insures that with the establishment of a thorough and sensible system you can be perpetually before the public through one media source or another. Mastering the three basic article formats by you is a critical portion of this system.

CHAPTER 7

PRODUCING ARTICLES BY YOU: THE THREE CRITICAL FORMATS

The unabashed self-promoter will write many articles during his shimmering career. These articles help establish his credibility as an authority, propogate his message, and promote his products and services. Resign yourself to one crucial fact: one article will not be enough. You must produce articles at regular intervals to continue to keep your name and services before the proper public and underscore the fact of your indispensability.

Producing articles by you, the acknowledged or perceived expert, could be difficult as your other responsibilities grow. If, however, you keep in mind the following formats you will produce the articles you need quickly and relatively effortlessly. The benefit of mastering these formats is considerable. You will know just where your material goes, how much material you need, and what each section is supposed to accomplish. Once having mastered the various formulas, you can write these articles in a very short time, even under the less than ideal circumstances of air travel.

The Problem-Solving Process Article

Whether we are selling a product or a service, each of us needs the basic Problem-Solving Process Article, (See samples page 312.) This article demonstrates your mastery of a subject which is important to your potential customers or clients. It says in effect:

- I have studied your situation. I know what your problems are. I know why you are worried about them and what may happen to you, or your organization if they are not solved.
- I have solved problems like yours before, so often in fact that I have invented a process for dealing with them efficiently, economically, effectively. This is called the Problem-Solving Process.
- As a humane, solicitous problem solver interested in your welfare, I have set down this Process.

The ostensible purpose of the Problem-Solving process article is clear: it is intended to lead the reader step-by-step through a related set of difficulties and demonstrate to him that they can be dealt with expeditiously. The purpose of this article thus seems avowedly educational, a clear public service piece. In theory the reader, having considered what you've written, should be able to implement your advice on his own. In theory, what you've written is the Compleat Self-Help Article.

In theory.

In fact, this article is not a public service piece. It is a lure to your prospective clients and customers. It should demonstrate to them your complete mastery of the subject, and, while complete in its own terms, should make it very clear that it would be easier to implement the advice if they had your service or product to work with.

This article is not, therefore, primarily or even largely a *self*-help article; it is rather a free ad with the considerable difference that the unwary reader approaches it in a less guarded, defensive fashion that he does recognizable advertising.

To get the most benefit from this article, you, the writer, must give thoughtful attention to how you will appear in it. Here are some suggestions for tone and posture:

- Empathetic. The reader wants to believe you care about the only thing that interests him: his own problem.
- Helpful. You should be perceived as someone who wants to assist the reader solve his problem.
- Experienced. You must look as if you know what you're doing. It helps, of course, if you do.
- Authoritative. The ring of of your words must be crisp, knowledgeable, definite. Experts stand forward. Even if they are not exactly certain how a problem can be solved, they can be quite precise about how many available options there are and the risks and benefits of each one.
- Brisk. No nonsense. We are all busy people. The expert wants to move you to problem solution with dispatch.
- Confident. The reader must be left with the strong feeling that you are certain your method brings results.
- Positive. Your message must be upbeat. You need not denigrate competitors. You can even comfortably acknowledge their good points, while being sure to indicate that what you know goes far beyond their rudimentary attainments.

Having read the Problem-Solving Process Article, the reader must be left with the strong feeling that you have made a difficult, complicated subject comprehensible. He must look at your method rather like the Sunday sports fan watches an Olympic swan dive; it must appear easy, graceful, do-able. No problem must appear to be insoluble. If your reader feels it is, he will first give way to momentary anxiety and then look elsewhere for a solution. It is not, after all, in our national character to admit that any problem is insoluble.

The reader's delight that his problem is soluble by him is necessarily short-lived, however, just as our thought that we, too, could master that easy swan dive. In fact, upon sober reflection the reader knows he will need assistance. And that is where you, your product, or your service come in.

A Few Tips About The Problem-Solving Process Article

- Solve only the problems that your clients and customers think they have. If you're not sure, ask them what they think they need to know or to have. They will have no trouble accepting what they know they already need.
- Focus your discussion on the results they need to attain, *not* the processes which produce the results. Never, never detail each specific step the reader needs to master. This obviates the need for you and your services. Be brief, be precise, but do not be exhaustive in detail.
- Offer a series of results which the reader needs to master in sequence. The reader knows he must accomplish several objectives to reach his goal. As his experienced leader, it is your responsibility to demonstrate which results he needs.
- Keep the language simple, compelling. Readers rightly mistrust experts they cannot understand. Remember: Humans have a deep-seated need to believe. We want to believe; we must believe to be complete. Humans believe first and most fervently in what they think they can thoroughly understand. Do not think, therefore, that you are furthering your cause by the use of high fallutin palaver and opaque jargon. You're not. You are merely making it considerably more difficult for your reader to accomplish his goal: to believe in you.

Final Thoughts On The Problem-Solving Process Article

• Length. Your article can be from 650-2500 words in length depending on where you are going to publish it.
• Tone. To think in musical terms, your article should be more Cole Porter than Mahler. It should have a sureness of touch which compels admiration, invites emulation, but ultimately leads the reader to conclude that he cannot do it on his own.
• Feel. Each sentence should feel substantial. The article as a whole should breathe authenticity and prolonged experience. Even if you are not such an expert, you must be perceived as one.

The Problem-Solving Process article is a superb way of indicating your familiarity with a set of problems and for showing the reader how to deal with them — by bringing in that really accessible expert: you.

The Sentinel

Most people are chary of salesmen. They are afraid they will be gently gulled into buying what they don't need and cannot use or something that will not live up to the exalted claims of the seller.

Such client mistrust — and consequent failure to act — can be discouraging to the ingénue self-promoter who realizes that every successful practitioner of his art is necessarily a super salesman, too.

Fortunately there is a way for the unabashed self-promoter to gain the trust of his client prospect easily and to transform himself from an unwelcome salesman into a colleague, a fellow trench fighter working towards a common end. This way is enshrined in the Sentinel article.

The Sentinel presents information to client prospects about either threatening developments of interest to them or about an opportunity which will be lost to them unless they take quick action. Common instances include a proposed government regulation with severe consequences for the industry or a favorable piece of pending legislation with dimming prospects.

Such situations call for the Sentinel to take the lead in advocating the interests of his client prospects.

The posture of the Sentinel is this: while you, the client prospect, are going about your usual business, I, Sentinel, am monitoring the Big Picture, those developments which can threaten your livelihood or which could, if properly advanced, bolster your security. You are so busy, the Sentinel says, with all that you are doing, you cannot expect to keep abreast of these crucial matters. But I can. (And I can, in the process, not only gain your trust, the first job of every successful salesman, but I can assume a position of leadership and respect, too, someone, that is, who you will be honored to work with.)

The Sentinel is, at all times, an advocate — an advocate for the important interests of his clients and his client prospects. Just how the Sentinel approaches his advocacy task will vary, however, depending on the nature of the publication where the article will appear.

A publication founded to advance the interests of your client prospects would not only welcome but also probably demand a more unrestrainedly partisan article than would a general interest publication without an ax to grind. The example (see samples, page 313) was published in the **Boston Globe**, a mass market general interest publication. This article is, therefore, restrained in its advocacy. Nonetheless there can be no doubt on the part of the reader just where the writer stands on the issue under discussion.

I happen to find this relatively restrained approach the stronger. I want my prospects to know that I am advocating their point of view but (particularly in a general interest publication) I do not wish to threaten my status as an objective observer. Indeed this status gives my advocacy on any given issue the strength it needs to be persuasive. The trick, then, is to be perceived as objective while taking a strong advocacy position on behalf of the interests of your client prospects.

The Sentinel allows you to pull this off.

The Sentinel article presents you as the cool fact finder who has assessed the situation calmly, rationally, thoroughly and then — and only then — adopted an advocacy course.

The article you write should be in tone:

- olympian
- detached
- omnicient
- rational
- statesmanlike

You should begin by presenting the relevant background information about the issue, both immediate and historical. This presentation should be as nonpartisan and evenhanded as possible. In this way you establish your position as the informed expert, which is pivotal to your image.

Go on to give both the leading arguments in favor and those against the measure. Clearly those arguments that do not support your position must be dealt with but in a cool, professional manner. As the olympian fact finder there is ordinarily no need for pyrotechnic language unless your opponent's case is ridiculously simple-minded or fatuous.

Having once made your case, as swiftly and completely as possible, make it clear to your readers what you want them to do, by what time: It is helpful if this article imparts a sense of urgency, namely that something irrevocable will occur unless readers take your recommended actions. By following your advice you have put them right where you want them — as followers.

The Sentinel is never just a detached fact finder. He is also a generalissimo marshalling first facts and arguments and then people — his client prospects — towards a definite objective: buying the writer, the leader.

One Specific Case Explored

The sample Sentinel article on page 313 illustrates both how to assemble this kind of piece and how powerful it can be.

I first became aware of the issue (charitable deduction credit for individuals filing short tax forms) from a specialized newsletter. The proposed change in the law was of definite benefit to my client prospects, had not yet broken into the general media (and because of competing news items was not likely to) and allowed me the opportunity to present myself to my constituency as an informed leader-advocate. Importantly, all necessary information on the topic was readily available from a public source (namely the office of the chief congressional sponsor) in whose interest it was to supply me with material. (See Chapter 6.)

Following the procedures outlined in the preceeding chapter, I quickly came to have all the materials I needed to produce the Sentinel. By then I had already made a determination of which publication would be most interested in it: a mass market general interest publication was the best bet, largely because of the nature of the subject (taxes) and the fact that most adult readers of the newspaper would be affected.

My decision to proceed was based on likely outcomes of the project. Here they are:

- promotion of myself as Sentinel/protector of the interests of my clients and client prospects ("JLA Never Sleeps!")
- general promotion of my firm
- increased perception of me and my firm as thoughtful, concerned, knowledgeable
- linkage with chief congressional sponsor
- contact with Massachusetts congressional delegation (all sent copies of article with letter urging their support)
- publication of article in **The Congressional Record** (by chief congressional sponsor in whose interest it is to secure maximum attention to his issue.)
- creation and strengthening of links with other advocates (individual and institutional) for nonprofit organizations
- creation of significant new leave behind to introduce me and my issue to electronic media which can further promote me and my company. This leave behind is an infinitely more valuable lever than any media release as it establishes you, through third party validation, as an expert.
- payment of $75 (standard fee from **Boston Globe** for this kind of article)

All this was predictable.

Here are the unpredictable outcomes:

- invitation to address regional conference of a United States government agency
- advance promotion and suitable on-site promotion to 250 of my preferred client prospects which constituted audience
- introduced at conference to corporate executive of Fortune 500 company (fellow speaker) whose company financed 20 nonprofit organizations to take later workshop program
- invited back as speaker to conference following year
- introduction at conference to trustee of two national non-profit organizations. Invited as keynote speaker to one, national conference presenter at other.
- advance promotion and suitable on-site promotion to preferred client prospects who constituted these audiences
- on site book and service-consultation sales, &c., &c.

Each of these items, and the ones which proceeded both from the initial conference and subsequent contacts, produced real yankee dollars. Each time I was invited to go to the next spot no one was skeptical, no one questioned my credentials or asked for a resumé. No one treated me with the doubt and mistrust which are so often the lot of the salesman. Never. Instead, each person I encountered, whatever their lofty positions, was grateful to have me and always gracious to me.

And why not?

The Sentinel article, in just 650-1000 words, establishes your:

- concern
- knowledge about what the readers face
- desire to bring about a beneficial solution

It establishes you as a leader, as a friend, colleague, public advocate and fellow fighter in the good and righteous cause. Wouldn't you be glad and grateful to secure the services of such a sublime personality whatever the cost?

You would indeed.

This is what the Sentinel mode of unabashed self-promotion can do.

The White Knight

The Problem-Solving Process article is a step-by-step demonstration by the writer-master of how an individual or organization can solve a related set of problems through mastery of certain crucial techniques.

The Sentinel article alerts this same individual or organization to a movement of events which presents either an opportunity for benefit or an opening for chaos and loss. It presents the writer as public spirited leader-advocate.

The White Knght article, the last of the three basic article formats to be mastered by the unabashed self-promoter, offers yet another alternative: the self-promoter as the inevitable master mechanic — ready, willing, able to solve your problems — ultimately with his product or service.

This article has four distinct parts to it. The first is:

• Create Anxiety

People are motivated to act because they are anxious about something, fearful that some fortunate result will elude them or that some unfortunate result will overtake them. The first of these, an elusive fortunate result, I term Upscale Anxiety; the second of these, an expected unfortunate result, I call Downscale Anxiety.

The White Knight article allows the unabashed self-promoter to capitalize on this pervasive anxiety and harness it to his success chariot.

It is the responsibility of the unabashed self-promoter to discern from his client prospects just what they are anxious about. Then he must gather detailed supporting information demonstrating just why his client prospects' fears are in fact reasonable (if not entirely accurate. This is not necessary.)

The unabashed self-promoter may use a wide variety of materials to support the anxieties of his client prospects:

- newspaper articles
- specialized studies
- legislative documents
- scholarly publications
- internal memoranda

Anything, in short, which will support and sustain the feeling of anxiety which the client prospects already have.

If you find that there are other matters about which these organizations and individuals should be anxious, add them cautiously and at your own risk. After all if they have not yet been perceived as anxieties you will have to undertake a perhaps costly investment of your time and resources to educate your client prospects about the new hazards. Such an effort might be a drag on your self-promotional resources unless you had some reason for assuming an early return.

Remember: If you must educate your public to an issue you have an extra, often costly and time-consuming step to go through. Knowing this the unabashed self-promoter is ordinarily quite content to work with the prevailing anxieties of his client prospect, perhaps spicing his concoction with one or two new worries, but not more.

The amount of anxiety that you need to impart depends very definitely on who is targeted as your preferred reader.

If you are aiming at prospering individuals or organizations you need not use much anxiety, often the barest hint that something beneficial is about to escape them is sufficient to induce activity. These individuals treat life as a race in which the glittering prizes go to the swift of foot and the ingenious of mind. To insure that they get these prizes they are willing to buy the necessary goods and services which assist in delivering success — including the goods and services which you have to offer. You need hardly stress to these people and their organiztions that time is of the essence and that uncertainty costs money. They know it.

With the upscale, then, it is your job merely to point out — with no heavy hand — the consequences attendant upon their failure to act and, more often than not, they will act — now. After all, they know from the Red Queen of Wonderland they must move twice as fast even to stay in the same place — and faster still if they are to have any chance of moving on.

It is rather different with the downscale. These people and their organizations are already well aware that life — and its pantheon of attendant glories — has already passed them by. They may, in moments of reverie, advance some bloated rhetoric as to why they are actually better off because they are no longer front runner, but they never loose sight of the fact that the race has moved far, far beyond them.

To get these people and their moribund organizations to act is difficult. They may know that to win life's race means taking chances, but they have run out of maneuvering room: any chance they take could turn out to be their last. Hence they are very, very cautious both about making decisions and committing scarce resources.

The downscale, then, need heavy doses of anxiety-producing words. They must be clearly shown that unless they act — now! — their poor situation will become even worse, that the hemorrage they are aware of will become, through inactivity, a death stream.

The White Knight article on page 314 is directed to a downscale population: post-Reagan nonprofit organizations, particularly those previously funded by the federal government. The unabashed self-promoter is advised to hit his downscale targets as I hit mine: with the full battery of anxiety producing words and a litany of very detailed, specific reasons for their anxiety. The more specific, the better. The clear message is: act now or you will die. Take as your first positive action buying me, my product or my service. This is the way to salvation.

• Indicate Desirable Outcomes, Do Not Explicate Processes

It is the foolish self-promoter who tells too much about *how* he works, thus obviating the need for his own services. This can be a problem in both the Problem-Solving Process article and in this one. Beware! The key to avoiding this problem is to concentrate the attention of your reader on results and to avoid supplying the detail about how these outcomes will be reached.

How do you know which outcomes to highlight?

Your client prospects will generally supply them. They know not only what their problems are but what results they must achieve to overcome them. Ask them. I have never known an individual to be at all reticent either about what ails him or about the blissful state in which he'd like to find himself.

The task of the unabashed self-promoter is to excite the interest of the reader (his future client or follower) by focusing his attention on a series of desired outcomes, which — by extension — the self-promoter can provide.

These outcomes should not be foreign to the reader. At no time can a self-promoter ever afford to be far in advance of his audience; here it would be fatal. The outcomes that you can provide to the reader-client prospect must be those which he himself values.

The point of this section of the article is to get the reader to acknowledge that you are an intelligent individual worthy of further notice and immediate patronage. The way to insure this result is to flatter the reader's intelligence. He will think you a creature of worth and insight if you:

- have him read what he's already read
- have him hear what he's already heard
- tell him what he already knows.

Such things he can agree with, and if you provide them he will have absolutely no trouble agreeing with you — and arriving at the not-so-startling conclusion that you, your products and services are worthy of his attention — and money.

Again: do *not* focus on the processes that will produce the results.

Remember: it is your task to excite the dreams of your reader and thereby motivate him to take the next step: buying from you. It is not necessary and is in fact detrimental to your interests to detail the exact processes and means which will produce *his* desired outcomes.

• Flip The Shame Switch

Every individual and every organization is susceptible to shame. And every unabashed self-promoter has come to know this blissful fact and unhesitatingly makes use of this interesting aspect of the human condition. The White Knight article needs a dash of shame to be entirely effective, just as it needs its quotient of anxiety.

It is perhaps worth pointing out what the difference is between shame and anxiety. Anxiety relates to self. Shame relates to others. People are anxious about what will happen to them and theirs, fearful about what they will loose or what will befall them. Shame relates to others — specifically about what an action of mine will do to someone else. This is a very helpful distinction to make, and it is very important to know that while all decision makers are anxious about the effect of their own decisions on themselves, they are also prey to shame about what their decisions will do to others. The unabashed self-promoter must activate this shame mechanism — and take advantage of it, the fear, that is, that because of a bad decision:

- employees will be laid off, with human frustration and deprivation the result
- stockholder dividends will be down with more human frustration and more deprivation the result
- town revenues will fall with more human frustration and even more deprivation the result
- clients and customers will not be properly serviced, with more human frustration and incalculable deprivation the inevitable result.

Oh, what a load of shame the unabashed self-promoter has at his disposal!

The shame which the unabashed self-promoter can call up varies in intensity with whether the individual or organization being addressed is upscale or downscale. I suspect that anxiety, being personal and applying to self, is probably always stronger than shame, which refers to the condition of others. Some, who have a residual humanistic streak, will no doubt cavil, but there it is.

I also suspect that downscale shame is a more potent force than upscale, although I am less certain about this. Perhaps a high tech panjandrum who makes a bad call feels not only personally anxious about the consequences but shameful about what he has done to the fortunes of untold numbers of others. I cannot say since these purveyors of the future are so seldom known to acknowledge human error.

When, however, the executive director of a special needs adoption agency makes an equally unfortunate decision, I suspect the shame is very, very potent indeed, because the consequences of that decision fall so heavily upon those who are least able to bear them. The unabashed self-promoter needs to keep these reflections in mind. And act accordingly.

• Indicate Your Specific Availability As The White Knight

All goes for naught, engendering anxiety, focusing on outcomes, spicing with shame, if no one knows you exist to provide the product or service which will insure the beneficial result. Ordinarily a brief biographical tag indicating your whereabouts follows the White Knight article (and the others, too). In the example on page 314, the tag is italicized and preceeds the piece. It is your right to have this biographical tag, and it should be as blatantly promotional as the publication will allow.

A Final Thing Or Two

The primary purpose of these articles is not, *not* to provide information. Newspapers and other publications print them because of their informational content, as a public service to educate and enlighten the public. But it should be perfectly clear that that is not your reason for writing them.

No, your reason for writing any one of these articles is:

- to promote yourself as a knowledgeable source
- to indicate your familiarity with information, processes, products, techniques, devices and on and on which are of use to potential buyers of you, your services and your products
- to stand forth as a leader in your field, not just as technically competent but as an empathetic leader concerned that your client prospects master their difficulties and — with your help — get ahead
- to avoid being thought of as a salesman and to be perceived instead as colleague, friend, technocrat, innovator — someone, in short, who it is a joy and privilege to work with.

What is delightful about these formats is that when you use them the articles which you must produce can be done quickly, easily as the information you have can be both sifted expeditiously and arranged with speed. Like any format, these can be used again and again. Moreover the products which spring from them — your promotional articles — can be printed and then reprinted again.

Finally and perhaps most importantly these articles — more than any conceivable media release — give you credibility with the electronic media and constitute your entré to it in ways which will be explored in another chapter.

Unlike a paid ad, no matter how bright, how vibrant, how ingeniously witty, these self-promotional articles have a dramatic life span. Articles that I have written using these formats have produced meaningful responses for up to two years. What ad has ever done as much?

Alas! Some self-promoters are obstructed on their road to success because they cannot produce the articles they need. They are poor writers, slow, unimaginative, wedded to every word they write, unwilling to prune to produce compelling prose. For them, then, a few additional tips and suggestions.

• Finding And Using Free-Lance Talent

If you cannot write the self-promotional articles you need, either because you are technically ill-equipped to do so or because you are just too busy, you will need free-lance writing talent to assist you.

The first problem is knowing where to find such talent. In any town or city with a smaller neighborhood oriented newspaper, write the editor and ask for the names and addresses of free-lance writers or stringers who may write for the paper occasionally. Do not tell the editor precisely why you are seeking these people; simply say you have a journalistic assignment and want to hire some help.

In a large city you can write the editor of a citywide magazine with the same query. The best place to look is with a magazine or newspaper editor who has to deal with these people on a regular basis. He can also give you some useful information about the going rate for free-lancers in your area. It is ordinarily ridiculously low.

Very few free-lancers, and those usually fairly well-known, make much money. It is therefore usually possible to hire a free-lancer to assist you for between $7-10 per hour or for about $75 per day. If you have done your homework, gathering the information you need and at least making an attempt at a first draft, a day is usually more than sufficient to produce the kinds of articles this chapter is about.

Of course, you can hire a free-lancer to do everything connected with your article:

- research the topic
- gather the necessary information
- draft it
- advise on where to submit the article for publication
- draft a query or cover letter

Everything, that is, except make direct contact with the publication in his own name; (it is perfectly permissible to call a publication to get relevant article guidelines and the names and addresses of contact people, but no more.)

While it is possible for a self-promoter to hire this kind of service, it is not very desirable. Free-lance talent for those in need is best used to gather the initial information (research assistant) and polish the final result (copy editor). Given the formats in this book it should be perfectly possible for any self-promoter with a modicum of necessary information to produce the articles he needs. Self help, after all, begins at home.

CHAPTER 8

GENERATING ARTICLES ABOUT YOU

There are two kinds of articles: articles by you and articles about you. The first of these establishes you as an expert; the second establishes you as a celebrity and is the more flattering. Everyone, after all, loves to be thought worthy of attention. Interestingly these celebrity articles are by far easier to get in print. The key is knowing how to generate them.

Here's where the wealth of America's civic, social, fraternal, political and business organizations come into play, ripe for use by the unabashed self-promoter.

Background

The United States is still a remarkably parochial nation. A succinct comment by one man-on-the-street illustrates the matter nicely. This man, a resident of neighboring Somerville, Massachusetts, said to me with quiet earnestness, "What happens to you guys in Cambridge is of no interest to us in Somerville." Somerville, mind, is contiguous to Cambridge. I, of course, have always had scant interest in Somerville, but I had no idea Somervillians emulated my own studied insularity.

The fact is most people have only the narrowest concerns. And media mirrors their interests. Most media stories in the nation — upwards of 85% in fact — have a local angle. They are written *by* local people *about* local people *for* local people — or at least about people and events with some connection to the locality. Even national stories are likely to get more play in any given area if they have a local dimension.

This situation is to the advantage of the unabashed self-promoter whose task is to transform himself into a local story — and hence get local publicity.

Note: The alternative to the local/geographical angle is the affiliation angle. That is to say, if you can demonstrate that you are related to the media source through affiliation to the group which publishes its publications, this is often a sufficient link. Alumni publications, trade magazines, fraternal publicatons may all be national; your membership in the relevant group constitutes local affiliation.

Knowing Where To Speak

Each day hundreds of thousands of speeches are given across the nation. Each day. Not only are many of them of forgettable content, but they do not succeed in advancing the self-promotional objectives of the speaker, and so are not worth doing. And this is not just because many of the speakers were not paid for their work, either.

Cash payment is not the *sine qua non* of a self-promoter — not immediate cash, that is. Self-promoters realize that a speaking engagement handled properly (e.g. so that it results in maximum media exposure) can produce much more money than a simple speaker fee. Self-promoters always have money in mind, and they pursue promotional possibilities because it produces more of it. Thus the unabashed self-promoter is perfectly happy to accept an unpaid speaking assignment if certain other conditions are present. It is, however, very important to know where to speak and under what circumstances. The goal of any speaking engagement for the unabashed self-promoter is maximum media exposure — and hence the delivery of information about him and his products and services to the maximum market of potential buyers. Speaking engagements must be selected based on their ability to realize this goal.

Here is how you make your decision about whether to speak to any given organization:

- Is there a newspaper in the town where the organization inviting you is located? If not, if the local newspaper covers several towns, is the town important enough to warrant coverage and is the organization in the town sufficiently significant to command coverage?
- Is there a radio station in the town where you'll be speaking? Once you have appeared in print, you'll want to use this print interview feature as your passport to local electronic media, or you'll want to alert newspaper and radio simultaneously to your presence.
- Is there a television station locally? Same principle as above. It is more likely these days that any local television will be cable.
- Does the local organization have a newsletter which can promote you both in advance and following your presentation? Does it have any organized means of communicating with its membership and hence of bringing your name, your product and your services to their attention?
- Is the organization affiliated with a regional or national organization which has a newsletter or magazine? It is often possible to get excerpts of speeches which are of interest to local chapters in the publications of their national organizations. These regional or national organizations also have conferences at which you can be invited to speak.
- Is the organization inviting you of importance in the community where you are speaking? Is it, that is, media worthy? Certain prestigious organizations in a community (the hospital, Chamber of Commerce, Sports Boosters, &c) easily attract media coverage. These are the kinds of organizations to be associated with.
- Are there immediate client prospects in the audience?
- Will the organization work with you to help meet your self-promotional objectives?

If you cannot answer "Yes!" to at least 4 of these questions (with the last being the most significant), you should probably not waste your time accepting an invitation from any organization.

How To Get Invited

When you start on the road to unabashed self-promotion you may wonder how you are ever going to become an honored and sought-after guest. You may, in fact, be daunted. Don't give in to this self-indulgent mood. Remember the immortal words of one of my favorite novelists, William Makepeace Thackeray, who supplied the necessary remedy for all of us. "If you're not invited, ask to be invited."

Your first task is to find out who to ask.

The associates in your existing circle of friends, acquaintances and business colleagues belong to dozens of organizations. It is now your responsibility to find out which ones they are and to decide which of them are appropriate for you.

I meet hundreds of people each year. With each of them I launch a networking conversation so that I can decide where they fit in my life and which contacts and associates they possess which may be of use to me. You do the same.

Here are a few of the things you want to know about the people you associate with:

- Where did you go to school? Are you an active alumnus?
- Do you belong to a religious organization?
- Are you active in a fraternal organization (Moose, Elks, Kiwanis, Rotary, Lions, &c)?
- Are you involved in a trade or professional organization?
- Do you sit on the board of a nonprofit organization or are you otherwise involved?
- Are you active in a political organization?

The purpose of these questions is to provide you with the leads you need to organizations which can provide the basis for your self-promotional activities. You are trying to discover through these — and related questions — not only whether your associate has appropriate contacts but whether he can be turned into your agent introducting you to people who can be of further service to you.

Here's how it works in reality:

My printer is a member of the Westwood Lions Club. I came to know this in casual conversation, but the piece of information was of more than casual interest to me.

- Westwood is covered by a well-distributed newspaper circulating in five affluent communities. Many client prospects could be made aware of my firm, its products and services through a successful, staged self-promotion.
- The Lions Club is the kind of significant local organization (composed of important local leaders) which insures media coverage, if the event is properly handled.
- The Westwood Lions Club is part of a major international organizaton. This organization holds both state and national conferences. A successful appearance at a local chapter therefore could be parlayed into subsequent appearances at others (and thus future self-promotional possibilities).
- Client prospects would be in the audience.

This sequence flashed in my mind the minute my friend told me he was a member of the Westwood chapter. Sad to say, however, there was no real likelihood that this group would ever seek me out on their own initiative; it saddens me to acknowledge this fact about them, but there it is. I had to take the initiative.

Remembering my Thackeray, I asked my friend to get me an invitation. Now when you do this, remember the person you ask has probably never proposed a guest before, doesn't know how it's done, doesn't know what to say about you, and doesn't see you as the mandarin you wish to appear before his organization. All can be — and must be — dealt with to insure that you are properly received.

Briefing Your Contact

It is your responsibility to provide your contact with all the information he needs to sell you to a program chairman. You provide:

- the subject of your talk
- reasons why it will be of interest to the target audience

- background materials about you (a simple fact sheet if you have not spoken elsewhere or have not yet received media coverage; this fact sheet supplemented by leave behinds if you have received such coverage.

Tell your contact that what you want is an introduction which can be handled in this way:

- Contact to organization program chairman: "I have a wonderful suggestion for a feature program. I've asked my friend to write (or call) you direct to see about arranging something in the near future."

If the organization program chairman is at a distance, a letter may be necessary. This is handled in the same way (See samples, page 334).

This is the theory behind the exercise: a member of an organization has a platform to speak on your behalf. As a professional courtesy (if nothing more) his suggestions will at least be heard, where a cold letter from you might well go unacknowledged no matter how beneficial the program to the intended audience.

Your contact should also indicate that you, the speaker prospect, are expert at working with the media and will help produce materials which will secure notice of the event and thus help promote the organization. Note: the unabashed self-promoter must early become an expert in framing actions which are to the seeming (or actual) benefit of the individual he wishes to turn into his agent. In this case what you propose to do (officially) is promote the organization by assisting them promote your appearance. In actual fact, of course, your own self-promotion is your first objective.

Note: even in situations where you have provided your contact with all the information he needs to make a good case for you, where you have suggested the best means of selling your appearance, and where (as will often happen) you yourself have provided the name, address, and telephone number of the proper contact person, you may have to remind your contact — more than once — to move on the matter. I am an advocate of persistent, gentle persuasion. If you have decided that the organization is important to you — with suitable self-promotional prospects and the likelihood of a significant dollar return on your investment — then keep urging your contact to act. I have discovered that after two rather less gentle reminders, it finally becomes more agreeable for my contact to do what I want him to do than for him to listen to the mellifluous tones of my voice.

Assisting The Program Chairman Assist You

Pity America's poor program chairmen. Consider their problems: they have imperfect knowledge about where to seek speakers and limited ways of checking on speaker quality. Yet they will undoubtedly be blamed for providing a mediocre product, a fact of which they are only too sharply aware. Allied to these problems is the fact that for them selecting speakers is not their first priority and that they have decidedly limited time. No wonder they need help! Help which the unabashed self-promoter is only too happy to provide. And which the harried program chairman is ordinarily equally happy to accept.

The role of the self-promoter in the process is this: he provides a quality product and says to the program chairman, in effect, "You are too busy to promote this admirable product — me — and, if truth were known, you don't know how in any event. Yet the promotion which will result is good both for you (as having brought such a sensational program), your organization (as being important enough to sponsor it), and, of course, for me (about which the less said, the better). So let me get on with the promotion — and help relieve the burdens of your considerable office."

It would be hard for anyone to disagree with this sentiment, much less a program chairman, whether of a local fraternal organization or a national trade convention. And they usually don't.

Occasionally however, it does happen. The program chairman may say, "We've never promoted our programs before," the implication being strong that they don't wish to begin now. Should this be the case in which you find yourself, you need to be diplomatically firm. Just how you act at this moment is crucial. You must act as if you are worthy of sustained media attention even when you haven't yet gotten it, and, of course, this is precisely the moment when this posture is most difficult to adopt.

Say, first, "Perhaps there hasn't been any media mention of programs before. But I'm sure you want the organization to be known for the good works it does and the quality of the speakers it attracts. The media helps insure this result. So let's use them to get our message across."

If this doesn't work, escalate.

If you are not speaking for a fee (or for a figure which is less than your regular fee,), say, "You know, of course, that I am speaking to your organization without fee. I can afford to do so if and only if I am able to get my message publicized. Since it is in the interest of your organization, too, I hope we can work this out. And, remember, I'll be working with you to ensure an appropriate result."

If the program chairman remains adamant, obdurate, obstinate, you must decide whether the organization is significant enough to address. Will there be client prospects on hand? Does the possibility exist to leverage your connection to a state or national affiliate? In either case the engagement might still be worth doing.

I have rarely been put in this position. On only one occasion in my career has a program chairman been unreasonable. She sought me out with an invitation to participate in a panel discussion, without payment. Now, the panel is not a form I either like or recommend for the unabashed self-promoter; we prefer the monopoly of the platform. And, of course, it goes without saying, that it is never palatable to be without payment. Yet I did not immediately rule out the possibility of appearing.

Here were my questions to this program chairman (as they would be to any program chairman):

- Does your organization have a newsletter which can promote me and my products or services both in advance of my appearance and subsequently in an article about my remarks.
- Would your organization mail a media release to selected publications in your field both with an announcement that I will be speaking and with a follow-up report on what transpired?
- Can I provide literature about my products and services to your audience and can I sell products (books) at the time of the program?

To each of these questions, the organizer returned a manifestly unacceptable answer:

- There was a newsletter, but it could not be utilized as a promotional vehicle. (The contamination argument.)
- By policy, media releases were never sent. ("We prefer mindless obscurity.")
- By our ground rules, no mention of products or services could be made or offered for sale. ("It's too, too, vulgar.")

Having (with increasing incredulity) listened to this rendition, I allowed myself the luxury of expressing both my amazement and pique about such inconsiderable, selfish arrangements. Program chairmen and self-promoters work together in mutual self-interest. On the (gratefully) infrequent occasions when one of these chairmen fails to understand the compact, you may, as I did, point out the lapse. It is for certain of these occasions, those beyond repair, that I maintain a reserve of wintry smiles, haughty manner, and clipped Ivy League condescension. I can testify to their effectiveness when properly used.

Preparing Your Media Materials

Your part of the compact with the program chairman is to provide all the media materials which are necessary. What follows is a list of these and tips on how to prepare and submit them:

Advance Newsletter Listing

Do not leave it to the imagination of the program chairman as to how you should be promoted in the organization's publication(s). Write the material yourself. The advancement announcement should contain the following information:

- your name
- name and location of your company or way to contact you either in case an individual cannot attend or wish to contact you afterwards
- date, time and place of presentation
- name and description of relevant product or service
- mention of last significant media coverage
- indication of any special connection with the organization you are addressing.

Here's what an advance notice about me might look like:
"Dr. Jeffrey Lant will address our next dinner meeting on Thursday, April 13 in the Thoreau Room of the Holiday Inn. Dr. Lant is well-known both as the president of Jeffrey Lant Associates, Inc., a consulting firm in Cambridge, Massachusetts specializing in nonprofit technical assistance, and as the author of the best-selling book **The Consultant's Kit: Establishing And Operating Your Successful Consulting Business**. Dr. Lant's book is now in its sixth printing. You may have read about Dr. Lant in the April issue of **Boston Magazine** or heard some of the enthusiastic comments made after he addressed our Pittsfield chapter. He will be speaking on "Unabashed Self-Promotion," and you can be sure it will be a provocative presentation."

You should ask the program chairman whether he needs a photo of you to accompany this notice. People like to have a face to associate with this information, and it is your responsibility to find out whether the organization can use a picture and to provide it if they can.

Media Releases

Media releases are best individually prepared and targeted to the appropriate promotional vehicle. When I spoke to the Westood Lions Club, I had only one media source to worry about and only one advance release to prepare. For towns with more than one newspaper, the unabashed self-promoter (if he wishes to derive full value from the event) will need to prepare multiple releases. Novice self-promoters may find this taxing, but by following the suggestions below the task need not be. Moreover, it serves a very real purpose, particularly for those individuals who lack the volumes of media clips of experienced self-promoters. You can in a very short time built up an extremely impressive array of leave behinds by producing tailored releases and by systematically making use of available print media outlets both before and after your presentation.

The point of doing multiple, tailored releases is this: each newspaper (indeed every media source) likes to have exclusive material. The more they feel they are getting such material, the more likely they are to use it. The unabashed self-promoter makes good use of this insight.

Let us assume that you are making a presentation in a community with two newspapers, one a daily and one a weekly. You thus have the possibility of *at least* four newspaper stories in connection with this single presentation, two advance, two subsequent.

To insure that you get these two advance stories, you will want to prepare two distinct media releases, each specifically prepared for one of the targets. It is to your advantage to do so because each release, and thus each printed story, can be used to accentuate different aspects of your presentation and highlight your different credentials, products and services.

Here's how to prepare the advance release:

- Paragraph 1. This paragraph gives your name, an identifying clause, and the who, what, where, specifics about your speech. It conforms in style to the advance announcement made by the organization in its publication.
- Paragraph 2. This paragraph sets forth the topic of the speech. It is sometimes incorporated in paragraph 1.
- Paragraph 3. This paragraph is designed to arouse the interest of readers and to indicate that the subject of the presentation is an important one. One good way of handling this paragraph is to have it conform to the introductory, or "anxiety" section, of the White Knight article by you (see Chapter 8). This paragraph poses either an implicit or explicit question to the reader, who by asking "Why?" or "What?", or "When?" is motivated to read on.
- Paragraph 4. This paragraph gives specific reason for reader anxiety. Depending on the length of the article, two or even three more paragraphs of specific anxiety detail may be added. It is important to point out that the authentification for the anxiety should be the speaker-expert himself, not a study, statistic, or report produced by someone else. This is the opportunity to establish yourself as the perceived expert and strengthen your credibility.
- Paragraph 5. This is a transition paragraph. It gives not only a summary statement designed to reinforce reader (and, don't forget, potential client) anxiety ("The situation is as grave for the nation's nonprofit organizations as it has ever been.") But it also makes a suggestion about how this anxiety can be dealt with: "The inescapable conclusion . . ."
- Paragraph 6. In an advance article, this paragraph suggests that the specifics of how to handle the problem will constitute the heart of the speaker's presentation. There must be an element of suspence which induces the readers to attend; this is it. Importantly, this paragraph paves the way for the subsequent article which will present in detail a report of the speech — and of the speaker's suggested ways of dealing with the problem.
- Paragraph 7. This paragraph offers additional information about the speaker and is designed to reinforce the reader's perception (and the perception of prospective clients) that the individual featured in this article is indeed worthy of notice.
- Paragraph 8. This paragraph has several purposes. It can be used by the unabashed self-promoter to compliment the organization having invited him. This will help insure a positive reception. He can also use it to establish a compatibility of interest and outlook with related organizations. In the sample article (page 317) this paragraph says, in effect, "I am an expert who is familiar not just with the YMCA but with all comparable organizations." This being the case, this article can be sent to comparable organizations as your point of entry.

- Paragraph 9. This paragraph continues the self-promoter's job of both complimenting his host organization and establishing him as the expert who can assist related organizations.
- Paragraph 10. The final paragraph gives the self-promoter a final opportunity to stand forward not just as a person of consequence but as a humane, solicitous problem solver, an appealing personality to the reader, someone the reader (or client prospect) would like to have around. The unabashed self-promoter takes advantage of this last word which gives him the opportunity of appearing as an individual of personal appeal as well as technical consequence.

The Clausal Principle

One of the keys to what makes this such a useful article for the unabashed self-promoter is found in the Clausal Principle. Each time your name appears in the article, and it will appear in nearly every paragraph, modify it with a clause that sets forth something important about you:

- a product
- a service
- an educational attainment
- some civic or professional recognition
- an award you've just been given, &c.

These modifying clauses are of the utmost importance to the unabashed self-promoter. They bring to the attention of general readers and more particularly to buyers of your products and services significant facts about who you are and what you can do, and they are presented with third party validation about their importance. Through the use of these modifying clauses you will stand forth as the acknowledged expert — and be taken as such.

Exclusivity

As previously mentioned, your media release becomes more attractive to a source if it is solely directed to that source. Thus it is helpful if, in the body of your release, you mention the source's name. In the sample this is accomplished in paragraphs three and six. The editor of the **Melrose Evening News** knows when reading this release that it was drafted exclusively for his newspaper. The result is an article that seems the result of an exclusive interview you have given.

Producing The Advance Media Release

The sample article from the **Melrose Evening News** reads as if a reporter from the **News** had interviewed me before the event. But I never talked to any reporter. I wrote this article word for word as it was printed. In theory organizations where you will make presentations will have a public relations or publicity committee. In actual fact most of them don't. Even the ones that do, however, are often amateurish; none, of course, has the interest you do in seeing that your self-promotional objectives are met. You are thus left to take matters in hand, and do it yourself.

Here's how the production process works:

- Know the available media outlets. Either check media reference directories or ask the program chairman about local newspapers. Doing both is preferable. What you get from the former source is a list of available outlets. What you get from the latter is a necessarily subjective evaluation about which are worth pursuing and in what order.

- Get release submission information. It is your responsibility to call the newspaper and find out the name and title of the appropriate editor to whom the release should be submitted, the address of the paper, its telephone number and deadline for the last edition *before* your presentation. When calling do *not* identify yourself. If you feel compelled to give some identifying clue, say you are calling on behalf of the organization inviting you to speak. When I make these calls, I just ask my questions, write down the information, and end the conversation, all very brief and to the point.
- Write the release. As should by now be very clear, the release you write should in fact be the article as you wish it to appear. The more closely it resembles an actual article (that is, the less an editor need do to it to make it acceptable for publication), the more likely it is to be used. As you write it, imagine yourself being interviewed by a reporter from the newspaper. You would wish this person to perceive you not only as an individual of consequence but also as personally appealing, charismatic. Both purposes can and should be realized in your release, the purpose of which is to establish you as an authority, an expert and person of note *and* one of compelling human interest, too.
- Prepare the release. To prepare the release, type it in the format suggested in Chapter 4 on plain white paper. It is not a good idea to request the stationery of the organization where you are speaking; however helpful you are trying to be, this suggestions seems presumptuous and is subject to misconstrual. Instead, send your typed draft to the program chairman (or to the publicity chairman, if such a person exists) along with a covering memorandum. This memo should invite your contact to suggest suitable changes in the text, and then to type it on organization letterhead and mail by a suggested date to the appropriate editor.

Follow-Up

All creatures great and small benefit from oversight. About 4-5 days before the publication's deadline, call your contact at the organization and inquire about whether the release has in fact been sent to the newspaper. If it has not, urge celerity. In fact, don't hesitate to suggest at this point that the release be hand-delivered if there is any question of missing the deadline. Advise your contact that the day before deadline he needs to call the editor and make sure that the material has in fact arrived and inquire whether any supplementary materials or information would be helpful.

Photographs

Newspapers like photographs to accompany articles. Do not expect the newspaper to send a photographer for you, however, particularly for an advance article. Have it produced yourself and submit it with your draft release. For an advance release a simple head shot is quite sufficient. Make sure that your name, a brief description of you and the date of the photograph appear on the back. Type these on a sticker and affix this to the photograph. Do not write on the back of the photograph in ink or type on it; these show through. The newspaper is unlikely to return this photograph, so don't expect it. (For further suggestions, see Chapter 11.)

Hints For Producing The Second Advance Media Release

Once you have finished the first advance media release, you are ready to go ahead and deal with any other print media sources. This is your opportunity to develop your perceived credibility, your status as an expert, and to produce another useful, compelling leave behind for future use.

Here's how your second release might look:

- Paragraph 1. This paragraph containing basic facts about your appearance will stay largely the same. You can, however, change the description of your firm and expand upon it. Mine might now read, "Dr. Jeffrey Lant, president of a Cambridge consulting firm specializing in raising money for nonprofit organizations."
- Paragraph 2. Describe your product or service, "Dr. Lant, author of **Development Today: A Guide For Nonprofit Organizations** (which recently went into a third printing)."
- Paragraph 3. Alter the structure of the sentence, add another self-descriptor but do not delete the implicit or explicit question which motivates the reader to continue. "The 36-year-old Lant ought to know what he's talking about. He has both worked directly with nonprofit organizations and researched their condition. He told the **Chronicle** that, 'The nation's 800,000 nonprofit organizations are today facing their most severe challenge.' "
- Paragraph 4. Cite salient facts increasing the anxiety of client prospects and bolstering your case. You can cite some of the same facts as appear in your first release but change the order. These paragraphs should not be identical. Remember: in theory two separate reporters are writing them.
- Paragraph 5. Rewrite so that the anxiety is reinforced and so that the transition is made to that which can be done about it. The paragraph might read," 'I've been working with organizations in 38 states myself,' Lant said. 'And the situation is pretty grim. My research has confirmed my own direct experience. Fortunately there are many, many committed citizens working along with us professionals to improve matters. In my remarks I intend to tell just what is working — and why.' "
- Paragraph 6. This paragraph can stay largely as it is.
- Paragraph 7. This paragraph should be rewritten to stress other credentials, products and services you want to promote. It might read, "Lant, who in February received an Official Citation from the City of Cambridge for his distinguished services to nonprofit organizations, has also recently been featured in the new book **Maverick: Succeeding As A Free-Lance Entrepreneur.** He said he has developed a Capital Campaign Fund Raising Program which should 'help nonprofit organizations raise the money they need to protect themselves against bad times like these.' Lant, who is Development Counsel at the YMCA, said that he has had the 'opportunity to perfect his model right here in Melrose.' "
- Paragraph 8. Praise the client and indicate that the experience you have is useful to other client groups. " 'Yes,' Lant continued, 'The Board of the Melrose YMCA has been most cooperative in making my model work. It has been a joy to work with them. The perfecting which has occurred in Melrose will be of the utmost value to other organizations — YWCAs, Girl Scouts, Boy Scouts, &c. — with which I'll be working in the future.' "
- Paragraph 9. This can stay largely as it is.
- Paragraph 10. Change to reinforce the point that you are more than technically competent; you are individually compelling. "Lant said that he welcomes these exchanges with community leaders. 'The real business of saving the nation's nonprofit organizations will take place in the hearts and minds of those who benefit from them. We technicians can do much,' Lant said with his quick smile, 'but we cannot do it all. I have something to say tonight, surely, but I also have something to learn.' "

Deciding When To Standardize Your Advance Release

It is clear that customized releases work very well for the unabashed self-promoter. The problem is, however, that they are not always feasible. If, for example, you were sending out 20 releases on any given day and speed was of the essence, it would not be possible to draft an individual release for each media source. Here are my rules of thumb for deciding when to standardize:

- Whenever possible, customize your releases, particularly in situations where you have fewer than five media sources to contact.
- When speed is important as when you are piggybacking on another story — see Chapter 10 — or when you do not have adequate time to invest in customizing releases, produce a standardized release. Note: even under these circumstances, you might designate 1 or 2 places worthy of individual attention and mass produce a general release for the rest.

The chances of your customized release being used by one or more of the places you contact are very, very good. There are three significant benefits that result when it is printed:

- When you arrive to make your speech, you will be accorded substantially more respect and consideration by the organization and by the audience. No wonder. The press has transformed you from yet another run-of-the-mill speaker into a mandarin, someone worthy of notice and attention. This is particularly true of the other mandarins who are present. They will have been alerted to the fact that you are one of them, an individual of consequence deserving of their notice.
- Your audience has been expanded exponentially. Now it is of no great concern to you that your promised audience of 100 has shrunk because of a rain squall to barely 20. In fact your audience is as numerous as those who take the time to peruse the article. These people, too, as well as those in the hall, have been exposed to your message, products, and services.
- You have created for yourself an Alternative Credential, a leave behind which can serve as your introduction to the electronic media, to comparable organizations, and to client prospects. You now have something tangible which describes what you do — and, more importantly, which indicates that others have found you worthy of notice.

One Last Word About Advance Announcements

Many newspapers frown on advance press, although they engage in it continually. This is because they realize that advance press is closest to outright promotion of an event — that is, free advertising. This is, of course, just why the unabashed self-promoter wants it. Don't be discouraged, however, if you are told by a newspaper or other publication that they cannot consider an advance article. In this case, see whether there is an alternative available to you. At the very least see whether the publication has a notice column about forthcoming events. And ask whether your announcement can be printed with your photograph (or have the program chairman do so). The unabashed self-promoter is not interested in engaging in time-wasting disputes arguing about company policy. Instead he seeks to find the best available means of promoting himself and uses it to the uttermost.

After Event Publicity

In a two newspaper town advance publicity will garner you two articles — or at the very least two announcements. Now, you must pursue the same media sources for post-event publicity. There are two ways of doing so: getting a reporter to attend and cover the event directly, or doing it yourself.

Getting A Reporter To Cover Your Speech

Reporters are overworked, underpaid creatures, who have in selected circumstances enormous power to assist you by promoting your message. It is your job to make it easy for them to do so. Here are some ways:

- Whenever possible it is desirable to ask the reporter(s) from a local newspaper to attend your speech. They are likely to come if:

    - the organization is a significant one within the marketing area of the publication
    - your topic is both significant and is of local interest
    - you are perceived as a consequential speaker
    - there is no other competing event of greater significance.

- It is your responsibility to mention to the organization's program or publicity chairman that you want a reporter present during your speech. Not surprisingly this thought ordinarily does not occur spontaneously to such people. It needs to be induced. It is the organization's responsibility to request that a reporter be present. The best way of accomplishing this is to write the assignment editor (in smaller towns the general editor performs this function) advising him of your event and requesting coverage. When the program chairman calls to see if the advance release has been received and will be used that is the moment to enquire about whether a reporter — and a photographer — will be sent to the actual event.

- If the editor sounds doubtful, at least two courses are open to the program chairman. Both should be used.
    - The program chairman, having been briefed by you on the importance of your talk, should advance the most cogent reasons why a reporter should be present. If the program chairman feels inadequate to accomplishing this task, he should suggest to the editor that a call from you, the presenter, might be helpful. The editor will probably agree to take such a call, and you yourself will have the opportunity to make your case.
    - If the editor still sounds disinclined to send a reporter, find out why. If there's another event taking place at that time, suggest another alternative: your remarks can be taped and the cassette delivered to the newspaper. You can also indicate your availability to speak to a reporter the day after the speech (for daily coverage) or within a day or two (for a weekly). It is a good practice for the unabashed self-promoter to tape his presentations. They are useful for self-criticism and perfecting your style; they are also helpful as introductions to groups which are considering using you as a speaker, and they can also be used as suggested above when reporters are otherwise personally unable to cover your speech.

You can also indicate your availability to drop by the newspaper's office and give an exclusive interview to the paper, an interview which will result in a news feature. Remember: if the editor is unable to send a reporter to your speech, whether it be in the day or evening, you can visit the newspaper *before* your event and give an interview containing the flavor and substance of your later remarks. This is a particularly helpful technique when you are only going to be in town for just a few hours or a day. Make the best use of your time.

Note: Even when a newspaper (or any other media source for that matter) has declined either to interview you or to send a reporter to cover your speech, do not despair. Find out from the program or publicity chairman the names and telephone numbers of the media people he contacted. Upon arrival, give them a call, tell them who you are and that you are now in town with some available interview time. Do not remind them that you have already been turned down for an interview. If you are told that say, firmly but politely, "Why don't I tell you one or two reasons why I think you'll go for this story."

Then tell the media source:

- why you have come
- what you are speaking about
- why it's important
- whether there is a local angle
- the organization you are speaking to
- that you are available — right now!

There is nothing so constant in the media business as change. Media people pride themselves not on their planning skills (which are negligible) but on their ability to react quickly to changing developments — to the here and now. This can be to the advantage of the persistent unabashed self-promoter.

If you are courteous, helpful and direct, you may well get the interviews which you had previously been told were out of the question. I remember, to bring up only one instance of many, arriving one day in Hammond, Indiana and being told that three major media outlets (in this case, two radio stations and one cable television channel) had declined the opportunity to interview me. By no means discouraged, (though admittedly amazed at their short-sightedness), I sat down to call each in turn. In each case I booked the desired interview — after having been turned down. In one case, the on-air personality of the most popular mid-day talk show, previously abundantly disinterested, virtually hugged me through the wires. "Can you get over here right now?," he shouted into the receiver. "Our afternoon guest has just cancelled and do we ever *need* you. If you can be here in 15 minutes, you're on." I was there.

The unabashed self-promoter cannot afford to take "No!" for an answer. He regards the person who declines the chance to use him, to hear his message, to learn about his products and his services, as benighted, and, alas!, a little dim, but, fortunately, educable. That is why "No!" to the unabashed self-promoter is just an embryonic stage of "Yes!". Remember that.

Writing The Follow-Up Article Yourself

If all else fails and the editor remains disinclined to make a reporter available either before, during or after the event, the program chairman should ask whether the organization might submit a news story based on your speech. Almost no editor will decline this suggestion. From his perspective it gets you off the line without promising you anything. From your perspective, it gives you, the unabashed self-promoter, yet another opportunity to get your message in print. Remember: you should be able to find out at least a day before your speech that no reporter is being assigned. Thus you will have at least one day (for a daily) and three or four days (for a weekly) to prepare and submit your article so that it meets the appropriate deadline.

- It is now time for you to swing back into action. It is perfectly all right, and indeed eminently sensible, for you to write the article about your speech *before* it is given. You therefore do not have to rush to produce it; instead, you can write it in advance and merely edit after the event. In this way it should be perfectly possible to drop off your article the next morning at the newspaper office.

Producing The After-Event Article

Review the sample article on page 318. It is a good after-event piece written by a reporter who had covered one of my seminars. There is, however, nothing in this article that I could not have written *in advance* had the need arisen. Here's what's in it:

- Paragraph 1. The opening paragraph of the after-event article is comparable to the opening paragraph of the advance article. The same particulars of date, city, and organization sponsorship are included, this time obviously in the past tense. Because the example is in news feature format (a very congenial form for the unabashed self-promoter) the writer, from the very first sentence, introduces details which show the subject to be an interesting, compelling, provocative individual, the kind of individual meriting this treatment. In your own case, you will shape the words to the dictates of your image and the desired effect upon general readers and client prospects.
- Paragraph 2. This paragraph expands upon the first. It contains more specific details about the event (cost, number of participants, place, &c). This paragraph continues to give a flavor of the event. From the self-promoter's standpoint it is important that the presenter and the event both look compelling, as offering useful information which might have enriched the reader had he attended. The point of the entire article is that this result is still possible if — and only if —the reader purchases the products or services of the self-promoter.
- Paragraph 3. Because this is a first-person news feature, the writer here interjects herself in the article as an outside observer-evaluator. Unless you arrange with the program or publicity chairman for one of them to sign this piece ("the byline"), you cannot use the word "I." It is perfectly possible, however, to get the same message across in the third person.
- Paragraphs 4-11. In this article each of the subsequent paragraphs concentrates on one or more self-help tips along the lines of a Problem-Solving Process Article. Note, however, that the paragraphs, like the best of the Problem-Solving Process articles, focus on outcomes not on specific process details. In other words to make the system promoted in the accompanying article work, you need Jeffrey Lant. So it should be with you. The point of these paragraphs is to indicate to the reader that: you are the expert and that you have a problem-solving process and so satisfy the reader's need for security. It is not to present a detailed outline of how the process works and can be applied in the readers' lives. For that they need you, your products, your services.

One Or Two Hints About The After-Event Article

Like the advance article, if you find yourself writing the after-event article about your speech or presentation, be unabashed. The sample after-event article offers a nice array of compliments about me, my products and my services. Had I been forced to write this article, the same kinds of sugarplums would have appeared. After all in theory this article is being produced by someone else, not me; under the circumstances I must then act — and write — as that person would. You do the same.

Next, don't wait to produce this article. The media stream is swiftly-flowing. If you lag in the production of your article, you will lessen the likelihood of seeing it in print. Self-promotion is a demanding business; it keeps strange, lengthy hours and makes extensive demands upon those who indulge in it. The pay-off, however, in terms of money, respect and recognition is worth it. So don't dawdle when you have a deadline to meet.

Creating Your Own Events As A Source For Articles About You

So far the chapter has largely dealt with your use of already-existing organizations as self-promotional vehicles. This is a course I advocate, particularly for novice self-promoters, and one which I ordinarily follow myself. However, from time to time, you may wish to generate additional media attention through mounting your own events. You should consider doing so if and only if:

- the subject of your event is a fresh one of interest either to general media or to the trade media which your client prospects read. Novelty and timeliness are both important when you create an event.
- client prospects will be in attendance. Since you may lose money on your event (especially the first time you produce it), you need the reasonable expectation of recouping your investment elsewhere. The most likely place is from client prospects who attend.
- it offers the possibility of being a continuing event (usually annual). Since the first event is usually the least cost effective (in terms of your time and money), you need to know that you can in future reap greater benefits from a diminished investment.
- media that you generate will help promote a product that is generally available and can be bought both by those attending your event as well as those who do not.

The Boston Consultants Convention

A good illustration of how and when to create an event is offered by the Boston Consultants Convention. I created this event and co-sponsored it with a local firm (Creative Connections) in 1982. While both firms went into the event hoping and expecting to make money, both could still do well even if the convention itself actually lost (a limited amount of) cash. That is because the preconditions of success stated above applied:

- The subject of the event was a fresh one. There had never been in the Boston area a convention dedicated solely to the interests of consultants and entrepreneurs. This made the event, if properly handled, media-worthy.
- Client prospects were in attendance.
- It offered the possibility of being a continuing event; moreover, it could serve as a model when exporting something similar to other large cities nationally.
- Media generated could help to promote other items generally available. In this case, I was interested in promoting my book on consulting, **The Consultant's Kit,** which is available in all local book stores. Maya Staver, the president of Creative Connections, could promote her firm, memberships in her networking organization and other forthcoming events.

All too often people who decide to create events both for self-promotion and profit rely too heavily on the actual event itself to bring them their return. Events often take two or more years to become profitable and well-attended. In the meantime, the promoters need to use the media coverage they get to generate profits elsewhere. Thus, if a self-promoter does not have such products and services he should think twice about the advisability of investing his time and money in an event. If the preconditions mentioned above cannot be met in your case, consider abandoning the proposed event.

Nonprofit Technical Assistance Institute

One way of minimizing your risk in event creation is to affiliate with an existing organization and offer to co-sponsor with them. This is what I have been doing with Cambridge College for the last three years with my Nonprofit Technical Assistance Institute.

I had two major alternatives to consider in creating this event: producing it myself through my company or offering it through an existing educational organization. The first course entailed substantial up-front investment for brochures, printing, mailing, room rental, &c. Resultant revenues, however, would be mine alone. The second obviated the investment of any funds by my firm, thereby lowering the risk. This was, of course, a real benefit.

Did this course lower my return? Not necessarily, I reasoned, since the college could offer something I could not: graduate credit and a certificate which would probably augment the audience. However, even had this decision lowered my dollar return somewhat, it still left me with several additional ways of capitalizing on the event which made it worth doing.

- Self-Promotional Possibilities
- Distribution of general brochure to several thousand nonprofit organizations (JLA client prospects) promoting me, the instructor, as an expert provider of nonprofit technical assistance and author of a critical resource on fund raising. The college can give me that which I cannot give myself: third party validation.
- Advance media coverage. As an unabashed self-promoter in good standing I can, of course, generate my own press. But why not have a public relations department do it for you whenever possible?
- After event media coverage (as per the sample article on page 320). Self-sponsored events rarely get this kind of coverage.
- Income Possibilities
- Identification of client prospects and book sales from those unable to attend, but who are now aware, through both the college's brochure and advance media, of me, my products, and services.
- Identification of client prospects and book sales to those in attendance.
- Speaker fee
- Creation of a program which not ony can be repeated annually in Cambridge but can also be replicated elsewhere in the country.

The Mobile University

So lucrative is this Cambridge College program, both directly and because of the self-promotional opportunities that it affords, that I have since created The Mobile University which operates on the same principle with major colleges and universities around the country. Under this concept, we offer directors of continuing education of such institutions a range of programs which they then promote through their regular catalogues or though special mailings.

This concept has been a very fertile source of self-promotional possibilities as well as actual dollar revenues. Because of my experience with the Nonprofit Technical Assistance Institute and The Mobile University, I am an unabashed advocate of affiliating with suitable trade, technical, professional, and educational institutions and making use of them to promote you, your products and services while simultaneously structuring your involvement with them to produce immediate revenue. I have found this approach easier to arrange — and ultimately more lucrative — than ordinarily setting up and promoting my own events (see Chapter 17). However, whichever alternative you adopt, don't forget to squeeze every ounce of self-promotion out of the event you create; otherwise, you have not derived maximum benefit.

CHAPTER 9

ARRANGING AND HANDLING THE PRINT MEDIA INTERVIEW

Chapter 8 dealt with getting articles about yourself in print. The clear message of the chapter? Often it is necessary for the unabashed self-promoter to write them himself. Fortunately, that will not always be the case — and will, in fact, be the case less and less as you become more prominent. The chapter reverses the emphasis of the last. It deals with:

- how to set up a print media interview
- how to persuade an editor you are newsworthy
- how to brief an editor or reporter about you
- how to prepare yourself to be interviewed
- how to handle the print media interview
- how to follow-up an interview once completed

Finally, this chapter will tell you how to assemble the interview package, a technique favored by print media sources and concentrating on several individuals, not just one.

Setting Up The Print Media Interview

The unabashed self-promoter knows that scheduling interviews can be a long, exhausting process. Media people are not like other mortals. They have long ago shed the elementary courtesies and social graces of life. They are in fact rather like animals in their natural state. They have patterns of behavior, but these are not always obvious — or even discernible — to the outside observer. Like these animals, journalists must be stalked, this time by the unabashed self-promoter whose task is to work with chary persistence until he has bagged his quarry. One of his most important trophies is the print media journalist.

It is important to understand how these people see themselves. Often older than their electronic media counterparts, print journalists look with mild contempt and annoyance at their electronic colleagues. They regard them as slapdash, superficial and empty-headed mannequins. Well mixed wth this assessment is a heavy dose of envy, for reporters are generally less well paid than their electronic counterparts and do not have their visibility. They compensate for these very real irritations by a general attitude that they are the only "real" journalists, the only "true" media professionals. Those who seek them out need to make an obeisance to this notion on which their collective self-esteem insecurely rests. So be it. The unabashed self-promoter is always happy to use the misdirected hubris of others to his own advantage.

How then to schedule the print media interview?

Begin by identifying your targets. I shall suggest now — and reiterate later — that when approaching media sources you utilize a Media Activity Chart to mark your targets and chart your progress in approaching them. (See page 321). It should be clear that under ordinary circumstances you cannot simply pick up the telephone, reach the media source, and schedule an interview. That's why you need a plan of attack.

Deciding Whether The Media Source Is Right For You And Your Message

Every successful self-promoter not only knows his message backward and forward, he knows why it will interest the specific media source he is pitching it to. This he thinks through in advance of any contact with that source. Do not assume that inspiration will strike you when you have that source on the telephone. It is more likely that you'll be nervous and awkward rather than inspirational and eloquent. Advance preparation is absolutely crucial, not least because media people have long memories for the sins of bumblers. Consider then:

- Who you are trying to reach with your message (your product or service)
- Is this print media source in touch with these people?
- How do you know?
- Why should the print media source be interested in your message, product, or service?
- Is something you do or have timely right now?
- Is it of particular interest to readers of the source?
- How do you know?
- Are there others offering a similar message, product, or service?
- Is there a distinct local angle to what you're doing?

Particularly at the beginning of your self-promotional career write down the answers to these questions and keep them readily at hand as you talk to media sources about interviews.

Here is why these questions are important:

- Who are you trying to reach?

Each print source (or, in the case of large metropolitan dailies, each print section) has a preferred readership. The editors of these newspapers and sections of newspapers give much thought to who they are reaching and what will interest them. You must do the same. You must gain a specific sense of who they are trying to reach and whether enough of these people are interested in what you've got to warrant coverage.

- How do you know?

The best way of knowing is to be familiar with the publication. Even reading just one or two issues will give you some initial familiarity both with the audience which is being targeted and what kinds of material the editors think will interest the readers. The unabashed self-promoter, perforce fascinated with all aspects of media, must be especially interested in this information. The bottom line is that you must be able to show an editor that his readers are interested in what you've got. If you can do this, he will want the story as much as you do.

- Is it timely?

Never forget how capricious the media is. It is whimsical and superficial with a fleeting attention span. This has some truly alarming consequences for the nation, but it is a fact which self-promoters can constantly use to their benefit. The media is constantly starting and propelling new trends. It is your task to identify — and, if you're good, to predict — them and so interpret and package what you've got in terms of what will interest the media — now.

- Are there others offering your message, product, or service?

If you have a unique message, product or service of general utility and interest, I salute you. Exploit it quickly, however, because you will not have it for long. Americans are an imitative people and take the greatest pleasure in duplicating the successful ideas of others. Not, however, that you do not have to offer a unique service to get coverage. Quite the contrary. The more people who are doing are doing what you're doing, the better it is — up to a point, so long as there is no promoter as unabashed as you among them. The involvement of many people in an activity indicates its importance and thus the likelihood that it deserves and will get media coverage.

- Have they been featured recently in the source you're interested in?

It is not the number of competitors which diminishes the possibility of coverage; as you see, a large number of people in a business actually improves the possibility of coverage — for the unabashed self-promoters in the field. What diminishes the likelihood of coverage is whether the media source in question has recently done an article on the subject. If this is the case, consider how you can repackage your material and so interest another section of the same newspaper or another print source altogether. Unabashed self-promoters aim to regularly cover all the appropriate media outlets, but they do not expect — or even wish — to do so at once. The unabashed self-promoter aims for constant, continual exposure through the media not just periodic thunderclaps of attention.

- Is there a local angle?

Never forget that most media is local. Even if your subject has been covered in a recent story, you, the unabashed self-promoter, are entitled to regard it as incomplete if it has neglected the local angle — you!

Every self-promoter, even the most advanced, must consider these questions before contacting the media. My work as a consultant to consultants is a good illustration of how this preparatory process works.

- Who am I trying to reach?

Consulting is of potential career interest to professionals in any field. My audience therefore is extremely broad and heterogeneous. It consists of:

- highly-trained professionals with technical competence
- individual service providers
- retirees with a lifetime of professional skills and experience
- people (such as women with younger children) interested in rewarding part-time professional work

Articles about my work in consulting can be slanted to many different kinds of publications and in many different ways to different sections of large general interest publications like newspapers.

- Is it timely?

Articles about my work in consulting can be defined in different ways to take advantage of significant national trends. During the heyday of the women's movement, consulting could be promoted as yet another way for professionally-trained and careerist women to both work and attend to family responsibilities. During the recession, consulting was of interest and offered promotional possibilities because of its job creation potential. As we approach Alvin Toffler's "electronic cottage," consulting will be of interest because consultants are prime candidates for establishing self-sufficient home-based businesses. My task as the unabashed self-promoter is to discern that which is most immediately of interest to the media and to package my subject accordingly.

- Are there others offering the service?

I am not the only one in the nation consulting to consultants, independent contractors and service-oriented entrepreneurs. It would be nice if this were so, but it isn't. However, the fact that there are others can work to my advantage, because I can sell it to the media as an indication of the importance of the subject. "Look," I am saying, "I am in the forefront of an important national trend, a trend which is of the highest interest and importance to many people (who read your newspaper). You guys in the media should be reporting this trend and helping your readers make good use of it."

Once I have so used my competitors (bless their hearts!), my task is to posture myself so that I am perceived as offering the best version of the service, the most timely, thoughtful, provocative, useful, comprehensive, &c. I do this, of course, by exploiting the media to get this message across — both to my client prospects and to other media sources which must also be convinced to promote my message.

- Have my competitors been recently featured by the media source in which I'm interested?

Every time any journalist mentions anything about the subject of consulting, anytime, (and particularly when it is a local source featuring an out-of-town competitor without mentioning me), I send him a note saying, "Don't forget about me, the local angle."

The unabashed self-promoter is in for the long haul. We intend to be featured today, featured tomorrow, featured forever. In their unending, sisyphean search after something new and different, media people are constantly in need of knowledgeable sources and perpetually perplexed about where to find them. The purpose of my note to the erring, uninformed journalist is to:

- establish contact with an individual who can promote me
- indicate that I am an authority
- send articles and other information which confirms this status
- state my availability for future interviews and as a source

I have had exceptionally good responses from journalists I have contacted in this way, not least because I never fail to compliment them on their original story and their grasp of the subject matter (though without me in it, it is obviously sadly lacking!)

With the media graceful persistence pays off.

Both at home and while traveling I am an obsessive reader of local publications and a compulsive radio and television dial switcher. I do all this to find openings which I can exploit and to identify journalists who have already covered my subject — either directly or indirectly. I reckon that those individuals who have covered a subject once will later do so again. Then, of course, I have so prepared them that their initial error of omission can easily be rectified.

Having done this homework, knowing why your message is both timely and appropriate for the publication in question and having identified an appropriate journalist to present yourself to, you are now ready to make contact.

Contact By Letter

I prefer that the initial contact with any media source be by letter. Having so advised you, I want you to know that I break this rule with impunity whenever the need arises. Here are some occasions when it might:

- A story has appeared in the morning edition of your daily newspaper. It is sufficiently important (a fact you can gage by its length and placement, e.g. on or near the front page of its section) so that there may be a follow-up. You want to be included.
- You are on the road and have either read in the local newspaper (or have heard over the air) a story about your subject. It is certainly permissible to call the journalist who produced the story, introduce yourself, and ask whether any follow-up story is intended, and, if so, when. If there is, indicate that you may be able to be of assistance. You can yourself follow up this call by sending the kinds of material and information you would ordinarily send in advance of a contact. If there will be an immediate follow-up, you may have to hand-deliver the material; this is a good time to remind you that whenever you travel, you should carry at least two complete sets of media materials for occasions just like this.

Remember: Journalists are trained to respond quickly. If there is to be a follow-up story, the person you contact may very well wish to enrich it by including you as another source. If not, you have at least succeeded in bringing yourself to the journalist's attention for future contact and have thereby broadened your contact network.

- You know the reporter. In this case, you will surely want to call and see if there is to be a follow-up and to indicate that you stand ready, as usual, to be of quotable assistance.

Under other circumstances, an introductory letter is usually the best course.

This letter is called a query letter. Its purpose is to indicate to the journalist (or editor) you are contacting why a story about you would be timely and of interest to his readers. When writing this letter (see samples, page 332), refer to the section of this chapter which outlines the questions you need to master before approaching any media source. These constitute the significant points of your letter.

Your letter should conclude by stating that you will call the journalist to discuss the suggested article. Do not expect the journalist to call you. Every succesful self-promoter must learn that telephone calls to journalists are only rarely returned and only at the convenience of the journalist.

Along with this letter, send materials and information which confirm your status as an expert and which illuminate you as an interesting, compelling personality. Be most careful about what you send. Your leave behinds should be up-to-date and in good condition. It is, of course, entirely permissible to send out-of-town clippings, particularly from sister publications of the one where you wish to appear. Never, never send materials you want to have returned or clippings from rival publications. Thus, do not tell the **New York Daily News** that the **New York Post** has covered you. It will undercut your desirability. And may indeed eliminate you from consideration.

This rule holds true for electronic media, too. It is perfectly acceptable to give the evening radio talk show clippings from both the **New York Daily News** and the **New York Post,** but heaven forbid that you should mention in attempting to book this program that you have just appeared on its rival talk show. Media sources don't want total ownership of you; they want selective servitude — ownership in their slot.

The query letter should be typed on your stationery. It should be composed to reflect the image you are crafting. There are, of course, certain kinds of people who could get away with a hand-written communications (a prisoner complaining about prison conditions, for instance), but most of us cannot.

Always, always keep a copy of this letter. Before sending it, note on your calendar when you should follow it up. Ordinarily you should do so about 10 business days after mailing. Also, before sending it, don't forget to add this transaction to your Media Activity Chart. This letter, after all, is only an introductory stop on the road to scheduling your interview.

The Telephone Call

Just what the best time is to call a journalist can be perplexing. And yet it is most important in establishing his receptivity to you and your idea. Thus, you should not call journalists connected with morning newspapers in the late afternoon and evening. Then they are on deadline. Similarly, you should not call journalists connected with afternoon newspapers in the morning. They, too, are on deadline. And you should discover what day of the week dailies close and avoid it. Journalists can be charming, but they seldom are when on deadline.

I like to make my calls to journalists early in the day or the period when they will be most receptive 9:30 a.m. or so for day journalists; 4 or 5 p.m. for afternoon journalists, and the day after publication for weekly journalists.

In placing your call, sit down at your desk with:

- a copy of your letter
- copies of supplementary materials
- your background sheet listing reasons why the media source should be interested in you
- your calendar
- your Media Activity Chart

Now, place your call.

Ordinarily you will not succeed in catching your quarry on the first attempt. If you do not, *always* leave a message. This message should include:

- your name
- your telephone number
- the name of any contact person who may either have referred you or who called in advance of your call
- the best time to reach you.

Ask the person who takes the message the best time to reach your target.

Unless there is a special reason for doing so (e.g. the story is developing quickly), do not call again the same day. You do not wish to be perceived as overanxious, a pest. Hard though it is for the unabashed self-promoter to accept, journalists do legitimately have other things to do than promote us. (Know this, but do not dwell on it.)

In fact, I would advise you to wait two full days before calling back. Then if your call has still not been returned, place it again. Call at the time of day you were advised that the journalist could best be reached. If the reporter is still not available, leave a second message. This should be identical to the first except that it should indicate that this is your second call.

Again, wait two days and place yet another call.

If the journalist still not available and still does not return your call, write a follow-up note (See samples, page 324). This note should indicate that you have attempted to call on several occasions and that you will try again, but that you would appreciate the reporter's consideration in calling you back.

This note should evince no evidence of the pique and frustration you probably feel. It is intended to show you as the consummate professional who will persist until successful. Continue this process until you connect or until you have decided that the reporter cannot be motivated to behave decently, professionally and cover you — for now.

Before you finally abandon this damned soul, however, try one more tactic: if your messages have continually been taken by the same individual (you'll know by the sound of the voice), explain your problem. Ask this individual if, at the very least, he could ask the journalist or editor you are seeking whether he is interested in your story and would leave a message with the person you are talking to now. In this way, you may be able to move the matter along.

Making Contact

At last you will succeed in getting through. Very, very rarely has anyone eluded me for good and even in these infrequent instances I have written a note expressing my disappointment in being unble to make contact and suggesting, à la Douglas MacArthur, that, "I shall return." I feel that such a note also gives me the moral edge.

It is very important just how you handle this first contact. Remember: you stand to gain much if the article about you is published, not least a friend in the business who can provide you not only with an immediate story but also future promotion and contacts at other media sources. Thus, handle this well.

The initial conversation should go like this:

- Self-Promoter: "Hello, is Editor Smith there?"
- Editor: "Yes, speaking."
- SP: "Mr. Smith, this is Jeffrey Lant. I'm following up a letter I sent you on April 1 about my work with nonprofit organizations and our Capital Campaign Fund Raising service. Is this an appropriate time to explain why I think this would make a good article?"

Note the following in your introductory gambit:

- Do not call the person you are telephoning by his Christian name. This is a gross presumption best left to young secretaries and dead-end junior executives, neither of whom know any better. If, however, the individual calls you by yours, reciprocate.
- Be brief and to the point. Mention the date of your letter and the subject of your proposed article.
- Ask whether this is a good time to explain your idea. Don't just presume that it is.

Here are some likely responses from Editor Smith:

- "Your letter? What letter? I haven't received any letter from you."
- "I remember receiving something, but I haven't had the chance to look at it, and besides this really isn't a good time for me to talk."

"What Letter?"

The situation regarding the delivery of correspondence to media sources needs to be the subject of a federal investigation. I know from the depths of unhappy experience that a substantial portion of mail correctly addressed and sent to a specific media person will not arrive. Where it goes is another inscrutable perplexity, but it does not come back, either.

I have on occasion had to send as many as five or even six packets of materials to my media targets; two or three packets is, unfortunately very, very common. On one notable occasion my Los Angeles publicist decided to take direct action after a particularly irritating experience. She had (after having mailed packets which did not seem to get to their destination) hand-delivered material and, finally, had a guard sign for it and pledge to deliver it personally. She then called the next day and was amazed (to say no more) that the journalist still hadn't received it. Resolved to do or die, she then took yet another packet of material and marched it personally into the journalist's office. While she was there she saw, in plain sight, two of her previously "undelivered" packets.

Was he careless? Busy? Arrogant? Inconsiderate? What does it matter! The unabashed self-promoter becomes (virtually) inured to the "What letter?" response. Here is what to do about it:

If the journalist has not received your material, do *not* take this opportunity to explain what you are writing about. If you do, you are necessarily on the defensive. The telephone is best used as an instrument of assertion: you use it to quick-step into someone's life and territory and to hold a tactical advantage. If you use it to explain yourself, however, you lose this advantage.

Instead, tell the individual that you will send a duplicate of the materials you have already mailed and that you will call in three days (if he is local), five days (if he is not).

Do, however, take advantage of the contact to inquire about the best time to call. And if you are at all unsure about whether this individual is the right person to be contacting in the first place, mention the subject of your story and ask whether you've reached the appropriate person. If not, ask for a referral and start over.

"Not A Good Time To Talk."

Don't push this. Remember: you are establishing a relationship. Instead of staking everything on a wild attempt to snag your listener's attention, just ask when it would be convenient for you to call again.

Real Contact

Call back when you've been told to do so. Ask again whether your material has arrived. If not, send another batch. Ask whether the journalist has had the opportunity to read your letter and the supporting materials. If not, ask whether he has the time to do so in the next two or three days. Do not explain what you've sent. Wait until your putative reader has comprehended it. Next, discover whether yours is a subject and an approach which would be of interest. This is a critical moment in the development of the contact.

Self-Promoter: "Is the subject and approach of my article of interest to you?"

Possible responses:

- "No, we never do this kind of thing."
- "I'm not sure. Tell me a little more about what you've got in mind."
- "Yes, it is!"

"We Never Do This Kind of Thing."

This statement means one of two things: either you are a novice self-promoter who has failed to do your homework and have therefore made the profound and costly mistake of suggesting a topic and approach to someone who is really acutely disinterested, if not hostile, or you have been brushed by a bit of journalistic hyperbole which actually translates into, "No, not now."

I am not a novice self-promoter and if I heard these words (which I confess I occasionally do), I would interpret them in the latter sense. In the metaphysics of advanced unabashed self-promotion, I assume the editor has misspoken himself.

Having heard these words, your first reaction might be to mumble a hasty, "Oh, I'm sorry!," and thrust the telephone back into its cradle, wounded. Don't do it.

Say, instead, "I'm terribly sorry. It seemed to me that this might be something you'd be interested in." Tell him why:

- you recently read an article in his newspaper on a related subject
- the subject is most timely
- due to the particular readers of the publication, you think the subject is appropriate.

This is a moment for the unabashed self-promoter to shine as a salesman; if your article is going to go, this is the time to propel it ahead.

You must now be very voice conscious. Is your target loosening up? Is he showing any understanding of why you have proposed this topic? Is he more congenial? If you sense that he is, press home your advantage.

Ask whether he has done anything in the last six months on the topic or on something related. Ask whether he himself is interested in the subject or think it is either intrinsically important or significant to his readers.

If there is still no discernible interest, ask whether the person can give you a referral to someone else at the publication. If you have adequately researched your topic, you know it is important. If the journalist does not want the story, he wants you to believe it is of no earthly interest so that it does not show up elsewhere challenging his judgement. If this is a deadend, at least plant the seed of doubt in the journalist that you have something of interest and will persist until it is published. But be nice about this. It is not necessarily the journalist's fault that he is shortsighted, benighted. Or perhaps he is just stupid. In any event, you may have to deal with him again.

"I'm Not Sure."

This is an opening. Take it. You have done your homework. The results should be right in front of you pointing out why the subject is important and who's interested. Marketing points all. Now, go for it! Your underlying thrust must be assertive, but you should state your points simply, professionally in a friendly way calculated to make a well-disposed acquaintance of the journalist and demonstrate your expert status.

At the very least, an opening of this sort should result in a good referral and the prospect of future coverage from this source. Make the most of it.

"Yes, It Looks Interesting!"

A conversation begun in this fashion ought to result in a sale. What you're primarily looking for now is specific information about:

- how the interview will be handled
- who will do it
- when it will be done
- how the journalist wants to follow-up this conversation (e.g. Should you call back tomorrow or await his call? If the latter, will he be calling or someone else? &c.)

At the very least, do not end this conversation until you have established just when you and the reporter will talk to finalize details. Perhaps these can be accomplished right then and there. If so, do it. Then hang-up the telephone. Do not gush your gratitude. A simple "Thank you" will do for now. After all, you don't really know whether you have something to be grateful for or not. You haven't seen the actual article. Fortunately, if you handle the next steps properly you will be able to utter a more heartfelt bit of gratitude to the journalist and congratulate yourself on your self-promotional mastery.

Preparing For The Interview

You have already done much preparation for your forthcoming interview. The fact you are having it proves that. Now you simply need to focus so that you can derive maximum benefit from it and achieve your self-promotional objectives. First, review your objectives. This interview should:

- reinforce and enhance your crafted image
- heighten knowledge about your products and services and excite potential buyers
- create a friend in the media who will extend your media contact network and provide you with subsequent coverage
- insure an article which can become a persuasive, useful leave behind.

As you think about how to reach these objectives, consider what kind of article will be most helpful: one which elucidates your Problem-Solving Process; one which has you stand forward as the Sentinel guarding your clients' interests, or one which clearly shows that you are the White Knight daringly delivering solutions to troubled client prospects. It is your objective to consider what product you want to derive from the interview and to steer it so that this product results.

In the beginning of your self-promotional career, before you appear for an interview, particularly for a print interview which will result in a tangible, re-usable leave behind, review these three formats. Make sure that you know how they are constructed. Also make sure that you have gathered the necessary information which each format needs and have considered the techniques and solutions which your clients need. *Don't go into any interview without them.*

It is awkward for you to bring such outlines to an interview, but there is absolutely no reason why you can't bring in a list of the salient points you need to cover to turn the resulting article into a valuable self-promotional piece. After a while, of course, you will have both the structure and your points down pat; until that time comes, however, write down what you need.

More Mundane Matters

Your most important preparation involves securing the article content you want. But there are other matters which deserve attention and which can adversely affect the final outcome.

The Interview Room

Just where you will be interviewed may well affect the article. For the inexperienced self-promoter I recommend holding your first interviews, whenever possible, at the publication's office. True, you may be rather anxious there because of the unfamiliar surroundings, but this is not necessarily a bad thing. A decent reporter (and there are some) will then have to work to put you at your ease, thereby establishing a human connection. Don't be a basket case, though. What is wonderful about being interviewed at a publication is that your words (and your back up materials) are all the writer has to go on about you. Thus you can weave your magic, advance your information, and reinforce your desired image with the least likelihood of jarring discordancies. What I mean by this is: if the interview is held at your home or office, you may not yet have created a unified environment in which to showcase yourself.

Your furnishings and the general ambience may detract from your image and how you wish to be perceived. When I was still in graduate school, for instance, I had no problem conceiving of myself as a mandarin figure but the cramped, monk-like cell I occupied on Boston's Beacon Hill did not sustain my proclaimed status.

If you intend to have reporters interview you in your office or at your home, make sure that you have given careful attention to your surroundings, the furniture and to the general ambience. Remember: reporters will incorporate some mention of this ambience into the article, because it gives a flavor of you and helps make the article more interesting. Just be sure that these interesting details confirm the image you are promoting and do not work against it. In the same way, it goes without saying that dress is significant. Let me say again, however, that the general books on dressing for success are not of much use to most self-promoters. They have absolutely no bearing on me, for instance. The style of dress you adopt for your interview must take into account two significant factors: the practices and prejudices of your client prospects and your own carefully-considered image. Many people, made insular by books on dressing for Fortune 500 corporate success, find it difficult to fathom that I do not own a suit (much less a three-piece suit) or a watch or any of the other minutia presumed necessary for big league success. But for me they are not necessary. They are not consonant with my image and my clients feel more comfortable because I don't look like a freshly-minted Harvard MBA. Learn the same lesson.

Just Before The Interview

Always confirm your interview. Journalists feel no compunction about abandoning what they see as a small, less universal story if something more appealing comes along. This is the way they are and no amount of Sunday-School lectures on the utility of the Golden Rule will ever change them. So protect yourelf by calling in advance to confirm your appointment.

At that time request directions to the publication if you have not already done so. If possible, have a friend drop you off at the interview rather than drive yourself. The last thing that will benefit your image and composure is arriving breathless, frustrated and late because you couldn't find a convenient parking space. Don't chance it. Remember: if some mention of your breathlessness appears in the article, you will be exposing your ill-preparedness not just to the interviewer but to thousands of people.

Finally, make sure you bring with you a complete packet of supporting documents — other articles written about you, articles by you, &c. Do not bring as part of your packet materials by and about others. It never ceases to amaze me when I find as part of an individual self-promoter's kit articles by and about others. No doubt they think such information makes them look well-prepared, as having thoroughly researched an issue by being the knowledgeable expert. Not to me, it doesn't. Your packet should consist solely of materials by and about you. Bringing the materials of others in your kit makes you look less an expert and should, therefore, never be done.

The Actual Interview

Your interview begins the moment you and the journalist see each other, the instant you shake each other's hands, the minutes you spend arranging your chairs and throughout your introductory pleasantries. Whatever you say or do can be legitimately used in the resulting article. Remember this and act accordingly. Remember, too, you have several objectives to reach during this interview not the least of which is adding a contact to your self-promotion contact network.

Here's how the print media interview should be handled:

- Wherever you meet, introduce yourself. Even if a reporter is interviewing me at home, I greet him at the door and say, "You must be Mr. Smith. I'm Jeffrey Lant. Very glad to meet you." Note that I do not introduce myself with my doctoral title. This would be presumptuous and *mal vu*. I want this person to like me and to treat me like a peer and colleague. In the article, of course, I want this title used. To make sure it is, I might say during the interview (if I am not asked, as I usually am), "Just for your information I go by 'Dr. Jeffrey Lant, president of Jeffrey Lant Associates, Inc.' professionally. I hope that's how you'll refer to me in your article."
- After introducing yourself, sit as close to the journalist as you can. You want this person to feel

your energy and your enthusiasm so that he can transmit it to his readers. Sitting across the room often creates an unnecessary barrier.

- Don't begin the interview process. Allow the journalist the courtesy of opening the interview. His first questions will ordinarily be:

    - name, title (how would you like to be referred to in this article?)
    - age
    - educational background
    - other information which can be used to add a personal touch to the article

As you answer these questions you will begin to direct the interview. Let us say, for example, that you want the article to follow the White Knight format. The details you present about yourself should all reinforce your image as a problem-solver, as someone technically competent, cognizant of the problems of your client prospects, with the ability to solve them. You will in fact filter the details of your life (which are necessarily complex and diffuse) so that they show an inexorable progression to your present eminence. You want to be shown as a person of directedness, not someone (like most of us really are) who has sometimes just been lucky and at other times really didn't know what he was doing. Unabashed self-promoters necessarily apply a selective filter to the complicated details of their lives, because media — print or electronic — can handle only stark, simple impressions, not complex ones.

As you proceed in demonstrating how you moved surefootedly to your present position, introduce the products or services you have, products and services which are the result of your experience and which can help others achieve the kind of beneficial position you are now occupying.

Any point that you want included in the article, you must bring up. It is your responsibility to do so, and it is your own fault if you don't. The individual interviewing you is a wordslinger; his technical competence does not lie in knowing your subject matter, about which he in fact may know nothing, but in understanding how to string words together in a coherent, interesting fashion. It is your responsibility to give him what *you* want to see in print; it is his responsibility to put it there. In actual fact, however, if you have aptly handled the interview *what* you have said will inform the final result.

It should go without saying, but probably doesn't, that there is nothing, nothing to be gained by arguing with a reporter. Many of the journalists who have interviewed me have not been the kinds of people I would choose to spend my leisure hours with. Many have been arrogant, some stupid, others ill-prepared. I allow none of this to bother me — when I am with them. They are the tools of my self-promotional trade, and I must make the best use of them I can. You do the same.

This is not to say that you must agree with everything a reporter says to you or with the direction of his questions. Feel perfectly free to correct any apparent misapprehension you feel he has, but do so in a professional manner, without raising your voice, without rancor, without condescension. Talk to him as to a good and valued friend who was unfortunately erroneous on a given point.

Print media interviews generally last between a half hour and an hour. This is quite enough time for you to get your message across if you handle the interview in a directed fashion.

If after 35-40 minutes you still feel you have not made your points, be firm — but gentle — about bringing them up. You must regard this as *your* interview. A good reporter will have the sense and courtesy to ask you, at the end of his questions, whether you would like to add anything. Take this opportunity to do so, but do not necessarily prolong the meeting. Five or, at the most, ten minutes are usually quite enough for you either to reinforce key points or to introduce others.

At the conclusion of the interview, ask the journalist whether it would be helpful for him to have another set of your leave behinds or any other material. If he asks for something you do not have with you, make a note to mail it. I *always* carry a notebook with me to every media interview. During the interview I'll occasionally jot down a note and in it I also log things I'm to do afterwards.

The Notebook

This notebook is also a good place to log information about the person interviewing you.

During the course of an interview, particularly in a journalist's office, I learn one or two particularly significant points about him, a predilection for skiing, for example, or an interest in bas relief. Such an interest may actually constitute his abiding passion. Note it. Later you may have a chance to reinforce your connection by sending information on this subject, passing along a tip about it, or introducing a friend who shares this interest. Don't suppose that you can keep all this information in your head. Write it down and act on it. The unabashed self-promoter is an unreconstructed activist; he knows the world will come to his door only after he has beaten a path to it for them and created an excitement about what they will find there. Your notebook allows you to log significant personal details about the people who can help create this excitement.

Interview Conclusion

At the conclusion of your interview, ask when the article will be appearing. You want to keep on the alert for it. If you have been interviewed by an out-of-town source, ask whether the journalist would kindly mail a tear-sheet of the article to you. I have always found them happy to oblige. Indicate that you are available when the journalist is actually writing the article if he needs a thought refined or a quotation clarified. Advise the journalist as to how you can be reached, particularly if you expect to be away from your office.

If you have been interviewed at the publication's office, the reporter will often ask you to stand by to have your picture taken after he's finished. This usually takes no more than 10-15 minutes, and the bulk of this time is generally spent locating the photographer.

Last Words About The Actual Interview

I have written nothing about handling a hostile print media interviewer. There is a reason for this. In all my years of being interviewed by print sources, great and small, I have never encountered someone overtly hostile. Bored, apathetic, disinterested, difficult, grumpy, yes, but not hostile in the sense of an individual actively trying to disconcert me, make me look bad, contradict me or otherwise inflict harm on me through the interview. It is my belief that if you follow the methods and suggestions of his chapter, you, too, will find print media journalists if not always a delight to work with at least substantially professional in their approach to their jobs.

And why not? You have made it easy for them by thinking through your objectives, gathering your information and behaving appropriately, assertively during your interview. If, however, you do meet a hostile interviewer, remain cool. It is hard to argue with someone who does not argue back. Only under the most extreme provocation would I ever end an interview because of a journalist's hostile manner, although I would always reserve the option of doing so. Instead I would continue to deliver my message, persistently, professionally. It is not part of my image to be rattled.

Interview Follow-Up

Ordinarily I do not send a thank-you note to an interviewer until the article has appeared. However, use your discretion. I would follow-up an interview if and only if I had promised to send certain supplementary materials and if I wished to reinforce a critical point made during the interview which I did not believe the journalist had absorbed or because I had neglected to mention something pivotal. My preferred method of doing so is by letter. I try not to call the interviewer after our time together not just because I am fearful of appearing pest-like but because such a call could undercut my image as the in-control professional. I cannot think of an instance over the last year or two where I have done so, although on numerous occasions reporters have placed a subsequent call to me. On these occasions I am brief and to the point. I close these conversations with an expressed and hearty thank you, glad that the reporter is being so conscientious about the result and certain it bodes well for me.

It usually does.

A Package Of Self-Promoters

This chapter has dealt with one-on-one interviews, just you and the journalist. Every print source publishes this kind of interview.

Print sources also print articles (like the sample on page 349) in which many experts are featured. In fact, such an article is often the best way for a novice self-promoter to break into print. The wonderful thing about this kind of article is that you can:

- suggest it
- sell it to the media source
- pack it with your friends and colleagues
- be in it yourself

To begin the process, go back to the moment when you first spoke with your prospective interviewer or his editor. If he then evinced some interest in your topic (that is, he acknowledged that it was both important in itself and significant to his readers), but was not willing to interview just you about it, propose the Promoter's Package. The Package is an article which will deal with the topic and quote several sources — not just you.

In suggesting this approach to the topic, advise the editor that you are willing and able to suggest others who could provide both perspective on the subject and helpful information. In short, you are willing to become the copy consultant.

Most likely an editor or reporter will not agree to this suggestion right away. They will want to ponder it, thinking about their own resources for rounding off the article. I have never yet been in a Promoter's Package where I have supplied *all* the other sources, even though I have usually supplied most of them. Reporters usually like to seek their sources from various quarters, even when they are happy to rely on one person for the bulk of their leads.

Pursue your suggestion pertinaciously, particularly with large metropolitan dailies which have the possibility of syndicating material. Promotional Packages are likely to be so used since they invoke many experts often drawn from many cities or states. These articles are often most appropriate for broader distribution. Thus while the initial article may not focus on you exclusively, a syndicated version in which you appear, but with others, may actually be much more in your interest.

Last Words

When your interview at last appears in print, be grateful. Just for a moment, give way to radiant self-congratulation. You are now an individual of consequence. Whether this consequence lasts merely until the next edition rolls off the press obliterating the firefly celebrity, or whether it lasts the duration of your lifetime and casts a rosy glow thereafter depends entirely on you and your further efforts. As you ponder this weighty thought, sit down and send a thank-you note to the writer — and to the editor, who may have initially approved the idea. You'll need them both again.

Be generous in this note even though you may not have agreed with every word in the article about you. At 6' 170 lbs, I am hardly the "slight, bespectacled" creature I was described as being in one interview, nor do I have manicured nails as one major magazine said. What of it?

It would take a lot of such errors before I seriously took issue with the writer and even then I would think twice — or more — before I registered any complaint. I suggest you follow my lead here and adopt a lenient approach to slipshod, overly-imaginative journalists unless some truly vital interest is involved. Remember: the only bad press is no press.

And One Final Caution

The objective of this chapter is to prepare you for all eventualities. It is a noble goal but one, I suspect, doomed to failure. The more I am out on the self-promotional circuit, the more the unexpected becomes my norm. My final word then is be prepared to improvise in pursuit of your objectives.

I leave you with this story. I was one day being interviewed by a major New York City daily. A particularly inept cabbie dropped me off at the wrong place. It was, as it turned out, only three blocks away, but it was also raining cats and dogs. I arrived at the newspaper soaked to the skin, my hitherto dapper blazer sodden, my khaki pants looking like props from the African Queen. This was not the image of the engaging entrepreneur I wished to project to the Big Apple.

Rather than despair, I resorted to the men's room and the blown air hand dryer — under which I crouched for several cycles, including two interrupted by incredulous, grinning employees. But I had the last laugh. When I walked into the press room, dry as a bone, I looked — and smelled — as if I had ironed my clothes in the hallway.

I gave a smashing interview.

It was syndicated.

CHAPTER 10

PIGGYBACKING AND MULTIPLE USE

The unabashed self-promoter is an inventive creature — of necessity. His time is limited and his expectations astronomical. He must therefore make the best use of every opportunity and continuing good use of that which his ingenuity has helped create. That's why the unabashed self-promoter must become adept at piggybacking and multiple use.

Piggybacking

All of us have seen the successful manifestations of piggybacking. It is impossible to pick up a daily newspaper without seeing them. These are stories which are either related but subsidiary to major news stories or which are printed because they connect us or tell us something interesting about a significant person, place, event, date, &c which looms larger in the public consciousness. Here are some possibilities:

- connected to a major news story
- connected to a significant person
- connected to a significant place
- connected to an important event
- connected to a major date

Each day around the country hundreds of piggyback features are printed, each helping to promote some individual, his product or service. Unfortunately most of those featured in this way rest content with one story about themselves. It goes without saying that these are the lesser lights of self-promotion. The unabashed self-promoter aims for regularity of coverage and sees piggybacking as yet another way of achieving his objective.

I first became aware of the possibilities of piggybacking when I was 13. I had begun an ambitious campaign button collection, and in connection with the presidential election of 1960 brought it — and me — to the attention of the local press. The result was a glowing article which piggybacked on the more significant national news story of the hour, the national election. The headline was hoaky, "Jeffrey, verily has all his buttons!," the accompanying photograph showing me weighed down with my trophies, the same. But the result was gratifying: various people contacted me to offer their collections, free, just to insure a good home for them. Having once discovered a winning formula, I was keen to repeat it. As a result my collection grew large and began to include some quite valuable pieces, all donated by admirers gleaned through the media. Such enrichment, of course, is one key reason for self-promotion, and it was a valuable lesson to learn at the onset of adolescence.

I have used piggybacking techniques ever since and will share with you one crucial example of how they have worked for me.

Insubstantial Pageant

British royal pageants occur at regular intervals and unfailingly delight not only the English but also the American public which has a touching enthusiasm for the gewgaws of monarchy. As a self-promoter I knew that if I could somehow attach myself to the monarchy, I could reap my entire life some bit of the glorious media harvest of the Windsors. My book **Insubstantial Pageant: Ceremony And Confusion At Queen Victoria's Court** was my way of doing so.

This book is an irreverent look at the abundant *faux pas*, errors and indiscretions which punctuated the gloomy court ceremonies of Queen Victoria's reign, the coronation, thanksgivings, funerals and jubilees. Each of these events is repeated by the current court. Now the fact of the matter is that while there is intense media interest in these events, there is very little substantial news about them. In part this is because of royal policy: no releases are put out about how they are organized, just what has been decided. Thus the situation is: great interest, limited news. This is the perfect situation for the unabashed self-promoter.

My book, in effect, constitutes a series of sidebars, that is stories related to the major event, but of lesser importance. Fortunately sidebars fill a very real media need.

I tested the utility of my theory in 1977 at the time of the Silver Jubilee of Queen Elizabeth II. Like most royal events, this one was accorded more media attention than the media had substantial material for. Ah, tailor-made for me, the young self-promoter.

I discerned two marketable angles:

- historical sidebars dealing with past jubilees
- a feature concentrating on me, "The Massachusetts Yankee at Queen Victoria's Court." (With apologies to M. Twain.)

I was, I confess, less adept in 1977 at the art of unabashed self-promotion and uncertain how it would go with the veddy reserved and promotionally retarded English. Rather than follow the considered, technically perfect, tested methods of this book, I did the best I could.

Unlike the United States, in England all the major newspapers both British and foreign, maintain their offices in and around Fleet Street. It is a long street burning with frenzied activity. I simply started at the top of the street seeking outlets with packets of my proposed articles, a page of biographical background, and a thin reserve of audacity.

The results were not initially encouraging. The **Daily Telegraph** snubbed me; I was thrown out of the **Guardian** (so much for liberalism!) and was given a polite but firm expression of disinterest by **The New York Times**. But two very good things happened at the foot of Fleet Street.

As I was explaining my mission to a very bored receptionist at The Associated Press, a young American popped his head around the corner, fortuitously. The receptionist gave a lackluster rendition of what I was doing, but fate was at hand. "Anyone named Jeffrey from Massachusetts can't be all bad," he smiled. It turned out he was named Jeffrey and was from Massachusetts, too. The result was the "Massachusetts Yankee" story syndicated around the world on the AP international wire.

Just a few blocks away sits the headquarters of **The Times** of London, signifying by its very detachment from Fleet Street that it is somehow different, important. There yet another bored receptionist directed me to the Features Editor who said, as a good journalist should, "Why don't you give me a thousand word column, and we'll see what it looks like."

It was on her desk the next day.

On Jubilee Day, a stunning June day, I sat in the back of my highly-polished taxi speeding down The Strand, a copy of **The Times** open on my knee, nonchalantly peering down (for the hundredth time) at the banner headline of my article. I confess to being aglow with excitement. I received dozens of compliments on the article which, of course, was superbly timed.

During the course of that long, brilliant jubilee summer **The Times** commissioned five more pieces from me and **The Irish Times** yet another. The result was my first book contract from that very eminent publishing house, Hamish Hamilton, Ltd. (I would like to point out that **The Daily Telegraph,** which had shunned the series, waxed eloquent over the book itself. How sweet it is . . .)

The benefit of **Insubstantial Pageant** did not end there, however. Not by a long shot. Each time the English monarchy mounts a pageant, I have a variety of self-promotional possibilities; I did several commentaries, for example, in connection with the wedding of the Prince and Princess of Wales, both in print and via the electronic media. Each time some ceremony related to my original work recurs I don again my media mantle as America's foremost authority on the English monarchy — and capitalize accordingly.

Planning To Piggyback

Most piggyback features can be planned. Either they involve your using an annual event like St. Patrick's Day or Thanksgiving or an occasion or event the date of which is known far in advance, like the presidential election or Harvard's 350th anniversary. Thus there is no excuse for not taking advantage of them by offering the media a story about something which will enhance the event — you.

Here's what you should do to exploit a piggyback opportunity known in advance:

- Keep a list of all those piggybacking opportunities which are available to you. One book will be of particular value.

  Chases' Calendar Of Annual Events
  Apple Tree Press
  Box 1012
  Flint, Michigan 48501

  This book lists both the official and unofficial designations of all the days of the year. We all know about the major ones which themselves offer prime piggybacking opportunities, but we can also take advantage of ones not yet household words.

  Identify appropriate media sources for your piggybacking. The more universal the event, institution, individual, date, &c., you are using, the more appropriate general interest publications are. My work on the British monarchy, for instance, is clearly of the widest possible interest and ought to go to: national radio and television, major newspapers and the wire services, AP and UPI.

- Send a letter to the assignment editor at the publication (see sample, page 322) explaining:

  - what important event, anniversary, commemoration, &c is forthcoming
  - what you've got that connects to it
  - enough about yourself to be perceived as interesting copy

Follow-up this letter in the ways suggested in the preceeding chapter.

Do not just limit yourself to one media source, especially if the thing you're connecting yourself to happens rarely; (there won't be another English royal jubilee until 2002, for instance.) Beware, however, of offering the same material to competing media. It is perfectly appropriate to offer your story to the **San Diego Tribune** and the **Los Angeles Times,** but don't give the identical information to the **Los Angeles Times** and **The Los Angeles Herald-Examiner.** Work up distinct angles. And never, never offer your material just to newspapers if there are also television and radio possibilities.

For the unabashed self-promoter the aim is never just one story, one television interview, one radio story, but many, many.

If Nobody Nibbles

If your event is getting uncomfortably close and no one has yet made a definite commitment to cover you, consider putting out a media release and either mailing or hand-delivering it to your major targets. A story about the gourmet Halloween delicacies you have up for sale will be worthless the day after the event, so don't hesitate to give urgency to your proposal by putting it in a media release.

Remember: most piggybacking opportunities can be planned in advance. The key is to know your target dates and to arrange your material so that it can be published as a neat, interesting addendum to a major story, something which will add human interest to an event which is going to get coverage anyway. Think of it this way: for the unabashed self-promoter holidays, anniversaries, institutions, great personages, significant events, and all the other piggybacking opportunities have been put here for us — and we should gratefully use them.

Each day hundreds of opportunities like these exist. Most are not properly utilized. I think, for instance, of the aeronautical engineer who was interested in the commercial possibilities of space travel and who told me, at the time of the first Columbia space mission carrying commercial cargo, how my theories were all very well and good but did not apply to him. How should he promote himself, he wished to know? I stood incredulous. "Sir," I said firmly, "you say you are an expert in the commercial possibilities of space travel. What is your opening? Your opening is the Columbia space mission now circling the earth. You should be giving an interview to the **Los Angeles Times** today or sending out a media release rather than moaning to me why my theories don't apply to you. For shame!"

Take notice the rest of you before you tell me you have no self-promotional vehicle.

Spontaneous Piggybacking

The first thing I do every day is sit down with the **Boston Globe** and the **New York Times** and a pair of scissors. Like Jimmy Carter (one of his more admirable traits) I read during most meals. I look for:

- information of use to my clients
- data which can be incorporated into one of my three basic article formats
- stories about personnel and format changes in the media
- media people who have done something notable
- stories which I can use through piggybacking.

I have included one such story in the samples section (see page 348). Here's how I created it.

Every day the media creates openings for the unabashed self-promoter to exploit, openings, however, which must be followed up with the utmost speed or they become useless. Unlike the items of the previous section of this chapter, these openings are not predictable. When I saw the article in the **Boston Globe** reporting that former Massachusetts Governor Edward King had taken a job as a consultant I had no advance information this would happen. Fortunately, however, the prepared unabashed self-promoter needs no such information. A true professonal, he is ready to swing into action as necessary.

How To Take Advantage Of An Opening

The key to utilizing an unexpected opening, particularly in a daily newspaper where editions follow each other rapidly, is speed. Under these circumstances you do not have the luxury of planning, of researching, of deliberation. You must already know your subject well enough, your media prospects well enough, and the techniques of media release production well enough so that your release can be sent off quickly. There are also, of course, a couple of tricks to the trade.

Look closely at the original article from the **Boston Globe** (See page 348). Now look at my media release. As you will see, I have mined the original article for the facts I needed in producing my release. Everything else in the release I have in my head.

Piggybacking articles succeed in being printed because:

- the original article is about a newsworthy subject
- you have added a new dimension to the subject
- what you have to say about the subject is interesting
- you have placed your interesting material in the hands of the media quickly enough so that they can update their original story with what you have given them.
- the material you have given them is in a form which can be immediately used.

The sample shows how this works.

- The job taken by the last governor of the state is front page news.
- My angle of welcoming him to the profession is offbeat. The governor is better known than I am.
- The substance and, importantly, the tone of the release are engaging.
- The release was distributed properly, quickly.
- It is a pithy news item which could be immediately used.

Getting The Release Out Promptly

Self-promoters who live or work near their state capitals or in large cities where several media may be housed together in a city hall, &c have an unquestionable advantage in this game. My office, for instance, is just 15 minutes by subway from the state capital where all the major media of the state maintain boxes where the governor, members of the legislature, lobbyists, &c can easily distribute their releases — and which are, of course, equally accessible to other unabashed self-promoters, too.

Thus, if I wish to piggyback on a story in the **Boston Globe** (a morning newspaper), I can produce the copy, duplicate and distribute it — all before noon — to the two wire services and to all major print and electronic media. This kind of quick turn-around is the essence of the game and is, of course, the reason why legislators and others with easy access to media are so often quoted. It is not necessarily the case (as every citizen knows) that they have something particularly notable to say. So what? They have succeeded in their objective: getting attention.

If you live or work far from a media nest, it would be wiser to concentrate on piggybacking opportunities which can be planned and where you can use the post and telephone follow-up. Still, don't abandon the notion of piggybacking when you are not near the media sources. Consider using the following:

- If you can present yourself as an authority on a matter of ongoing media interest, write (or if time is short, call) a reporter covering the issue and announce that you have an angle on the topic which would enrich his coverage. Be sure to follow-up such a call immediately with the material the reporter needs.
- Write a Letter to the Editor. Most people who use this format don't consider it self-promotional piggybacking but that's exactly what it is. Letters to the Editor are particularly useful to the unabashed self-promoter who wants to stand forward as the Sentinel guarding the interests of someone important to him.

I remember, for instance, a particular occasion when the **Boston Globe** ran a particularly capricious and gratuitous attack on a woman who has a local radio show. The editorial, complete with a string of unnecessarily offensive adjectives, struck me as pointless and malicious. And I said so in a Letter to the Editor which went out, like all my piggybacking responses, on the day of the attack.

Under the media self-initiated Doctrine of Equity, this letter stood an excellent chance of being printed, and printed it was.

Now, I did not know when I opened the newspaper that I would be, within an hour or two, responding to a self-promotional opening, but there it was. And there was good reason for taking it.

The woman in question had been unnecessarily victimized, but she had not done anything wrong. That is, she would live to broadcast tomorrow. Since there was no burning emotional issue involved, I might be the only one to rush to her rescue ("The White Knight"), and I could anticipate some later rewards, perhaps a spot on her show.

As it happened (note the cool nonchalance of this phrase), I was negotiating just then with that same radio station, a very important one in the Boston market, to do a show, but had been getting stuck in an unending game of telephone tag and disinterest. The printed letter changed all that, promptly.

On my next call, the man I was seeking said, "I saw your letter in the **Globe**. In fact, everyone here saw it. And it's been posted on the bulletin board in the news room. Just between you and me, you're the only one who defended her. I'd like to have you on my show."

As a result of that introduction, and a good show, of course, I went on to do not just one broadcast but more than a dozen on that station.

Yes, I believe in piggybacking through Letters to the Editor, but I choose my subjects well and think through just what I might get. In this case there were several good possibilities:

- a new friend in the media
- a possible broadcast
- at the very least, publication of a letter which would show me, before 1,200,000 possible readers, as someone both humane and solicitous, quick to jump to the defense of someone pointlessly attacked. My image can always stand such reinforcement.

Multiple Use

Because the unabashed self-promoter is a very busy individual, he needs always to be aware of methods showing him how to use and reuse material already composed and printed. To the unabashed self-promoter a word once printed is nice, but it is not sufficient. *Each* word that you write should appear again and again in a variety of printed media sources around the nation, reverberating your message more and more strongly but with less and less of your time and resources committed. The Principles of Multiple Use provide the critical guidelines you need to achieve this objective.

Principle I: Particularization By Place

Remember, remember that most media is local. Knowing this, the unabashed self-promoter can take advantage of it for his purposes. Here's how:

As previously discussed, the best place to start your self-promotional career is in your local newspaper (or in the publication of an organization with which you are connected). This article should be in one of the three recommended formats (Problem-Solving Process, Sentinel, or White Knight). It should be sprinkled with one or two local examples of what you are writing about. These examples particularize the piece.

As soon as you have written the piece and mailed it off, begin to collect facts which support your case from neighboring cities and towns. You can gather this information from direct experience or from publications.

Note: Some degree of flexibility in particularizing your article is permissible and helpful to keep in mind. Refer back to the sample article on page 314. This piece was published in the **Cambridge Cronicle** for a Cambridge audience, yet there are no examples from Cambridge in the piece. The theory is that readers in a suburb of the nearest metropolitan area are necessarily interested in and affected by what takes place within the larger community. By the same token the editors of a larger metropolitan newspaper (like the Boston **Herald American**) are amenable to using facts about a suburban area if their paper circulates in that area. Thus facts about Cambridge can be utilized both in a Cambridge article and in a metropolitan Boston newspaper but ordinarily not in another suburban newspaper. There is one exception, however.

If the suburban newspaper is part of a chain circulating in several communities the head office will often publish a piece with facts from one community in all its newspapers, particularly if the point of the article is generally applicable. Even in this circumstance, however, the editor prefers the article to be particularized.

The sample article is a good illustration of how this process works:

- It was originally written for the **Cambridge** (Massachusetts) **Chronicle**, my home-town newspaper. This market, however, will never be large enough to sustain my business — or my pretensions. Right from the first, I knew that too much time was being invested in the piece to warrant single publication. I had my eye on a major Boston daily and thus used Boston examples to support my argument.
- At about the same time the article was mailed to the **Chronicle**, I rearranged it sufficiently to mail to the Boston **Herald American**, the city's second largest newspaper. It is never a good idea to send the duplicate article to print sources where the same readers might see both. It is, however, perfectly possible and indeed desirable to utilize the same information and examples. The whole point of this exercise is to get maximum publicity at a minimum investment of time and other resources. This article was published about a month after the first.
- As it happens, the **Cambridge Chronicle** is part of a chain; it also publishes weekly editions in neighboring Watertown and Somerville. About the same time my original piece ran in Cambridge, it also ran in these towns, without changes.

The next logical step is to particularize your piece so that it can be published in each of the other newspapers in and around Boston. Note: like many large cities Boston has newspapers which are designed entirely for sections of the city. For purposes of this discussion, they can be regarded as comparable to suburban newspapers. Thus I would be seeking a fact about an Arlington nonprofit organization for the Arlington newspaper, something about a Winchester nonprofit for that town's newspaper, &c.

Considering that there are over 100 newspapers in and around Boston, I could easily have gotten two stories *per week* for a year without repeating any newspaper. Each story would use the same matrix and promote the problems of my client prospects and my availability to solve them. And, of course, this quota would not even take into consideration articles about me, piggybacking opportunities, &c, &c, to say nothing of electronic media.

The next stage of the particularization principle is to expand your coverage area (and hence your marketing area) to new places. Again, utilize your basic format and add a dollop of local information that will particularize the piece. I have included, (see page 316), to carry on with my example, a piece of mine appearing in the **Baltimore Sun**, the state's largest newspaper, in November, 1981, several months after my **Herald American** column appeared. You will notice that I have not particularized this piece; please, however, do as I say not as I do. If you do not particularize the piece you run the risk of an editor saying it has no local applicability and hence cannot be run. This is where my status as an author and frequent newspaper contributor are of the utmost assistance to me. I rely on my reputation and on the coherence of my article to persuade editors they should run an article of mine. To be on the safe side, at least at the beginning, you should particularize.

Principle II: Exploiting Newsletters

In the case of Principle I, you must type each article anew and add the particularizing information which will make the piece relevant to the audience perusing it. In this case, you simply need to distribute a copy of the actual article to newsletters and similar information publications with the requirement that they reprint it along with follow-up information about you and your product or service.

I long ago learned that the publishers of newsletters constitute a superb source for the unabashed self-promoter. Unlike editors of newspapers and magazines, they do not ordinarily have large staffs trained to gather material. Yet they must produce an information-rich product at regular intervals. We unabashed self-promoters have an uncalculable advantage with these people. Here's how to exploit it:

- As soon as your article goes to a newspaper, begin to research the names of newsletters and other publications outside your metropolitan area which might be interested in the topic and the information you have available. Remember: there are more than 75,000 newsletters in the country. Type the envelopes or at least the address labels so that you can mail copies of your published article speedily.
- Produce your leave behinds as quickly as possible. On the day of publication, give the article to your printer so that he can print up leave behinds. There are many examples of leave behinds throughout this book: articles printed on your stationary with the name of the publication, date of the article, your company name, address, and telephone number. Each item must be included.
- Draft a cover letter to the newsletter editor. This letter need not be personal. I have found that a "Dear Colleague" salutation is perfectly adequate. This letter should:
- indicate that the enclosed article is available for them to reprint
- that you expect no fee for allowing them to do so, but would appreciate renumeration if this is the newsletter's standard practice
- that in return for foregoing compensation you would like to be identified so as best to promote a product or service. Here are a couple of such identifications about me:

"Dr. Jeffrey Lant is president of management firm Jeffrey Lant Associates, Inc. providing technical assistance to nonprofit organizations. You can reach him at 50 Follen St., suite 507, Cambridge, MA or by calling (617) 547-6372."

"Dr. Jeffrey Lant is president of Jeffrey Lant Associates, Inc. JLA specializes in managing capital fund raising campaigns for nonprofit organizations based on the methods of his book **Development Today: A Guide For Nonprofit Organizations** ($24.95) He can be reached at . . ."

Note: Unlike daily newspapers and most magazines, newsletters allow and encourage the publication of complete follow-up information about people, products and services they have featured.

- that you give the publication freedom to edit your article in any way so long as the sense is not altered and so long as you are identified as specified
- that if the publication does not reprint articles in this fashion, you wish the editor to know either you are available for an exclusive interview or that you would be happy to submit a piece more in keeping with the newsletter's format. In this case, ask them to tell you what they want.
- If you have a product available, also ask the publisher whether he would be interested in a Cooperative Marketing Agreement with you. Under such an agreement your product gets promoted by the newsletter in return for a percentage of the sale. Such an arrangement insures you of continuing coverage in the newsletter. Publishers who enter into Cooperative Marketing Agreements are usually agreeable to regular articles about you. Note: Such agreements usually do not begin with your first mention in the newsletter. Another way of handling a Cooperative Marketing Agreement is to recontact a newsletter *after* they have run an article about you and inform them about the good response you've had. Then suggest a Cooperative Marketing Agreement. (See samples, page 330)
- Finally, make sure you request a copy of your article when it's published.

(See samples, page 328, for first letter to a newsletter.)

Remember: the article you send to a newsletter may be either a Problem-Solving Process article, a Sentinel, or a White Knight article. Any one will do.

Do not expect to get paid for submitting this article, although feel perfectly free to ask for standard renumeration if they have it.

Each time one of my articles appears, I send out between 10 and 100 copies to newsletters. Some publish the entire piece; some adapt it to their format (often the article becomes an "interview with Jeffrey Lant"); some request me to adapt it to the format; some like to do something entirely new. All these possibilities are perfectly alright with me. The important thing is that my products and services are being promoted —without cost to me.

Principle III: Particularizing By Industry

Some of you, like me, have developed specialties which transcend any particular trade, industry or profession. I have several such specialties. My problem solving methods of raising money for nonprofit organizations are equally applicable to small day care centers, inner-city poverty organizations, or suburban arts councils. My advise to aspiring consultants is useful in all professional and trade specialties. This book on self-promotion is equally universal.

Take the sample article on consulting on page 312. This is a Problem-Solving Process Article originally written for the **Cambridge Express.** The first sentence particularizes it, "All Cambridge is divided into two parts. Those who are consultants and those who wish they were." The article which follows, however (except for one or two small, local items which can easily be deleted) is universal and hence offers many multiple use possibilities.

Principle III, Particularizing by Industry, suggests writing universal articles which can be used and reused *and* particularized by including one or two words or phrases directed at a publication's specific readership.

Thus, note the inset on page 312. This is the first paragraph of the identical article to that appearing in the **Cambridge Express** as it was printed in **Mass High Tech,** a computer publication. Between the two publication dates, a year apart, this same article also appeared in a Los Angeles business newspaper. While that newspaper might have chosen to particularize it, "All Los Angeles is divided into two parts . . . . " they simply reprinted, apparently concluding that the universality of the piece was not adversely affected by the specific mention of Cambridge.

In each of these instances, I did not bother to type out the article again and pretend that it was new. I simply sent the published article (in my offset, leave behind format) with a brief letter noting when and where it had appeared and why I continued to think the readers of this publication might be interested in seeing the piece. Photographs accompanied this letter.

Ordinarily I would direct such a letter to a weekly newspaper or specialized publication. Note: in my example it was specialized publications in business and high technology which used my consulting article. You can send the article in this fashion as your property if you have not disposed of all rights to the first publication printing your piece. In selling an article for publication, I advise the editor that I am selling *first rights only*; that is, they can publish the article in one issue of their newspaper or magazine, but that I retain all other rights, including reprinting in other publications.

Note: you must be most explicit with a publication on this point. Otherwise they will (probably rightly) assume that they have bought all rights to a piece. The unabashed self-promoter must become keenly aware of rights issues. For the unabashed self-promoter America is like a mediaeval kingdom made up of thousands of media baronies. Your task is to be able to arrange your self-promotional articles so that everything, *everything* you write can be printed not just once but dozens of times in every kind of publication. If you sell all rights to a publication (unless it has a whopper circulation like **Reader's Digest** or **Changing Times**), you have probably made a mistake: first, because the money you have received is probably inadequate recompense for the resources you have spent to produce the piece and the likelihood of expected return; second, because you have unnecessarily deprived yourself of other markets and all the money and promotional possibilities which accompany them.

True, if you have sold all rights that by no means precludes an article from being published elsewhere. It just means that if it is sold the original publisher shares in the proceeds of the sale. To be sure, many publishers, recognizing the pittances their writers are paid for articles, waive their rights (if the amount in question is small), but why take the chance?

These rights questions can be complicated, and at the very least the unabashed self-promoter should have some nodding acquaintance with them. For further information the Library of Congress has published a handy pamphlet on the matter called "Copyright Basics" (Circular R 1) Request it by writing:

Copyright Office
Library of Congress
Washington, D.C. 20559

One further word about payment. Many, many publications are cash poor, perpetually. This is a small fact which can benefit the unabashed self-promoter who is not himself similarly situated and who can afford to take some risk. Get paid for your article in advertising space — with a premium. If the publication, for instance, offers to pay you $100 for your article, say that you'd rather be paid in ads and suggest they give you $150 worth of space. It does not, of course, cost the publication this amount to run your ad; indeed it costs them considerably less that the $100 they would actually be paying you in cash. The editor may very well agree.

But make sure this ad does *not* run in the same issue as your article. The whole point is to get maximum exposure. The first issue will have your article with complete information about how to contact you; the second will be a standard ad with copy designed to follow-up and reinforce your original article. I make a regular practice of offering this alternative to cash-poor publications, my posture never being one of self-interest but rather *noblesse oblige.*

Principle IV: Multiple Use Through Updating

What should by now be very clear is that it is the responsibility of the unabashed self-promoter both to stay alert to promotional openings (piggybacking) and to the myriad opportunities for reusing every word he writes.

Some article of mine is popping up all the time. Often when a buyer calls me to follow-up a piece, I have to ask not only where he saw it but how it started, for, of course, a reader always is sent his copy of a publication long before a courtesy copy is mailed to an author.

To the reader, of course, the article seems not only enlightening, but fresh, invigorating. That's as it should be. In fact, I may actually have written it a year or two before and just particularized it or updated a key paragraph. People have continually asked me how I am able to produce so many articles, so quickly while attending to my other enterprises. Until now, I've answered them with a sphinx-like smile, knowing but unfathomable. Now you know. There is really no secret. There is just masterful technique.

Each year I add to my stockpile of possiblities a few new serviceable pieces, so many more arrows in my quiver, reusable like all arrows. Each year I take the time to review my existing stock. It is always, always easier to update pieces already written than it is to write new ones, and it is this updating process which leads to my fourth principle of multiple use.

Let us say that you have published a certain Problem-Solving Process article a year ago. Now it is time to update your readers on both the process itself and the common errors made by those who attempt to follow it or who deviate from it at some point. Where my original article a year ago was about "Mastering The Consulting Game," my update might be "Ten Mistakes Along The Way To Mastering The Consulting Game," or "Why You Aren't Mastering The Consulting Game." You will not be surprised to learn that this second article borrows heavily from the first, growing naturally from it.

A Sentinel article has wonderful update possibilities. Take the sample on page 313. As I mentioned before, the legislation discussed in this article is now the law of the land. An updated Sentinel article would focus on whether the legislation is working or not, advance reasons for success or failure, and make suggestions for further reform in the interests of your client prospects. Who could more naturally write this article than you, already a published expert on the subject?

The White Knight article, too, needs an update. What are the anxieties of your client prospects today and what do you, their White Knight, propose to do about them? Your readers await you.

In writing these updates, one word of warning. Although every politician is a self-promoter, not every self-promoter is a politician. Those of us who are not running for office (and most of those who are) need not necessarily worry about squaring this year's analysis with what we wrote last year. I hope you have the depth and breadth of technical knowledge so that your articles will always be correct. But even technical experts have bad days.

"Never complain," the old saw says, "Never explain." In point of fact, an article you have written in the past may have been ill-advised. Perhaps you're now sorry that the legislation you advocated in last year's Sentinel article is now the law. But be very careful about how you handle a matter such as this. Is it necessary to your image that you issue a public "Mea culpa!"? Does anyone care that *you* were wrong? Or do the people now being adversely affected simply care about what they can do to protect themselves? You tell me! Better yet, you tell them — in your next self-promotional article.

Principle V: Create An Informal Syndicate For Multiple Use

So often ingénue self-promoters bound up to me dog-eager, exuberant like adolescents who have just discovered sex. "Syndicates," they say, "if I write one article — just one — I can get it carried by hundreds of newspapers, just like 'Dear Abbey.' I'll be rich and famous!"

It's a touching notion, gentle reader, and, as I have previously written, it works for articles about you, but not so well for articles by you. I have perused the **Boston Globe** and the **New York Times** for years now for evidence of syndicated articles, and the names which crop up are the names we all know so well: Bombeck, Abbey, Ann, Buckley, Porter, McGrory, Evans and Novak, &c., &c. There are others, of course, less well known, but I suspect that the regular cadre of syndicated writers, outside the wire services, is under 100.

There are several syndication services in the country. I have written to each in the preparation of this book for useful information. This I have included in the Appendix (see page 286). Additional information is available in **Literary Market Place** and **Writer's Market.** What is clear from both my informal and formal research on syndicates is that it is very, very difficult to break into them.

What works better is producing your own informal syndicate of various publications which will print you on a regular or irregular basis. I have assembled a group of such publications, and I know other unabashed self-promoters who have, too.

Here's the deal: certain kinds of publications, principally low-budget weeklies and specialized tabloids need high quality material but have limited means of paying for it. Thus syndicated pieces are ideal for them. Approach these sources as you would when offering to have them reprint an article:

- Ask whether they are interested in a regular column of specified length.
- Tell them why you think their publication is right for such a feature.
- Indicate your familiarity with what they already do. (Don't for heaven sakes, just presume that they don't have a comparable feature. Know it!)
- Send two or three ready-to-use samples, or if you are already publishing your feature elsewhere, send your last two features as leave behinds and your next feature in typescript.
- Suggest the amount of money you want. Generally you cannot expect to get more than $25 per thousand words.
- Indicate whether you would be willing to be paid in ad space in alternate issues, thus cutting down on the number of pieces you need to write but keeping your visibility high.
- Say you will follow-up with a telephone call. Don't expect them to track you down. (See samples, page 326).

A Few Last Words

To the unabashed self-promoter self-promotion is a game. It is a game, however, in which the rewards are both very high and very substantial. It is fun for the unabashed self-promoter to think of ways to exploit the media. Fun to think of how to piggyback on great events and institutions. Fun to jump on breaking news and know that a timely comment will appear on breakfast tables around the nation. Fun — indeed thrilling — to know that every word you have published as a self-promoter is like a seed which can be planted and used again and again.

Of course, as the special piggyback sequence on page 348 indicates, there are equally mirthful journalists about in the land, who, because they so admire our audacity and inventiveness, occasionally place creative obstacles designed to spur us to great achievements. The way Margo Miller of the **Boston Globe** no doubt gleefully suppressed my name in her column when I welcomed former Massachusetts Governor King to the consulting profession is herewith trumped.

Margo, you should know it's very, very difficult to outsmart a seasoned and thoroughly unabashed self-promoter.

CHAPTER 11

THE UNABASHED SELF-PROMOTER IN THE DARKROOM

Every unabashed self-promoter needs photographs. They are as much a part of our stock in trade as the standard media release. Yet you need not become an expert in photography. Leave that to the technicians. Instead, concentrate on knowing what you need, when you need it, and how to use it. This, for our purposes, is quite sufficient.

A Few Introductory Words

Having said this, however, a few words about how to produce a decent photograph are in order. Most photographs are both thematically insipid and technically imperfect. Sadly, the photographers you work with are quite capable of producing just this kind of flawed product. Thus you cannot afford to be entirely oblivious of the process of producing good photographs.

A good photograph is a paradox. It invites the viewer to suspend belief for an instant by approaching with a sense of anticipation an event which he knows intellectually has already occurred. This is the magic of photography. Keeping this feeling of anticipation alive in your photographs is the challenge of the art.

Here are a few suggestions which should help achieve your objective:

- The center of a photograph is static, dead. Keep yourself out of it. If there is action in the picture, its direction should be *into* the picture, not away from it. *N.B.* If you are being photographed with two people more important than you are, break this rule. Get firmly into the center of the picture and stay there. Insignificant folk tend to get cut from photographs by newspaper editors. Position yourself so this can't happen to you.
- Don't chop the picture in half either vertically or horizontally. Keep the horizon either above or below the center of the picture. If the picture is divided in the middle, it has conflicting centers of interest and is inherently less interesting than a strong, dramatic, unified shot.
- Watch out for confusing backgrounds, whether an open window or a Jean Miro painting. Watch out, too, for those ubiquitous trees and posts which, given the opportunity, immediately sprout from a subject's head.
- Give your subject more space to move and look *into* than out of. Remember the sense of anticipation. You can sustain the impression of movement if you think of the side of the print as a wall. The subject should be placed so that his back is to the wall, not his face.
- Consider the frame. A dark sky is more acceptable than a light one, because it serves as a frame. Beware of a picture which is light along the edge. This is called bleeding, and it directs the attention of the reader away from the shot, beyond its edge, towards something more interesting. Your objective is to keep the viewer focused on your picture — and on you.
- But not for too long. Beware the picture that is too rigidly framed. This is called the donut. Editors dislike it because the eye gets trapped and won't move along to other articles and photographs in the same publication. Your task is to get the eye's attention for a reasonable period without, however, holding it prisoner.

The Photographs You Need

Keeping these few simple rules in mind, you should be able to produce the basic photographs you need. Fortunately most of us don't need anything more than the basics, because our photographic requirements are not extensive. The unabashed self-promoter can make do quite nicely with the following kinds of photographs:

- Basic head shot
- Basic action shot

Finding The Photographer You Need

It is no surprise to me that the television couple "The Odd Couple" should have a professional photographer as a leading character. Photographers are a strange, disorganized breed who very much march to the beat of a different drummer. Finding one of them is not difficult. Finding a good one is.

In practice, you should maintain as part of your Self-Promotion Network a list of photographers. There are at least two good ways of finding candidates for inclusion:

- Note the photo credits under the pictures in the local newspaper. I have found that staff photographers often have a private practice on the side and are perfectly happy to schedule an appointment with you. Just write and ask. The cost of such private sessions varies considerably. You should expect to pay between $25 - $75 per hour and up to $5 per print.
- Ask for the cards of photographers who take your picture at newspapers. As you become more and more active on the self-promotional circuit, you will necessarily come into contact with many newspaper and magazine photographers. *Always* get their names and addresses. Whether a photographer is staff or free-lance, you should ask to review his contact sheet, all the shots he actually took.

  Remember: Even a bad photographer can take a good picture. You know, of course, the story that enough monkies given enough typewriters could produce the works of Shakespeare. Keep it in mind when dealing with even the most fatuous photographers.

  You may simply want to buy extra prints of the shot used by the publication, or, more likely, you will decide that another shot, foolishly overlooked by a philistine editor, better represents you and will want copies of that. Note: Photographers keep their contact sheets for months or even years, but if he is a free-lancer don't expect the publication to know where to reach him. Keep the information on file yourself.

You And Your Photo Session

Once you have selected your photographer and scheduled your photo session, you must plan for the outcomes you desire:

Don't Leave The Selection Of Result To Your Photographer.

A photographer, however good, is only a technician. He can and should give you the benefit of his advice, but he must not make the decisions about the result. You must tell him, directly and pointedly, what audience you are trying to reach, what effect you wish to create, what image you want to portray. You are not a model to be twisted into an appropriate shape; you are the active agent in this scenario. If you don't think these matters through, the photographer will give you what he wants you to have, which may or may not bear any resemblance to what you actually need.

Therefore, before your photo session, answer the following questions, as specifically as you can:

- What audience am I trying to reach? What are their likes and dislikes? How do they dress? What postures do they take? What would most impress them about me? Least impress them? Your photograph is not designed for everyone. Try as we might, whatever photograph we take, we are unlikely to impress all people. So what? It doesn't matter so long as the audience we are trying to reach sits up and takes notice. What matter the rest?
- What effect do I want to create? Consider your image. Write down a series of key words that relate to your image and the effect you are trying to create. Ordinarily these will be action words or words that imply action: power, authority, intelligence, caring, concern, humanity, empathy, &c. Write down the words which most suggest what you'd like the viewer to think about you as he considers your picture. For myself, I like people to think, however fleetingly, "Here's a bright, empathetic individual. I bet he can help me solve my problem."
- What image do I want to portray? Image is all embracing. When promoting any particular image, you must consider the clothes you wear, the place where you are photographed, fabric, color, your expression, hair style, in short the totality of effect. Each must do its part to produce a single, strong, unified message. Perhaps a picture is worth 1000 words, but a picture is meaningless unless the words are thematically unified and produce one intense response from the viewer.

Where To Be Photographed

When you have control over who is taking the picture, select the location where you feel most comfortable and which is most consonant with the image you are trying to promote. This might be just about anywhere. In practice, it should be a place where the photographer can take not only a series of head shots but also a series of action shots.

The word action may initially be confusing. It does not necessarily suggest pole vaulting. The action in any given shot must be appropriate to your image. The All American Mother may be a champion poker player, but she is better photographed giving her adoring children glasses of nutritious milk. The Sage is best captured pondering the illusive *mot juste* rather than on the golf links. Those of us in the persuasion business, like me, may well be talking. It's scarcely surprising there are so many photographs of me with an open mouth.

Your photo session must produce both head shots and action shots. Furthermore it should produce a variety of each. This suggests changes of clothes, locations, and props. Even an experienced self-promoter needs to see which of several locations, costumes, and activities best represents what he is trying to get across. Don't settle for less.

If you go to a photographer's office, you will very likely have to settle for a limited array of possibilities. Arrange for him to meet you where you will have the greatest number of options.

A Word On Props

Props help foster and sustain an image. Some work. Many don't. I recall, for instance, a celebrated photograph of one of the nineteenth century Professional Beauties, ladies of social standing but limited resources. Dazzling in her beauty, the one of my memory stands before the world holding a large, very glassy-eyed, quite evidently dead fish. So much for the photographer's febrile imagination. Do give adequate consideration to the props which appear with you in any photograph. Do they really add something? Do they augment and amplify the image you want to get across, or do they merely look contrived?

- Don't be photographed holding a telephone receiver. This is a cliché which always makes you look posed and artificial.
- Don't be photographed at your typewriter. Ditto.
- Do use animals. These undiscriminating creatures give you a human touch and desirable quality which might otherwise be lacking.
- Do be photographed with books or other appurtenances of learning. This, too, is a cliche, but such backgrounds still suggest intelligence and scholarly objectivity.

Hands And Hair

Every American mother's impulse about hair is correct: keep it out of your eyes. Most hair photographs badly and detracts from the subject. I know; I have very unruly and recalcitrant locks which, when falling over my forehead, give me a look of having been seized by an intergallactic alien intent on mayhem. Hair should always be brushed off the face and pulled back, if necessary. Americans prefer a freshly scrubbed look, and this is seldom achieved with mounds of hair.

In the same way keep your hands away from your face. A favorite author shot has the writer's fact-filled head lightly resting on an equally lightly clenched fist. In real life no one has ever taken this pose. Moreover, in the more avant garde circles of body-conscious California such a pose gives particular offense: if any portion of the hand obscures the subject's face, this is thought to be a clear signal that that subject has something to hide. In a culture like that of Los Angeles where people tell their all within a quarter hour of meeting, the very idea of discretion, much less secrecy, is anathema.

When The Shutter Clicks

Millions of Americans have participated in the cult rite of saying, "Cheese!," before the camera's probing lens. It's an absurd little event, but it affirms our membership in the body politic. It is, however, insufficient for the unabashed self-promoter.

I have two ways of handling this moment of truth, the moment when the shutter snaps an uncompromising image:

- I recall the effect I am trying to create. I recollect my key words. And I visualize a situation in which I am acting out these words. The camera merely records the activity.
- Alternatively, I stare hard into the lens, eyes wide, lips moist, and begin the kind of mating ritual with the lens which Margaret Mead in other circumstances captured so well in **Coming Of Age In Samoa.**

I acknowledge that the resulting photographs have very different uses.

The Contact Sheet

Once the actual photo session is over, there is more for the unabashed self-promoter to do before the actual prints are made. There remains your session with the photographer and the contact sheet.

Before you engage a photographer, you should know how long it will take him to produce a contact sheet. If time is of the essence, they can be produced overnight. A week is very liberal indeed.

First, the photographer should allow you to review the contact sheet at your leisure. Do not be discouraged by what you see. You are now at an intermediate stage of production, and much, much can be done to produce a superb picture.

Examine each frame on the contact sheet. Use a magnifying glass if necessary. If you don't have one, ask to borrow one from the photographer. You need it to examine each frame closely.

What you are now looking for are photographs which either wholly or in part contain your desired look and which can, if properly treated, produce the effect you wish. Mark those that look promising, even if only marginally so. Once you have done so, you are ready for a conference with the photographer.

Remind him of your objectives, the effect you wish to create, the image you want to produce. Now show him the photographs you have selected which you think contain the necessary qualities.

The question now is: Can the photographer by cutting, slicing, airbrushing, cropping, enlarging or erasing leave you with the effect you must have. These are technical questions, and you need technical answers. It is not necessary that you be fully conversant with the technician's art, but it is necessary that that technician be fully clear on what you wish to achieve and that he be capable of producing the desired effect with the raw material which is available. Moreover, this effect must be delivered in both a head shot and in an action shot.

Once the photographer has given you the assurance you need, send him back to his work. Before he goes, however, get a date by which you will have the completed samples you need. Do not at this time order more than 1 print of any sample photographs. You will need to approve the samples before stocking up.

Again, the photographer should be able to produce samples for you within a week. Again, if time is of the essence, they can be done more rapidly. Be clear with the photographer what you need and when.

The Sizes, Color And Number Of Prints You Need

You need photographs in both 5" x 7" and 8" x 10". These are the standard sizes. Your photographs should be black and white. I myself have never bothered to have color prints done and have never regretted the decision. Color prints are expensive, and I see no reason to have them around unless they are absolutely necessary.

For the same reason, be conservative as you buy your black and white prints. Not only are all photographs expensive, but I guarantee you your tastes will change as you develop as an unabashed self-promoter. What seems so eye catching and appealing today may well embarrass you in a few months. Thus, do not order too many photographs right away. A dozen of each size and type should be more than adequate.

Captions

Every photograph must be marked. The best way to do so is with a caption. Captions should be brief and to the point. They should be typed on a sticker and placed on the back of the photograph. Include the following information on a head shot:

- name of subject
- professional affiliation
- title
- location
- current notable achievement
- last most recent notable achievement
- telephone number for follow up

Here's how the caption of my head shot might read, "Dr. Jeffrey Lant, president of Jeffrey Lant Associates, Inc., a Cambridge, Massachusetts management consulting firm, is author of **The Unabashed Self-Promoter's Guide.** He also wrote the national best-seller **The Consultant's Kit.** For further information call (617) 547-6372."

This caption is also appropriate for any action shots. Yours may need some alteration. At the very least each photograph should have your:

- name
- company
- title
- location
- telephone number

This shorter version is called backing and should also be added on a sticker. Neither backing nor caption should ever be written or typed directly on the photograph as these marks show through.

Using Photographs

Ordinarily you will need your photographs for the following situations:

- With an advance article about you. Unless the publication you are dealing with is major, you will probably have to send a picture along with an advance article or media release. A 5" by 7" black and white head shot is usually best.
- With an article by you. Many publications are quite happy to run a photograph of the author along with his piece. But not all. It is usually better to ask the editor in advance whether he wants a photograph and will use it if you send it along.
- With small publications. Smaller publications, weekly newspapers, trade and technical publications, newsletters, are usually understaffed. However they usually like to run photographs. Again, ask the appropriate editor whether he cares to have a head shot of you.
- With organizations where you are speaking. Oftentimes such organizations have publications in which you can be promoted if you supply not only the copy but also the accompanying photograph(s). Ask your contact.

Because photographs are expensive, I do not automatically mail them along with a story. I either:

- call and ask the editor if he wants a picture, or
- query with the same question in a letter

Indicate at the foot of a standard media release that photographs are available if requested. I use this technique only where I am sending out many releases and cannot write an individual letter. If I really want my photograph to accompany an article (and I usually do), I either telephone an editor or write and follow up with a telephone call. Since a photograph is to my benefit, giving my story additional space and prominence, I do what is necessary to insure that it is used.

PHOTOGRAPHS IN SPECIFIC SITUATIONS

Events Where You're Featured

It is unfortunately true that most unabashed self-promoters will not have their photographers as permanent parts of their retinue. Could we but afford this amenity many problems would be spared us. There does come a moment when we have to rely not merely on the kindness but on the competence of strangers. This can be irritating.

Whenever you are speaking or making a presentation, arrange with the host organization for a photographer to be present, if only for a few minutes. There are several reasons for this desire:

- A photograph should accompany any story about this event.
- A photograph with a caption may be a sufficient story (as, for instance, in an organization's newsletter).
- You want the opportunity to review another contact sheet to see whether there are photographs worth producing in quantity.

I have discovered in my considerable travels around the nation that most organizations are lamentably ill-equipped to provide the photographic services which you as a speaker and unabashed self-promoter have every right to expect. Under the circumstances it is best to place your request for a photographer as early as possible, provide suitable reasons for wanting one (frame them in terms of publicizing the organization and not you), and be persistent until the arrangements are made. It is unfortunately true that most organizations do not begin to glimpse the public relations potential of their speakers and programs and act, in consequence, with amazing obduracy when asked to provide a service which is to their own benefit as well as yours. So be it. The unabashed self-promoter never minds forcing others to do something good for themselves. It is a decided bore, that's true, but there is often no alternative.

Ensuring The Greatest Number Of Pictures From Any Event

Remember: Just as all news is local, so are all photographs which are in fact mini-stories. As you approach any event, do not think in terms of getting one published photograph but consider how you turn one event into dozens of published pictures. You do so on the basis of location of participants, first and foremost.

At Conventions

Each year thousands of state, regional, and national conventions are held. Most pass without any general photographic report despite the fact that they include distinguished speakers and often thousands of participants. If you have ever attended such an event manqué, pay close attention.

- If you are organizing a convention, explain to your speakers, particularly to your keynote speaker, that there will be a Photographic Receiving Line. If you are the (especially keynote) speaker, let it be known that you would like and expect a Photographic Receiving Line.
- To prepare for this event, the organization needs to engage a photographer, develop a standard caption, arrange a suitable spot near the speaker's presentation, have volunteers on hand to distribute and collect an appropriate information form.
- Immediately following the speaker's presentation, those desiring to be photographed should gather at a specific location. If there are several representatives from a city or town, these may be gathered in one place; if there are large numbers expecting to be photographed, different sections of the alphabet can be assigned to different rooms.
- Upon arriving at the appropriate location, each person being photographed should be given an Information Form. This form seeks the following information:

    - name of person being photographed
    - company affiliation
    - title
    - complete address
    - telephone (business and residence)
    - name of local newspaper(s)

  Individuals completing this form should be asked to print, not write. Note: There should be a question on the form asking whether the individual would like to purchase a copy of the original print for a specified price (say $5-$10). This is a good way for an organization to raise unrestricted income. Checks should be collected when the Information Form is turned in.

- All photographs should be taken before a banner inscribed with the complete name of the organization. Some organizations print up a special banner for each convention with their name, the city in which their meeting was held, and the year. This makes good sense if you can do it.

Distributing The Photographs

It is a wise idea to take these photographs as early in the convention as you can. If you are involving the keynote speaker, this should not be difficult, as this speech is usually the first delivered. Even in the case of a three-day meeting, it should be perfectly possible not only to mail the photographs from the convention but have them available for convention participants. This will save mailing costs.

While the photographer is developing the pictures, volunteers should be preparing both the captions and mailing envelopes. Here's how:

- Those being photographed should be asked to fill in a standard caption form with their names. If only one person is in a picture, simply mail this form to the newspaper.

- Type a sticker with standard backing information:
  - name of subject
  - company affiliation
  - position
  - town, state
  - follow-up telephone number

  When the pictures are developed, place this sticker on the back and clip (not staple) to caption.

- Prepare mailing labels for newspapers by using **Ayer**'s or any other standard print media directory. If you have an advance list of participants, you may even be able to type these labels early. Note: Inevitably some hapless soul will be left out of the proceedings or will call to complain that his name was misspelled. These problems are trifling. *Non illegitimi carborundum.* Remember: The fame of your organization is being spread far and wide (and with it the fame of that person of distinction, the unabashed self-promoter). See samples, page 350).

At Your Parties

Don't hesitate to do something comparable at your own parties. At my publishing parties, for instance, I customarily organize a photographic receiving line. There I stand, author with book in hand, pulling my guests into photographs which will, in the next week or two, appear in their local newspapers. Wednesday is a good day to have such parties as many local papers print on Wednesday, and you therefore have the maximum amount of time to have your photographs developed, captioned and mailed. In any event, you must work with dispatch, since you are facing a deadline.

The Inevitable, Usually Intolerable Group Photograph

No chapter on photographs could conceivably be complete without a pass at that great American institution, the Group Photograph. We begin with it as schoolchildren and it accompanies us through life, at anniversaries, reunions, company picnics, and on and on. Such photographs, like death and taxes, will always be with us. What is worse, they have a tendency to linger, irrefutable evidence of a profound lack of imagination.

If you must indulge, keep the number of participants to a minimum preferably no more than seven. Add a diverting prop or two. And try to have your subjects doing something other than staring glumly into the camera. Even Harvard rugby shots from '09 have, regrettably, no allure under such circumstances.

The Obligatory Obituary: It's Your Funeral

Remember: Just because you have slipped under the daisies, your self-promotional activities should not prematurely abate. Besides, you owe it to your public to go out in style.

If you have followed the techniques of this book conscientiously, you will in due course become a personage. Personages get obituaries, and their obituaries get photographs.

The photographs accompanying obituaries have always struck me as unsatisfactory. They are usually blurred, habitually unflattering, and always seem to be at least a generation or two old. I have, to be sure, nothing to say against their age. If you looked your most recent best in 1962, God knows you're entitled to that shot to accompany your obituary. Only make sure, please, that the local paper has it.

It is entirely proper and by no means morbid to send an appropriate letter to the obituary editor with both important facts about you (for the copy) and the photograph you'd like to be remembered by. Don't rely on your necessarily addled and unsettled heirs to perform this service and don't expect a mere journalist to give adequate consideration to the proper eternal image.

Helping these journalists makes eminent good sense. Neglecting them is undoubtedly a mistake. After all in this case, they really do have the last word.

One Last Point

It seems hardly possible, but I believe people are even more careless and unimaginative about photographs than they are about the other matters discussed in this book. At least you won't be. Not only do photographs add a significant dimension to whatever appears about you in print, making you a more human, more compelling individual. They also significantly augment the amount of space you can get. And surely if anything ought to make sense to the unabashed self-promoter it is this.

CHAPTER 12

ROCK AROUND THE CLOCK WITH THE UNABASHED SELF-PROMOTER

As should be very clear by now, to approach the media as if they were somehow monolithic would be a great mistake. What makes the media so complex is the fact that they are highly differentiated. The unabashed self-promoter must become attuned to these differences and learn how to position himself so that he can be most appealing to the decision makers within each sector. On first glance this may appear to be an awesome, time-consuming process.

To outsiders, the electronic media seems to resemble nothing so much as a mediaeval kingdom of infinitely complex, variegated units, each with its own codes, perquisites, and peculiarities. The novice self-promoter may experience some bewilderment at this situation. Fortunately as this chapter demonstrates, electronic media breaks down nicely into generic types of programming. Every major media market has virtually all of the patterns which follow; most lesser markets have a fair number of them.

The key for the unabashed self-promoter is understanding just what each type of programming is, what its purpose is, its audience, and just what kinds of guests it wants to feature. This is the first problem for the unabashed self-promoter to solve. The second is to re-package oneself, one's product and service, to redefine, reposition, shade and emphasize oneself in such a way so as to become the perfect guest for *each* type of program. This is not difficult, but it does demand constant thought and continuing flexibility to take advantage of the shifting circumstances of the media.

Ultimately the high degree of media differentiation, which may at first have alarmed the novice self-promoter, is the unabashed self-promoter's chief delight, for what it means is that there is an infinity of available markets to exploit, a never-ending number of programs on which to appear. What a challenge! To the unabashed self-promoter, knowledgeable about the markets, protean in his media characterizations, the problem is not whether he'll get on; he knows that that is a given. It is rather how to handle the daunting task of keeping a significant presence in all the major markets of the country.

GIVING THE MEDIA WHAT THEY WANT

In The Morning (Radio And Television)

Between 5 a.m. and 9 a.m. electronic media is the equivalent of strong black coffee. It helps people wake up and prepare for the day ahead. These programs, which are universal, provide a mixture of news and feature material rendered in a distinctly light fashion. The programs are designed for an audience which is only episodically tuning in, since its primary responsibility is getting ready for the day's work. Because of the way most people are listening, news and features are handled in a short, brisk, fast-paced manner. There is nothing lazy or laid back about wake-up programming. The guests on such programs must act accordingly.

Interviews on these programs must be so compelling and authoritative that busy listeners, hastily getting ready, feel obliged to stop in their tracks and pay attention. The successful morning talk show interview can make them do just that. Long disquisitions on any subject are inappropriate and are discouraged.

Often these wake-up shows like a news tie-in with their guests. "Good Morning America" and the "Today" show are prime examples. They bring people on each morning who are intimately involved with the headlines — or who can comment on them intelligently. If you have some knowledge about a pressing event in your community, or have a product or service which gives you authority to speak on the subject, you have a self-promotional springboard. Let us say, for example, that you are a botanist, tree surgeon, gardener, &c in a town infested with Dutch elm disease. You have the self-promotional lever you need.

Because wake-up talk interviews are brief and chatty, you as the unabashed self-promoter must necessarily paint with a broad brush. That's all right. You are not writing a definitive treatise; you're passing on information in an interesting, conversational fashion. Your audience wants to feel, not overwhelmed by your erudition (or cheated because you have left out useful information), but warmed and enlightened by their brief but thorough contact with you, the expert source. As an unabashed self-promoter with a product or service to sell, you will, of course, provide necessary follow-up information so that your listeners can contact you after the show for more in-depth handling.

Wake-up shows can be maddeningly informal. First, most of them take place before the radio or television station is actually open for business. Very often there is just a skeleton crew on hand and a producer and host who can be very sleepy.

I remember one occasion on a radio wake-up program in Fall River, Massachusetts which has always struck me as symbolic of the genre. I was scheduled to go to this rather grim old mill town to do a 5 a.m. wake-up show. It happened that it had snowed heavily the night before and that it was tough getting from Cambridge. There was only one person at the radio station, a droopy-eyed fellow who doubled as producer and host and redoubled as receptionist, weatherman, coffee maker, and technician.

I knew it was going to be a long day when, after we had been talking "on the air" for five minutes or so after the first commercial, the host remembered he had not turned the microphones on. Nothing was being broadcast! After this happened again, I took it upon myself to remind my host to turn on the station after every commercial.

Things got worse.

I had come to Fall River to talk about a bill I had introduced in the legislature, Massachusetts being perhaps the sole state in the Union where any citizen has this right, a real benefit to the local unabashed self-promoter. No one on a grey, wintry, snow-drenched day in Fall River wanted to hear about my plans to reform secondary schools in the Commonwealth. They wanted to talk about — snow removal and why their drive-ways hadn't yet been plowed at 6 a.m.

All, that is, except for one agitated woman who decided that reform of the secondary schools meant SEX EDUCATION, that bourgeois bugaboo. Why, she demanded in strident tones, did I want sex education in the schools? (Needless to say, I hadn't mentioned the subject.) Didn't I know that this would threaten the virginity of her three young daughters, all beautifully brought up but apparently susceptible to dark primordial currents.

All self-promoters have days like this.

I've capitalized on mine by writing this book.

What will you do?

Mid-Morning Talk (Radio and Television)

The pace of the wake-up shows cannot be sustained over an entire day. It is too fast, too frenetic, too disjointed. People, bless their souls, are too slothful and lethargic. At about 9 a.m. therefore, the early morning staccato format changes to something more slow-paced, leisurely to meet the needs of a different audience. By now the breadwinners have gone, the kids are at school, people whose lives are bound by a 9-to-5 routine have disappeared. In their wake are the housewives, pre-school children, retirees, and, to my continuing delight, a hefty number of the self-employed who work from their homes —one of my prime audiences.

This audience is looking primarily for entertaining feature material, often of a personal nature. They want to know how to improve their lives — but they do not want to be overwhelmed with complicated advice and techniques which defy simple implementation. Instead they are looking for the kind of conversation they might have with a solicitous friend. Indeed, friendship, companionship is the keynote of mid-morning talk.

I am my most endearing on mid-morning talk shows. I become the tow-headed darling of grandmothers and women over forty, the serious, empathetic, yet deeply adorable grandchild and boy-lover everyone always wanted. I am not the intimidating expert, never the brash self-promoter, but a knowledgeable, enthusiastic friend who can make the lives of my listeners easier, more comfortable and more fulfilling.

This audience loves the quick fix. It has the time but neither the energy nor inclination for schemes which demand a sustained commitment and persistence. It wants results, but it does not want to work hard for them. The unabashed self-promoter facing this audience must be gently urging and confidently upbeat that better times are around the corner — if his listeners use his product or service. Good anecdotal material is important here. "Look!," you are saying, "octogenarian Mrs. Smith did it. Betty Jones with three toddlers did it. Old man Merriweather with his gout did it, too." If you have the kind of product or service where you can identify satisfied users and these users fit into the demographic of the mid-morning audience, bring them along.

Mid-Day News (Radio and Television)

At twelve noon the pace changes again. Media people want us to believe that the news is a seamless garment rendered on the Mount of Olives and delivered by cherubim. It must be as terse as the Ten Commandments and as authoritative, for, after all, it is Revealed Truth. Anything less, even a blooper, derogates from its carefully-cultivated image of control and infallibility. Thus all features aired at this time must conform rigidly to a very rigid format.

When appearing on such shows either in person or by telephone hook-up, get to the heart of your subject quickly and do so with short, thrusting statements. Despite the fact that much of what the media peddles at this hour is highly subjective opinion, pap and political grand standing (often manufactured by professional self-promoters who prefer to be called "statesmen"), the station wants to maintain the illusion of an objective truth machine. In appearing on such shows, you must seem to be the in-command expert, facts, figures, key concepts, all down pat and ready to be delivered in a pungent, trenchant way.

Such interviews because they are generally short (2-3 minutes is often thought extensive) need to be practised, especially if they will be live. At the very least know exactly what points you need to make and keep in mind your key words or quotable phrases for easy delivery. Don't expect to practice in the studio. The people you'll be dealing with don't have time for practice, for mistakes, or corrections. They are, after all, dealing with immutables, truth received from on high. Practice suggests the existence of human frailty in their midst — but the perception of such frailty is anathema in America's news rooms.

People on wake-up and mid-morning shows are so very human. Witness my bumbling friend from Fall River. They come across as the friends of their audiences, and producers hope for and expect a very real rapport between the on-air personality and his listeners. This person can make mistakes and gaffes, just as any acquaintance might do. If they are not encouraged at least they are tolerated in the comfortable live-and-let-live atmosphere of these programs.

Not so in the news room. There is always an urgency, a bristling electricity, a nervousness about those who deal in the news. Very often in person they are distracted, jerky, too-quick talking, uncomfortable to be around. No wonder. They are the priests of a very demanding, unforgiving, unrelenting deity. They are in this role capable of any rudeness in behavior to lesser mortals in service of their unloving god. Remember that young cub Chris Wallace, the very archetype of the stern, unyielding juvenile reporter, barking at a lackadaisical, rambling Senator Charles Percy during the last Republican National Convention. "You're on television, Senator!," that unbending acolyte thundered. What matters the dignity of a senator to the demands of the voracious behemoth?

Prepare thyself or find yourself similarly victimized. Be objective, authoritative, knowledgeable, in control and brisk and you will find yourself tolerated — on the first step to acceptance in the news room.

Afternoon Talk (Primarily Radio)

From about 1 p.m. until 4 p.m., interviews again become chatty and amiable. They are designed to inform but, as with their matutinal counterparts, they must not overwhelm with their complexity. Such interviews, of course, demand expertise, but it is clear that these experts must not appear austere, formidable or distant. Like mid-morning talk show audiences, those in the afternoon want a friend. This friend — the unabashed self-promoter — must be capable of improving their lives. Your job is to appear as the accessible expert — to be cordial, kind and concerned, but knowledgeable. The kind of friend most people desperately need but so seldom have. Eschew the technical in favor of sensible conclusions which get accepted less because of your credentials than because of the confiding, empathetic, ingratiating way in which you deliver them.

Drive-Time Talk (Usually Radio)

This is the perfect slot for the hope purveyors — the unabashed self-promoters who say, "There is a better way for you. I used to be in your situation, but I found the way out. Listen closely and take heed from my good example."

Picture your audience. It is five o'clock and already rush hour is on. In large cities helicopters chop the air locating the sources of traffic confusion. Trapped behind the wheels of their cars, fatigued in mind and body is your audience. This is the moment of their utmost disspiritedness — they need a pick-me-up. They need a tonic reviver. They need hope and inspiration. They need you, the unabashed self-promoter.

The unabashed self-promoter from 5 p.m. should be a dreamspinner, someone offering the weary and worn a constructive vision of a better world — for them. The self-promoter at this time can, without difficulty, conjure up in his listeners their not-so-hidden feelings of frustration, irritation, brooding rage. He remembers Thoreau's words that, "Most men lead lives of quiet desperation," and moves at this particularly vulnerable moment to provide an alternative — which he himself commands.

Drive-time shows allow for this performance — and are the perfect vehicles for it.

Like all talk shows, drive-time programming is geared to the presentation of news and public affairs. All such programs peddle hope, attempting to inform and motivate their listeners, but drive-time programming is the zenith of its kind.

There may be problems, invidious trends, trying circumstances, the flotsam and jetsam of life on a troubled planet at a troubled moment in its star-crossed history, but the listeners want to know not just the dimensions of woe but what they can do about it. This is their general question, "How can I take advantage of circumstances and become (or remain) healthy, prosperous, ahead of the pack?" Fellow feeling, after all, at 5 p.m. in the midst of a traffic jam is at a decided minimum.

The self-promoter at drive time is an inspired, inspiring visionary — an individual who has, after perhaps an uncertain start, found the way out, the way to realizing the hopes and aspirations of his audience.

In such circumstances, I first attempt to establish empathy and a sense of identification with my audience. I, too, I say, once was as you are, but no longer.

My presentation is based on a variation of the Redeemed Sinner image of Chapter 2: when I was a 9-to-5 employee I was a sinner, a depraved man who knew not the ways of salvation. Then I came to the light, and it is this light, my product, my service, which can lead you towards your objectives, too.

Every unabashed self-promoter becomes a master at purveying hope. He must conjure up, sometimes subtly, sometimes in graphic detail (leavened with humor) the current plight of his listeners. Then he must convince them that there is a better alternative, an alternative which he can help make available.

No one delivering drive-time programming need be unduly coy about the state of his listeners. The bulk of them will be depleted, baffled at the conditions of their lives, annoyed (if not worse) at their present circumstances, ripe for ideas and techniques which will liberate them. Hail, the emancipating self-promoter!

I had a curious experience one day of just how powerful such an emancipator can be. I had had two hours on a Detroit drive-time radio show and then rushed instantly to the airport. While running to my plane, I heard the same station on the air (I always ask my drivers to tune on the station to see if the host or callers say something about me after I'm off the air).

As I went by I overheard a very well dressed businessman and an elderly black shoe shiner earnestly engaged in discussing what I had said. Both were favorably impressed. The name of my book even came out in conversation. I had to hurry ahead after thinking, just for an instant, of going over and introducing myself. I decided against it.

As the olympian dreamspinner, a majestic disembodied presence, I had if perhaps only momentarily touched the lives of two very dissimilar people. As yet another harried traveler en route to nowhere, I would inevitably appear diminished, even demeaned. I went on, however, happy at this demonstration of drive-time hope purveyance.

There are a million such stories in the naked city . . .

Evening Talk (Primarily Radio)

What is evening talk? I think it's the contemporary version of vaudeville. Consider my nocturnal experience on a major New York City talk station. I arrived in the green room and was seated next to a grandmotherly woman with a captivated look on her face. No conversation was possible, since her transfixed expression suggested an immediate "Shoosh!," if interrupted. She turned out to be the mother of the on-air guest.

The guest, as it transpired, was a dowdy suburban housewife with an unappealing monotone, and an outrageous tale. She had, it seems, been kidnapped by aliens, not once, mind you, but twice, and taken to see "The One," an interstellar Ming the Magnificent with plans aplenty for spaceship earth. Unfortunately whatever "The One" had told her was now lost because of an unfortunate amnesia which had not, however, precluded her writing two books, one following hard on each audience.

After this mind-clouded messenger of future events, there was a woman who made dresses for parrots, delectable concoctions designed to be color coordinated with their motley plumage. And following her, a telephone call to San Diego to a man who makes historically accurate costumes for bull frogs.

And then me.

Evening talk shows usually run between 8 p.m. and midnight. Ordinarily they utilize a call-in format which permits the audience to get immediate access to the guests. Every night millions of Americans tune in to hear their favorite on-air personalities tackle the most interesting and controversial guests on topics designed to prick the audience.

These audiences are akin to the readers of the lurid grocery store tabloids. They have an insatiable thirst for the odd, strange, and different. They tune in for information and to have their prejudices confirmed and reinforced; they tune in, too, however, for color, controversy and contumely. Like the fans of Roman gladiators, they thrill to see their highly-paid (but similarly short-lived) favorites, the talk show masters, pitted against the guest, themselves generally well-known authorities on any given subject.

As the guest on such a program (often the most highly-rated radio show in the market), you need to come across less as the solicitous friend of the mid-day programs and more the in-command expert, less as black coffee and more as a tangey, very dry martini, comfortably well-informed, diamond-hard when necessary, very much the cultural mandarin. Have information, good humor, and a quick, penetrating response as part of your arsenal on such programs.

I have appeared on many, many evening call-in shows. I regard them as low to middle-brow entertainment and on them, more so than with other formats, I am very much the entertainer.

I recall, for instance, one evening I appeared on the "David Brudnoy Show," the top-rated radio call-in show in Boston. It was the eve of Harvard Commencement, and I had been invited to appear as the editor of **Our Harvard** with the author of another new book on the University, Toby Marotta, who wrote **Men of Harvard: Gay Men From The Class of '67.**

Although I had some serious reservations about both the content and thesis of Toby's book, the program had proceeded amiably enough since both the host and Marotta are silky smooth and congenial. Indeed, that was the problem, there was no spark. And hence no calls. Until at last one obviously older gentleman called and asked Toby if there was any sex in his book between "you know, older men and younger ones." Brudnoy set the scene for what followed in his ever-quick way, "Like 60 and 40," he said. "No," said the soft-voiced caller, "Like 45 and 15."

"No," I now chimed in, "You'll find that kind of stuff in **Our Yale**."

It took just a minute but Toby, Brudnoy, the technicians, everyone, gasped — and then guffawed. Every mike in the room had to be covered, we were all laughing so hard.

"Where do I get it?," the now aroused caller persisted.

Where, indeed.

Pederastic self-promoters of Yale, get on the stick.

All-Night Talk (Primarily Radio)

All-night talk, which ordinarily begins at midnight, seems by comparison with its predecessor to ramble. All-night talk is the friend of the insomniac and of the unheralded legions who toil while the rest of us sleep. There is something comfortably worn and down at heel about all-night talk, like a drowsy conversation between intimates. The all-night self-promoter needs to suggest confidence and empathy. He must develop, in short, a bedside manner. Doing so can lead to great results. George Murphy, the former senator from California, attributed his election to the fact that, in movie reruns, he constantly found himself in the bedrooms of his voters. His pal Ronald Reagan benefitted from the same phenomenon.

On all-night talk shows, I am informative, of course (I am always that), but also soothing, seductive, the sought after friend and companion. To be sure, there have been exceptions. On one television show in Boston, trying valiantly to be the local equivalent of the "Tonight" show, I was featured with a gigantic poster which read "Are you a consultant?", a companion piece to similar sociological studies like "Are you a preppie?" and "Are you a nerd?", my poster featuring the salient aspects of the genre. On that same show there was a dancing bear, three golden retrievers, members of a strange group called "Ladies Against Women," and a monosyllabic real estate czar. It seemed an apt mix.

More normal was the four hours I did after midnight live by telephone hook-up on the National Black Radio Network fielding calls from around the nation or my nightwalking stints on KABC in Los Angeles.

Listeners of such programs want usable information to be sure. They want a forum to express themselves, too. But they also want an all-night friend who brings solice, inspiration, hope. After midnight I am that friend and my message is clear: buy me, buy my goods, buy my services, and the solice, inspiration and hope you now feel because of me will stay with you.

Who can resist such a deal?

Week-End Public Affairs Programming (Radio and Television)

These programs are usually taped during the week to be played on Sundays, often at hours which repel even the most civic spirited.

These programs are designed to address public issues and to impart other vital information. They are, despite the odd hours at which they are broadcast, most useful to the self-promoter, so long as the unabashed self-promoter appears to be solving public problems and disseminating crucial information — not promoting. At all times the unabashed self-promoter must appear to address an important issue in constructive fashion. In the process, of course, it is not very difficult to suggest that those who are really serious about solving the problem buy you, your product, or your service.

Public affairs programs take their subjects from the pages of the daily newspapers; they deal with the perceived significant issues of the day. As with so much involving the media, the unabashed self-promoter succeeds in getting air time on such shows as he can make himself coincident with the buzzwords, themes, concerns, and anxieties of the moment. I received an avalanche of public affairs time in 1982 because the subjects I most talked about — nonprofit organizations and consulting — had news hooks, nonprofit organizations because they were being adversely affected by federal budget cuts, consulting because I could sell it as a job creation mechanism which ought to be seriously considered by professionals out of work because of the recession. I didn't so much invent these hooks as gage what would be of interest to the media — in this case public affairs programmers — and package my material accordingly.

Given the fact that American politics is determinedly middle-of-the-road and traditionally avoids divisive polemics, the unabashed self-promoter should use public affairs programs as a moderate in search of common sense solutions to vexing problems. While your commitment to a distinct point of view is self-evident, you must, for the sake not only of your credibility but your audience appeal, appear as an individual of reason and constructive conciliation. If you have opponents (or competitors) whose names the host unfortunately raises in the conversation (you never do so), do not paint them as devils incarnate, but rather suggest that they are good men — gone astray to be sure — unhappily incomplete, erring indeed but good men notwithstanding.

As a mandarin in good standing, it is your part to patronize the unfortunate and attempt to bring them to the light, at least officially. Praise them when you can. After all clear evidence of your genteel rationality will make any deep, incisive criticism the more plausible.

Week-end public affairs shows are among the easiest to get on in part because of their strange hours, in part because many (particularly radio) stations attempt to encourage and increase community involvement through this mechanism. I myself made my radio debut on such a program on station WCRB in Waltham, Massachusetts.

Public affairs programming allows the unabashed self-promoter to stand forward as a statesman, the very embodiment of civic concern and respectability. It goes without saying, of course, that you will present yourself as such a statesman only if you have already created the product or service which will further help your listener.

Otherwise keep your bromides to yourself and leave the airwaves to those who have already done their homework.

Last Words

The unabashed self-promoter is an inveterate television and radio channel switcher. He wants to know at any given moment all the program options which exist on each station in each market in which he wants to be featured. Once knowing the options, once knowing what the host is trying to do with his program, who he is trying to reach, it is your task to package what you've got so that it is of interest to both host and targeted market.

Don't make the classic mistake of those approaching the media and assume that each program is the same and that one letter and one line of reasoning will fit all. It won't.

Treat your program content as a lump of clay and mold it in such a way that it is appealing to the audience of each show on which you want to appear. This is not as difficult as you might think.

I have myself taken such subjects as fund raising for nonprofit organizations and consulting and made them appealing both to senior citizens shows and those explicitly directed to the disco market. The trick is constantly reworking your material so that it fits, like a hand in glove, the individual program you are approaching.

As you become adept at doing so, you, too, will rock around the clock as the twenty-four hour a day, luxuriously unabashed self-promoter.

Just give me a little credit for helping you along.

CHAPTER 13

ARRANGING YOUR ELECTRONIC MEDIA INTERVIEW

Now that you know the available formats, you are ready to take the next step to getting on radio and television. This chapter is an important one. If you master its content you will stand head and shoulders above your competitors for precious air time and have the very real likelihood of getting the exposure you want and need to promote your product or service.

Prepare Your Message

If you have been reading this book in sequence, you already know how important it is to be clear about what you are saying — and why. You must know who your target audience is, why they should care about what you're doing, the benefits they will derive and why you are the best person to speak on the subject. If you have any questions on this subject, review Chapter 9. Media people have limited attention spans and very limited interest in any subject. By following the methods outlined in this book, you will get access to them, but the access will be meaningless unless you are prepared to say, crisply and directly, just why they — and their audience — should be interested. Remember: you may have only two or three minutes to make your case. Under these circumstances it behooves you to be very, very clear as to why anyone should pay attention to you.

I like to present my message in terms of who will benefit from what I have to say. How will the specific audience of a given program (whose demographics I have researched) be improved because of me, my message, service, product. On air personalities are always concerned about keeping their audiences happy. If you can show them and their producers how you can be of assistance in meeting their objectives, you are very likely to get the exposure you require.

Prepare Advance Documents

Once you have thought through your message, it is time to draft a series of helpful documents, some or all of which you will present to the program producer to make your case for air time. These documents are very important. They clearly demonstrate that you are a professional, concerned about meeting the needs of the station personnel, well versed in what they require, desirous of helping them in what they must do: produce a superb program. Remember: there are people in the media business who pride themselves on their willingness to break in fresh talent, people who have not yet been on radio or television. It was my very good fortune to stumble across such a man when I began on radio. But they are very, very rare.

Most media people, anxiety-ridden anyway, living in an industry which is inherently unstable and where careers can be ridiculously short-lived, are conservative. They don't like taking chances, although they love the deceptive rhetoric of innovation and progress. In fact, they are largely forced by circumstances to deal with people who are known quantities and can deliver a known result. They don't like experimentation, risk, or uncertainty.

If you are without experience, therefore, and you present yourself in a casual or unprofessional way, you are very much lessening the likelihood that you will get air time. By carefully preparing both your case and your support materials, however, you present yourself in the best way, that is as someone who can dependably deliver a product and who can minimize the risk of a very risky business.

Leave Behinds

It should be clear by now that I think the unabashed self-promoter should first deal with print media before going into electronic media. This is not just whimsy. Electronic media has a warmth and an immediacy that print media can only rarely match. But it is also ephemeral in a way that print media is not. Print media remains behind, tangible evidence with substance that can be viewed and reviewed. Not so electronic media.

To be successful in electronic media, the unabashed self-promoter ordinarily needs to be successful in print. This success in print gives you legitimacy and desirability in the eyes of the electronic media. I am firmly convinced of this. Success in print gives the unabashed self-promoter what I call alternative credentials, alternative that is to the licenses, degrees and certificates which delight the middle class professional and give him the security he craves.

Unfortunately, these licenses, degrees and certificates do not unduly impress media people. They deal daily with the great and near great (even if only circumstantially so), and besides as repositories and deliverers of The Truth, mere earthly consequence is of no significance. What matters to media people is demonstrated success in the only area they regard as worthwhile — that is media itself. And this — for most self-promoters — necessarily means print media since this kind of exposure abides.

Production of Leave Behinds

At the beginning of your self-promotional career, all articles by or about you should be turned into leave behinds. After awhile if you are conscientiously following my suggestions, you will have so many articles that you can pick and choose which to use as leave behinds.

As should by now be apparent, speed in producing these leave behinds is critical if you intend to use them as inducements to the media to give you further coverage. In this regard, having a beneficial relationship with a printer is of the utmost significance. I have carefully cultivated such a relationship. On the day an important article by or about me appears, I have my printer drop by and pick it up; I get 1000-2000 copies within 3-4 days.

Note: Just how many copies you order of an article will depend on how much self-promotion you intend to do. At times, I have printed up as many as 50,000 pieces.

Remember: a good article by or about you has an effective life span of at least a year, maybe more. From one particularly good piece in the Business Section of the **Boston Globe,** we drew calls for *over* two years. This, I think, is unusual.

Finally, make sure that all leave behinds are printed on your stationery with your name, address, and telephone number. The samples in this book will give you the idea.

Introduction

"Who are you?", the caterpillar demands of Alice in **Alice in Wonderland.** Who indeed? Media personnel will want to know.

You need to produce a 50-word introduction of yourself suitable to be read over the air which you present as part of your initial media packet. The purpose of this introduction is twofold:

- it will establish you as an expert worthy of notice
- it will allow you to control how you are introduced on the air.

Most media people are only too happy to give you, the unabashed self-promoter, the opportunity to present yourself in the best light. The self-written introduction allows you to do so.

This introduction should list:

- your name
- your company affiliation
- your title or position
- relevant educational background
- recent articles by or about you
- recent books
- citations or other awards
- relevant products or services
- follow-up telephone number or way you can be reached

Here's how a couple of my own introductions might read:

"Dr. Jeffrey Lant is president of Jeffrey Lant Associates, Inc. a Cambridge, Massachusetts management consulting firm for nonprofit organizations. Dr. Lant, a graduate of Harvard, is author of **The Consultant's Kit** and **Development Today: A Guide For Nonprofit Organizations.**"

"Dr. Jeffrey Lant is president of Jeffrey Lant Associates, Inc., of Cambridge, Massachusetts. Dr. Lant and his firm specialize in Capital Campaign fund raising for nonprofit organizations. These methods are the subject of a recent article in **The Grantsmanship Center News,** a leading publication in the field."

Never, never leave anything as important as your introduction to chance, either to your media target, or, ultimately, his audience. Craft it yourself.

You may title this document, "Who is the guest?," and type your material on an 8½" by 11" paper.

Context Document

Once you have suitably established who you are, you next must clarify what your subject is and why it's important. Understand this: media people know surprisingly little about issues. That is why they have such short attention spans. They are experts in packaging and delivery, but most have ridiculously little background in program content. Even if they have good, well-rounded educations, however (something we can only wish for), they would still not know about your subject as you do, and would very likely have no idea of why it is important or worth dealing with.

Your leave behinds go far towards filling this gap, of course. Electronic media people get many of their stories from print sources, a fact which consistently rankles many print journalists. Your third-party validation by a print source (either through an article by or about you) makes you more interesting to electronic media. However, it still helps to clarify just what your subject is and why it is important. Like all else regarding the media, you must do so in just a few well-chosen words.

In about 100-250 words, provide information on:

- what your subject is
- a definition of terms if your subject is likely to be unknown to the reader
- compelling statistics about the dimensions of the subject. How many people are involved? How many of them are in the marketing area of the media source?
- how the subject relates to the listener population of the media target
- any other helpful information which will clearly demonstrate to the reader the importance of the subject, the number of people affected by it, and why it is of consequence now.

Here's what one of my Context Statements might look like:

Why Talk About Nonprofit Organizations Today?

Everyone is affected by nonprofit organizations, everyone. They educate us from kindergarten through post-graduate school. The provide us with medical assistance. They enrich our lives culturally. They are our day care centers, churches, civic groups, professional and trade organizations. There are one million such organizations across the nation. Yet many of these organizations are in trouble. They face:

- unprecedented federal government budget cuts
- state tax-cutting initiatives
- a lower return on their long-term investments
- higher personnel costs
- fewer Americans giving to the charity of their choice.

24,000 of these organizations are in Massachusetts. What can be done to help?

Dr. Jeffrey Lant, president of a Cambridge management consulting firm for nonprofit organizations, knows the problems of the nonprofit world. He has also devised some timely solutions. The author of **Development Today: A Guide For Nonprofit Organizations,** Dr. Lant can put the problems in perspective and offer a series of constructive, efficient, economical solutions.

There's nothing new about nonprofit organizations. There is something new — and dangerous —about their current plight, however.

This plight will be well known to members of your audience, for without exception the lives of every member of your audience are affected in one way or another by nonprofit organizations.

As a guest on your show, Dr. Jeffrey Lant will help them help themselves — by offering not merely an overview of a troubled situation but also practical steps they can take to help their organizations raise the money they need to provide the services that are so important to all of us.

Note: You, the unabashed self-promoter, are clearly brought into the Context Document as someone who is an authority on the subject and can deal with it. Remember: media people are constantly publicizing problems. Through their public affairs programs, however, they like to suggest solutions, too. The Context Document allows the unabashed self-promoter both to suggest the importance and dimensions of the subject, and how he as a problem solver fits into it. It gives media people the "hook" they are always seeking.

The same Context Document above shows that your subject area need not be new. Nonprofit organizations have been around a good long time. But you must have a new wrinkle, in this case the funding crisis and what can be done about it.

Media List

You have now produced materials which demonstrate that there is a subject of interest to the listeners, that you are the expert who can deal with it in a helpful way and that, through your print media leave behinds, you have already been doing so. Now indicate that you have already done so on the electronic media.

As you begin to appear on media, keep a complete list of all the programs you do. Demonstrating that you are "media worthy" means that you have an enhanced likelihood of garnering even more air time. Remember: media people are not risk takers. They want to stick with a known quantity, the tried and true. By submitting a media listing of other programs, you demonstrate that you are this quantity, not only that you think you can produce a valuable product but that you have already done so.

Clearly this is a list you maintain until you are a household word. Clearly, too, it is not something you have on your first day as an unabashed self-promoter. Don't worry about it. Just plan to produce it as soon as you can. Here's the information you need:

- name of program
- call letters of station
- city, state
- name of host and/or producer
- kind of program
- market position, if known
- date of broadcast (or taping, if broadcast date unknown)

Thus, " 'David Brudnoy Show', WRKO Radio, Boston, MA. Jon Keller, producer. Evening call-in. #1 in time slot. April 23, 1983."

You have now demonstrated that you are a pro, that you've had experience, that you have been deemed acceptable by colleagues in the industry. All this is important. Given the incestuous nature of the media and the peripatetic nature of practitioners, it is entirely possible that either the host or his producer is known to the people you are now approaching. This, too, will strengthen your case.

Note: you may occasionally have to alter your list to suit an individual case. Let's assume you have done only the Brudnoy show above and no others. If you wanted other Boston evening call-in show exposure, it would not be in your interest to let them know that you appeared on a competitive program. In this case you are actually better off without a demonstration of experience.

By the same token, however, the moment you moved out of the Boston market to, say, Providence, you would want to go after a comparable program to the one you had already done, in this case evening call in. Your appearance on the Brudnoy show indicates expertise with a particular radio format. As you approach other markets, capitalize on your experience, and get in touch with comparable programs. You will be in a particularly strong position if the station you are approaching is a sister station to one on which you have already appeared or is part of the same network. The next chapter tells you how to discover this important information.

Sample Tape

Again, I want to stress how seldom media people are willing to take risks with the people they put on the air. All the material for which you have now been given guidelines is designed to reassure them, to soothe their anxiety and prove that you will not be an embarrassment, such as they all too frequently encounter.

But all this material is written — and hence rather foreign to electronic media personnel. They prefer tape. Thus, whenever possible, you should have a tape available of a recent media appearance.

It is no problem getting these tapes once you're on the air. All you need to do is ask the producer of either a radio or television show — in advance of your arrival, please — whether he can produce a copy of your performance. He will tell you whether:

- he has the facilities
- he has the cassette tape
- you can buy the cassette tape or get it gratis because of your appearance
- you need to bring your own cassette (in the case of a radio program).

The producers are quite prepared for this request, less because of unabashed self-promoters and more because of the media ingénue who wishes to share a copy with Aunt Harriet and so confirm his celebrity standing.

As far as television is concerned, audio-visual cassettes cost between $25-50. Audio cassettes for radio shows are much cheaper, under $5; in fact, ordinarily the radio station simply gives them to guests. I have found that in practice you need about one television tape a year, just enough to indicate that you continue to be fetching and charismatic; you will have more need for radio tapes. If I were you, I'd duplicate these tapes for future use. It should go without saying that you should never send an original tape as you are very unlikely to get it back.

Make sure that on the cassette you number the sides, write your name, the subject of your remarks, the radio station call letters, program and play (or tape) date, at the very least. If you have a cassette of an entire show on which you were only featured in part, note the area of the tape (by number) where the listener can find you. No media person wants to take the trouble to hear last April's weather and stock quotations. Do everything you can to make the listener's job easier.

"But I Haven't Been On The Air Yet!"

No problem. There is an acceptable alternative. As mentioned in an earlier chapter, make sure that you tape all your speeches and oral presentations, the speeches you are having covered by articles about you. Tapes of these speeches, particularly if they deal with the subject of your proposed program are not as good as an actual broadcast, but they will do. They indicate to the producers or on air personality that you know what you're talking about, you are a recognized expert, you can hold an audience's attention and that an organization has thought well enough of you to invite you to come. All this is in your favor.

As with on air tapes, make sure these cassettes are clearly marked with:

- your name
- the subject of your remarks
- the name of the sponsoring organization
- city
- date of presentation.

And, again, never send your only copy.

Sample Question List

The Sample Question List is particularly helpful at the interview itself, but it is also worth sending in advance of scheduling because it gives the producer or on air host a fairly clear indication of how the interview will proceed and what material it will bring out.

In preparing your question list, consider what a moderately intelligent, reasonably informed individual might know about your subject. Not much, right? You cannot assume any prior knowledge about your subject. Thus, the questions must begin at the beginning and carry through to unveil who is affected, how many are affected, what difference it makes whether what you are proposing is done (or is not), whether the current trend will continue, &c. Your interview must be an entirely self-contained package, even though it may only last 90 seconds. Clearly, the shorter the interview, the more artful the process of producing this result.

Here's what a Question List might look like for me, if I were being interviewed as the author of **The Consultant's Kit:**

- What is a consultant?
- Where did the word come from?
- How many consultants are there?
- What fields do they practice in?
- Can anyone be a consultant?
- What special training do you need to become a successful consultant?
- What makes a successful consultant successful?
- Do you have any advice for beginning consultants?
- Can you run a successful consulting business from your home?
- Is consulting especially interesting to retirees and women who want to work part-time?
- How did you, Dr. Lant, get into consulting?
- What does your consulting firm do?
- You've been featured in a book called **Maverick: Succeeding As A Free-Lance Entrepreneur.** What's that about?
- How's **The Consultant's Kit** doing?
- You're associated with 23 universities around the country teaching workshops on consulting. Who takes these programs?
- What is the future of consulting?
- Are you, Dr. Lant, going to keep writing about consulting?

The questions you write are designed for several purposes:

- They give the broadcaster who might use them a framework and a sequence, thus making his job easier.
- The answers provide the listener with two kinds of information:
  - background material about the subject so that he has a listening context, and
  - material about you, the expert.

The Sample Question List is designed for an interview of about one-half hour. 15-20 questions should be more than adequate for this amount of time given the fact that you must take into account commercial interruptions and the fact that the host will presumably have a couple of questions of his own.

Basically, in my Sample Question List, the first ten questions are designed to provide the reasonably intelligent but otherwise uninformed listener with a context so that he can understand and appreciate the information you are providing.

The remaining questions, by and large, are intended to give you, the unabashed self-promoter, the chance to speak to your place in the field (image enhancement) and the special worth and value of your goods and services.

The Question List is effectively divided between what the station sees as its first responsibility, namely providing listeners with valuable news and public affairs information, and your own needs and objectives as a self-promoter. The successful self-promoter early learns how to balance these potentially conflicting but actually quite symbiotic goals.

Announcement Of Forthcoming Event

If you are promoting an event such as a workshop, speech, &c, then you should also produce in advance a brief (25-50 word) announcement which both confirms your status as an expert and can be read on the air. Such an announcement should include:

- your name
- your title
- the subject of your presentation
- sponsoring organization
- date
- time
- place
- telephone number for follow-up information

Thus, "Dr. Jeffrey Lant, president of Jeffrey Lant Associates, Inc. of Cambridge will speak on 'Unabashed Self-Promotion To Build Your Consulting Business' at the Boston Computer Society at MIT on Thursday, May 19 at 6:30 p.m. For further information contact John Sturm at 536-5390."

Draft Cover Letter

Now that you have completed your basic packet of materials, you have one more document to draft, the basic cover letter which will accompany these materials and which will, in fact introduce you.

This letter only helps you to the extent that it persuades the media target to peruse the remainder of materials you have developed. It can, however, hurt you substantially, for if it is not good, well-written, cogent and alluring, you will already have a strike against you as your reader may decline to review the remainder of your material. Thus, though the cover letter will probably be written last, it is of the first importance. It should contain:

- an opening paragraph about the subject on which you propose to speak. Cite the existence of a current article or pertinent local leave behind.
- a second paragraph indicating who you are, the source of your expertise
- a third paragraph listing enclosures
- a fourth and final paragraph indicating that you will contact the media target by telephone in the near future (see examples, page 332).

Production Of Media Packet

All materials should be produced on your stationery with your name, address and telephone number clearly visible. Each page should be headed with the title of the item following. Short items can be put together on one page such as the Introduction, Context Statement, and Media List. You may use both sides of the page to minimize the number of sheets you have to send, but it is good to keep the different formats on different sheets, if possible.

Optional Item

Particularly when you are dealing with television where bright white teeth and angelic smiles are at a premium, it is wise to send a photograph. Or you can do as I do, namely indicate that a photograph is available if they require one. Since my photograph appears in most articles about me and several articles by me, media personnel have at least some idea that I am not a latterday troll.

What Not To Send

The materials which I have suggested you prepare should give any media person all the information he needs about you and your subject. Beware of how you deviate from my suggestions. Do not, for instance, place letters of recommendation or a résumé in your packet. You are not applying for a job. One of my acquaintances (whom I regard as sunk amidst the innumerable lost souls of this earth), makes it a point of sending letters from past employers and his résumé to media sources. This strikes me as most unprofessional and detrimental to your status as the perceived authority in your field. Job applicants carry these negligible materials; the unabashed self-promoter is a mandarin figure whose credibility is confirmed by the thorough preparedness of materials designed to reassure the media target and by the fact that members of the print media have already found him worthy of coverage.

Note: the materials which you prepare must be continually updated and revised as you receive more and still more print exposure and air time. The media business is fluid, very, very fluid. You must be, too. I am constantly at work tinkering with my introductory packet, updating it, deleting items past their usefulness, adding more compelling pieces.

Don't be like the man who, with deep pride, showed me his media packet only to be told by me, in a burst of characteristic candor, that it was absurdly unsatisfactory: there was nothing in it, nothing, not a date, a clipping, a speech which was not at least a year old. What that packet proclaimed so very clearly was that my poor friend was passé, a fate worse than death to the unabashed self-promoter who must be perceived as forever *au courant.*

Selecting Your Media Targets

Now that you've prepared your background material, you're ready to select the first people to receive it —your initial media targets. Your leave behinds provide you with a guide.

As suggested earlier in this book the unabashed self-promoter ordinarily begins in his own backyard, with his home town newspaper. If you have done so, then your first electronic media exposure should also be in the neighborhood since it will be easier to get.

Again, let us take the sample **Cambridge Chronicle** article on page 314 as the example. Once I knew that this was going to be in print, my next task was to discover whether there were any local radio stations. In fact, there are several, most affiliated with local colleges, a few entirely independent. From them I needed:

- name of program director
- name of director of public affairs
- names of producers of shows I had decided were appropriate for my suggested program
- address
- telephone number

An article in the **Cambridge Chronicle** usually has most impact in Cambridge. If the subject is of widespread interest or has applicability to surrounding towns or the nearest metropolitan area, you can approach stations there, but for the most part a Cambridge article is most useful to you with Cambridge media. This article makes you a local authority and hence of further interest to local electronic media.

Clearly an article in the local newspaper opens only a limited number of electronic media possibilities. Cambridge happens to be well supplied with local radio stations, for instance, given its size, but ours is an unusual situation. The average community of 100,000 people might just have one station, perhaps not any.

You may decide, however, that — for now — one program is all you want to do. In that case use your print leave behind to leverage your connection with the electronic target, and leave further self-promotion to another day. As you might gather, however, for me one program is never enough.

Those who share my sentiment must do as I do: either reprint their basic article (adding local detail) in another newspaper in a city with additional radio and television targets, or do so for the nearest metropolitan area. My sequence of examples beginning on page 314 demonstrates that I did the latter.

I took a version of the article appearing in the **Cambridge Chronicle** and updated it for a major metropolitan daily. When this article appeared, I then had access to all the radio and television stations of Boston, a major media market.

Given the subject you are writing about, the importance of your material, your own standing in the field, competing stories and the like, you should have a fair surmise as to whether your article will be printed or not. If you do not now have a good grasp of possibilities, you will quickly develop one.

If you feel confident your article will be printed, draw up a list of media sources, both print and electronic, to which you will direct it once it is published. Chapter 10 gives you more help with other print possibilities. Now you must also decide how much electronic mileage you can get out of the piece and how much time you are prepared to spend to get a beneficial result. Targeting is the result of your deliberations.

As each print media piece of mine goes to be published, I make a determination about how valuable the subject matter is and how much electronic media coverage I need now and can milk it for. Let us say I have done my last complete sweep of the media (see Chapter 15) two months before, but that I was then unable to schedule two radio stations and one television station which said, in effect, "Get back to us." The article is my chance to do so.

If, however, I have not done a media wave in 4 or 5 months and have nothing planned for a comparable period (actually inconceivable in my case, since I plan for a minimum of two sweeps a year or more, usually three), then I will want to leverage my article to get a goodly harvest of electronic media.

Just what a "goodly harvest" constitutes depends on such variables as:

- the subject of the article
- the "news hook" you have developed
- your perceived expertise
- the professional completion of your media packet
- competing stories

If I had no sweep of the media planned, if I had not had one recently, if the variables listed above were auspicious, I would aim for at least six or more programs. The final key is time: once having contacted a media source, remember that it will ordinarily take you several telephone calls, very likely the mailing of several additional packets, much aggravation and irritation to complete the sale. Moreover, I think it unwise for the unabashed self-promoter to drop a connection without seeing it through to the end, yes or no. If you drop it midway, it is not only unprofessional but it indicates to the media source that you can be put off. This is not the message that I, as an unabashed self-promoter, want to communicate. I want media people with whom I do business to know that I intend to carry through on every connection I initiate and that nothing, nothing will put me off. If they learn this early about you, you will spare yourself much subsequent frustration.

At this point it is important to remind you that tracking down media personnel is dull, thankless work, but a considerable part of the self-promotional game. The people you are dealing with — unless they want you (in which case they regain their manners) are all too often thoughtless, rude, ill-bred. They do not return telephone calls, lose materials with reckless abandon, and disdain organization. That is why the novice self-promoter can only handle a limited number of possible broadcast options at any given time. For myself, the paradigm, 20 contacts is quite sufficient. This number constitutes a media wave or sweep.

One final point: remember that the object for the unabashed self-promoter is continual exposure. Thunderclaps are all very well, but they are of limited utility. The unabashed self-promoter seeks continuing waves of exposure over his target audience. If waves are what you want (and they should be), you only want to use a fraction of the media available in your local area at any given time. If you live in a community with only two radio stations and are unwilling to expand your horizons, the worst thing would be to appear on both simultaneously unless you had a hard news angle. For feature material on you, you need one to feature you today, the other in six months. This would be the best use of available outlets.

Draw Up Your Media Activity Chart

Once you have selected your targets and you have the names of suitable programs, their on air hosts, producers, addresses and telephone numbers, it is time for an electronic media activity chart. (See page 321). This chart will allow you to track progress and will come in very handy when you set out on your next media foray, which you as an unabashed self-promoter are duty bound to do.

Contacting The Electronic Media

(Note: At this point it would be useful if you reviewed the steps used in contacting the print media. See Chapter 9.)

Before you write a cold letter to any media source, think twice. Do you have a contact who can help you? If so, refer back to Chapter 5 and the Pyramid of Contacts. This is the point to use your sales skills to get your contact to move on your behalf. Remember that you want to hear, "I'll take care of it for you." Press hard to get your contact to do the selling job for you. He can give you automatic acceptance with the media source and ease your way in. Don't, however, wait forever. If you have a contact who refuses to act on your behalf, then call and use his name. This is not the best alternative, but as your options narrow, use it.

The Telephone

As with the print media, you will have to make numerous telephone calls to electronic media personnel before you get through. That's part of the game. The steps you will probably have to go through are outlined in Chapter 9. There is one major difference, however: electronic media personnel will be much more concerned with how you look (for television) and sound (for both radio and television) than print media journalists. If you have done your homework, however, you are prepared: you have both photographs and tapes available, if necessary. Never hesitate to suggest that you have them and to ask your contacts whether they would like to receive what you've got.

Dangling On A String

In my experience, electronic media people do not like to say "No!" to a project, and they will generally avoid doing so if there is even the most remote likelihood that they may use you and your material. There is a reason for this deliberate vagueness, and it isn't a charitable disposition on their part either. It's anxiety about having enough material on hand to produce the product they must have ready at a designated time.

Within both the print and electronic media an intricate puzzle is being assembled, every minute. The problem is that unlike a jigsaw puzzle, no one really knows how the pieces fit together or whether there are even sufficient pieces to make the final result. That's why media people keep us on strings, dangling, both unable and unwilling to give us a definite response until their deadline is very near at hand.

One situation among several underscores why media personnel are anxious — and why they keep their options open. In April as I was walking out the door of a Milton, Massachusetts radio station having completed two hours live on the air, the producer of the show tapped the host on her shoulder and broke the bad news: tomorrow's guest had just cancelled. She was stricken, visibly stricken, and asked me if I had any suggestions. I now had a gift of two hours of air time at my disposal and had I not been en route to another city I would have spent some time on the telephone putting another self-promoter in my debt through a very handsome gift.

- guests cancel
- guests forget (Yes, even this is true.)
- news developments alter circumstances

The media world is necessarily fluid. Under these necessarily uncertain conditions, it is little wonder that media people keep us on strings, infuriating though it is.

There are two things you can do:

- **Be Persistent**

As I have often said to aspiring self-promoters, particularly those who are after media in cities other than their home town, keep after producers until the moment the show you are aiming for is aired. Call producers and let them know how they can be in touch with you. If they have evinced any interest in your topic (and if you don't know, ask), let them know you are at their disposal if they need you. Work with media people as with any other colleague, for the unabashed self-promoter and media personnel are necessarily colleagues in a curious but symbiotic relationship. Remember the old Beatles' line, "I get by with a little help from my friends." Let your media colleagues know that you can provide that help if necessary.

- **Do The Same Thing In Your Home Town As Out Of Town.**

I customarily let my Boston-based media friends know that if they find themselves with a hole to plug, for *whatever* reason and at *whatever* time of the day or night, I am at their disposal. I am unabashedly willing to step into any situation and pinch hit, and my quite earnest desire to be of assistance to them has provided me with many media spots I wouldn't have otherwise received.

I recall, for instance, the day I got a call from a local television host who said, "Jeffrey, we were going to have a boxer on the show today, but he forgot. Can you get over here in 15 minutes?" "What do you want me to talk about?," I said. "Something in the news," he replied, "like terrorism."

As it happened, I was about to teach an adult education course on terrorism and had just written an article on the subject. It was a good topic for him to have selected.

The host so liked the program that he decided, half way through, to make a mini-series on it. He told me to go home, change clothes, and come back ready to tape "tomorrow's" program.

I did.

On another occasion, also involving a television channel, I was called to appear immediately, in the urgent, peremptory way television personnel have. This time I named the subject — one of my books. I arrived just in time to calm a very nervous host, who was so grateful, she asked me whether I'd like to go on her Sunday evening show, syndicated in 10 states. I gratefully accepted.

Why do I put myself at the disposal of beings who are notoriously disorganized, capricious, unmannerly? To be given, without asking, a half hour of television time in 10 states, that's why.

The unabashed self-promoter must be ever conscious of the peculiar restraints and conditions under which media people work. The chief of these is the ever-pressing uncertainty about program content. While this is infuriating when we are unknown quantities and media personnel are unwilling to make a commitment to us, it can work to our advantage once we have proven we are a good guest, knowledgeable, charming, empathetic, endearing to all sorts and conditions of men.

Handling your interview in the proper way leads to this blissful result.

CHAPTER 14

THE SUCCESSFUL INTERVIEW

So, you're about to go on the air. It's a thrilling sensation, isn't it? Savor the moment. It is one of the undeniable delights of unabashed self-promotion that you have been selected from among the thousands who crave this opportunity. Congratulate yourself. You've earned it.

But don't stop thinking or preparing. Remember: you could still defeat your purposes — and emerge much worse off — by bumbling your interview. There's nothing much to be said for obscurity, unless you're stupid, ill-prepared, myopic, sloppy and disorganized in which case, believe me, you're a lot better off.

Your forthcoming appearance will allow you to achieve one or more of the following results:

- become better known
- publicize your product or service
- enhance your image
- make money

When I go on the air I aim to achieve all of these.

So should you.

The steps in this chapter will allow you to successfully meet your objectives and stand forth as a cool, calm, empathetic professional eager to help producers and on-air personalities produce the high calibre products they want — and must have if they are going to remain in the business.

BEFORE THE SHOW

Getting Your Materials Together

To get your interview date, you have had to make ten telephone calls, deal with two different producers because of a characteristic staff change, send three sets of material, and schedule and then reschedule your appearance. Surely all you have to do now is appear, right?

Think again!

First, no matter how many sets of information you have sent ahead to the producer never assume that any will be on hand for your interview appearance. Make sure you take a *complete* set of information, a copy of each document you wish either the producer or on-air personality to have. Make sure, too, that you bring a duplicate of any product you intend to have displayed on a television show or that you wish the host to discuss on radio.

I am usually very good about this. From lamentable experience I have learned that the axiom "out of sight, out of mind" applies no where so much as with media personnel. Therefore I customarily travel with complete media packets and assorted copies of my books.

Needless to say on the one occasion I did not do this, I was tripped up. I arrived at a television studio in New York for a nationally-syndicated broadcast. My New York publicist, a very dogged fellow, had sent — count 'em — *three* copies of one of my books until he was finally sure one had arrived (that is to say, until the host actually held it in his hand and said, "I have it!"). All for naught. The host's office and the studio were not in the same building.

Thus when I arrived one of the dewey-eyed production assistants said, "You did bring a copy of your book, didn't you?" Didn't I? Didn't I?

I was the only guest on the set without a brightly-colored gewgaw thrust in the eye of the electronic polyphemus filming us. And I was very, very chagrined — at myself, mind you. For it does no good, no good at all, to be irked at the childlike creatures who frolic on the set and purport to be in charge of production and program delivery. Like any other two-year-old, they are legally incompetent and while decidedly irritating are beyond criticism.

So be it.

Bring duplicates of everything. If you don't have it with you, it isn't available.

Confirm The Date

Don't assume that the date you have written in your calendar is in fact the date. Call — a day in advance —to confirm. Also, if you are a live guest, call again the day of your appointment if a major news story breaks. For safety's sake, do the same even if you are only taping.

Again, I have learned to confirm from harsh experience. But what I have also learned is that even a confirmation doesn't necessarily mean anything. I remember one occasion with a Boston radio station where after confirming my date, I appeared, only to be told — by a secretary — that "something has come up for the host."

A few months later this negligent host had moved to another radio station where she again scheduled an interview and again, after reconfirmation, pulled the same trick after keeping me waiting in her office. On this occasion I allowed myself the ultimate luxury of writing to the general manager of the radio station a stinging letter of complaint. Needless to say there was no answer. Media people constitute a law unto themselves. Knowing this, you will be sure to reconfirm — as close to your appearance as possible.

Dress

Dress in conformity with your image and with the product or service you are promoting. As an All American Whiz Kid, I can comfortably forego tailored three-piece suits, Rolex watches, Gucci shoes and the other outward appurtenances of corporate arrivism. So can the Frontiersman, the All-American Mother, and, most often, The Sage.

Other books in dressing for television universally dispense the same advice:

Men: Don't wear white shirts, go for a cute number in blue.

Women: Avoid polka dots, loud stripes, hot colors like irredescent oranges and flaming reds. Dress cool. But avoid white.

This advice is acceptable as far as it goes. But it doesn't really go very far.

The clothes you wear must be consonant with your image. This is the important thing. If you do this, you can break the rules with impunity.

I remember one occasion last summer when I was doing a television taping on a very hot day. I arrived at the station in a bright red blazer, red tie, white ducks and penny loafers — no socks. I thought I looked dazzling, and I wasn't worried about the absence of socks because, I reasoned, no one was going to be shooting my feet, right?

Wrong.

This particular talk show involved the host and her guest sitting on a raised dais. Both the opening and closing shots were long — and neatly encompassed my naked feet.

After her initial shock had abated, the host shrugged and the show went on. Months later when I returned she said, in a very pointed introduction, "Well, Jeffrey, I see things must be going better for you than last summer, since you're wearing socks."

Still, the absence of these socks went neatly along with my Tom Finn demeanor. On the whole, however, I recommend podostical propriety.

I suggest it for radio, too.

Although I have broadcast for radio wearing clothes of the utmost casualness, my general advice, particularly for beginners, is to consider both the format of the program and your objective and to dress accordingly. If you are doing an all-night call-in show and need to come across as sultry and seductive in your selling, by all means wear something soft and caressing (I have a Pendleton shirt which is most appropriate) to get in the mood. This outfit, however, would be manifestly inappropriate when you are doing the news, which must be clipped, quick-moving and authoritative. Pajamas with feet just don't package you properly here.

The late Lord Reith, a founding father and authoritative titan of the British Broadcasting Corporation, had the right sartorial idea. When doing the news he had newsreaders (which is just the right word for them) don evening dress (whatever the hour) so as to deliver the received word with just the right degree of sonorous solemnity and seriousness. For this alone his lordship deserved his coronet.

Transportation

Mandarins don't drive themselves. The ultimate mandarins, of course, have limousines and chauffeurs. This, I reluctantly confess, is still only an aspiration for me, though I suspect the royalties from this book will enable me to ascend to another celestial plateau. (Not a moment too soon, either.) Even so pocket mandarins of relatively pinched circumstances should not drive themselves to their media destinations. This is not just a matter of status either.

Those who drive themselves to media appointments often arrive out of breath, out of sorts, surly and agitated due to the transgressions of other drivers who cannot be made to see the importance of your arriving in time and in pristine condition.

Either take a taxi or get a driver. Then you don't have to worry about finding a convenient parking place or about how your hair will look after you've walked seven blocks in the rain.

Use this extra time to your best advantage. It is amazing to me how much of people's lives are absorbed by the mere tiresome business of commuting, getting places. This is time for the unabashed self-promoter to be thoughtful and creative, an opportunity to get yet another jump on the run-of-the-mill mandarin. I am therefore abrupt in discouraging conversation by garrulous cabbies or from drivers who presume that my physical proximity to them is an invitation to get better acquainted. Instead, I use the time to:

- read material for further articles, books and broadcasts
- draft these articles and books
- draw up lists of activities to be accomplished
- outline speeches
- refine piercing epigrams
- review the status of pending media engagements
- scheme about life in general.

As a matter of course, I arrive at the station in a very chipper mood, even if this is contrived, as it sometimes must be.

I recall, for instance, a very blustery February day when I was scheduled to do a television show in New Bedford, Massachusetts. My driver's car broke down half way there, fortunately outside a gas station. Alas! The source of the problem proved elusive and, as my desperation grew, I got later and later.

The situation was saved, perhaps, by repeated telephone calls to the station reporting progress (or lack of same), although I was given a stern admonition about how long the production crew could be kept. When I finally arrived at the studio, very cold, very dissheveled, but too late to wash my face before taping, it took a moment, I'll confess, to compose myself. But Truman Taylor is a superb interviewer, and he conducted one of my best performances.

If you are going to be late, even 10 minutes late, call and alert the show's producer. Media people thrive on instant communication even of essentially pointless information. Give it to them.

In The Waiting Room

At last you are in the building. You should feel a quickening of the tempo which began, at the inception of your desire to appear, *lentement* and accelerates by air time to *furioso*. You have important work to accomplish before you go on, however — work which can be of significant value to your continuing career as an unabashed self-promoter.

If you are placed in an exterior waiting area (before being passed into the electronic inner sanctum), try to accomplish at least the following:

- Discern whether you'll be meeting alone with the producer or host.

If you are, you have some work to accomplish, work that relates not only to this particular appearance but to further appearances on other stations.

Ask the receptionist whether you will have the opportunity of meeting with the producer in advance of the show (or the host, if he doubles as his own producer). Whatever you may have been told in advance about a pre-air meeting may or may not hold true at the time of your arrival, so ask again. What you do depends on what you're now told.

If the receptionist informs you that you will have a pre-show producer interview, you can go on to the second task below.

If the receptionist says you are not going to have this interview, inquire (if you do not already know) whether you are the last guest on the program, that is that the host finishes for the day with you. If so, and if you have time to do so, you can stay behind five or ten minutes to accomplish some important objectives. If not, at least one of these needs to be accomplished now.

If you are not going to have a pre-show interview and either cannot wait at the end of the broadcast to talk with host or producer or the show continues, ask the receptionist this question:

- Is this station (television or radio) part of a chain?
- If so, can you get me the call letters and cities of your sister stations and their addresses and telephone numbers?

It should by now be obvious why you want this information: It is most useful for networking purposes. If you have appeared on station XYZ in Baltimore, it is likely that you can parlay this into an appearance on sister station ABC in Toledo. Moreover, if personnel at one station are not actually acquainted with personnel at another, at the very least their names will be familiar.

It goes without saying that the receptionist will not know this information. Secretaries and receptionists make a point of destroying excess brain cells by prolonged inactivity and disuse; since there is no compelling reason why they should bother knowing information about sister stations, they ostentatiously ignore it. Your inquiry will, I guarantee you, be the first of its kind, unless, of course, I have preceeded you to the station.

If the receptionist does not have this information you have several options:

- You can ask her to request it of the producer.
- You can request it directly from the producer at your (no matter how short) meeting.
- You can request it when you send your thank-you note.
- You can ask your publicist (or driver) to gather it while you are on the air; (any opportunity to keep these people active while you are at work is to be seized.)

Don't forget it, however, just because the receptionist is determinedly obtuse.

Listen To The Station

Whenever possible (including during transportation to the program), listen to the station, and, if possible, to the program on which you'll be appearing. This latter will be possible if you are not to be the first guest on a live program.

Knowing your place is important and should not be left to your arrival at the studio. Media people are, perhaps justifiably, concerned that they deliver a complete product; they are not, however, concerned at all about your schedule and your other responsibilities. They therefore habitually ask *all* guests on a program to arrive for the first segment, well knowing that the rest will have to cool their heels for longer and still longer times with nothing to do but wilt and grow dropsical.

They arrange matters thus to allay their own considerable anxieties. Often, even when pressed, they will not disclose the order of appearance, just so you are compelled to appear early — or risk missing your slot. This is jejune but frequent. Whenever possible, however, find out just when you are going to appear and act accordingly.

Unless you are going to be made up for television (more and more rare these days), you seldom need to arrive more than a quarter hour before your appearance. Arriving much before this is not so much irritating for the producer as it is bad for you. From time to time in waiting rooms, I find myself losing the adrenalin edge that insures a good performance. Being keyed up is definitely to the advantage of the unabashed self-promoter. Remember the 1976 presidential debates between Carter and Ford? Jimmy had a quiet dinner with Rosalynn before the first debate in Philadelphia. Jerry got revved up by the staff. Carter's performance was wooden, mechanical, programmed, thoroughly unappealing. Ford's was, for the man, admirably enticing. No wonder. You want to exude charisma and attractive electricity, vitality; time to get droopy in the waiting room is not to your advantage.

Peruse The Trade Press

As you sit waiting to be moved to the next step, take advantage of the trade publications at hand, publications such as: **Ad Age, Radio and Records, Earshot, Billboard,** and **Broadcasting.** Scan the columns about format changes and personnel moves. You want to see whether:

- a nearby station has changed into a format beneficial for you. Perhaps a country-western station has gone all talk. This is a good time to move since they probably won't have a backlog of guests.

- any media personnel with whom you have worked have gone on to other positions. One of the ways your Self-Promotion Network naturally grows is when someone you've already been interviewed by moves on. The unabashed self-promoter keeps that contact and retains the contact with his successor. One of the ways to find out where the media tumbleweeds are blowing is through the people columns of trade publications. These you can conveniently peruse while waiting to be interviewed.

With The Producer

More often than not you will have some time alone with the producer of the show; the exception will be at smaller radio stations where a harried host performs this function and is spread too thin to do more than shake your hand before airtime.

The time you spend with the producer must generate several results.

Information About The Producer

I have found that I get very little time with the producer of a show, and there is much to accomplish in it. Primarily what I want is networking information. When I go into a broadcast situation, I expect to do well. Moreover, I expect to have this good result work for me beyond the confines of this single show by leading to other broadcasts. The list of sister stations can be helpful in achieving this objective. So can knowledge about the connections of both the producer and the host.

In practice I have found it necessary to gather this information while being whisked through a vast expanse of unfamiliar corridors by a quick-talking, usually very young producer who is escorting me, the product, into another storage facility there to await ascension. His task is simply to move me into take-off position and replenish his depleted store of documents by taking from me the background material I have already sent again and again.

I have far greater expectations of him.

I have developed the Principle of Assertive Courtesy for such situations. The Principle of Assertive Courtesy advances the unassailable proposition that any individual certain of his objective will always more successfully reach it by lavish and ostentatious attention to the interests of the parties he is dealing with rather than through any comparably ostentatious solicitude regarding his own needs. In short, define everything you are doing in terms of the other party's interests not your own, so that you are perceived as empathetic, not pushy. The more crass your own goals, the more necessary this gymnastic.

Here's how it works. You could simply say, "I need networking information about your prior work history so that I can use it to my self-promotional advantage." You could say this. It is very honest, but it's not very astute. Or you could say, remembering the Principle of Assertive Courtesy, "I've enjoyed working with you. You obviously have had a lot of experience in the business, and it shows. Where have you worked before?"

Here's what you need to find out from the producer during your brief time together:

- prior employment with specific call letters of stations and cities
- types of stations
- other shows with which he is connected both for this station and others (a radio producer may, for instance, have a connection with a non-competing television station)
- whether the producer has his own show.

You also need to know whether:

- the producer can make a tape of your show and will do so
- the station can syndicate your show to other markets
- the station uses snippets of your (radio) show outside the actual program.

You also want to leave the producer with your complete name, address, telephone number and the subject and date of your remarks in case individuals call the station wanting follow-up information about your product and service. I try to leave this information, too, with the receptionist if I am to be the guest on a live program where the calls will be immediate.

Finally, I alert the producer to what my *next* promotion will be, my newest book, a workshop, a forthcoming article, &c. My hope is to snag one or two braincells and begin the process of acclimatizing him to my next venture. As an unabashed self-promoter, I know that I want to come back. I want to use this time, this opportunity with a key decision maker to best advantage by alerting him to another project which will surely be of interest. I have got this date. I want him to know I do not wish it to reside in majestic isolation but be part of a splendid sequence.

All this I must accomplish in startlingly little time with an individual who is probably never giving me more than a moiety of his attention. That's all right. I succeed as well as circumstances allow. Ordinarily it will not be convenient or possible for me to get most of the information in other ways, so I have to do the best I can. That's life.

What makes it easier, however, is that I try to begin the conversation with a compliment about how grateful I am to be appearing, how well organized the producer has been, how conscientious and easy to work with.

To be entirely candid, I may or may not believe these things. But the fact of the matter is that the juvenile producer galloping me down the hall, the producer who barely made it out of college, the producer who hasn't a clue about the great issues and events of our time, is in a position of considerable power and consequence. I may dislike it; I may hope for divine retribution. But there it is. And the unabashed self-promoter is nothing if not a realist. Hence my academy award winning performances in the cool, dimly-lit corridors of media stations around the nation. I am "on" whenever I am dealing with media people and never more than in an initial meeting with a producer. "Was ever contact in this humor woo'd?/Was ever contact in this humor won?" (with apologies to W. Shakespeare.)

In The Green Room

At last, and not so very long after you have met, either, the producer will deposit you in The Green Room, that final waiting area from which you will be called to greatness. From time to time the producer will wait with you there, but not often. He has other duties to perform.

In the green room you, too, have things to do, for it is here that you will find the other guests for the program, some unabashed self-promoters just like you, many new to media and finding refuge either in an avalanche of annoying banalities or a silence so frozen it resembles the frosty aura of a Boston brahmin. You, however, are in the green room not just to wait for your summons but to squeeze advantage from your colleagues.

As anywhere else in the world, the green room has its own peculiar social customs and ranks. The rank of those present corresponds to the amount of time they are getting on the program. Considerations such as wealth, position and intellect are extraneous. Unfortunately, you do not at first know just how much time people are getting, but you can quickly discern as much by the demeanor of the participants.

The unabashed self-promoter cannot be put off by such artificial dividers, however. There is gold to be gleened in the green room, and he must to it.

I have two separate strategies for making myself a success in the green room and gathering the networking information I need. If I can discern from either the receptionist (usually a lost cause) or the producer (who always knows) just who the guests are on the show today, then I either go about the room once greeting all and then seating myself in the midst so that general conversation is possible, or I make the decision which single guest I'd like to meet and position myself accordingly.

I have, however, used other ways.

At one all night television talk show in Boston (very self-consciously modeled after the "Tonight" Show), I arrived in the green room only to discover the guest I most wanted to meet was asleep on the couch. This was not promising. Two jugglers were engaged in practicing their tricks. All that remained was to talk to my publicist and somehow get noticed.

During the writing of this book getting noticed has not been difficult, since I had simply to take out my note pad and begin writing critiques of the guests, thereby gathering useful information and arousing interest. It wasn't long until other guests arrived and started asking what I was doing (*sotto voce* comments to my publicist aided the thawing process). Even the jugglers, who proved to be charming if stilted, were captivated. We ended up with a general exchange of business cards — and some useful information for us about where the others had been appearing. This is, of course, networking material, and my new friends from the green room are critical links in my Self-Promotion Network, because they have direct access to the producers and on-air personalities who can, in their turn, help me.

Meeting The Host

At last, at long last, your air time, your all-too-brief air time has arrived. You have been making good use of the lead-up. Now you must indeed be smashing.

At this point, either a production assistant or producer will call for you or the on-air personality himself (no doubt a bit distraught if he is performing several roles).

You should have ascertained by now whether:

- you will have more than five minutes alone with the host prior to air time
- you will be able to spend a couple of minutes alone with the host after your segment.

If you are going to be able to spend a minute or two with the host after your segment, you need not rush things now. You can concentrate instead on the program itself instead of having to think, as well, about later possibilities.

The Greeting

Don't be shy with the host. Media people, even at the smallest radio stations in the smallest burgs, are in the public relations business. Their trademark is the freely-given hand and the wide-open smile. Reciprocate. All of us, of course, are shy. People who don't know me well are amazed, incredulous when I say that I am shy and inhibited about meeting strangers. But it's true. I always wonder what everybody wonders: will he like me? Will I be good? Will I measure up? Experience, to be sure, suggests the answers, but that was definitely not the case at the beginning. Then it takes courage. Courage, that is, and an abiding belief in yourself.

You know your own very palpable weaknesses and inadequacies. And these may make you shy and hesitant. It's rather like the scene from one of the Hope-Crosby "Road" movies where they are describing what two dancers on the screen really felt like when filming. ("Her feet were killing her." "Don't forget their argument.") But on the screen itself they look dazzling, alluring, forever young and captivating. Which is as it should be. This is the image business, and every self-promoter is in it.

Thus, when you are called into the on-air personality, throw your shoulders back, take a deep breath, and follow the advice of Phyllis George (former Miss America, now wife of the Governor of Kentucky) who reminds herself before going into any room to, "Flash them pearlie whites!"

One last word on the subject. Remember: the host wants to like you. He wants you to be good, and he wants the program to be a knock-out. True, he has sat through an infinity of lesser lights, the ill-prepared, the braggarts, flashy con men, the tongue-tied. But he is, like his colleagues, both a perennial optimist and an avid enthusiast of the human comedy.

If as you extend your hand you feel one last tremor, remember this: you are in a much better position than the host. You can make a fool of yourself on his show knowing that there are thousands of other outlets around the country on which to redeem yourself; he will be left behind to explain to his management just how a turkey like you got on the air.

Think about it.

Now, knock 'em dead.

The Minutes Before Air Time

The time you spend with your media host will be brief and must be well used. Either:

- he is already on the air and is coming to get you during a news or commercial break
- he is just going on the air in which case he is preparing for the whole show, or
- he is about to tape and must get final directions and signals from his technicians.

In each case, you will probably not have his full undivided attention.

To begin with, state your name slowly and clearly. If you have a complicated last name, write down the phonetic pronunciation and include it with your introduction. Most hosts are concerned about getting your name right and will ask you to repeat it until they have it correct. But not all. The host of one television show in New York on which I appear is maddeningly cavalier about his guests' names. Fortunately mine is relatively easy; I remember one occasion on this man's show when he garbled the names of every member of his panel but mine. He seemed beyond caring whether he came across prepared or not, but it embarrassed the guests.

Despite your best efforts the host will sometimes get your name wrong. Do one of two things:

- The first time it happens, whether on air or not, simply say, "Actually, my name is pronounced . . ."
- Pass the host a note with your name and pronunciation during the first break. Ask him to make the correction.

I prefer the first method.

As soon as you arrive in the studio the host will direct you to where you are to be seated. Don't make an assumption about this. Wait until you're directed. Particularly in radio stations, there are often several microphones, not all of which will be hooked up. Sometimes, too, you and the host will have to share a microphone, and you need to be positioned just so: usually the end result resembles the starting point for a kissing marathon.

Just before air time (or taping), you and the host have distinct, if compatible, objectives. He wants to make sure that you are technically ready for the show:

- Is your microphone on? Either it is a stationary mike, in which case you must be properly positioned for it, or it is a lapel mike (more often used in television).
- Is your head set working?
- Do you have a cough switch? Where is it?

Don't assume these things automatically happen. They don't. Within recent memory I have:

- appeared on a radio call-in show where no one checked on my head set. I was left totally in the dark when the first telephone call came and only the scurrying of the technicians quickly saved the situation.
- broadcast on television without a lapel mike, since one technician thought another had put it on, and I didn't check.

It is the responsibility of the host and his technical assistants to insure that you are both properly positioned and technically equipped to broadcast, but they occasionally forget or get their signals crossed. So you'd better keep on the alert and remind the host if it looks like nothing is being done.

Your chief objective is to familiarize your host with just who you are, your product or service and pertinent background information. Fortunately all this is contained in the information packet discussed in Chapter 13. There should be at least two complete packets in the room, the host's and yours. The most important single page in yours is the one listing your telephone number and follow-up information. Keep it next to you. In the excitement of a broadcast it is often easy to forget a telephone number.

In the very brief time that you have, go through this packet of information with the host explaining what you've prepared. Sit next to him if possible and pick up each specific piece of paper and hand it over physically. "Here's an introduction of who I am and what I do." Hand it over. "Here's a description of my product." Hand it over. You get the idea. Finally, "Here's a number where people can call me for further information. I'd be glad if you used it on the air."

If this is going to be a television show, you might want to inquire of the producer whether this telephone number can be flashed on the screen. Each program has its own guidelines about doing so, and you can find out what they are when you've booked your appearance. If possible, you do want your telephone number flashed, however.

Once you've had a chance to present your packet of material, allow the host to tell you a little bit about his show and its format. This show is his spaceship, and he is its captain. He is proud of what he does and wishes to let you, the guest, know both why what he is doing is distinctive and what he wants to achieve with you. Listen to this soliloquy. Insofar as you can key into the host's aspirations for himself and his show, you will be made more welcome.

One Or Two Final Preparatory Items

Make sure you have both a glass of water at hand and a note pad. I have found that the water should be room temperature, and that prior to the program you should avoid beverages which are especially cold, hot, or carbonated. They can have unfortunate side effects. It goes without saying that you should avoid the sauce.

Make sure you have a note pad. You need it to record the networking information, of course, but you also want to write down points which need answering or ideas which occur to you during the show. I find my mind is especially fertile during a broadcast and that I am always scribbling notes to myself.

Finally, ask whether there is a cough switch. This is a button you can press in a radio station whenever you feel an irritating spasm of coughing coming on. Not all stations have this item. Some prefer that you remain entirely natural, hacking on the air.

One final note before you go on the air: stay cool. There are situations in the life of every self-promoter which, at the time, seem unbearable, but which serve, in retrospect, to prove my point that we are truly superior beings. Just recently, for example, I was leaving a publisher's office to proceed to a radio interview in Boston. He took me a "short cut" through a back section of the building, and he managed in the process to get my finger smashed in an inconvenient door. Moments later I noticed a disconcerting amount of blood oozing to the floor. My first problem was: can one suck one's bloody finger in front of a businessman? My second: what can I do about the blood while I'm on the air. "I just hope your broadcast isn't live," a very sorry publisher wailed.

Of course it was.

As I arrived at the studio, I was literally dripping blood and had to forego my customary handshake. I was given a piece of toilet tissue, wrapped myself up and for the next 30 minutes had to watch the interviewer (a young woman) keep fascinated eyes on my ever-reddening wad. She was solicitous, and the interview was — smashing. Despite the blood, perhaps *because* of the blood, I gave a truly bravura performance. On the whole, however, I prefer a more prosaic introduction.

Handling Your Interview

Whether you are being broadcast live or taping doesn't matter. What does is how you present yourself. What follows is a series of tips for making your interview pointedly successful.

Be Upbeat

When I first began in radio, which is where many unabashed self-promoters begin, I was earnest, zealous, and grimly purposeful. No longer. I was taken from this course by an anecdote which a helpful radio host told me in the hope that he would lighten my style and delivery. "Remember," he said, "if you want to be a media success the story of how to report the sinking of the **Titanic.** Don't say, 'Today the **Titanic** sank, 1400 passengers were lost.' Say, brightly, 'Today the **Titanic** sank. Of 1438 people on board, 38 were SAVED.' " Put the emphasis on the upbeat word, not the loss.

Deliver what you have to say in a clean, crisp, fast-moving, decidedly upbeat fashion.

Always Cite The Name Of Your Product Or Service

Pronouns are anathema to the unabashed self-promoter. So is any language configuration which stands between your listener and your product or service. Never say, "The reason I wrote this book." Say instead, "The reason I wrote **The Consultant's Kit . . .**" Never say, "This service is intended for nonprofit organizations." Say instead, "My Capital Campaign Fund Raising Service . . ." Be complete. Each sentence you say can, unobtrusively, become a mini-ad. This is hard to do and needs practice. In your daily speech, excise pronouns and other language which forces your listener to exert himself excessively. Talk in short, vivid bursts and always cite the complete name of your product or service.

Don't Be Argumentative

Everyone who hears you is not going to like what you have to say. So be it. Your job is to present your case as fully and completely as you can, but not to argue its merits. Argument demeans.

One evening I was making a joint appearance on a Boston call-in program with another author on entrepreneurial subjects. He and I had had a long day of interviews, and he wanted nothing so much as bath and bed. He managed to get through most of the show without misstep until a woman named Loretta called. "Hello, my name is Loretta, and I'm a first-time caller. I have an unusual question for your guests. I keep coming up with ideas that other people run with. Like, I invented home-based word processing services — before they were even popular. How can I get people to stop stealing my ideas?"

"What's your current idea," my colleague asked.

"Oh, no, buster! I'm not telling you! You're so smart, you'd probably steal it!"

"Okay. Have you written out a business plan, Loretta?"

"No, I'm not too good at writing."

"Well, Loretta, I suggest that the first thing for you to do is write it down and see whether you have any competitors."

"Like I said I don't write so good."

At that moment, the hours of fatigue, frustration, and the absence of his favorite martini struck. Into the microphone my colleague just shouted, "WRITE IT DOWN, LORETTA. AND HOLD ONTO YOUR DREAM."

Everyone, including the hapless Loretta, was stunned. Loretta hung up. The show went on. But my colleague's veneer as the unflappable business sage was cracked.

There is a happy ending to this story, however.

The next day when we were finishing our media sweep, at the end of one of our television shows, I looked straight into the camera and said, "Loretta, wherever you are, hold onto your dream!"

There is no point arguing with your guests.

By the same token, there is no point in arguing with your host, either.

As should be very clear by now, most hosts do not want an argument. The objectives of most television and radio shows would be shattered by dissension and discordance. Most hosts are, accordingly, willing to take you at your optimal self-estimate and to give you the opportunity to make best use of the time available, so long as you recognize that they, too, have objectives to meet.

Very, very rarely do I encounter a host who is inclined to be difficult.

On one occasion, again on a Boston television show, the host was a very belligerent, aggressive advocate of senior citizens. I was asked to come on his show and defend the policy of the college where I was then employed charging full tuition costs to old folks. On the same show was a college administrator from a competing institution which offered senior citizens free courses. The studio audience was composed of senior citizens.

Let's face it, this was not a wonderful situation to be in. In this case, the best that could be accomplished was to stake out a reasonable position — namely that people should pay a reasonable price for a worthwhile product — and defend it to the best of my ability. A good defensive position.

The host, however, made my inglorious if completely understandable position much, much easier. He told me before the show that he was completely appalled by my position and would 'cream' me on camera.

Curiously, his attitude made my task easier. He was so aggressive on camera, so arch, so utterly partisan that the feeling in the room began to change — in my favor. "Of course," the audience was reasoning, "people should pay a fair price. Why not us?"

What was, therefore, a basically unwinnable proposition came out very, very well by the end of the show, because of the host's sniping, interruptions, and generally uncordial attitude.

N.B. Later this man was appointed Secretary of Elder Affairs by a Governor of Massachusetts. A few days after his appointment, the **Boston Globe** disclosed that the three degrees he listed on his résumé were all false. He never made it into the Cabinet.

Hosts will duel with guests, particularly on radio call-in shows. Your task, however, is a consistent one: stay cool, present your case with the utmost lucidity, don't get rattled. A heavy-handed host makes your life infinitely easier. And remember, too: don't get distracted by hosts who pound the desk à la Khrushchev, raise their voices, thrust their bodies towards you. This is theatre.

Cultivate a pattern of icy, controlled response.

Beware The Discursive Host

You will meet hosts who, paid to talk, become enamored of their own dulcet tones and regard guests as unfortunate distractions. Bear with them, but only up to a point.

Far more menacing than the angry, argumentative host are those who either cannot or will not keep the discussion on target or cannot or will not let you participate.

I have some hints for each situation.

One day I was broadcasting on consulting from a radio studio in the middle of a cow pasture near Ann Arbor, Michigan. I may have been the most urbane guest ever to appear. The host had many, many hours to fill and was only too glad for the help. He noted that I have a Ph.D. in English History and as it was the height of the Falklands Islands War asked me, on the air, to speak about it. Question after question followed on a subject I was not prepared to discuss and which would not result in any money in my pocket.

In this kind of situation you need a bridge.

A bridge connects, moves you from a conversation which is not in your interest to one which is. Here's how my Ann Arbor situation could be bridged.

"Yes, having a Ph.D. in British History as I do, people often ask me how I came to be offering workshops on consulting. I tell them . . ."

Use the "People often ask me . . ." approach. This moves the conversation back to your objective.

Also see how your subject connects to the topic. As a consultant I might have said, "The Falkland situation is really tailor-made for a consultant. Now my work in consulting is really very applicable here."

The key is to always keep in mind just how much time you have. If you have a very short interview, say 15 minutes, you bridge earlier, after a minute or so. Only if you have the luxury of time can you affort to let the matter run on.

It is important to point out that bridging is both important and tricky. You need to get back on track but without perceptibly short-changing or offending your host. This is where your ingenuity comes in.

The Garrulous Host

By the same token you need to take into account the garrulous host. One day at a Boston television studio, I had to sit on the stage while the producer ran a taped interview between the host and a well-known Hollywood director. "How did I do?," the host asked the producer when the screening was finished. "Fine," the producer said laconically. "It would have been better though if you had allowed the director to say more than 'Hi, mom.' "

Garrulous hosts can destroy your interview, and, not so incidentally, make themselves look both amateurish and boorish in the process. You should help them avoid this needless fate using the Principle of Assertive Courtesy.

As with a host who does not stay on the track, you must give the garrulous host a chance to say his piece. It is, after all, his show. But as in the other situation you are not obliged to remain forever passive, uttering monosyllabic replies to verbose questions. Break in and stand your ground.

Also use the first break to your advantage.

Most shows will be interrupted by various commercial messages. Even taped programs get stopped at regular intervals to allow commercials to be inserted. This is a good opportunity for you politely to remind the host that you have a couple of items you'd like to bring up. Do not say, "I've had trouble breaking into your monologue." Do say, "There are a couple of points I'd like to stress in this upcoming segment. Here they are."

Remember something a garrulous host often forgets: no matter how devoted the audience is to a favorite host, it wants to hear you, the guest. It is the host's responsibility to give you that opportunity and your responsibility to create the opportunity if it does not otherwise become available.

Use Humor

No matter how grim your subject, don't forget the power and persuasiveness of humor. Also, don't forget that humor can defuse difficult situations and, properly used, can establish you as an attractive, compelling individual.

One evening I was on a very popular call-in show when a young woman called and got through the producer. The minute she got on the air she said, "You're still the same arrogant élitist you were in school," giggled, and hung up.

"Who was that?," the host said.

"Oh, that's a girl I refused to marry a couple of years ago. Can you blame me? I obviously made the right decision," I replied, deadpan.

It worked.

Use humor both to establish a rapport with your host and your audience. But don't clown. The unabashed self-promoter becomes an expert at knowing just how much humor to use and when to use it. He carefully steers between the Scylla of tendentious dullness and the Charybdis of backslapping mirthfulness. Both are equally treacherous.

Don't Laugh At Your Audience

What can also be treacherous is laughing at your audience. This can be hard not to do. Particularly on call-in programs you will be confronted with the totality of the human comedy, and it can be very, very funny, often pathetically so.

Several years ago I was a frequent guest on an afternoon radio call-in show in Boston as a commentator on "young adult lifestyles," that is people who were always exactly my age.

One day the topic was singles bars. I approached the topic with characteristic aplomb, although I had never been to one. The host asked a series of questions about the manners and mores of such places, including the cost of drinks. I hazarded a typically specific response, which one caller telephoned to dispute. "The cost is much higher," he said, "especially at the nicer places."

"Which you obviously go to," the host said. "Well, since you're clearly an expert on the subject, tell us what pick-up lines work for you."

"Hmmmm," replied the caller, giving the question the serious deliberation it obviously deserved. "I have a lot of 'em, but I'll tell you what works best for me. I spots the girl I want. I stares at her. And then I walks over, cool like, and says, 'You and me was made for love, babe.' "

We were broadcasting from a glass-enclosed studio where the public could watch the proceedings, and in an instant both our audience and the two of us were howling. We literally fell off our stools.

The host choked, "You and me was made for love, babe?"

"Yeah, that's it," an obviously-pleased caller said. "And it works, too!"

I bet it does.

Having been unable to follow this, my own sage advice, on occasion, I can only hope that you will try and avoid laughing at your audience. It often can be patronizing. We may feel it, but we ought not to show it.

Don't Be Monosyllabic

Hosts consistently complain to me about the guests who come on their programs and answer questions with answers which would have made the laconic Silent Cal seem verbose. Just as you wouldn't be monosyllabic with your friends, avoid being so on the air.

Your host wants relatively short, very conversational answers. He wants them to be fluid, with anecdotes rather than statistics. Clipped, abrupt answers just will not do. Remember: the purpose of media is not to impart truth (which may be monosyllabic) but to amuse, entertain, and instruct.

Raise Questions, Answer Them

If the unabashed self-promoter is not hearing the questions he wants, he answers the ones he would have preferred to have. We must become past masters at this art.

Again, try "People often ask me why."

- "Most people want to know whether . . ."
- "In a recent letter I received, the correspondent asked me if . . ."
- "When I was lecturing in Dubuque, a member of the audience wondered . . ."

You get the picture.

Richard Nixon used this trick to great effect. Now don't back away just because of this taint. Remember RMN won the 1968 presidential election because of a superb strategy for dealing with the media he despised. But that, as they say, is another story.

The trick to using this technique is to cite individuals with whom the audience can identify. If I am broadcasting to housewives, I transpose my examples to be housewives; if to students, then undergraduates, &c. I want my audience to know at all times that people like them have already found me indispensable. It makes it easier for the audience to come to the same conclusion.

The Break

By the time the break arrives you should be well into your stride commanding the interview but in the very nicest way. Use the time now available to fine-tune your broadcast. Advise or remind the interviewer:

- about your introduction for the second segment
- to give your telephone number
- about where your product is available
- of questions you'd like to have raised.

If you are truly a pro, that is to say an unabashed self-promoter who seeks not only to advance his own causes but to deliver a worthwhile product so that the host can think back on this program with satisfaction, the interviewer will oblige you. I am not only an unabashed self-promoter, I am a perceived unabashed self-promoter, which is a position no one else who reads this book need ever be in. Nonetheless, I meet my self-promotional objectives time and time again, because I am concurrently meeting the objectives of my host.

Use the break both to clarify how your own objectives can be met *and* to discover if there is anything that the host would like to bring up. You, the unabashed self-promoter, and the host are in a symbiotic relationship. Now is a good time to refine it.

The End Of The Beginning

As your time comes to an end, your host will usually give you a signal. Use what remains to reinforce that point which you most want your audience to remember.

On one occasion an erudite colleague, approaching summation, gave a long learned disquisition on the hazards of setting up a home-based business. He was grim, determined, candid. Then the television host turned to me and asked for my last remark. "Buy **The Consultant's Kit,**" I quipped, "and you can avoid every problem so soberly stated for you."

My colleague had a product to sell, too, he just forgot about it in his final, precious seconds. I didn't.

When you have finished your final comment, don't move whether you are on radio or television. Take your cue from the host. As soon as he takes off his microphone and gets up, you may do the same.

If you know that the host must continue with this show or even do another taping with yet another guest, don't linger. You are a product, and you have done what you were supposed to do. Ordinarily a host will walk you to the door of the station, but not always.

However much time you have available use it well. First you want to know when the program will be aired. Ask. The host will usually know. Also, the host can point you in the direction of the producer, so you can pick up your tape of the show. Don't forget it; it is most useful.

Spend a moment after the show to reinforce and extend your personal rapport with the host. This relationship is important to you. Consider:

- he can broadcast you again
- when he moves to another station, you can get another contact
- he is at the top of the Pyramid of Contacts for the Self-Promotion Network and can provide you with other important leads.

Yes, you want this relationship to go very, very well.

Here's how to handle the wrap-up conversation:

- Compliment the host. Even on the occasion in Pittsburgh when the unfortunate host stopped the tape on two occasions to ask me if he was doing all right, I left with a compliment. Even on the occasion in Worcester, Massachusetts where a young woman on her solo run ran the equipment so that the first 15 minutes did not get on the tape. Even then. I give some compliment and express my gratitude, which can really be heartfelt particularly in situations like those cited. (After all, we were finished without further mishap.)
- Ask the networking questions you previously asked the producer. Yes, now that you are done with the matter which ostensibly brought you to the station, carry on. You want to discover how this contact can be of further assistance to you.

- Mention a forthcoming project. Toss out the lure. Every unabashed self-promoter is looking ahead to his *next* broadcast on the station. I am seldom very interested in what I have just done, and rarely listen to myself. Why should I? What interests me far, far more is how and when I am going to be back. Hence the mention of my next project. Will it be a product currently being developed? A new service? An educational program? It doesn't matter, tell the host. As glad as you that the broadcast is history, grateful to you for your deft, professional approach, the host will probably say, "I'll be looking forward to hearing from you when you're finished." Given what you've just done for him, he probably means it.

Some Final Words

If your broadcast has been live, leave your name, address, telephone and product information with the receptionist as you leave the building. She can forward calls to you.

As you leave the station, if you have been on a live radio broadcast and the show is continuing, ask your driver to turn on the channel. Often a host has had several very complimentary things to say and callers have had the opportunity to keep the discussion alive. Not always, though.

I once left a New York radio station and jumped into a taxi headed to LaGuardia Airport. I asked the cabbie to turn on his radio to a disco station he obviously wouldn't ordinarily listen to. "Why?" he grumbled with typical Big Apple politesse. "I was just on, and I want to see if the discussion is continuing."

"Now," said the radio host, "I'd like to continue our discussion with this question: 'Have you ever made love in a public place?' "

"You were just on this station, huh?," the cabbie said. As he eyed me in his mirror, it was with a look of considerable interest, even respect.

The Thank-You Note

If the host is grateful for what you have delivered, you should be grateful, too, for the opportunity. Don't just say so. Put it in writing.

The media people you are working with don't get much fan mail. Add to the meagre volume with a note of appreciation. And, as an unabashed self-promoter, send something even sweeter about the producer to the host and about the host to the general manager. That's a very good way to cement this oh-so-perfect symbiosis.

CHAPTER 15

ARRANGING YOUR MEDIA WAVE: THE COORDINATED APPROACH TO UNABASHED SELF-PROMOTION

You have now mastered the basics of unabashed self-promotion. You know how to craft a Quintessential American Success Image, what media outlets are available, how to contact them, and how to make your interview productive. You have now reached the baccalaureate level of self-promotion.

There is, however, more to learn and much to refine. Too often, however, the self-promoter who reaches this point gives way to a decidedly premature self-congratulation. He may have had an article published, may also have been the subject of a brace of electronic media interviews. He feels good. His adoring family feeds his perception of himself as pocket celebrity. It is very, very heady and satisfying.

It is also quite dangerous.

Although any given print media article may have a lifespan of a year or even two, and you may get calls from a radio appearance six months after, the value of any single media appearance is limited.

I remember one day sitting with an august group of businessmen who were fretting about how some protest group was going to invade on a certain day ten major corporations and issue florid revolutionary rhetoric. "They'll be on all the national networks," was the prevailing lament.

After sitting unusually quiet through a maelstrom of indignation and plans for counter-insurgency, I could bear it no longer. "Gentlemen," I said, "how many of you watched the national news three nights ago?" Much rubbing of temples. "How many of you remember the lead story?" No one. No one.

Unabashed self-promoters take heed. Not only are myopia and oblivion the public's reigning deities, but this same public has a collective attention span of infinitesimal duration and a memory which is even shorter. All of this will dishearten the ingénue. It only spurs the promotional veteran to greater lengths.

The Idea

The unabashed self-promoter cannot simply rely upon the publication of single articles and the broadcast of single radio and television programs to disseminate his message, no matter what immediate impact they have. The unabashed self-promoter rather needs a strategy which enables him to take one single message, one single product or service to as many media sources as possible during a short, concentrated period. This strategy is contained in the Wave Theory of unabashed self-promotion.

The Wave Theory posits that the major objectives of the unabashed self-promoter can only be realized through successive waves of media within a given market, waves that succeed not only in reaching the audience once but on several occasions from several directions. Each wave "coats" a market, raising the consciousness of the audience from naught to negligible and on through successive stages to immortal bright-shining fame.

These waves must come at regular, considered intervals so that that unabashed self-promoter, his goods and services, are perceived as inevitabilities. It is easy, of course, to generate these waves with paid advertising. Each of us, each day is subject to a wave of paid advertisements. It is trickier to accomplish when you are asking for the time without paying for it.

Step I: Produce The Basis For The Promotion

To have a successful promotion there must be something to promote. The unabashed self-promoter must become expert at generating promotional vehicles which can capture the attention of the media while at the same time enabling him to be individually featured, too. Thus the unabashed self-promoter has always before him twin objectives:

- to conceive of the vehicle which will most interest fickle, capricious media
- to insure that the promotion of this vehicle insures his own promotion.

The promotional vehicle can be:

- a product (like a book)
- a report, study or article (such as appears on page 313)
- an event (like the Boston Consultants Convention, see page 319)
- another individual or organization (see page 354)

It does not much matter from a promotional standpoint what the vehicle is so long as it will generate sufficient coverage both for itself and for you, the unabashed self-promoter.

To be sure, there are seasoned promoters who are perfectly content merely to gain the public's attention for their products, events, clients, &c. This is all very well, and they will, of course, benefit greatly from the methods delineated in this book. They do, however, fall short of the ultimate challenge: achieving coverage both for the perceived object of the promotion and its presiding genius, too. So be it. All may gaze upon Mt. Everest; some few may scale it; only the trifling few may stand upon its summit, transcendant.

Step Two: Selecting The Media Targets

The novice self-promoter will want to select very few media targets to approach, two or even one are perfectly satisfactory. These may — or even should — be small, with limited audiences and of limited consequence, a college radio station, a weekly newspaper. The reason for this selection should be obvious: practice makes perfect. The unabashed self-promoter, like any embryo professional, needs a place where he can comfortably afford to fail, where suitable standards for beginners apply.

With the Wave Theory matters are different.

The key to the Wave Theory is hitting a number of targets, enough so that there is a reasonable chance that the average listener or reader will have heard of you more than once. Just how many media sources, print and electronic, do you target, however?

There is always a tension between the maximum extent of possible coverage and your available time. Your task is to make a very conservative estimate both about how many media outlets are appropriate and how much time you have.

Analyzing The Sources

Most of my media waves begin in Boston, which is the nearest major market. Once I have selected my promotional object and thought through just why I feel it will be of interest to the media and how I will present it to them, my next task is to ascertain just who I should approach.

As Chapter 3 demonstrates, we here have it rather easier than you in some other markets since there exists for Greater Boston a very comprehensive media source book. Surprisingly many major markets do not have such a helpful compendium. If yours is one of these negligent markets, you will have to complete one yourself; (once you do, let me know, I'll list it, and we'll both make some money!)

I carefully review each newspaper, magazine, radio and television source within the marketing area. The first time you initiate a wave you will not have much of this information which makes subsequent waves easier to arrange. That is why you have to look upon all your early work as an investment that pays off bit by bit.

When you begin, even if there is a helpful general media guide available, you will not have the detailed specialized knowledge of your market which can come only from working with it. Were you told last time you appeared on a radio station that entrepreneurial features were most welcome now? It is very unlikely this kind of insiders' information is published.

Review each possible media source in your market attempting to discern whether you should invest in an approach to it.

- Have you ever appeared in or on this medium before? Were you favorably received? Were you told to wait awhile before returning? Have you done so?
- Do you know anyone at the source? Can you telephone and see whether an approach now would be fruitful?
- If you have not worked with this target previously and do not know anyone there (or have no suitable contact), why do you think your subject would be of interest to it? Is your material popular? Is it original? Is it especially newsworthy just now? Has the target somehow demonstrated an interest in what you'd propose?

Unless you have satisfactory answers to these questions, don't proceed. Creating a media wave is very time consuming under the best of circumstances; you want to pick your targets very carefully, very thoughtfully.

Write down your reasons for selecting a target. Even today after I have dealt with hundreds of media targets, when launching a wave I carefully think through what I am trying to achieve and who will be most responsive.

In fact, of course, as you consider which targets to adopt you must also consider the time you have available.

Out-Of-Town Waves

The unabashed self-promoter on the road has very, very limited time. The unabashed self-promoter at home just has very limited time. As the unabashed self-promoter considers his out-of-town targets, he should consider them in terms of an ideal day. Here's what it looks like:

- wake-up radio (or television) show
- mid-morning television show
- twelve o'clock radio news
- early afternoon print interview, major metropolitan daily
- late afternoon print interview, major suburban weekly (or daily) or public affairs radio taping
- evening radio call-in show
- all-night radio call-in show

On a good day, doing a wave, the out-of-town unabashed self-promoter should be able to comfortably schedule up to 7 interviews. The pace is brisk, even frenetic but bearable. I have on my best days done 10 interviews, but I have been vegetabalized at its conclusion.

Now, planning your out-of-town day should be easy. You need to list the prospects for each type of vehicle, and you need to prioritize them. How many programs are there from 6 a.m. to 9 a.m. in your targeted market? Once you know that, you will begin to jockey for position. You will begin with the most important vehicles and (if you are not successful in getting them) work down your list until you have the required number of appointments.

The unabashed self-promoter, as I have said before, is a stark realist. He knows that he may not, particularly on an original outing, get the top-rated show in every slot, but that doesn't bother him unduly. He knows what he must have to make a complete, rewarding day.

Here's what an alternate schedule might look like, for those who have not succeeded in getting their first media choices:

- wake-up radio. Search out smaller station.
- mid-morning public affairs radio taping or interview with smaller newspaper or specialized magazine
- radio taping at college radio station
- meeting with newsletter editor
- print interview, small suburban weekly
- meeting with producer of call-in radio show for future scheduling

This second schedule shows, first, that if necessary you will lower your expectations until you find a media vehicle which will promote you, and, second, that as part of your scheduled time you may have to *meet* with decision makers to convince them that you are media-worthy. The important thing is that where you have made the decision to go to a foreign city, you must make the best possible use of your time.

Remember: not everyone starts off on the "Today" Show. The unabashed self-promoter understands that he must make a considerable investment in himself. This means beginning with programs and in publications which may not be your ultimate objective. Still, be grateful to them. They give you the opportunity both to define and refine your approach and to develop a series of very worthwhile contacts.

N.B. Despite my best efforts, I have from time to time found myself in various cities with an incomplete day of media. In such cases, I systematically work my way down my target list, calling both those who said "No!" and those who were not yet interested. Sometimes I get no farther than a secretary; sometimes I get through to the media target directly. My purpose? At this point just to say "Hello. How are you?" That I'm in town and that I'll try them again when I come back. I want these people to know that I will never, never give up and that for all that they've made a pivotal error of judgement either in failing to schedule an interview or even in their unwillingness to discuss the subject, I'm big enough not to hold it against them (at least not perceptibly).

In-Town Targets

You have a flexibility of time when you're at home that you rarely have on the road. Use it.

In preparing for a wave of Boston, I both identify more targets and give media targets the utmost latitude in scheduling. I expect, therefore, to have a much higher success rate with Boston-area targets than elsewhere, because if there is any interest at all I can accommodate myself accordingly. You should do the same.

In a foreign city, I am usually forced to choose a day or two when I shall be available, and must then work around the existing commitments and priorities of the targets. Even here, however, there is some flexibility. Identify the chief media targets in your designated market in descending order of significance. When contacting the first of these, indicate, if at all possible, that you will accommodate yourself to any reasonable date. Once you have this major program cemented, you are in a much stronger position to schedule noncompetitive media targets.

In Boston, I generally select a window period during which I want my wave to begin and end; this window is usually 30 days. If the media targets are at all interested in working with me, it really ought to be possible to do so within this frankly liberal time period.

The Media Activity Chart

The Media Activity Chart, which I have mentioned before as an admirable idea, is absolutely mandatory when you are scheduling a wave. Using this chart, you should be able to tell at a glance, not only who you are approaching but also the exact state of the case. I cannot stress enough that once you have initiated contact with a media source, carry it through to its conclusion, whatever that may be.

I think it should go without saying by now that this means a telephone call not returned by a media source within a reasonable period needs to be replaced, and that you must continue to send your supporting materials until you are sure that they arrive.

Telling Prospective Media About Scheduled Media

When arranging a wave, you may very well encounter the media's penchant for exclusivity. "If I decide I want you," so the reasoning goes. "I don't want to share you. But I can't say just now that I do want you. Be careful anyway."

This can be infuriating.

I have learned to cope with this prejudice by giving a media source exclusivity in its format and time slot. That is to say, I don't schedule 2 competitive evening call-in shows, even if I have the time available, nor do I allow myself to be interviewed simultaneously by two competing major newspapers. This is not to say that I do not send general mailings to all media sources at any given time. I do, on a regular basis. But anything that suggests exclusivity — as an interview might — I ration. There is no problem about this approach when you have control over it. If I have the time to do so, I approach one media source in each format at a time, and if not successful there, go on to the next. The problem, of course, is that one always does not have time in such luxurious abundance and may have to approach competing media sources simultaneously.

In such situations, I attempt to schedule my preferred media first. If these media do condescend to be malleable, the correct thing to do is to let other competing media know that you have such an interview and that you feel obliged to give this scheduled source first priority. If the second source wishes to go ahead on this basis, there is no conflict.

If, however, a secondary source schedules you first, you have a different game to play. Then call your preferred target, and tell them what has happened. Tell them you prefer your interview (or whatever) to be with them, and let them advise you. While you play this game, remember the old addage: A bird in the hand is worth two in the bush. Don't ever give up a scheduled interview, despite the fact that it may not be your preferred target, simply in hopes of thereby landing something better.

In a wave, the unabashed self-promoter looks for a range of varied media that will allow him to get at his audience in different ways. Fewer and fewer places are two newspaper towns. In practice if you are interviewed once by a newspaper it is harder to get a subsequent interview within a reasonable period. That is why I like to hold certain media targets in reserve. I know I'll be back to them for my next wave.

How Many Waves, How Often?

The question of how many waves to organize is rather complicated. Each wave needs a promotional spearhead, a product, article, event, individual, &c. The more of these the unabashed self-promoter has the more waves he can organize, both in the nearest major media market and in other media markets, too.

In practice, I have found that I am able to launch two or three waves in Boston each year and an equal number in selected major cities nationally. Nowadays both in Boston and elsewhere I have come to rely upon publicists for assistance in this demanding task. (See Chapter 18.)

Each of these waves has a distinct theme. These themes may be related, and often are, to the waves which have preceeded them, but each is also quite separate. Each wave I begin has several purposes:

- to promote the particular object of this wave
- to promote again goods and services of earlier but related waves
- to promote me.

A few examples would, I think, be helpful.

Waves Launched By The Author

While I have had a long and fruitful relationship with the media going back to my adolescence, I was an adult before I fully fathomed the significance of media waves as opposed to isolated articles. For purposes of illustration I shall utilize the significant waves I have launched since the beginning of my company, 1980. As is clear, the best and most productive waves piggyback on trends, events and developments of perceived importance to the media. The unabashed self-promoter develops a feel for what these trends, events and developments will be — and prepares accordingly.

Nonprofit Wave

During the summer of 1980, it became perfectly apparent to me that whoever would become president, Carter or Reagan, there would be significant cuts in the federal budget, particularly relating to social programs. President Carter had already begun this process; a putative President Reagan promised more of it. I, therefore, made the very calculated decision to write a book designed to assist organizations already feeling a pinch which would only get worse. The result was **Development Today: A Guide For Nonprofit Organizations.** This book was publicized simultaneously with the election of Ronald Reagan.

The President-elect was a very dramatic boost to my nonprofit wave. In virtually his first public statement after his election, he said there would be sizable, even traumatic budget cuts. These were sure to impact social service organizations, thereby heightening their perception of a problem needing a solution — my product (book), my service (fund raising consultation). Importantly, I had no educational job to perform.

The developing circumstances, which bear looking at, were very much in my favor:

- The issue was national and important.
- There was no perceived competitor dealing with it.
- The media would need constructive material advising concerned individuals how to deal with this situation.
- My product and service were timely.
- My product and service were ready.

The first nonprofit wave had as its theme, "The President is serious, folks. Fortunately there are things you can do not only to prepare yourself for the brave new world ahead, but also to be better off altogether." This was a message best put forward in a White Knight article of the type found on page 314.

The initial White Knight article laid the groundwork for successive waves (multiple use) with other print sources both general and specific to the affected organizations and to the electronic media, too, both in Boston and elsewhere.

As with so many waves, quick action was important with this one. Given the fact that the Reagan Administration was serious (which was not initially perceived by the media), it was inevitable that in due time I would have competitors advancing their own theories about what the affected population should do to stay alive. Since the media's interest in this topic was decidedly limited (as it is with most subjects), as the number of competitors surfaced my initial advantage would necessarily lessen. Fortunately, I was well prepared to move: I had thought through my self-promotional objectives, prepared both the theme of the wave and the product, and identified media targets all before the subject had attained a high degree of significance. Preparation, prescience, and luck all must be handmaidens of the unabashed self-promoter.

Given the fact that the media's interest in my subject was not elastic and that competitors were bound to emerge (there being money to be made, as Rhett Butler sagely observed, in the plight of others), it was important to plot the next phase of the wave, Nonprofit Wave II.

The first nonprofit wave had both local and national dimensions but principally was focused on Boston as was entirely natural for a company seeking to build, first, a local client base for secure income.

The next wave was built on the article on page 313 which was published in May, 1981. I first became aware of the issue involved (individuals using the short tax form getting credit for charitable contributions) through a newsletter as I have already described. I at once glimpsed the possibilities for a wave, a wave which I then needed.

The sample article on page 313 is a Sentinel article geared to a Massachusetts readership. The issue, however, is national. A very few changes in this article turn it into a piece for Kansas or Minnesota. That is the chief benefit of a Sentinel piece and our federal union.

This article was both perfectly timed for a second nonprofit wave and well constructed. It offered a public issue on which to comment and grew nicely out of my first nonprofit wave. It was a very neat package offering as it did a strong public service dimension (ostensibly the reason for the piece) as well as the possibility of promoting my book, firm, and nonprofit consulting services.

The next phase of the now-continuing nonprofit wave I launched in the fall of 1981 with a series of Development Training Workshops designed to enable me to take my practice, my message, and my products national in a more systematic fashion. The theme of this wave was, "Hands On Training For Afflicted Nonprofit Organizations."

You must always keep in mind that Americans in general are tremendous self-help boosters. We like to breast-beat about problems, but we very much like to see people getting on with the business of moving on, working things out, improving — not just bewailing. From a self-promotional standpoint, my workshops were very timely in content and were, of course, designed to take maximum advantage of our self-help leanings.

This part of the wave was aimed less at Boston, where I had already had substantial coverage, and more at other major cities around the country where media opportunities were sought. These media opportunities were not just promoting workshops, however. They were promoting my firm in general, **Development Today,** our client services, the workshops *and* me, the now widely-acknowledged expert in the field. A very neat package.

This wave took place throughout the autumn of 1981.

In the spring of 1982 the action returned to Boston, now ready again for another coating of the market. The ostensible objective was a special Nonprofit Technical Assistance Institute which I organized with Cambridge College (see page 320). The purpose of this wave was, of course, to promote this activity. In fact, however, it was to promote the now-extensive string of goods and services listed above as well as the Institute which was the hook the media swallowed.

Once they had done so, however, I needed to think carefully about what my next nonprofit hook could be. How could I get this wave to continue? I needed a new product, a new service, a new vehicle of some kind.

I chose to do a second edition of **Development Today,** an edition which would take into account developments in the post-Reagan universe. Because I was also involved with other waves (see below), I did not need this product instantly. That was fortunate since my time was very limited. The book was published in February, 1983 in time for a mid-winter-spring media sweep which concluded in April. (See Chapter 20 for further details.)

The mid-winter, 1983 wave for **Development Today** was the most extensive in Boston since my Sentinel article in 1981. That is because I had two other waves to deal with, one major and one minor.

The Consultant's Kit Wave

Again peering deeply into the crystal ball (which is a necessary apparatus of all aspiring self-promoters), I discerned in the summer of 1981 that the recession we were in was really part of a basic transformation of American society, Alvin Toffler's famous Third Wave of post-industrialization.

In any such period of rapid change, the unabashed self-promoter is presented with glorious opportunities. Here were a few of the things I saw:

- professional people unaccustomedly thrown out of work
- inflation eating away at the pensions of the elderly, who were forced to look for ways to supplement their incomes
- a greater number of households headed by a single parent with children
- increased dissatisfaction with the standard corporation, not least because of a shrinkage in the job market and a narrowing of opportunities
- a quickening of the never-long-dormant national entrepreneurial spirit. Whereas the previous epoch had been marked by a growing attitude that "government should do it," now there was growing interest in the role of private citizens and private industries — and a growing enthusiasm for the money that such private entities could make.

The time was ripe for a product that could key into these trends and take advantage of them. The result was **The Consultant's Kit.**

This book was launched on its first wave in the late fall of 1981. As you will remember, this was at a time when my media efforts were otherwise concentrated on securing publicity outside Boston in connection with nonprofit workshops, books and services. It was thus time to hit the local market with something entirely different.

Now the problem is the media often find it difficult to visualize an individual as an expert in multiple fields. Media people like tags. The richness of human experience and intellect is, therefore, unnecessarily confusing. The protean, unabashed self-promoter with schemes and projects aplenty will have to work especially hard at being perceived an expert, media worthy in *each* of his fields. I have, and it works, but it does take effort.

The initial promotion effort for **The Consultant's Kit** was, therefore, aimed at Boston media who had been taught to regard me as the nonprofit technical assistance expert and were now being encouraged to add a new dimension.

Note: while the initial targeted efforts were done in Boston (and later New York), untargeted efforts were in progress elsewhere. That is to say, we mailed media releases to print media which could not, however, because of time considerations, be followed up. This is acceptable so long as you do not stake the success of your efforts on these untargeted mailings. Ordinarily I have found that such mailings do result in short items being published or even in requests for further information, interviews, &c. For me, however, the targeted waves are by far the more important activity.

Too Much Media? The Waves Create A Tsunami

There are problems involved in generating concurrent waves of media, problems perfectly exemplified by what happened to me in June, 1982. Three dissimilar waves jostled together within a 10 day period leaving me exhilarated — and exhausted.

As I noted earlier in this chapter Cambridge College held our second annual Nonprofit Technical Assistance Institute in June, 1982. At the same time the first Boston Consultants Convention took place, and, not least, my book **Our Harvard** came out the day of Harvard Commencement, appropriately enough.

This kind of a situation necessitates deft planning. Here we have three separate, distinct waves occurring simultaneously, any one of which could generate sufficient local media and one of which (**Our Harvard**) is a quite likely vehicle for national exposure.

How, then, to handle a situation rich with possibilities, fraught with possible perils?

To begin with, you must prioritize your waves. Which of them offers the possibility of greatest return? How you define return is your call. For me, it is dollars. This was a toss up between the Nonprofit Technical Assistance Institute (which most significantly promised clients) and the Consultants Convention, which offered in addition to convention-entry fees, book sales for the firm. Upon reflection, the decision was made that in circumstances where a media source might be equally receptive to all three possibilities, the consulting aspect would be stressed. And so it was.

In the meantime, however, all likely local media were targeted — for one possibility or another and pursued accordingly. Here was the strategy:

- Give priority to Consultants Convention which offered both pre- and post-event promotion possibilities.
- Give secondary attention to Nonprofit Technical Assistance Workshop which as an event had been held before. Attempt to secure post-event coverage, which had not previously happened.
- Piggyback **Our Harvard** (and party accompanying it), on Commencement, which is treated as a news event by significant media sources.

These objectives were met.

In a case where you find yourself with several promotional objectives, make sure that you control the entire promotional process. This I have learned from hard experience. That way you can decide which event to push first and which next, which materials will be sent when and how you will follow-up. Otherwise the media people may be confused by successive waves of material on totally unrelated subjects. This will probably not be in your best interest.

Successive Consulting Waves

Following the extravaganza of media coverage in June of 1982, I did no further waves until November of that year. At that time Geoffrey Bailey's book **Maverick: Succeeding As A Free-Lance Entrepreneur** was published. This book presented me with an ideal local self-promotional vehicle because it included a chapter on me and my work. While this book is also discussed in Chapter 16, it is important to note here how we transformed this chapter into yet another wave.

You must remember that the average author who is regarded as worthy of general media attention (a small fraction of all authors, by the way), usually gets one sweep of a market. I had at this point already had 2 — when **The Consultant's Kit** was first published; again when the Consultant's Convention took place, thereby allowing me to promote the book, too.

Maverick presented a joyous third wave which is very, very unusual because of the average author's inability to conceive of the Wave Theory and his publisher's inability to implement it.

There were two angles for this wave, one local, one seasonal: "The Maverick Master and the Master Maverick," and "This Christmas Give Yourself A Job." The media went for these angles very heavily. Over the course of three or four days we had 15 interviews of one kind or another. The predominant attention, as was only proper, focused on **Maverick,** not only the new product but a book dealing with entrepreneur-ialism, a subject of wider interest than **The Consultant's Kit.** Without difficulty, however, I was able to piggyback on **Maverick**'s prominence to push my product. The result was a fifth printing of **The Consultant's Kit** in January, 1983.

What Lies Ahead With JLA Waves?

As I write we have just finished our latest nonprofit wave, another dozen interviews or so spread nicely over about 2 months.

What next?

The next wave will accompany the printing of this book. This wave, which will start in Boston and move quickly beyond, will promote:

- **The Unabashed Self-Promoter's Guide**
- accompanying workshops
- JLA's public relations division
- **The Consultant's Kit** (its precursor volume, now in a 6th printing)
- accompanying workshops
- consulting services to nonprofit organizations
- **Development Today**
- accompanying nonprofit fund raising workshops
- your humble servant

The trick now becomes writing the articles and handling all interviews, print and electronic, so that as many of these items as possible are clearly promoted, so that the audience knows sufficient about each and has specific follow-up information.

Last Words

Between waves, the unabashed self-promoter does not rest. Why should he? Sporadic interviews can occur. Published articles about your goods and services; the stray radio and television show which could not previously be scheduled; a letter to the editor; a quote; a quip, a mention here or there — all happen. All this is pleasant and keeps your name before the public.

But it is the waves of media which establish you as a known entity, the elusive household word. Never forget it.

Oh-so-mistaken and glum self-promoters continually suggest to me that the success of this system is based on a book. Make no mistake about it, books help, hence the following chapter. But it is nonetheless true that most authors, notwithstanding their creations, get no wave coverage, while lesser mortals without such an intellectual credit do succeed in regularly attracting it. An article, a report, a bill in the legislature, an event, an individual can all generate a wave.

The key is to produce an item of sufficient interest to the media that they can hook their story, your interview on it — and which will in the process promote you, too. As you see, many things do nicely in this regard.

Having said this, why not create a book, too? In books lie manifold self-promotional possibilities. Alas! Even most authors scarcely know them.

Read on.

CHAPTER 16

BOOKS BY AND ABOUT YOU, THE UNABASHED SELF-PROMOTER

This is not a chapter about how to select a suitable topic for your book, how to write or produce it. For that you will have to go elsewhere, although, to be frank, what's available is not very helpful. This chapter is about how to use a book as a self-promotional vehicle — from the very instant that you've decided to do it.

Alas! Most authors haven't got the slightest idea how to do so; if they're lucky they can handle selecting a suitable subject and producing good readable copy.

Alas! Most publishers don't know either; if they're lucky, they are expert at producing an attractive eye-catching and aesthetically-pleasing product.

That's it.

But when the content is finished and the product manufactured, then, only then, does the real fun begin — what to do with it.

This chapter offers a few characteristically astute observations.

First, it begins at the beginning: unabashed self-promotion using a book as the promotional vehicle begins from the time the title is chosen, before a single word is written. Its promotional value should continue through a series of steps: pre-publication excerpting and the fashioning of material into spin-off articles through actual production and into post-publication excerpting.

The unabashed self-promoter sees myriad promotional possibilities in a book; he looks at a book as a process, not an object, and he understands that the mere sale of the book is not the sole or even necessarily the chief reason for its production. Publishers, bless their hearts, will disagree; for them the sale is all, all that matters. That's reasonable. But it is insufficient for us. An unabashed self-promoter produces a book for many reasons:

- to enhance his credibility
- as a vehicle with many, many promotional possibilities
- to make royalties

Money, as you see, is only one of the possibilities, undeniably important though it is.

Sadly, because a publisher's chief reason for producing the book is the money, his interest ordinarily begins only when the product itself is available, much later than yours. This is why, as an unabashed self-promoter in very good standing, I have established my own publishing company. Previously I worked with "regular" publishing houses both in Britain and this country. You will benefit from my (not always satisfactory) experience by following the advice given later in this chapter.

You need not, however, follow my example and create your own publishing company to get the full self-promotional benefit from your book. It is, though, often the right course if you have:

- a high visibility subject
- the ability to write well and quickly
- organizational skills to handle distribution
- extraordinary stamina, persistence, and a deep belief in your product.

If you choose the traditional route of placing your book with a publishing company, you must understand that it is chiefly your responsibility that you derive all the potential benefit you can from your book. Remember this: 80% of books published actually lose money, according to recognized trade sources. Publishers are well aware of the fact that a book has a considerably below-average chance of returning a profit. Thus publishers put promotional money into books only when they have *already* demonstrated their success, not before. This is, of course, a catch-22 situation. It is, however, the truth. Thus, if you want your book to be successful, first as a self-promotional vehicle, then as a profit center, you must undertake its promotion. There is no alternative.

The Title

You may not be able to tell a book by its cover, but you can certainly sell a book — and create interest in it — by its title. Note the title of this book: it is different, attractive, compelling. It may even be the reason you bought it. If so, don't be surprised. I planned it that way.

For me, the self-promotional benefit of a book begins once I have selected the title. Unlike many writers (generally novelists with uncertain prospects), I am not coy about keeping my work in progress a secret. I want people to talk about it even before the product exists; I want to excite their interest, whet their appetite, get them to ask me, "When is it coming out?" "How is it coming along?" The title is the first means of stimulating this interest.

I like my titles to be both descriptive and if not provocative, then different. I write them for two sets of people: the media who I want to write about them and the buying public, who will make my investment of time and other resources worthwhile.

This book is an excellent illustration of how the naming process works to the advantage of the unabashed self-promoter. The media, in this case, are mentioned right in the title. The word "exploit" is designed to provoke them. I know, and now you know, that media people are always on the *qui vivre*, afraid of being exploited. This title, deliberately provocative (and hence risky), utilizes this source of provocation and anxiety and turns it into an actual selling point.

Ever since I adopted this title, media people have been fascinated by it; not all, to be sure, have been enamored of it. Some have been offended. But no one has been apathetic about it. More to the point, they have been anxious to discuss it — in their articles, columns, and on the air.

Without a word of the book written, the **Hartford Courant, Boston Globe,** and **Boston Magazine**, all important print media, published stories on this volume, something that existed solely in my mind.

Second, the title should be directed to a specific market segment and should excite this market to buy. This book is directed to a very broad market, and it excites these people to buy by keying into some of the important subliminal truths of our time:

- Resources are finite.
- Everyone can't have enough of them.
- Those who are to succeed must distinguish themselves in some way.
- Omnipresent media can help me distinguish myself.
- Media, while omnipresent, is enigmatic, mysterious.
- To get ahead I must reveal the mystery.
- To get ahead I must buy this book.

It is an unanswerable, compelling sequence. Something very like it probably went through your head when you decided to buy. My title started the process. Your purchase completed it.

When I conceived this book, I developed a flyer about it, a flyer which was bound into printings of **The Consultant's Kit** and which I made generally available to both individuals and the media.

Do the same.

From the moment the idea is born, and more specifically, from the moment you select your title you have a product to promote, a vehicle for self-promotion. Don't neglect it.

Pre-Publication Excerpts

I look at material as a mine. Unlike the usual subterranean variety, however, one lump of material can be mined and mined again. This process begins with producing pre-publication excerpts and articles.

My goal when I write a book is to get media attention from the moment I conceive of the title through post-publication articles and excerpts. In this regard each word I write, each, can be published at least three times — in the first pre-publication excerpt, in the book itself, and in the post-publication excerpt. A word which the author prints only once had either be destined for a sublime home like the **New York Times,** or it will rest in oblivion.

As I produce my books I simultaneously consider how best I can utilize the material:

- Shall I reprint chapters as is?
- Shall I mine chapters and material to produce articles, columns, &c?
- Can I use an article or excerpt so produced as the basis for a media wave?

The answer to each of these questions ought to be "Yes!"

My book **Insubstantial Pageant: Ceremony And Confusion At Queen Victoria's Court** is a good illustration of how this part of the promotional process works.

As previously mentioned the book was originally run as a multi-part series in **The Times** of London, with some appearing in **The Irish Times.** You are not surprised to learn that each word published there was reprinted (with permission) in the actual book.

As the librarian of Windsor Castle told me, however, in expressing his opinion of my decision to publish in newspapers, "But they are so ephemeral," he lamented. So they are.

It is, therefore, my rule of thumb that as much of my material as possible printed in newspapers should also be put in a more lasting publication, a general interest trade or even academic publication. Thus the same material on English ceremonial coinage published in **The Times** turned out in a more dignified, refined (but substantially similar) format came to rest in the annals of an official numismatic journal published by the British Museum. Likewise, the amusing piece on the amateurish way nineteenth century naval reviews were handled, which made such an impression when published by **The Times** on the day of the Queen's Spithead Review in 1977, was suitably ensconced in a full-dress version in England's premier naval magazine. My piece on the snubs given to Queen Kapiolani of Hawaii went first into **The Times**, thence into a Hawaiian magazine. And so on.

So it should be with your material.

As you are working on your book you should carefully review the material which you have available and the totality of self-promotional outlets. You should be continually asking yourself, "How can I make what I've got both interesting and suitable in format for this media source?" I ask myself this question every day as I seek to discover how the information and material which I have will meet the objectives of media people.

Excerpting

If you want your material to be excerpted in magazines (and why not?), you must remember that they often have considerable time leads, 4-5 months is not uncommon.

Generally excerpting is a process that you begin to consider only when the book is actually finished; up to that time, you can refashion the material you have into articles, &c. With **Insubstantial Pageant,** I refashioned material. With **Our Harvard** I excerpted both prior to and at the time of publication.

If you are looking to magazines excerpting (as opposed to that in newspapers which can move faster), be prepared to begin hawking chapters as soon as they are in final form, even if the book itself is not yet in production. This is because magazines often take their time about deciding, and because it is generally not a good idea to have more than one publication at a time reviewing the same material.

A Caution Or Two

Beware of publishing too much of your material too far before your book's publication date. As in all self-promotional matters, I prefer a controlled process. In general, I advise you to begin publishing the bulk of your articles and excerpts 90 days before the official publication date, that is just about the time books are actually available.

If some material is published even earlier, don't worry. Just make sure to get leave behinds to the publisher's promotion department and to the sales representatives who are presenting your book to the stores. You want them to proclaim it a "comer."

What I have so far discussed pertains exclusively to print media. Reserve, whenever possible, your appearances on radio and television to such time as your book is actually printed and available in stores.

Much of what happens before a book is published will be the responsibility of the unabashed self-promoter. You must interest people in your title and subject, and you must fashion the articles and mine your material to best advantage. The excerpts, however, if you are publishing with a regular publisher will probably not be your responsibility. This does not mean, however, that you should not be aware of how the publisher works — or should assume that he is handling the matter properly and to your best economic and self-promotional interest. So saying, it is time to explore both this aspect of the relationship with your publisher and other important ones, too.

The Unabashed Self-Promoter And His Publisher

In general I have found publishers particularly inept and infuriating on the subject of book promotion. My feeling is echoed by most authors of my acquaintance. Publishers tend to dismiss this talk as the usual grousing of authors, but they are sadly mistaken to do so. I have therefore developed the following check list which should help you decide, before you sign a contract, whether a publisher is going to give you anywhere near the assistance you need.

- **Talk to your prospective publisher's promotional representative**

Find out what manner of creature you will be dealing with. If this individual cannot give you detailed answers to your questions today and strikes you as insipid now, think what it will be like later when the initial pleasantries are history. Understand, first, that a publisher is not doing you a favor by publishing your book, that it is in your mutual interest to come to an understanding. You have labored long and hard in the production of a product. You have every reason to be thorough in investigating the abilities of the publisher and his personnel to do justice to it.

- **Ask about promotion for the average book**

Ask the publicity representative to tell you, in detail, *exactly* what is done to promote the average book, not **Jaws**, not **Gone With The Wind**, the average title with a 3000-5000 first printing. Unless you are the exception you can expect to be similarly treated. Ask to see some standard media releases. Too often they are so bland and unappealing that even your own mother wouldn't buy your book if this is all she knew of it. Ask whether all material, all, can be sent to you in draft form to review prior to printing and mailing? Demand the right of review.

- **Who will you work with? How aware is he of media sources?**

Find out whether you are going to be assigned an account representative. If not, find out who you will be working with. Don't just assume you'll end up working with the right person. Far more likely is the reverse. Once you know, find out how much he knows about the right media sources for your book. It isn't just a question of knowing that a certain show exists, but knowing a particular host or producer. Find out what sources of information your representative has available. Is he using standard media directories, or does he have some contacts? If he has contacts, will he use them for you? Don't assume the answer. Is there the right chemistry between you and your publicity representative? This is incredibly important. Does he share your vision of the book and its possibilities, or is this just another prosaic assignment for him? Find out in advance. After you've signed your contract, it's probably too late.

- **Will the publisher target media and follow them up?**

As you are now well aware, unselect mailings to media rarely have great impact. Thus a publisher must be willing not only to draw up appropriate materials and mail them but follow them up with telephone calls, and, in the case of the most important media, meetings. Will this happen? Media people ordinarily need to be sold on an idea; they need to be shown how the material in your book relates to their format. They need to be convinced both that the subject is of interest to their audience and that you can deliver it in an interesting fashion. This involves salesmanship — and targeting. If your publisher can promise no more than the standard fare, producing a standard media release to accompany the standard mailing of 100-200 review copies, you are probably in the wrong place.

- **How will your publisher handle expenses?**

These days precious few authors travel around the country doing major promotional tours. Their expenses are covered. Will yours be? Say you live in Boston and you want to arrange a day of media here, one in Hartford, and one in New York. Your travel and accommodation expenses need not be extravagant. But will the publisher bear them? Moreover, if your publicity representative proves inept and unforthcoming (all too likely), will the publisher supply you with sufficient funds to:

- produce an acceptable media packet
- distribute it
- cover telephone expenses, &c.

If not, think again. Think of your irritation if the publisher cannot provide you with suitable publicity assistance, decides not to cover your own expenses, and yet you decide to go ahead on your own. You will benefit from your labors, of course, but the publisher will still make more from the sale of the book! I doubt you will enjoy knowing this.

- **Know the rights representative**

Most large publishing companies have on staff an individual who handles rights, permissions and excerpts. Smaller publishing companies contract out for this service. Because you now know that excerpts are most important, you will want to know the individual handling them. Ask him the questions you need to have specifically answered:

- How do you work?
- When do you begin to submit material?
- Where do you think my material can go?
- Who do you know there?
- Will you multiply submit?
- How long will you allow a source to retain material?
- What other projects will you be dealing with when this project needs attention?
- Are you prepared to negotiate on the price with excerpt publishers?

This last point can be most significant. I remember one particularly irritating experience in connection with my book **Our Harvard.** The Editor of **Harvard Magazine** told me one day they had made an offer for one of the pieces of the book. It was, though a good offer, less than what the excerpt consultant had wanted. The sale was not made, and, in fact, the piece in question never did get excerpted. A nice promotional opportunity lost for both author and me because of the obtuse stubbornness of the individual handling excerpts.

As you discuss your book and its promotional possibilities with your publisher and his representative look for clear, detailed, specific answers. Don't be satisfied with bromides. Also, ask for the names, addresses and telephone numbers of a couple of current authors. Find out from your literary colleagues just how happy they are.

The Publication Party

Most books these days are not given a publication party. This is not only an unfortunate impoverishment of the literary and social scenes, it is a mistake from a promotional standpoint. I have in my own life rectified this alarming state of affairs.

A publicity party is not just an opportunity to impress your friends and colleagues that, after a long bout with poverty and obscurity, you have finally arrived. Instead, it is chiefly an opportunity to alert appropriate media to the existence of something worth covering, you and your book. The only possible reason not to hold such a party is that the media you need to influence are dispersed and cannot attend. Even so, I say go ahead.

I have often said what bears repeating here, namely that your party can be a smashing self-promotional success whether anyone comes or not. The event itself may or may not be of significance; how you follow-up the event and exploit it is very important. Remember that.

In this regard the guest list for your party is of critical significance as are the materials you produce about your book to accompany the invitation. First here's who should be invited:

- representatives of all media who can promote you and the book *in any way.* Do not hesitate to invite people you don't know, and do not hesitate to invite multiple representatives from the same media target. Here in Boston the **Globe** is our most significant newspaper. I may send our invitations and information packets to as many as 20 individuals on this newspaper including the publisher, selected editors, columnists, individual reporters, &c. Many of these will be people I don't know.
- people in your Self-Promotion Contact Network who are not themselves decision makers but who are connected to such people
- free-lance writers
- opinion makers in your marketing area. Such people by talking about you, your book, your party help promote it.

When I published my first book and had my first publishing party, the invitations were simple and eloquent. Now I have gone beyond. These days (as you will see from the material in Chapter 20), I accompany each invitation with an exhaustive packet of materials, in fact a media packet. I send these materials to each guest whether they are directly connected to the media or not. I like each guest to come prepared, of course (the residual pedagogue in me), but more than than that I like the media people to have all the material they need so that if they cannot come they can still write a wonderful story — as they so often do.

At The Party

I always have fun at my parties which have a justly-deserved reputation for an excellent mix of worthwhile people, superb food and drink, and an atmosphere of congenial bonhomie. Such events are rare.

But I regard these parties as work. As an unabashed self-promoter I know that the most important benefits to be derived from this event come after it is over. This, however, takes work while the event is on.

First, never fail to make use of this event as a massive photo opportunity. As you learned in Chapter 11, now apply. A photographer should be on hand to take photographs of you and individual guests. This should be the picture: you, the author, with Mr. and Mrs. Adams of Manchester. All other people from Manchester should also be in this picture, although you should avoid overcrowding. In a party of 50 people, you can probably get 30 or more such photos. Do them quickly and in an organized manner.

You want these pictures developed *as soon as possible* so that you can dispatch them to appropriate trade newspapers and magazines and (usually) weekly newspapers. If you have significant guests in attendance, or either you or your book is of local importance, the major daily newspapers may also publish a photograph, but this must be developed promptly. Don't forget pictures for the magazines of organizations with which you are associated: religious, alumni, fraternal, social. All need photographs demonstrating the exaltation and success of their members. Not neglecting to invite editors and writers from such sources will, of course, help insure publication.

Even if they don't come.

After all, parties are not cheap. They are not, however, expensive either. A very nice party should cost, for invitations, accompanying packets, food, drink, bartenders, room, flowers, &c., between $750-1000.

Just how you follow-up this event will determine whether this is a lot of money or a reasonable investment.

Follow-Up

All the media people you have invited get followed-up, whether they came or didn't. Of course if they came, it will be easier. Under the influence of that delectable third martini, one may have let slip that fatal phrase, "I'd like to have you on my show." You have only to call up and reap your rich, very much earned harvest. Gratefully such circumstances do occur, more and still more as your promotional career matures.

At the beginning, however, expect matters to be rather more demanding. As before, you need a Media Activity Chart. Systematically begin to contact (usually by telephone) all media sources.

If the individual was in attendance call and remind him what a good time he had. Ask whether he needs any further material (there should have been extra packets and copies of the book at the event) and whether he has given any thought to what program you should be on or how else to feature your book. Frankly, you should be prepared to be helpful — suggest your preference. Be prepared to give your reasons. While the extent and duration of the salesmanship will probably be reduced because of your hospitality, you cannot forego it. If you do not, on your first call, get the specifics you require, at least arrange a time when you can call back and wrap matters up.

If the media representative did not accept your genteel invitation, you have more selling to do. Face it, many media people (but significantly, not all) get many, many invitations. Thus in following up, you cannot even assume they remember receiving yours. Significantly, too, given the general laxness about media mail delivery, you cannot even assume it was received. Thus:

- Keep calling until you get media target on telephone. In your message say you are following up an invitation sent on a particular date.
- When you get the media target on the telephone, express your regrets that he was unable to attend. Tell him what a swell party it was. (Maybe next time, he'll look livelier.)
- If he indicates he got no invitation, tell him why you held the party. Say you'd like to send some material before speaking in detail about your idea.
- Send material.
- Telephone again.

Now you are into the same sequence that I have previously presented, the sales sequence. The same is true if the media target has the material, for you must still present a compelling case and persuade the media target to turn over some of his scarce space and air time to you.

As before, pursue every lead. You have opened the contact with your invitation. It is your responsibility to bring it to a conclusion.

Remember: a book nicely opens the possibility of a media wave. Take it.

Just one caution: before you launch this wave make sure that your publisher has books in the stores. Don't use up your exposure unless you are sure of getting maximum profit from this project. Just how the publisher can insure the delivery of these books at the appropriate time might be one of the questions you'd like to ask him before signing the contract. Don't overlook the desirability of speaking to the sales force sharing with them your vision of the book. They can impart this — and your promotional plans — to the book store owners whom I, as a matter of course, also invite to all my publishing parties.

After The Send-Off

You have now had advance articles, pre-publication excerpts and excerpts which accompanied publication, a smashing publicity party which produced dozens of targeted photographs as well as the entré to many, many media sources, both present and absent. Is that all there is?

No!

The existence of the final product, the book itself, opens the possibility for post-publication articles and excerpts. This self-promotional phase corresponds to that before publication except that you now have the final product to show editors.

Alas! This all-too-beautiful product gets less and less valuable as a promotional property with every passing day as its informational content ages. Act now!

Even before you have bound books, you should have drawn up a Media Activity Chart showing just what places you intend to send books to — and what your objective is in doing so.

Most publishers seem to concentrate on getting reviews. These are not nearly as significant to me. I want excerpts, features based on me and the book, &c., formats which will draw much greater attention to me and the book than a mere review no matter how complimentary. Of course, it goes without saying that I do not cavil when such a review is forthcoming. Neither will you.

This review, however, should not be your primary objective. Always aim for more major treatment and make sure that you have the publisher reserve to you a sufficient number of review copies so that you have something to send to editors.

A Book's Promotional Lifespan

Most books draw publicity for a single publishing season, not more. This is, however, less the fault of an individual book itself than the inexorable sequence of the publishing schedule which produces list after list, the newest pushing aside the last.

In fact, as I have discovered with **The Consultant's Kit**, there is no reason why you can't get media attention for years with a given book. By the time this book is published, **The Consultant's Kit** will have been out two years; throughout this time it has consistently drawn substantial media attention. This is, of course, in large part because of the wide interest in the subject and because of some significant national trends. Other books on other subjects may not have drawn so well even given masterful and ingenious promoting. But part of the genius of the unabashed self-promoter is not only that he knows *how* to handle promotion, but he senses just what will lend itself to his proven techniques.

One thing that helps is being featured in a book.

Books About You, The Unabashed Self-Promoter

The first time I was featured in a book was by accident, that is to say I didn't initiate the process. That was in 1977 when some of my dealings with the late Pulitzer Prize winning poet Anne Sexton showed up in a posthumous collection of her correspondence, **A Self-Portrait In Letters.** Mrs. Sexton and I had had a rather turbulent relationship surrounding a poetry reading she was to give at Harvard; as this proved to be her last public reading it took on a significance no one could have foreseen at the time. Still, I didn't like the way the editors handled the correspondence, and the fact that they printed it without knowing all the circumstances. I printed my response, drawn from my very copious journals, in a very reputable literary magazine.

That fact that I didn't entirely like the sections about me in the Sexton book in no way precluded me from using them to my advantage. Mrs. Sexton had a significant local following and **The Self-Portrait In Letters** graces many book shelves. Being included in the book gave me a certain caché that my eager-to-be-immortalized peers didn't have. It was one thing to write a book, oh-so-much better to be featured in one.

Quite.

More recently I have discerned how to stimulate the production of books featuring me and how to use them for maximum self-promotional advantage. I thought you'd probably want to know.

Maverick: Succeeding As A Free-Lance Entrepreneur

In the fall of 1982, Franklin Watts (New York) published **Maverick** by Canadian author Geoffrey Bailey. It presents an admirable example of a book format which does not only immortalize the unabashed self-promoter but also gives him a springboard for further media attention.

Maverick is a book modelled after the Problem-Solving Process article. It aims to give aspiring entrepreneurs a good introductory understanding of what they must know to succeed and offers in the process a step-by-step guide. Each step in this process is exemplified by one or two individuals. Bailey both personalizes each particular step and makes it accessible to the reader by presenting it through the work of his featured entrepreneurs. I am featured in a chapter entitled "Never Vaudeville: Introducing Jeffrey L. Lant" which deals with how to create a marketable proposal, something very important for any entrepreneur.

Any self-promoter worth his salt should be able to stimulate and produce a book similar to **Maverick.** Here's how:

- Think of a Problem-Solving Process book in your field. It doesn't matter whether it's "10 Steps To A More Beautiful Garden" or "How To Lobby Your Bill Through Congress."
- Identify all the steps in the problem-solving process. You must yourself be aware of just what it takes to produce the desired objectives and must outline them specifically. The reader of **Maverick** will, by its conclusion, have a good sense of what is necessary to succeed as an entrepreneur — step by mandatory step.
- Identify individuals who are good examples of each step. This may initially seem harder than it is as you wonder just who you know who ought to be included. In practice to begin the project you need to identify only two or three. These people will have their own contact networks and will happily refer you to others who can be of assistance. I myself was brought into **Maverick** in this fashion by Bailey's editor at Franklin Watts.
- Either feature yourself in a chapter or sprinkle the text with propitious examples of your techniques. Here I take issue with Bailey. He approached the task of writing **Maverick** as author to text, and therefore did not include himself as a subject in the book. This is, of course, perfectly standard, but he missed a splendid opportunity to promote his own business.

Producing a book like **Maverick** is not difficult. In actual fact, the subject of each chapter more or less writes his own material, or, at the very least, gives the author all the information he needs to fashion it himself. My section of **Maverick,** for instance, draws heavily from **The Consultant's Kit. Maverick,** therefore, becomes part of the multiple use of my consulting material, the chief expression of which is **The Consultant's Kit.**

What could be easier?

The tricky part, of course, is finding a publisher. If, of course, you have a trendy subject like consulting, you may want to publish it yourself. But you may wish to forego the delights and travails of self-publishing in favor of the traditional route, just as Geoffrey Bailey did. That's fine, too. Just be sure that if you do, you review the earlier portion of this chapter so that you are entirely clear and comfortable about what your publisher will do for your book.

What is wonderful about a book modelled after the Problem-Solving Process article is that it has a very neat outline, a definite beginning and end, it lends itself to including a series of experts, who themselves can either write the book or give you all the material you need to do so, and it is a very nice promotional vehicle for all concerned.

How We Used Maverick As A Self-Promotional Vehicle

My chief glory in **Maverick** is not so much having been included, flattering, of course, but not necessarily meaningful, as the way I used it as a self-promotional vehicle. As you will remember, I had had a wave on consulting and **The Consultant's Kit** in June, 1982 at the time of the Boston Consultants Convention. This wave had been the second whose actual objective (as opposed to its perceived objective) was promotion of **The Consultant's Kit.** It was unlikely that the Boston media would be amenable to a third wave on consulting unless the angle was substantially changed. **Maverick** did that; as such, it appeared at an ideal time for me.

The Angle

As stated before, we had two angles for this wave: "The Maverick Master And The Master Maverick" and "This Christmas Give Yourself A Job." The first of these keyed into the local angle of the story. Canadian author Bailey might or might not have been considered media worthy in the United States. As a Boston-based maverick, however, I gave him local credibility and a local angle. This suggests that when you are assembling your problem-solving process book, you will want to take into consideration just where everyone comes from. You will want to include individuals from all the major media markets in the country. This is clever planning and looks ahead to the day when they give you your local angle.

The second angle, "This Christmas Give Yourself A Job," was thematic and keyed into the top story of the hour: unemployment and the economy. We could easily piggyback on this top story by providing an interesting dimension and, importantly from the media's perspective, one possible solution to the problem. Everyone, everyone knew there was an economic problem in the nation. Now people wanted solutions. We provided at least one.

Timing

As soon as we had our themes, we determined just when we would be available to the media. In fact, our dual approach offered a good deal of flexibility. Geoffrey Bailey, coming from out of town, could only remain a limited time, in this case a little more than two days. This was our main period. During this time media sources had three interview options:

- Bailey alone
- Bailey and Lant
- Lant alone

Since I was local, I also had the possibility of providing interviews after Bailey left.

Predictably most media took the second option, the **Maverick** duo. It was, in fact, the most unusual. One or two stations preferred to interview Bailey alone, and after Bailey left I managed to get several more interviews by myself; in fact, ultimately I had more interviews in the Boston market than he did!

The Materials And Their Distribution

Our basic information was contained in **Maverick.** This was supplemented by a standard media release on the book and by supplementary leave behinds about me.

The standard release was, unfortunately, just that: standard.

The writer had not considered the possibilities of promoting the individuals featured in the book, and so their names were not in the release. Moreover, the text itself was flat and insipid. Inadequate though it was, we needed it, and we needed the books, too — fast. As is so often the case when working with the media, speed is of the essence. Extraordinarily, this is a hard point to impress upon publishers and their publicity representatives.

You have two courses of action when working in this situation: either you can send a list of media sources to the publisher, names and addresses, and ask that books be sent, or you can have a number of books sent to you directly and mail or deliver them yourself. I prefer the second option since it gives me maximum control; assured by the publisher, however, that books would be sent quickly, on this occasion we used the first option. It was so unsatisfactory that it only succeeded in reinforcing my predisposition to mail books myself.

Having been reassured by the publisher that books were in fact being sent, we placed calls to all the media people we wanted to work with. We assured them that they would have books in just a few days. Because of a predictable foul-up in New York, no books were mailed, and without this material most media people would not act. It is a testament to their faith in me and my record that some did decide to go ahead without having seen the information.

Ultimately a shipment of books was sent directly to me, and we hand delivered several to the most important media targets.

Learn from this experience: have books sent directly to you and ask the publisher to reimburse you for postage and delivery costs. At least this way you can be sure they have in fact been sent.

Because of the blandness and incompleteness of the standard media release, we also supplemented our materials with another release specially designed for Boston. This release highlighted our theme and both participants. Our final packet of materials included the following:

- **Maverick**
- standard media release on **Maverick**
- special media release for Boston
- leave behinds about me.

As before, we developed a Media Activity Chart to note which media targets we were pursuing, and then proceeded to follow-up.

The Interviews

In a joint project such as **Maverick,** there are several promotions going on:

- the book itself
- the author of the book
- the business of the author
- the individuals featured in the book
- their business projects

Both parties to the promotion need to be clear about what their promotional interests are and whether at any given point they conflict. In fact, they will ordinarily coincide quite nicely.

It is perfectly possible during the course of the average print or electronic media interview to promote all these objects. Certainly it is desirable to do so. Begin to do so in your introductions.

"Today, we have with us Geoffrey Bailey, author of **Maverick: Succeeding As A Free-Lance Entrepreneur,** a Canadian direct mail copy writer, and Dr. Jeffrey Lant, author of **The Consultant's Kit.** Dr. Lant is from Cambridge and is one of the mavericks featured in Bailey's new book."

During the course of the interview, it is very, very easy for each participant to plug the books, products and services of his partner. Here are some suggestions:

Bailey: "One of the key things in attracting new business is a persuasive marketing proposal. In Jeffrey Lant's book **The Consultant's Kit,** there is a really admirable section on this topic. I drew on what Jeffrey Lant wrote for **Maverick.**"

This is very deftly done. Bailey stands forth as a very likable figure as well as knowledgeable about his subject. I get yet another plug.

Note: whenever possible cite the full name of all individuals, their products and services. You are building name recognition. Continued repetition is important.

Quite properly the emphasis in all the interviews was **Maverick.** That was the ostensible purpose of the promotion and was of chief interest to the author. Thus during most interviews I let Bailey take the lead. Because our interests were mutual, however, he was able to meet both his — and mine. In my own remarks, I returned the favor.

The Results

The result of the **Maverick** promotion brought 15 radio, television and newspaper interviews in the Boston area, a superb result. This promotion secured its objectives. It:

- promoted the primary product, **Maverick**
- heightened awareness about the author
- highlighted his business and projects
- produced a third media wave for **The Consultant's Kit**
- promoted my goods and services
- broadened public awareness about me.

Other Promotional Possibilities

I also used **Maverick** as a means of promoting myself to the following kinds of publications:

- trade
- alumni
- civic
- social
- fraternal
- religious

Again, this announcement easily piggybacked on **Maverick** other products and services which I wanted promoted. Here is a typical announcement:

> "Dr. Jeffrey Lant, president of Jeffrey Lant Associates, Inc. of Cambridge is featured in the new book **Maverick** by Geoffrey Bailey (Franklin Watts, New York). Lant's own latest book **The Consultant's Kit** has gone into a fifth printing."

Don't forget to make good use of all the people columns which appear in most publications. My rule of thumb is that I like to do so at least twice a year.

The Book Package

Perhaps having read this chapter you wonder whether you have the time, patience and information to do a book or whether you yet have the determination to help put together a promotional project like **Maverick.** Don't be discouraged. There is yet another alternative, a good one for introducing you to the world of books, publishing, and literary self-promotion: The Book Package.

The Book Package is a book on a single theme composed of the contributions of a number of writers, perhaps as few as six or eight, or as many as 50 or even more. I myself have participated in two such projects, as editor of **Our Harvard: Reflections On College Life By Twenty-Two Distinguished Graduates** and as general editor and writer of the preface for **An Introduction to Planned Giving: Fund Raising Through Bequests, Charitable Remainder Trusts, Gift Annuities And Life Insurance.**

In this method, you, the unabashed self-promoter, make a calculated decision about a subject or topic which will be a suitable promotional vehicle. Perhaps you have neither the time, inclination, nor material to write a complete book on the subject yourself, but you do want to generate a self-promotional opportunity. The Book Package is perfect for you.

Take **Our Harvard** for instance.

I did not go to Harvard College, although I did get my Ph.D. from the university. I wanted, however, to create a project that would:

- link me to the heart of the university
- promote me both to the general public and to the influential body of Harvard alumni
- put me in touch with a select group of those alumni
- produce revenue.

Our Harvard was the result.

Because of my lack of a Harvard undergraduate degree, I would never have been asked to be in such a book had I left it to anyone else. Thus would have been lost a very admirable self-promotional opportunity.

As it is, all my objectives have been realized, handsomely. The last direct mail piece I received from **Harvard Magazine,** the university's alumni publication, had an attractive insert promoting my book and one by the president of the university. There they were, cheek by jowl, a very pleasant combo.

What **Our Harvard** proves it that through a carefully controlled process it is possible for the unabashed self-promoter to ally himself both in the public's perception and in fact with any group of very prestigious, powerful individuals despite the fact that he has little or no connection with them — so long as the project he proposes meets their objectives.

The reason people like Erich Segal, Arthur Schlesinger, Buckminster Fuller and all the other illuminati of **Our Harvard** agreed to do the book had little if anything to do with me, everything to do with the fact that I provided a convenient, desirable vehicle for them, a means of reflecting on a pivotal period of their lives and standing agreeably and preeminently before their fellow alumni. The fact that I was able to turn the project to my own self-promotional uses, while very important to me, was of utterly no concern to any of the participants.

Even before it was published, **Our Harvard** began to pay self-promotional dividends. Each chapter had excerpt potential; ultimately places as diverse as the **Boston Sunday Globe Magazine** and **Esquire** did excerpt it. Moreover, it offered electronic media possibilities, too; remember the story about "Our Yale"? That took place on a major Boston radio station.

The result was just what I had hoped: the boy who grew up in a small midwestern town and graduated from the University of California, Santa Barbara became, through a creative self-promotional project, prominently associated with America's most prominent, most mandarin university. It was a very, very heady feeling to see during Commencement Week, 1982 when **Our Harvard** came out all the book stores all over Boston with this book well displayed in their windows and to see the joyful parents of newly-graduated alumni with the book tucked under their arms. This is yet another reward for the ever fertile, ever inventive, ever unabashed self-promoter.

An Introduction To Planned Giving

I conceived this project in my role as publisher of JLA Publications and recruited the editor, Daniel Vecchitto, who in turn recruited the other contributors, technical experts all. I contributed the book's preface.

A book package like this follows the Problem-Solving Process model. Unlike **Maverick,** however, the contributors wrote their own chapters.

An Introduction To Planned Giving was not designed for the general public. Its primary audience is fund raising professionals, tax attorneys, accountants, and executive directors of nonprofit organizations. As a specialized book it was best promoted through specialized media, although as an aid in tax planning, it also has general media possibilities.

Books like **Our Harvard** and **An Introduction To Planned Giving** are good models for the unabashed self-promoter to follow:

- They are relatively easy to produce (although there are decided strains about motivating and encouraging individual authors).
- They offer the same pre- and post-publication article and excerpt possibilities as any other book.
- They lend themselves nicely to sequels and can be easily updated and improved.
- They can meet the professional and promotional objectives of many, many people.

The unabashed self-promoter with limited time and, perhaps, with limited confidence about his ability to produce on his own a full-length book manuscript (an admittedly daunting project) needs to consider carefully the Book Package, which, properly handled, can meet your self-promotional objectives.

Although I am no expert in planned giving, I am now prominently associated with a major book on the subject, a book which **The Grantsmanship Center News,** a key publication in the field, called "excellent" in its review and which was excerpted in two of the major trade publications.

> "Dr. Jeffrey Lant has contributed the preface to the new book **An Introduction To Planned Giving** edited by Daniel Vecchitto. Lant is the president of Jeffrey Lant Associates, Inc. a Cambridge consulting firm. His own book on fund raising **Development Today: A Guide For Non-profit Organizations,** has just gone into a revised Second Edition."

Thus the unabashed self-promoter, in this instance through a Book Package which he creates, deftly extends his credentials while, at the same time, promoting his other ventures. No, do not overlook the delectable promotional possibilities of the Book Package even though you may yet be daunted by the book itself and may not yet think yourself ready for the apotheosis of being the subject of a book.

And remember this: unless you have one or more of these possibilities in place, you will be denying yourself one of the great treats of unabashed self-promotion: the lecture circuit, where otherwise reasonable individuals turn over good hard cash for the privilege of beholding you at your oratorical best. Most within this curious pantheon got there via a book.

CHAPTER 17

THE UNABASHED SELF-PROMOTER AND THE TALK CIRCUIT

No unabashed self-promoter can afford to remain ignorant of the talk business. It offers both significant financial and promotional possibilities. The problem is that there is precious little written about it (and less of this of any real value), so that the ingénue is left to make his way alone — each step punctuated by some characteristic, unnecessary error. Pay close attention to this chapter, minimize your mistakes, maximize your beneficial return.

Breaking In: The Rubber Chicken Circuit

Very, very few people begin at the top of the talk business in demand nationally, represented by an agent, drawing princely fees of $1000 or more per performance. (Johnny Carson at $40,000 per speech, Henry Kissinger at about $25,000 and Alexander Haig a little lower constitute the upper limits and give you a handy yardstick.) My advice to you if you want to skip the necessary plodding and mundane first steps is to arrange to be captured by foreign terrorists, save the president from an assassin, or perform some other spectacular feat. Otherwise resign yourself to following my suggestions.

Off, Off Broadway With The Unabashed Self-Promoter

America has tens of thousands of organizations most local, all ready for you. As I have discussed previously (review Chapter 8), these organizations all offer self-promotional possibilities. The fact that most people fail to make the best use of these opportunities should be of no interest to you; after all, most people fail to make the best use of any opportunity. You, however, are different.

Getting Invited

Most organizations, whether the local Kiwanis, Knights of Columbus or PTA, are hard up for good speakers. Members constantly lament the tedium of the speeches they are forced to hear. Most lavish excessive praise on efforts which by any standard are mediocre. Thus, take heart! If you are bad, with thin content and abject delivery, you will be no worse than what they've already heard, and will quickly be dumped into the grateful darkness of oblivion. If you are anything other than bad, you will be remembered as the closest thing to silver-tongued Cicero who has ever graced their podium.

To get your invitation, ask your friends to arrange to have you invited. You must know what organizations *all* your friends and relatives belong to, all. In your immediate circle there are probably several dozen useful affiliations. Here are some of them:

- religious organizations
- alumni and educational organizations
- civic
- social
- benevolent
- trade and labor
- fraternal

Complete a questionnaire on all your friends and associates until you have at least 12 possibilities. Don't forget the associations of your children. These, too, are links which can be used and which you should not overlook.

Press your contact into service on your behalf. Have him:

- find out the name of his organization's program chairman
- discover what kinds of speakers are needed, when, and for what program formats
- whether there is the possibility of payment.

Let me stress that while payment is nice and certainly is your goal, you cannot expect it and will usually not get it as a new, untried commodity. Frankly, given the new speeches I have heard (granted those who delivered them had not had the chance to read this book), they really ought to have paid the long-suffering organizations which hosted them!

Your contact ought also to brief the program chairman about you and on what a fine, inspiring, informed speaker you are and so create an opening so that you can contact the program chairman directly.

Note: in the unlikely event that an analysis of your friends' organizational contacts turns up little or nothing of any immediate use, you will have to approach program chairmen directly. In this case use a variety of the Sample letter found on page 336.

What Should I Talk About?

Popular polls consistently show that public speaking is the greatest fear of most adult Americans far surpassing our alarm and anxiety over such trifles as nuclear annihilation and an IRS audit. If nothing else, this has given me a useful insight into the mental condition and judgement of my fellow citizens. I suspect there are two related reasons for this anxiety:

- We fear that we know too little about any topic to be of any interest.
- We feel diffident, if not worse, about submitting ourselves to the evaluation of an audience filled with, we are sure, masters of picayune and caustic criticism.

If this is how you feel, get over it!

While a detailed knowledge of any given subject is certainly helpful in giving a convincing platform performance, it is not, *not*, absolutely necessary. Seasoned speakers are inevitably masters of platform process and can, out of no more than a handful of illuminating anecdotes and supportive facts, weave a compelling performance. In fact, too much detailed knowledge in a speech is indisputably an error as the audience, without this rich detail set down before them, is overwhelmed by the niagara of information. Ergo, this rule: A speech or other oral presentation should have but one leading idea. All information, all facts and statistics, anecdotes should support and develop this one significant, structuring idea. If you can convince one person of one idea during your time together, you are a cogent speaker. To try and do more risks accomplishing nothing.

Do not worry about an over-critical audience. There are always, always people in any audience whose chief objective in life is to poke holes in what the speaker is saying and by successfully engaging the speaker in a species of guerilla warfare to emerge as the unquestioned victor. Don't worry. First, it is your show. The audience, even if they didn't know your name before you were introduced, and even though the name fled from their heads immediately after hearing it, has come to hear you.

Your audience has come to learn a little, to be entertained a lot, and to spend as pleasant an interlude as is possible. If you meet their objectives (and they are remarkably consistent whatever the educational level of the audience or the nature of their professional interests), you will be assured a warm, even enthusiastic welcome. Remember: it is undoubtedly the case that your audience has been burned before, generally often, by speakers who did not deliver this result. If you succeed in giving your audience what it wants, it will be quite prepared to overlook lapses of diction, mixed metaphores, improper subject verb agreement and other distresses. If you are engaged with your material and engaged with your audience, what matters such minutiae? They won't bother your audience, and they shouldn't bother you either.

Developing Your Core Program

This does not mean, however, that you shouldn't give consideration to what you are going to say. You have to. Successful speakers develop a Core Program, a program which they can repeat again and again and which can be changed, updated, expanded or even contracted as events develop and circumstances dictate. With such a Core Program, called The Speech, Ronald Reagan became president. No one should underestimate either its utility or its power.

Your initial Core Program will probably be technical, that is on a subject where you are the master of all details. Mine was on fund raising for nonprofit organizations. This speech will be delivered both to organizations or individuals who have need to use the information (and, if you have arranged matters properly, the service you have developed to assist your potential clients) and to other professionals in your field with suitable variations.

The Core Program you develop can parallel the three basic article formats (see Chapter 7).

- The Problem-Solving Process Speech sets out 7-10 steps which lead, in sequential order, to the solution of a problem.
- The Sentinel Speech alerts your clients and potential clients to either an alarming or salubrious development which calls for prompt action on their part.
- The White Knight Speech alarms your audience about inimical developments in the field but suggests what can be done (read: what you can do) to create a beneficial result.

Later, as you become more advanced as both an authority and a self-promoter, you will mine your Core Program to develop a series of related technical programs and the inevitable motivational component which people need to be spurred into action. This development will be discussed at length later. Your initial problem is to develop a Core Program which can be delivered to the widest variety of organizations and which is capable of being molded into programs of varying durations and formats.

The Promotional Possibility Of The Rubber Chicken Circuit: A Reprise

If you are not being paid for a speech you can still benefit considerably, not least of course because of the practice you are getting. It is, however, your responsibility, not the host organization's, to see to it that you realize your self-promotional objectives. Most organizations have never dealt with a thorough-going, well-prepared self-promoter. They know nothing about the publicity business and have never considered themselves a vehicle for unabashed self-promotion. You are, therefore, dealing with the greenest of the green, and if you expect to realize your objectives you will have to keep them firmly in mind and be patient with the amateurs you are working with. Here's what you must do:

- Find out whether the organization has a newsletter. Oversee what goes in it about you. Your entry must stress the points which you want both your prospective audience and other organizations to know: your depth of knowledge about your subject, the services and products you have developed, your problem-solving process, your renown as a speaker, the timeliness of your message. Note: You want to be in this newsletter both in advance of your presentation and afterward. Don't forget to inquire as to whether the organization can print your photograph with the entry. Your interests may well be served before your speech by the publication of your photograph and a caption story of 50-100 words.
- Develop suitable media release(s). Develop a media release of about 350-500 words announcing your presentation. Find out the name of the local newspaper editor. Have the organization type this release on its own letterhead and mail. They must follow-up with a telephone call to insure that the material has arrived and that it will be used. Don't forget your photograph. If there is more than one local newspaper, consider developing a tailored release for each.
- If you have previously appeared in print and have print leave behinds, assess local television and radio programming. Identify suitable programs (ask organization program people for their assistance). Have the organization send media releases and follow-up with telephone calls. At the very least the organization should send the release with a letter indicating that *you* will personally follow-up. If you have any question about the preparedness and dependability of the organization use this method.
- Assess the possibilities for a citation, proclamation or other civic award. Is the organization you are speaking to of significant local importance? Are you more than the ordinary Wednesday lunch speaker? If so, a citation and presentation may be in order.
- Arrange to have your speech taped. To be a successful speaker, you need tapes. Make arrangements to have your speech taped, even by a friend. If the organization cannot or will not assist with taping your presentaton, get permission to bring a friend. You probably need to ask, since extra food may be involved.
- Ask for a letter of recommendation and endorsement. Keep a file of letters from organizations where you have spoken. Don't expect the organization to offer such a letter spontaneously. It won't. In requesting such a letter, you have several options:
  - Simply let the organization write the best letter it can. Such a letter may or may not be helpful to you.
  - Suggest topic headings to be addressed in the letter:
    - professional approach to planning
    - program content
    - audience response
    - receptivity to questions
    - desire to have you back
    - send a letter from another organization as a sample.

When you are beginning your speaking career, each speech you make will take considerable time in preparation and will probably cause you mental stress and anxiety. You will, of course, learn by doing which is a substantial benefit. But do not let this be the only benefit. Use each speaking opportunity to hone your self-promotional skills, too, and develop your reputation and standing.

A Note For Beginners

If you are suffering from a particularly bad case of nerves or if you simply want additional opportunities for practice, consider joining Toastmasters International. I myself have never been a member, but I recognize its utility and suggest you attend at least one meeting to see whether it might be helpful.

Formed in 1924, Toastmasters has a variety of meetings; most clubs meet weekly and provide numerous occasions for speakers to get up before a live audience with prepared and extemporaneous presentations. For further information, check your telephone book or write the World Headquarters:

Toastmasters International
2200 North Grand Avenue
Santa Ana, CA 92711

Moving Ahead: Expanding Beyond Your Core Program

The successful speaker has not only one but several presentations, different both in content and format. The real practiced, polished speakers may have two or three dozen programs, one way and another.

As I mentioned, my initial Core Program was fund raising for nonprofit organizations. This was a particularly good core selection, since it addressed the basic needs of organizations, cut across professional lines, was national, had a large potential following, and could be mined for many other presentations.

Develop Programs Of Differing Formats

All too many people think the talk circuit is composed solely of celebrities who make after-dinner speeches. Nothing could be further from the truth. These people garner a disproportionate share of the limelight, but they constitute only a small fraction of the action.

The unabashed self-promoter, expanding beyond his Core Program, must develop a series of program formats. Here are the available options:

- 45-60 minute standard lecture presentation
- 2-2½ hour workshop presentation. Primarily lecture but may include limited audience participation.
- 4 hour (½ day) workshop. Allows for greater audience participation. Actual case studies of participants may be addressed.
- 7 hour (full-day) workshop. Allows for extensive lecture, elaborated problem-solving procedures as well as participant involvement.
- 2 day workshop. In this program participants should begin to perform written exercises based on your lectures and problem-solving methods.
- 5 day institute. Should be run very much like a college class with extensive lecture, homework by participants and in-class writing assignments.

Note: Every program I do begins first as a Core Program and is then developed into these different formats. Every one. The unabashed self-promoter becomes expert at developing programs for any conceivable situation using the same body of information.

Developing Additional Programs From Your Core Program: Your Speaking Conglomerate

Once you have defined your Core Program and refined it into each separate format, it is time to begin developing related programs of interest to your targeted market. Once I had developed my initial Core

Program it was developed into suitable vehicles both for nonprofit laymen (executive directors and board members) and for fellow professionals in the field (development counsel, directors of development, &c.)

Next, the program was developed into different time formats:

- 45-60 minute speech on fund raising for nonprofit organizations. Can be given at civic, social, fraternal organizations at lunch or after dinner. Can also be targeted to lunch or dinner meeting of nonprofit professional associations or even to the board of directors of a specific not-for-profit organization. As new technical information becomes available this information can easily be factored into this speech.
- 2-2½ hour workshop. This program can be given at local, state or national meetings of nonprofit associations. It constitutes an introductory training program for laymen. Also, as "New Developments in Fund Raising" it can be shaped to be appropriate for fund raising professionals.
- 4 hour workshop. Again, this is used for local, state and national meetings of nonprofit organizations. It is designed for laymen who have either limited or no fund raising experience but who are now raising funds. It gives them some introductory familiarity with problems they are likely to encounter and presents information useful to their own situations.
- Full day workshop. This is designed as a separate activity. Where the two-hour and half-day workshops are ordinarily run as part of a convention, often competing against other workshops on topics of interest to the members, this program customarily stands alone. A single organization may sponsor it as a training session for those involved in fund raising, including trustees and staff; it can also be sponsored by a local, state or national organization which charges participants an often-nominal cost to attend.
- Two day workshop. This workshop is also designed as a separate activity. It is most likely that an association, as opposed to a single organization, would sponsor this program, although, from time to time, two or three organizations co-sponsor it and either keep sessions entirely private or allow a few other local organizations to participate for a charge.
- Five day institute. This format is ordinarily arranged by a college or university which may offer credit for the program. Under this format, you act as lecturer in chief and master of ceremonies. Other speakers may be invited to make presentations on select subjects. There are numerous opportunities both for student participation and for more traditional homework assignments. Like all programs, this one should be capable of national replication. Three years ago I launched the Nonprofit Technical Assistance Institute at Cambridge College. This takes place in June each year.

Diversifying Beyond Your Core Program

One of the several keys to succeeding as a speaker and to making the utmost use of your opportunities is to reuse all your links. Once you have delivered one useful program to an organization, you are a known quantity. The goal is to be invited back. If your program is exceptionally timely and utilitarian, producing the avid enthusiasm of your listeners, you should offer it to the organization for future meetings (See samples, page 338). However, be apprized that there are many occasions when your speech will have been received with rapture and the organization still will not want it repeated right away, seeking instead something new, different, unusual, the characteristic American quest. In such circumstances, you must diversify or risk losing a beneficial connection.

If you have chosen your Core Program carefully, that is if it meets the essential needs of your listeners, you can easily add a series of supplementary programs. What are your listeners' essential needs?

- If your listeners are connected to an organization, they are probably looking for information which will increase their profits within the current fiscal year.
- If your listeners are individuals, they are probably seeking information on how to be more attractive to others and more successful in life — immediately.

If your Core Program falls within either one of these areas, you are likely to experience the least difficulty in securing speaking engagements — so long as you follow the other suggestions of this book.

You will be marketable, but not quite as readily, if your Core Program:

- advises individuals associated with organizations how to cut expenses in the current fiscal year.

You will be even less marketable, if:

- you advise individuals connected to organizations how to increase long-term profit beyond the current fiscal year and, similarly, reduce long-term expenses.

Note: All programs focusing on private individuals must get them to do something — now! You must put them on the road to greater riches, alluring beauty, a flatter stomach, today. Collectively, we have a ridiculously abbreviated attention span, but this can work to your advantage as both speaker and unabashed self-promoter.

Defining Additional Technical Subjects

Once you know what people are likely to buy, you can expand beyond your Core Program in this fashion: Create a series of complementary, supplementary programs which relate both to what people are likely to buy first and additionally to what they are likely to buy thereafter.

I diversified beyond my Core Program on fund raising for nonprofit organizations into the following areas:

- capital campaign fund raising
- corporation and foundation fund raising
- board development for nonprofit organizations
- public relations for nonprofit organizations

By the same token, my Core Program in consulting is entitled "Establishing And Operating Your Successful Consulting Business." I diversified beyond this program into:

- selecting your niche as a consultant
- creating your consulting Supergroup
- exploiting the media to become *the* nationally-known expert in your field
- creating and managing your Mobile Mini-Conglomerate

As you may imagine this book will spawn an entire series of programs based on the unabashed self-promoter theme. The Core Program is called "The Unabashed Self-Promoter's Guide."

What is important to realize is that each of these programs, developed from a basic core of information, can be presented in anything from a one-hour format to one running through five days. In this way for me, three Core Programs have become 15 program formats, all with significant self-promotional possibilities, national territories, and tens of thousands of listener-participants.

Your Move Into Trade, Technical And Professional Associations

Once you have diversified beyond your Core Program, you are ready to make a concerted assault on America's trade and professional associations and leave the Rubber Chicken Circuit behind. Today I rarely speak without a fee and very, very rarely to the host of civic, fraternal, and benevolent organizations which constitute the heart of the Rubber Chicken Circuit. I am nonetheless very, very glad that they exist and thank those that suffered through my early perorations for their stoic endurance. I can only hope the food was good! Like me, you should make good use of these organizations, shaping and perfecting your presentations, exploiting all media opportunities. Once you know what you are doing, how to create material you need, how to deliver it for maximum effect, how to work the media like a fine instrument, move ahead. You are ready to make dividends on your investment.

Begin With Your Own Trade Or Professional Association

The unabashed self-promoter in his role as speaker par excellence is an assiduous reader of convention programs. Keep them on file. Ask your friends to bring you the agendas of the conventions they attend. Get in the practice of sending for the agendas of conventions you would like to speak at. In this connection, you should be aware of a publication noting many forthcoming conventions and the cities in which they will be held:

World Convention Dates
Hendrickson Publishing Co., Inc.
79 Washington St
Hempstead, New York 11550
(516) 483-6881

To begin with, however, make sure you see the agenda of each convention, local, state, national, or your own professional organization.

The reason you need to review this material is simple: Is there a competing program to yours about to be offered or which was offered at the latest meeting? If not, you have the field to yourself: Take it. Call the organization and find out who is acting as program chairman for the next meeting. Find out, too, if any state or regional meetings are scheduled for the next year. Ask who is organizing them. Then write a letter requesting consideration. (See samples, page 336). This letter should:

- Indicate your familiarity with the organization's most recent or forthcoming convention agenda.
- Indicate that you have a topic which is or ought to be of considerable interest to the members. Give reasons for this conclusion if they are not self-evident.
- Propose one or two formats for your presentation and indicate that others are available.

Should you mention money in this letter? That depends. If you have become a practiced speaker regularly commanding honoraria, then you had better say so. Do not, however, mention any specific numbers until you have an expression of interest from the organization and a clear indication of what you might be doing.

If you are not yet a recognized professional speaker, don't mention payment in this first letter. Again, you need to have an expression of the organization's interest and an idea of what their objectives and expectations are.

Note: It is perfectly acceptable, often indeed desirable, to have a friend who is a member of an organization mention your name. This is another illustration of networking. I ask my friends *and* clients to recommend me to their professional and trade associations as a matter of course. It is your responsibility to direct conversations to their associations and memberships. Find out the complete names, addresses, telephone numbers and leadership of these organizations. Never be afraid to ask for it. Also, consult the **Encyclopedia Of Associations** for such information.

Remember: Letters such as this one should be accompanied by suitable leave behinds. You should also indicate that you have a tape available for review. Now's when you need it.

Follow-Up

Once you have sent this kind of letter (or had a friend do so), it is your responsibility to follow it up with a telephone call.

In my experience program planners of conventions are generally not difficult to track down. They are not professionals but amateurs given their positions for a year and often exceedingly unsure about how to proceed. Surprisingly, even the biggest and "best run" national associations do not keep a Convention Book, gathering from organizers information on what worked and what didn't for their meetings. Thus year after year program planners are left to reinvent the wheel. They will probably be very glad to hear from you, especially if you have had a good strong letter of recommendation or if you are a member or otherwise connected. Here's what to do:

- Find out whether the convention agenda is set. If it is, in cement, go no farther. Find out instead who will be the *next* program chairman. Get specific information on how to contact this person. If the next program chairman has not yet been appointed, contact the association's executive director and indicate that you will follow-up your letter immediately after the next convention. It goes without saying that if you are attending this convention, you should try to meet personally either with the executive director or the program chairman, if this person can be identified and is present.
- Do not end your conversation with the current program chairman until you have indicated that if plans change (as they so often do in this business), you'd like to be considered. Make sure the program chairman has all necessary information on how to reach you.
- If the agenda has not been finalized, ask whether the topic(s) you have proposed is of interest. Prepare to sell them to this pivotal decision maker. Dwell on their perceived value and benefit to the membership. If the program chairman informs you that there is something comparable on the agenda, ask him to read the description. Often programs with similar titles are in fact quite different. Often an identical program given by two different experts produces two quite distinct results. It is your obligation to explain this to the program chairman.
- If you have proposed only one program and the program chairman has declined to be interested, you can either say you'll be back with another idea or you can again indicate you are available if things change. In this situation, be sure to get the name of the *next* program chairman and write ahead with your suggestions. It is doubtful that many speakers who have

been successful in getting an assignment, protect their position by letting the next program chairman know of their continuing interest. So, you get in first. If you are later told that the original speaker again wishes to make his presentation, you at least have bargaining leverage and the opportunity to present something else.

If The Program Chairman Indicates Interest In You And Your Program

Once you have found out that the program chairman is interested, you need some additional information:

- What convention speaking spots are open? Don't automatically assume anything about what kind of presentation you will give. It is, of course, unlikely that fresh from the Rubber Chicken Circuit you will keynote a major national convention, but don't automatically assume otherwise. Ask the program chairman if the keynote speaker has yet been confirmed. If all breakfast and lunch speakers have been selected. If the speaker for the awards banquet has been determined. You have this objective in seeking this information:
  - You want to emerge with the best possible speaking assignment. Like everything else in American life, convention speakers are divided into their own hierarchy with the keynote at the apex. You want to be as near this apex as possible.
- It may be possible to combine appearances. Perhaps you can, on a given day, be both the lunch speaker *and* a workshop presenter. This is a very popular arrangement both for speakers who are not yet celebrities and for organizations. Under this package arrangement, you, the speaker, can make yourself more marketable by offering more services without a significant additional time commitment. The organization can thereby justify hiring you.
- How many people will attend the convention? As a general rule, the more people coming, the larger the budget for speakers.
- What is your speaker budget for this year? This is a pivotal question. If the budget is small, you will have to give consideration to cutting back the time you spend. Alternatively, you can suggest a package arrangement which will leave you in possession of the bulk of monies which are available.

Once you have heard the answers to these questions, you are in a position to evaluate your potential participation.

"We Want You, But We Have No Money"

This statement often puts speakers in a quandary. I guarantee you that you will hear it. So be prepared.

Is an unpaid speaking engagement worth accepting? The answer to this question is a strong, "It depends."

- Will you, your products and services be promoted in the organization's newsletter or publication in advance of the program?
- Will they assist you with general media? Will they make the necessary follow-up telephone calls?
- Will potential client prospects be present? How many?
- Can your product actually be sold at the meeting?
- Will the organization provide booth space in its exhibition area without charge?
- Can the organization arrange for a citation or other award?
- Are there local chapters of this organization where you might also make presentations? Would such presentations lead to clients?

- Will your presentation be covered in the organization's publications?
- Will journalists be invited to cover your presentation?
- Can you be given free advertising space in the organization's publications?
- If your remarks are suitable for inclusion in **The Congressional Record** (as being on a subject of national interest), will the organization bring them to the attention of an appropriate congressman?
- Will the organization record your presentation?
- Will it sell your presentation to members (in return, perhaps, for a percentage of sales)?
- Will the organization pay travel and accommodation expenses?

I do, I confess, occasionally give a speech or other presentation without an explicit fee. I am highly suspicious of other speakers (unless they are in the World Class) who say they never do. However, I do insist that my expenses be paid and that the organization cooperate in giving suitable alternative compensation suggested by the preceeding items.

"We'd Like You. How Much Do You Want To Be Paid?"

Ah, how sweet it is to hear these exhilarating words. Let me assure you, you have earned them. How much to charge varies depending on several factors. Here they are:

- What is the organization's budget? If the organization has a total speaker budget of $500, a very modest amount but a fairly common situation, you will charge a basic fee plus expenses, the whole totaling $500. For this amount of money you should not give more than a two-hour workshop presentation. Remember the rest of us!
- How much am I being asked to do? You need to develop a basic set of charges, such as: If the organization wishes you to make multiple presentations (or if you have convinced them that they wish to do so), you can, of course, give them a break in price, but you should charge proportionally less for two presentations than for just one. I like the format where I am the keynote speaker of a convention and also offer at least one workshop presentation on a pertinent subject. This format allows me to have my say and the members of the organization to get at me with their specific questions. Organizations like this format, too. It is more expensive, of course, than a single speech or single workshop presentation, but does not cost as much as those two prices together. I want to give organizations an inducement to hire me for additional presentations once I am present.
- How much preparation time is involved? If you are being asked by the association to develop a new, unusual program or in some other way being asked for research and development, you must figure your time expenditure into your charge.

Perceived Value Of Your Information To The Client

If you have material and information which will assist in improving an organization's profitability within the current fiscal year or will immediately make individuals more attractive, you can and should charge proportionately. Your fee always needs to take into account the perceived value to the client of the information you are imparting. This is a most important category. If you are at all unsure of the value of what you are disseminating, ask people in your field how useful it is. Act accordingly.

Your Perceived Standing In Your Field: Your Celebrity Quotient

People who are better known always get paid more than those who aren't — whether they are worth it or not. The entire purpose of this book is to raise your standing — and your perceived worth — by exploiting the media. Here is your moment of truth. If you have followed my recommended techniques, you have steadily, inexorably been transforming yourself into a celebrity, even though the field in which you are known may be a narrow one. Just how narrowly you are known is largely immaterial, so long as you get credit for your standing when it counts.

Your Competitors

Your ideal competitive situation is to be in a position where you possess acknowledged status in a field and are alone offering critical information of immediate value to the clients/audience. Under such circumstances you will command the highest speaking fees and get the greatest cooperation from the organizations with which you are working. Such situations are relatively infrequent (though much more common than is commonly supposed) — as are all things desirable.

More often you must be aware of your competitors. The unabashed self-promoter as speaker must keep and assiduously maintain a Competition File. This File must contain as much information as you can collect about your competitors:

- their names
- firm names
- addresses
- telephone numbers
- speaking fields
- preferred clients (e.g. who they market themselves to)

It is helpful in this regard to maintain on file all brochures, articles, speech transcripts, tapes, newsletters, books, &c of your competitors so that you have a very clear picture of what they are offering — and to whom.

Inevitably the most difficult information to get will concern fees. Many speakers are listed in the appendix of **World Convention Dates**, referred to above. Here you will find information about: speaker topic, availability, fees, &c. However, many speakers simply say that their rates are "available upon request." If you are really interested, you might like to have a friend write and request pertinent information. Don't do it yourself, especially if you have begun to get visible in your field.

One authority I consulted in writing this chapter suggested that when working out fee arrangements with an organization, you inquire of the program chairman how much your predecessor was paid at the last comparable meeting. This, he explains, will help you determine how much you should ask for. This is, also of course, a means to check on the speaker stipends of competitors who may have worked with these same organizations. Personally, I have never used this technique and doubt that I would. I suspect a program chairman would regard the question as impertinent and refuse to answer it. In the end, you must decide whether you need the information badly enough to risk being thought vulgar.

There is one final way, also of limited utility. The International Platform Association, to which I shall again refer, requests program chairman to mail in evaluations of paid speakers for inclusion in their column "The Marketplace of the Platform." This information includes the fee paid. However, it seems either that few program chairman know of this column or are too slothful to send in a report, since it is pretty brief. Nonetheless, here is the address:

International Platform Association
2564 Berkshire Road
Cleveland Heights, OH 44106

In point of fact, it is difficult to get reliable information about how much other people charge. Moreover in the long run it is very much beside the point. If you are following my suggestions about exploiting the media, your status and reputation are constantly rising. Unless you have a competitor as shrewd and dedicated as you are to enhancing his reputation through unabashed self-promotion, you will have a relatively clear field. If, however, a program chairman says, "We want you, but you're twice as expensive as Joe Smith," here's how to respond. "Madame, you are probably right. But you must know a Rolls Royce costs more than a Toyota. If you merely want to get there, use the Toyota. If you want the consummate experience, try the Rolls." If the decision maker decides for the Toyota, don't fret. There are people in the world, lamentably numerous, who will never be ready for the Rolls. Personally, I pity them, and you should be suitably eleemosynary.

Working With A Professional Association To Insure That You Meet Your Publicity Objectives — And Theirs

It should be clear by now that as an unabashed self-promoter you will be working with many people who do not understand the need for public relations and publicity and are sceptical about the methods used to get it. So be it. If they are benighted, we must nonetheless cope with them and move them along. Fortunately, if you have arranged matters properly at the time of fee and condition negotiation, the organization at least knows what you want and at least has some introductory understanding of what they are expected to do.

What I am about to write should by now seem old hat. If so, you are on your way, not only to accepting and understanding it, but to having it enter the marrow of your bones to become a very vital part of the way you function.

Work with the organization on how to promote you in advance of your presentation. Consider:

- an article about you in the organization's publication. If need be, offer to draft it yourself. Emphasize that this article is a draft which the organization may alter in consultation with you. Don't forget the beguiling photograph!
- an article by you. Most people need sustained contact with people and ideas before they actually register. As an unabashed self-promoter, you must never forget how little people know, how hard it is for them to grasp facts, and how few of these facts are retained after having been gathered. You must always, always work for repetition. An article by you in the organization's publication will help your cause by introducing your prospective audience to you and your ideas and allowing those who are interested to refer back to them as necessary. Again, don't forget an accompanying photograph.
- a general media release. Write this yourself or at least draft it, and let the organization review it before typing it on their letterhead. You should be willing to assist the organization in identifying general media contacts in television, radio, newspapers, magazines. Don't rely on the organization knowing where to send media materials. All too often this is the dismal road to disaster. Remember: make sure to ask for about 2 dozen of the releases for your own purposes.

You can send them to publications of the following kinds of organizations with which you are connected:

- trade
- civic
- social
- labor
- fraternal
- alumni

Note: Be sure to affix relevant organizational details to media releases sent out to such publications. For example, all such releases sent to alumni publications should include your class year. In these circumstances it is perfectly appropriate to write it in by hand.

It goes without saying that you should help the organization develop a Media Activity Chart for the most important media sources; these sources need telephone follow-up which the organization must be willing to provide. As likely as not the individual you are working with will have little or no direct experience with the media. In this case, you must provide your organizational contact with the story angles he can offer to the media about you and your program. This is most important. Do not allow these angles to be developed without you, even if you are working with an experienced public relations practitioner.

This year in connection with a trade association I was addressing, I had to work with such a "seasoned" professional who strongly resisted my suggestions on how to sell me, saying, with a notable touch of hubris, that as he was knowledgeable in the business he needed no help. The results proceeded directly from some mediaeval cautionary tale: our "seasoned" pro managed to arrange no significant media presentations. In such cases, be persistent. You really ought to know more about how to sell yourself than anyone else. If you don't, for shame!

- An article after the convention. Don't overlook the possibility of having your remarks printed or having a significant excerpt from your presentation enshrined in print. It's your responsibility to make the suggestion and to work with the organization to locate a suitable forum.

A Final Word Or Two

No matter how well scheduled you are at any convention or organization presentation, you will find yourself with free time. Use it wisely. While you are connected with an organization as a featured speaker, you are in an enviable position to approach other people who can be helpful to you:

- Arrange appointments at other organizations at which you want to speak which are headquartered in the same town. Check the Yellow Pages (under "Associations"), the **Encyclopedia Of Associations**, and the other reference books mentioned in this volume to see what other organizations are located in the town where you are making your presentation. Write ahead. Say you will be in town (tell them why) and that you'd like a meeting. Call for the appointment. If during this convention your client prospect evinces any interest, invite him to attend your presentation. Chances are he won't come, but even so he's gotten a critical message: you're a star.
- See media people. Don't hesitate to see media people even if they aren't interviewing you. After all you want to build your Contact Network. Send the media release along with a letter requesting an appointment. Be candid: say you'd like an interview (or what have you), but that at the very least you'd like to get acquainted. Good media coverage grows out of good personal

relationships between you, the unabashed self-promoter, and media personnel. Sure you want the story— now. But you also want the contact and the opportunity to see what kinds of stories and story angles are of interest to the person you're dealing with. Once you know, you can act accordingly. Don't hesitate to call and set up these meetings once you've arrived in town. Remember: the schedules of media people are always uncertain. Keep yourself flexible to fit in.

Visit Book Stores And Other Product Distributors

Once you have developed products, be they books, audio cassettes or whatever, do not neglect a call on your distributors (or potential distributors). As my friends have learned, whenever I pass a new book store, I drop in and introduce myself to the manager. If he has books, I tell him how they are doing nationally (and usually drop a pregnant hint as to how to display them to better effect). If he doesn't, I make a case as to why he should stock up and drop off appropriate materials. In a city where I am speaking, especially where media is taking place, I drop in on the managers and explain what is taking place. Under such circumstances, many managers are willing to give the product special prominence.

Note: whenever possible I deal with the manager. I always *ask* for this person. If he is not available, I reluctantly will deal with a subordinate but all too often their answers are vague and uninformative. This is rampant clerkism, the "Don't-Ask-Me-I-Only-Work-Here" school of infuriating behavior. In such circumstances, control your fast-rising irritation, work with this creature as best you can, and leave a hand-written note for the manager with suitable leave behinds. Say how sorry you are to have missed this decision maker; no doubt you mean it.

Speaking Follow-Up

Finally, don't forget to follow-up the convention appropriately:

- Send a letter to the executive director not only thanking him for your being able to participate but for the good work done by the program chairman and any additional public relations liaison with whom you may have worked.
- Send a suitably fulsome letter to the program chairman and public relations liaison.
- If you have addressed the organization in any capacity other than keynoter, contact next year's program chairman and indicate your desire to participate again. Such communications early in the planning process are most welcomed by meeting impressarios. If you have been the keynote speaker, of course, you will probably not return a second year in the same capacity. And anything less would, of course, be *infra dig.* I myself, of course, would be only too willing to overlook this problem if the money were right. "A foolish consistency," after all, "is the hobgoblin of little minds."

Breaking Into The College Continuing Education Market: Education's Golden Egg, Your Golden Opportunity

The traditional college-age student is becoming a rather rare and much sought-after creature. Four-year colleges and universities faced with the stark fact of fewer numbers are indulging in lavish admissions campaigns, promises and public relations to attract the necessary bodies to their campuses. This is a sad, sad scene. But it is, fortunately, no concern of ours, for adult education, now titled Lifelong Learning or Continuing Education, is growing quite nicely, thank you, in both traditional and innovative settings. In fact, anyone interested in self-promotion and the talk circuit who neglects this rich, burgeoning market is a discredit to the profession.

The Continuing Education Scene

In this section I am by and large focusing my remarks on the continuing education programs administered by colleges and universities. However there are many organizations which also create and sponsor such programs where, of course, these suggestions are also generally applicable. A good list of such organizations can be found in:

The Seminar Market: A Research Report On Open-To-The-Public Short Courses and Business Seminars In North America
by Dominick M. Schrello, Ph.D.
Schrello Enterprises
555 East Ocean Blvd., P.O. Box 1610
Long Beach, CA 90802
(213) 435-1789

There are many worthwhile reasons for working the continuing education market:

- It is national. There are nearly 3000 adult continuing education programs associated with colleges and universities.
- You can repeat your program around the country. Instead of offering your program just once, you can offer it in every continuing education market around the country. You should know, however, that an individual institution will ordinarily expect and request exclusivity within its market.
- Your program can be repeated between 2 and 4 times each year in each market. If your program is a money maker (and if it isn't it won't be repeated), the institution will want to repeat it at least twice a year and up to four times a year — once a quarter. Colleges like to stay with sure things and once you have proved that you're one of them, they'll want you, again and again.
- Programs can be offered evenings and weekends. Because this is adult education, the courses must be held when the adults are available, during the evening and, usually, on Saturdays. This is a wonderful way of making the very best use of time which, for most people, is ordinarily unproductive.
- The continuing education universe is a small one. As in any self-contained network, deans and directors through their professional organizations get to know each other. If you are bought by a pace-setting, respected member of the profession, this will be a cue to others that they should have you, too. And they won't be shy about contacting you.
- Affiliating with a college or university builds your credibility. Institutions of higher education are still able to confer legitimacy and standing. They give you a level of recognition and acceptance which you cannot confer on yourself.
- The institution puts up the venture capital for your program. When you affiliate with an institution, they put up the necessary money to attract the students both through advertising and public relations. If the program is cancelled for lack of participation you do not suffer by losing the money it cost to arrange it.
- You do not have to generate your audience. This gathers because of the general catalog, special brochure, advertising and public relations activities of the institutions. Your commitment is limited to coming in, providing a quality program, and cashing your check. This is most comforting.
- You can make extra money by mentioning your product either in the catalogue or special brochure which is developed. People who cannot attend your program can still be made aware of who you are and the product or service you have available. This can be a source of extra revenue for you.

- You can be well paid. Some I know teach for under $100 per day. However, those who develop a national reputation and became the acknowledged experts in their fields, delivering an academically acceptable program which consistently makes money for the host institution, can easily make more than $1000 per day plus expenses and product sales. This is not unusual.
- Institutions can help boost your reputation and image by assisting with public relations. This will be explored further in this chapter.

People often ask me why I am willing to give up a percentage of the profits by affiliating with universities. Now you know. When continuing education programs function properly, they earn their money. When they don't, it is a less compelling bargain. The purpose of this section is to help you so that you can help them earn their keep.

Developing Your Program

A university continuing education program will *only* buy your program if they can make money from it. No matter how germain, how socially conscious, how utilitarian, if it cannot be sold, they do not want to buy it. *Tout court.* Never forget this.

In considering which programs to offer:

- Examine the current catalogs of local divisions of continuing education. Colleges will be happy to mail them to you, happy to maintain your name on their mailing lists. Don't ever contact a program planner or dean unless you are either sure that your program is new, different, unusual, or it does not duplicate the content of an existing course which, at first glance, appears comparable.
- Develop a marketing letter. (See samples, page 342). This letter should:
  - outline the course content (a brief synopsis in cataloguese is appropriate to enclose)
  - identify the target market. Who will buy this course?
  - give reasons for the potential interest of the market
  - present reasons why you are the best qualified person to offer this course.

Don't expect a program planner to know why your course is important, who will want to take it, or why they'll come. You have to supply this vital information.

- Follow this letter with a telephone call and request for visit. Be brisk and professional. I have found continuing educators some of the most receptive people in the world to new ideas. After all, they make their money by seizing and exploiting trends, and they want to know whether you can help them reach their objective.
- Have the courtesy and good sense to be prepared for this meeting. Have at least introductory information on the following points:
  - course name (a catchy title)
  - descriptive subtitle
  - course description for catalogue
  - format (one hour a week for 6 weeks; one Saturday, &c)
  - target audience
  - marketing products (general catalog only; special brochure; advertising, &c)
  - instructor qualifications. (*N.B.* Personally I prefer a biographical narrative to a résumé. Mandarins don't use résumés. You must decide for yourself.)
  - sample brochure copy
  - media release

- course text and classroom passouts
- suggested price of course

Preparing this packet gets easier and easier the longer you are in business. It involves a significant investment of your time and creativity at the beginning. If you want to get ahead, you will make this commitment. Alternatively, you can risk going ahead without being so well prepared. Since a lack of thorough preparation inevitably casts a doubt on your professionalism, you face the very real likelihood of failure. It's up to you.

The Meeting

If you have either brought the necessary materials or (recommended) sent them ahead after making your appointment, you will be treated as the professional you inevitably are. In such circumstances, I have discovered meetings will be very, very short. After you have established a track record, they can and will ordinarily be handled by telephone, and you will be hired sight unseen. I know. This is how I get most of my assignments these days.

If you have thought through what you want to offer, who it should be offered to, and why they will buy it, the institution will probably be inclined to adopt it, so long as they have no competitive item. If they have something which is related in content, this may actually work to your advantage, since more and more institutions are grouping related programs and marketing them together, even going so far as to offer a special discount for enrollment in more than one of the courses. Don't hesitate to suggest this possibility.

Fee

As a general rule, the most lucrative speaking engagements in continuing education are in the noncredit area, that is adults taking courses for the sheer love of it and the desire to amass immediately-utilitarian information. Hence, your programs, as a matter of course, should be offered without credit. Fees in such instances are negotiable.

In practice, continuing education programs remunerate instructors in several ways:

- fixed, flat fee. If the program takes place, you, the instructor, receive certain remuneration plus expenses.
- per capita fee. You are paid a certain amount for each participant.
- percentage return after expenses. You, the instructor, split net revenues with the host institution after allowable expenses have been deducted. Generally this division is 50-50%, although different institutions arrange matters differently.

Because institutions arrange payments for instructors in often-idiosyncratic ways, I have found it helpful to tell them what profit I want from the day and to let them tell me how they want to arrange matters so that our mutual objectives are realized. My minimum figure is $1000 plus expenses and product sales.

There is no reason why an institution should not agree to this kind of figure. You are bringing in money to the institution for minimal work on their behalf, and you will only be paid if the institution makes money. They can afford to be liberal.

Unabashed Self-Promotion In Continuing Education

In my experience while continuing educators are most receptive to new product ideas and keen to make money by selling them, they remain unreceptive and often downright hostile to the notion of promoting their programs via the media. The usual reason they give for their disinclination to be creative is that they have many programs to promote and cannot show favoritism. In fact, I suspect most of them are technically inept and are not receptive to the shibboleths of lifelong learning which they regularly mouth. In all fairness, in many institutions their hands are tied. Unless a department of continuing education has its own public relations officer, it must work through the main publicity office of the college. In practice, this office usually ignores the promotional possibilities of continuing education despite the revenue it generates for the institution as a whole. In any event, the end result is that working with continuing educators to promote your program can be a difficult, frustrating experience.

Your introductory conference with the program planner, or, better yet, the dean or director can help matters considerably. Resolve:

- that your program will receive public relations attention. (Do not assume this.)
- who will provide the hooks for stories about you and your course. It should, of course, be you. Who knows them better?
- who will write the standard media release. Colleges will want to do this. Most of them define public relations solely in terms of these standard releases and will feel emasculated if they do not perform this task. I suggest, however, that you do it yourself. Releases produced by colleges, whether by divisions of continuing education or public relations, are relentlessly bland and uninspired. If the college is adamant about producing the release, graciously agree but insist on reviewing it in draft. I suspect you will be appalled.
- that the college will make follow-up telephone calls to the media. Find out who will make these calls and give them a training session on what to say about you.
- that media sources will be invited to sit-in on your program and cover it. If you are teaching Bone-Head English, it is doubtful journalists will want to attend, but if your program content is new, experimental or controversial, they may wish to review it. If there are meals to be served (as at an all-day workshop), clear in advance that the journalists can have one. Don't assume that one has been ordered, even if you have notified the central office in advance. Amenity is a foreign word to too many continuing educators.
- that you will be evaluated. Evaluations, along with audio cassettes, are necessary to the unabashed self-promoter in his role as speaker. These evaluations are a source of comfort to other continuing educators considering your program. When you have good ones, use them as a lever to get more business. When you have bad ones, consider whether the criticisms have any merit. If they do, learn from them.

After The Program

As always, write both the program planner and the dean a thank-you note. Compliment the program planner by name to the dean. If either the program planner or dean has been particularly helpful, write the president of the college. Such letters are rare. Indicate in this letter that you are already looking ahead to your next presentation. Suggest one or two dates and any format changes that will make your program even better. Finally, ask for the names of other continuing educators well known to the dean. You definitely want referrals. If you have done a good job, you deserve them. After all, the fact that he selected you reflects well on the decision maker, and he'll probably want others to have a clear indication of his intelligence and judgement.

One Final Promotion Note

Consider becoming a member of the International Platform Association. Its chief activity is a national convention where ingénue and experienced speakers get to perform, exchange horror stories, and promote themselves to program chairmen. They also publish books and a helpful publication called "Talent." As I've already mentioned, each issue features a column called "The Marketplace Of The Platform" which prints speaker evaluations (and prices) from program chairmen. Each time you speak for a fee, draft an evaluation paragraph and send it to your program chairman (planner, director, or dean) and ask him to mail it in on his letterhead. This is a way of building your name recognition among potential buyers.

At Last: Securing The Lecture Agent

It is a sad fact of life that no lecture agent will even deign to consider you unless he scents cash. I don't blame them. The mail boxes of lecture agents are stuffed with riotously optimistic requests for representation from every species of yokel, unknown individuals with a tedious subject, no experience but, Rumpelstiltskin-like, with every expectation of turning their dross into gold. Such letters cause lecture agents, who can be people of great charm, to rise to heights of unexampled vituperation.

Lecture agents work on commission. They only receive commissions if you receive bookings. You only receive bookings if you are either a household name or are in command of information on a topic of consuming public interest, are known as a dazzling orator, can motivate sluggards, or possess a technical competence which makes you of interest to other professionals needing that skill. All others had best keep practicing on the Rubber Chicken Circuit.

Selecting Your Agent

There are three kinds of agents:

- Symbiotic Agent. The Symbiotic Agent enters into a mutually-beneficial relationship with you, whereby your mutual interests of income and self-promotion are met.
- Benign Parasite Agent. The Benign Parasite Agent adds little or nothing to your professional life. He does little, delivers little but, correspondingly, takes little. While this may in fact seem benign, there is actually an opportunity cost, if nothing more, to involvement with such a creature. If the Benign Parasite is not actually developing and promoting you, you are actually missing out on other opportunities. If the Benign Parasite has enough instinctive sense to keep you alive, he is nonetheless a crippler.
- Malign Parasite Agent. This critter demands money in advance of service, develops no materials (or, even worse, faulty and unprofessional materials), and delivers nothing. Cormorant-like, this creature battens on your resources, an open maw his trademark and apt symbol. He weakens you, cripples, and leaves a dessicated remnant. He is, alas, common.

How To Find Agents

You may begin your search for an agent in three places:

- in the Yellow Pages of your telephone book under "Entertainment"
- in Richard Weiner's book **Professional's Guide To Public Relations Services** (See Chapter 3). This contains an introductory list featuring the biggest agencies.

- in the appendix of this book where I have listed the information sent me by lecture agents responding to a query of mine for this book.

Don't write them unless you have the very real likelihood of making money as a speaker. If you do, proceed.

The Introductory Letter

As with so many other letters in this book, your first letter to a prospective lecture agent needs to be a marvel of compact persuasiveness. It should:

- express your desire for non-exclusive representation
- give your background as a speaker (you may, of course, enclose a list of your major speaking engagements within the past year and forthcoming programs).
- set out your major topics
- suggest program formats
- indicate the availability of such support materials as books, audio cassettes, letters of recommendation, &c

Along with this letter, you should send a selection of leave behinds. While you may want to include one or two articles by you, the bulk of materials should be articles *about* you. (See samples, page 344).

Note: Refer back to the first point above. All but the biggest most prestigious lecture agencies will deal with you on a non-exclusive basis, that is to say you can be represented by more than one agency at a time. Until such time as you have become a recognized, compelling celebrity non-exclusive representation is in your best interest since it insures that your name will be brought before potential buyers not once but regularly — which is, of course, just what you want.

Follow-Up

You may gage whether you have cracked the oblivion that holds most people by whether the lecture agency writes back reasonably promptly and civally. You may take this as a measure of your arrivism. If not, don't despair. Surely by now you are used to making the necessary follow-up calls.

The Follow-Up Call

Many lecture agencies are small and most are called after their principals. Address your letter to this individual. If you are at all uncertain about whom to contact, call and ask for the name of the person reviewing new talent. Either call the principal or this person.

It would be nice if people still had the elements of civility and politesse. But most don't, at least not to people they don't know and haven't yet proven their ability to make them money. You can, therefore, expect the person you reach to be misinformed, disinterested, and often needlessly abrupt. This is our unsatisfactory world. Handle your call in this way:

- Ask whether your letter and materials have arrived. If not, say you'd like them to be reviewed before you call again. Confirm the individual who should receive your packet.

- If it has arrived, ask whether it has been read and received. If not, ask how long this process will take. Arrange to call back then.
- If it has been reviewed, ascertain any possible interest.
- If there is the slightest glimmering, ask for an appointment. If not, end the conversation in good order. Never permit yourself the luxury of telling the person you are speaking to what you think of him. (Break this rule often and colorfully when you've made it!)

The Meeting

Although the lecture bureau will call you the client, your agent works for you. Never forget this. You are interviewing someone for a job and while you yourself are inevitably being interviewed, too, remember who makes the final decision.

You have two main objectives for your meeting: to discern how your lecture agent will market you (techniques) and to whom (markets).

Selecting a lecture agent is not unlike selecting a publicist (in fact the two have significant similarities) and your selection process will be similar, too. (See Chapter 18).

Lecture Agent Techniques

Have your prospective lecture agent walk you through all his procedures. He should provide you with hard fact about:

- what information he needs about you
- what information he needs about your programs
- who will draw up marketing materials (brochure, leaflets, &c)
- how quickly they will be drawn up
- whether you get the opportunity to review and comment on them before they are finalized
- who is responsible for photographs
- what a typical client portfolio looks like.

Don't just talk about these matters. See them. Ask for samples of each item mentioned and not old ones, either. Something being used today. Also, ask who your account representative is. Talk to this person. Get a sense of who he is and how he works. This will be important to developing a successful relationship.

Lecture Markets

Once you have got a good sense of what materials will be developed about you and your programs and how they will be produced, you need to know how they will be marketed. Who will get them and how will they be followed up.

There are different segments of the talk market. College (undergraduate), trade, professional and corporate. Do you have programs suitable for all of these markets? If so, can your agent market to all, or will you be focused on one market or another. Know precisely.

Get your prospective agent both to show you how a campaign comparable to yours was developed and get his initial suggestions on how he might handle yours. Get a clear sense of what will be done, by whom, and how long it will take. I have discovered in practice that most lecture agencies move very, very slowly. Get a sense of how long you'll have to wait for results.

Thus you need to know how your agent will bring you up to date on developments. You will need regular communication with your agent, particularly as you pursue your own speaking engagements (as you must) and continue to develop your image following the techniques of this book.

Terms

Conclude your conversation with a discussion of terms. Most lecture agents take 1/4-1/3 of the gross speaker fee. They get this upfront from the booking organization in advance of your presentation. Your percentage is sent directly to you. Needless to say, your agent should receive no percentage of your expenses. Note: either request your agent to have your accommodation expense direct billed to the client or else have him make other arrangements which do not necessitate your advancing any money.

Beware of lecture agents who request or require advance fees. Some are reputable. After all, a new client costs a firm money, often for as long as a year or more before there's any return. In selected circumstances such fees, particularly for speakers who are not yet widely known, may be justifiable. In any case, I would want to check some current client references to see whether they had to pay the fees and to ascertain whether they felt the expense worthwhile. You should, of course, always ask for client references, but where you are being asked to advance funds, it is mandatory to do so.

The Unabashed Self-Promoter Emerges, Again

Before you sign any contract, get a clear sense of how your agent will handle the ancillary self-promotional opportunities which can accompany any speaking engagement:

- Who will work with the organization to arrange for an advance article about you?
- An article by you?
- Who will draft a media release and who will send it to both general and specific media?
- Who will arrange for your remarks to be taped?
- Who will arrange for excerpts of your presentation to be published in an appropriate publication?
- Who will write the captions for your photographs?
- Who will arrange for a photographic receiving line?

Sadly, most agents are either ill-equipped to perform these tasks, don't know how to do so, or are outright hostile to doing them. Lest you be surprised at this last point, consider: an agent makes his money from your lecture fee which he has received in advance of your presentation. Although more promotion will result in your development as a more marketable property, this may seem like a lot of bother for no immediate return to your agent.

Hence, if you want publicity you'll probably end up working directly with the organization to get it.

Or else you can hire a publicist.

CHAPTER 18

HOW AND WHEN TO USE PUBLICISTS

So, you have either read this far and become progressively more and more daunted at the prospect before you: the need for febrile inventiveness as you concoct a public image and your leitmotif; for a dazzling virtuosity of self-promotional form and substance, and for an awesome, dogged perseverance as you pursue your media quarry.

Or perhaps you have followed my maxims and advice with such dedication, such commendable thoroughness, that you are suffering from another problem: you now have so many self-promotional possibilities, so many shows on which to appear, so many articles breaking into print, that you cannot take maximum advantage of your galloping good fortune, that *embarras des richesses*.

Either way you decide it's time for professional help, for a technically perfect, splendidly connected, profoundly devoted partisan, your self-promotional champion — the publicist.

Such a person, in your beatific vision, will:

- understand your genius
- crystallize and capture it in words of compelling brilliance
- bring it effortlessly (both because of its radiant persuasiveness and his own universal web of high-level contacts) to the attention of media decision makers, who, upon hearing it, will confess to longing for just such a one as you, and
- therefore catapult you to the attention of an expectant world, which will, in gratitude and exaltation, shower adulation and untold riches upon you.

You have, perhaps, given way to such a fancy. And have looked to its realization at the hands of that midwife, the publicist. Be honest, now. I myself continually meet people who, while assuring me that they have an appealing product or service, are equally adamant about either their lack of time to market to the media or their lack of ability to do so. All want to know one thing: "How can I find someone else to take on this responsibility? How can I find a publicist?"

When to Seek A Publicist

There is only one correct time to seek a publicist: when you yourself have become thoroughly familiar with the self-promotional universe, are generating a steady stream of publicity, but are, because of manifold commitments and the lack of time, failing to exploit all the available possibilities.

At this point you are aware of how to sell yourself, you have some idea of what print and electronic media options are open to you, you have a sense of what written materials work for you and how media people respond to you. In short, you have benchmarks.

Others should beware. Individuals who have had little or no experience with the media and who find the whole business as detailed in this book distasteful and distinctly beneath them, who pine for that person who can take the burden from them, are positioning themselves for frustration, disappointment, disillusion.

Individuals who retain publicists, but who do not themselves have necessary background information on working with the media, have no standards by which to judge how their agent approaches the task of representing and selling them. They may, suffering from inflated expectations, take their publicists to task for failing to deliver media coverage, having no sense that the publicist may have succeeded beyond reasonable prediction. Conversely, they may passively acquiesce in a lazy publicist's assessment of a disinterested market when the problem lies less in what is being sold than in the publicist's own unimaginative and slothful marketing procedures.

The only way to deal with this problem is for the unabashed self-promoter to have at least introductory experience working with the media. That way he is in a better position to evaluate a publicist's record and to know whether it would be advantageous for him to retain any given agent, and, once having done so, could realistically evaluate just what was being done on his behalf.

The Search For The Compleat Publicist

As you get into the media business, publicists will become more and still more evident. Your fellow self-promoters, met in the green rooms of radio and television stations, will discuss them in conversations of startling candor. Regularly, the publicists themselves will appear with their bleary-eyed clients in tow, pinching them into shape like so many anxious coaches with prize athletes. To meet publicists, then, you must go where they go. Once there, you will have no trouble making contact.

Publicists are constantly hustling jobs. Like other consultants, they live by assembling a jigsaw puzzle of professional assignments; since many of these tasks are short-term, they must constantly look for the next. Thus you can expect publicists to evince a very forthright interest in you, if you give them the slightest opportunity.

As you know, I use my time in media green rooms to network. I like to meet not only the program's host and his producer but also all the guests and their mobile claques as well. Thus, I have come to meet many, many publicists. Without fail, they are quick on the card draw; they bless me with an engraved bit of cardboard, a brilliant smile, and the promise of increasing immortality and the love of multitudes if only I have the sense to call them.

Another alternative to picking up publicists in green rooms is simply to check the Yellow Pages under "Publicist" and to make some telephone calls. List all available options and be sure to call *all* of them for information.

I am always astounded when people tell me they retained the first publicist (or anything else) in the telephone book and didn't bother to contact any others. Such a procedure might make sense if you were acting on the ardent recommendation of a professional associate but otherwise seems downright stupid. You need comparative information to make an informed choice.

Clarifying Your Objectives

Before you approach the possibilities, you must be clear about what you want to accomplish. List your specific objectives, that is list specific measurable outcomes which the publicist can help you achieve. Be specific. Don't just say you want to be on television, say what show you'd like to be on. Know why that one is relevant for your purposes. Try, too, to estimate just how much media you'd like to do and what kind. Unless you have a very specific idea of what you want to accomplish you will not be able to advise the publicist, and you will be, as a result, at his mercy.

Do you have a specific audience of people you need to reach? Who are they? What do you know about them? What kind of message are they likely to be partial to? Think through the basic questions:

- Who do you want to reach?
- What do they want to hear?
- How should you be portrayed?
- Why should you be featured?
- How often should you appear?

A good publicist not only wants to hear what you've got to say on these parts; he needs to hear. Whether he asks these questions of you is one good indication of whether he really wants to work with you in your self-promotional endeavors or whether he is just interested in banking your fee.

Interviewing Your Potential Publicist

When seeking a publicist, remember one important fact: he works for you. He is a technical expert in his field, adept at tactics, but you are the generalissimo crafting strategy. How easy it is to forget this when meeting some high-powered creature who is aggressive, blunt, doctrinaire. Who's hiring who, anyway?

On The Telephone

Unless you do meet a publicist in the green room, your interview will ordinarily begin on the telephone. As stated before, call every available source in the nearest metropolitan area. You can discern much from this initial contact. If you reach a secretary, tell her you are interested in discussing possible representation.

Ask for:

- the standard brochure
- information on different retainer or contract relationships
- any background information on the firm which will enable you to make a decision.

Also, ask whether there is a cost for an initial consultation. Do not ask yet for references as this is premature just now.

See how cooperative the secretary is. This is a good indication of how well run the office is. See how quickly you receive the material you want. It should ordinarily go out the same day you request it. If they are not interested in securing your business, just how interested do you think they'll be in serving you?

Don't be alarmed if there is an introductory cost. See if this can be applied against the cost of an eventual contract. In my experience most, but not all, publicists will gladly agree to an introductory meeting without cost.

Before The Introductory Meeting

If the publicist is professional, he wants to know something about you in advance of your meeting. Unless he is just interested in securing your hourly fee, he'll have every reason to try and discover who you are and what kind of promotional services you are seeking. When, therefore, you decide to have your first meeting, it is a good idea to send the following materials in advance:

- background information on you
- a synopsis of information about your objectives (answers to the questions on page 244 would do nicely)
- information on the service or product you want to promote.

Prepare the publicist by submitting the kind of information which will enable him to:

- confirm your seriousness of intent
- understand the product or service you want promoted
- discern the audience you want to reach
- reach some preliminary conclusions about which of his services would be most appropriate and economical.

Never, never go to an introductory meeting with a publicist unless he has had the opportunity to learn something about you and your project. Make this meeting productive by submitting the most detailed information you can, but, please!, make it concise and to the point.

The Interview

The meeting with your prospective publicist should be held at his offices. You want to judge the environment and meet the people who will have a hand in fashioning a successful relationship, be it only a secretary.

A busy professional will only have limited time to spend with you; an hour, properly arranged, should do nicely. There is much to accomplish in this time.

First, reprise your objectives. Bring along a duplicate set of materials and go through your points one by one with the publicist. The publicist should follow the discussion with his own set. The introductory portion of the interview, perhaps 15-20 minutes, is yours. You want to give a full presentation on your objectives, and you want the publicist fully to understand what you want and need to accomplish. A good publicist will listen during your presentation. His words should be limited to questions which help refine your objectives and enable you to expand on what you want. Beware of the publicist who, during this part of the conversation, seems insistent on telling you about services he provides. He cannot offer a suitable service until he hears what you wish to do. At the very least, it is a courtesy to you to hear you out.

An informed professional will need the information you are providing. Do him the favor of bringing it and of being both prepared and focused in your remarks. If you are not so prepared and focused, the professional will very likely be disheartened and lose interest. His reckoning will be: if my potential client is so unfocused here, I doubt he will be suitable for media. I cannot risk my reputation by dealing with such an individual.

This does not mean that what you say need necessarily be exhaustive or definitive. It is the professional's job to assist you with substance, form and delivery, but it will not be to your advantage to appear ill-prepared.

After you have made your initial remarks, it is the publicist's turn to talk. In this portion of the conversation, the publicist should begin to inform you how he can help you realize your objectives. Please note the wording "help you realize your objectives."

A good publicist enters into a partnership with you. He can be of technical assistance but *at no time* can you, the client, be removed from the process. You must always remain active in the process. In no other way can your relationship with the publicist be successful.

Now that the publicist knows your objectives, necessarily incomplete though they may be, he can begin to tell you in detail just what his part will be in realizing them. Listen closely. You should be hearing process information, that is information which clarifies *what* will be done as well as result information, which deals with the final outcomes.

Each piece of process information you are given should be exemplified by a particular document. If, for instance, the publicist says he produces standard media releases, you need to see a sample. First, however, have the courtesy to listen carefully and completely to the publicist's presentation. He should detail just how your objectives will be met by him. Here are the questions which need answers:

- How will the pubicist gather information about you, your product, your service? Find out what kind of information you should submit, whether there is a questionnaire to complete, where meetings will take place to discuss this question, and how many of them there must be.
- What kinds of written materials will the publicist draw up on your behalf? Take into account the materials suggested in Chapter 13. Has the publicist mentioned these?
- How long does it generally take to produce these materials? Will you have the opportunity to review them before they are finalized?
- If the publicist needs a photograph (and he very likely will), who will arrange to take it?
- Once the final materials have been approved, how does the publicist approach media sources? What kind of cover letter does the publicist use with materials? What does the total media packet look like? Is the cost of producing and mailing these materials in the fee or is it extra?
- Does the publicist draw up a Media Activity Chart which can be shared with you? How do you know what media sources are being approached on your behalf?
- As these media sources are approached, will the publicist keep you abreast of *all* decisions, not just the positive ones. At any time in the career of the unabashed self-promoter it is important to know why he is *not* being bought; this is equally as important to why he is. How will the publicist keep you abreast of decisions? Through an updated Media Activity Chart? Through a memorandum? How often will you get it? What will it include?
- Can the publicist help get articles *by* you written and published, if you need this assistance? Publicists all too frequently overlook the importance of articles by you, concentrating instead on media interviews. If you supply the content for these articles, can the publicist produce them and direct them for publication?
- Will the publicist accompany you to media interviews? At least at the beginning of your self-promotional career, it is helpful if the publicist attends. You need a candid, objective source to criticize your performances, someone who can and will give you pointed, helpful suggestions during a break in a taping, for instance, when there is still time to improve.

In one way or another most publicists perform most of these tasks. Your job is to see how well they do them. You now need some examples.

Gathering Information About You

Have the publicist walk you through the information gathering process. Precisely what does the publicist want from you and precisely how will the publicist gather the information he requires? Don't be put off by generalities. This is terribly important. Unless the publicist gets thorough information on you, your product, your service, he can never hope to sell it to the media. You need to know just how he gets this information. You need to be sure that this information provides him with the context he needs and sufficient background so that he, in turn, can brief others on what you do and persuade them that it is significant. If a questionnaire is involved, or any other written materials, ask to review them.

Written Materials

All publicists produce written materials about their clients; most are regrettable and certainly not compelling advocates on your behalf. Every publicist, *every*, is a professional writer, and the documents produced for and about you should show it. They should be lucid, fast-moving, above all else appealing. If you do not look interesting in these documents, you can rest assured you'll never get the chance to prove otherwise in a media interview.

Ask to see the standard materials produced for a *current* client. Ask to take them with you (you don't need client photographs, of course, just written material). There should be no problem about your doing so. It is scarcely confidential since it is being sent to media sources everywhere, and you cannot rate the professionalism of the publicist without reviewing it.

Make sure you get a sample of each document the publicist puts out as a matter of course. If different documents are put out in different promotional packages, you should find out now.

How Long Does It Take?

How long will you have to wait for materials? Find out exactly. In practice, the answer the publicist gives you now will be optimistic. To be sure, you'll need to check with one or two current clients. They may remember how long it seemed to take before they had the opportunity to review draft documents.

Will You Have The Opportunity To Review Materials Before Printing?

Nothing, nothing should be sent out about you until you have approved it. Remember: it is your image which is at issue, not the publicist's, and your future relations with the media. Media people have long memories. Flooded with materials far in excess of their ability to use, they look for any reasonable excuse to exclude. Don't let your publicist give them such an excuse on your behalf.

All materials should be sent to you in a timely fashion so that you can review them at your leisure, and let a friend or two review them, too. Here is where your Self-Promotion Contact Network helps. If you have a friend in the media, he can easily review materials about you and make necessary editorial and content suggestions. If you have such a friend, this is a good use of him. But the exercise will be rather meaningless unless you are working with a draft document.

The Media Activity Chart

Just as you must do when you work alone, so must the publicist draw up a Media Activity Chart. Whoever deals with the media needs to maintain a convenient log of just what targets are being approached and how things are progressing. Different publicists, of course, will use different systems to track progress. But you should know what the system is. Ask for specifics and review documentation.

Will You Be Kept Abreast?

One of the most provoking things about working with a publicist is just being told where to go and when to arrive. The unabashed self-promoter needs a thorough briefing about who is being approached, how they are being approached, and what they are saying. You must know in detail why you are being bought — and what reasons are being advanced for not buying you so that you can make midcourse corrections.

Find out from the publicist just how he intends to keep you informed on developments. Will he send a weekly activity report? A detailed memorandum? Will there be a telephone or in-person conference? Don't be put off with vague answers. They are a mark of unprofessionalism, and a red flag that the reporting practices of the publicist are suspect.

Articles By You

Unhappily, most publicists seem unaware of the promotional possibilities in articles by you, the expert. You are, however. Find out from your putative publicist whether he can and will be of assistance to you in the preparation of the kinds of articles described in Chapter 7. Be prepared for the fact that you may have to instruct a publicist on the importance of such articles and in their use. While media releases are very much part of the stock in trade of publicists, helping produce articles by their clients is not — just now.

Accompanying You To Media Interviews

It is a sign of status on the promotional circuit to be accompanied to an interview by your publicist. It is as sure a sign of arrival as whispering to a dinner partner, "Of course, *I'd* love to do it. But you'll have to ask my agent." Publicists are a visible status symbol and as such have a distinctive value in presence alone. This is not, however, their chief value, however, flattering as it may be.

Particularly for the beginning self-promoter the presence of a publicist can be of the utmost assistance in guiding an interview to a successful conclusion. Did you get off to a rocky start? Are your answers to questions too long? Too short? Have you failed to make some telling points that ought not to be left out? The publicist can tell you. He will use the commercial breaks or breaks in the taping to point you in the right direction.

Of course, the publicist can also provide you with tips by reviewing the tapes of your lectures, broadcasts, and print interviews, but in the process you may sacrifice an interview or two as you became the suave, cogent media celebrity of your imagining.

Is your publicist willing to review your performance and critique it, or not? Beware of a publicist who is not willing to evaluate your interviews and give you some coaching. This person is purportedly a technical expert, and, as a beginning (or even experienced) self-promoter there is much to be learned.

Besides, reviewing your performance has an educational purpose for the publicist. He needs to know as much about what you're selling, about you, your product, your service, as you do. Accompanying you to interviews, otherwise evaluating your performances will refine his perception of what you are trying to do and make him a better salesman on your behalf. If the publicist seems unwilling to do this for you — look elsewhere.

References

You have now heard what the publicist has to say about himself. A good publicist will have listened to your objectives, explained to you how he can both refine them and help you reach them, and will have provided you with necessary written materials which you can review after your meeting.

If you have not been impressed by what you've heard, you can simply shake hands and leave. If there is an hourly fee to be paid, pay it joyfully for you have learned something more about the tricky business of finding a competent, compatible publicist. Moreover, you have probably spared yourself a lot of misery. An unsatisfactory relationship with a publicist can have ramifications far beyond the terms of your engagement; it may result not only in bad blood but opportunity costs, both now and later. If you have the slightest suspicion, if your questions do not draw forth the information and clarifications you now see you must have, leave.

On the other hand, if you have been dealt with fully, professionally, empathetically and are thinking about engaging the publicist, you have one more significant step: speaking with existing clients.

Human nature being what it is, any individual is going to put his best foot forward. That's fair enough. But you need to know just what the other foot is about. Current clients can give you an indication.

Ask the publicist for the names of two or three satisfied clients. A new publicist may not have so many; this is not necessarily a bad thing, but it does mean you have to place an increased reliance on fewer people. On the other hand, such a publicist may be willing to work hard so as to gain your good opinion.

When you telephone these references, make the call a thorough one. Go through the significant tasks which good publicists perform and see just how effectively your prospective publicist performs them for his client.

I have found that even the most circumspect client waxes eloquent and candid on the subject of what his publicist is — or, more commonly, is not — doing for him. Some of these sins are venal; some are not. It is your job to sift the evidence and arrive at a verdict.

Cost: The Final Factor

Up until now, I have said nothing about how much publicists cost. By design. While I am well aware that in practice cost is often a pivotal consideration, it is not always properly so. Cheap seeming publicists can be expensive; one which initially seems dear can, over the long haul, be a bargain. The problem is determining when this maxim is true and when it is merely marketing hyperbole.

In general publicists charge between $25-$100 per hour, a fixed, flat fee. Other publicists, admittedly rarer birds, charge by the number of interviews they book. One seasoned publicist of my acquaintance has an interesting fee schedule; it begins with a flat rate of $1000 when he delivers any nationally syndicated television show like "Today" or "Donohue," $500 for a comparable national radio show, down to correspondingly lesser amounts for shows with a purely local market.

How do you know which alternative to take?

My advice, if you decide to retain a professional publicist is this: find the one who will do most thoroughly the tasks I have outlined and who charges a fee closest to $25. This is a reasonable start.

Working With Your Publicist

Like any other consultant, you get the best results from your publicist by forming a working partnership. I shall reiterate this key point: you cannot delegate all promotional responsibilities to your publicist and retain nothing more than the task of sweeping grandly into an interview. This is the prescription for chaos and ultimate oblivion.

First, schedule regular conferences. Make it a habit to consult with your publicist for one hour each week. If your project is a major one with a tight deadline, you may have to schedule more and longer meetings. So be it. Ask for a detailed progress report. Ultimately these meetings should evolve into tactical sessions with the publicist giving you very specific information about what he has done and how things are progressing, case by case. Anything less fails to meet your objectives and may indicate that the publicist is not giving sufficient attention to your situation.

Keep Your Publicist Updated

Publicity is a fluid process. Its constant element is unending change. Each day you should be developing new and improved angles to your product or services; each day others are developing strategies and materials which may impact on what you're doing. You are also writing articles, giving speeches, receiving awards, &c. Your publicist needs all this information and needs it promptly. Whether it's a new flattering publicity photo or a sage and provocative article, send it to your publicist at once. It is your responsibility if the publicist is not kept up to date on you and your activites. This is the second key aspect of working with your publicist.

Third, speak up if you don't like something or don't understand it. Promotion is a process which, as this book clearly demonstrates, can be learned. You cannot begin to be an equal partner in the relationship with your publicist unless you understand why and how he does things. It is not smart to act smart if you're not smart.

More Tips For Working With Your Publicist: Meet His Contacts

One of the things a publicist can do for you is build your Self-Promotion Contact Network. Publicists, to be sure, may be wary about introducing you to their contacts for fear that they are writing their own dismissal notice. However, bit by bit, as you work with a publicist you will meet their significant contacts. Treat these like any other addition to your contact network and cultivate them accordingly. Remember: no consultant relationship lasts forever. It is your responsibility to derive the maximum benefit from your business relationship with your publicist. Supplementing your Self-Promotion Network is one good way of doing so.

Work At The Studio

In practice, I have found it most efficacious to have a publicist with me at the studio. Not just to add cubits to my stature, either. I rely on publicists to gather necessary directions and to deliver me to the door of my destination, to announce my arrival, and, from time to time, to amuse my tedium.

In addition, publicists have a very real role to play while the unabashed self-promoter is being interviewed. In the case of a novice self-promoter they can help redeem a flagging performance. For those of us who are more experienced, they can work the telephones.

No publicist should ever be allowed to sit and read the newspaper while you're being interviewed. This is prime work time for him, too. In practice all but the most perfect self-promotional days have holes in them; while there may be three interviews during the day, there is space for an evening call-in, &c. Particularly when the unabashed self-promoter is out of town, it is the task of his publicist to stay on the lines alerting media people to the availability of his client.

I am vehement when I say: when you are promoting an event, either in town or out-of-town, the possibilities of advance media are not exhausted until the event itself is finally, entirely over. Thus if I am in Los Angeles doing an event, I want my local publicist to stay on the telephone throughout my stay, no matter how short, alerting media people to the fact that I am in town, ready and available, and that they should act — now!

Media people respond very well to this urgency, this need to make an immediate decision. They reside in a penumbra of immediacy where nothing else matters but the here and now. Your publicist should know this and should make use of it.

When you and your publicist arrive at a studio (or a newspaper, &c), the publicist should ask for the use of a telephone. This will be given as a matter of course even if at the smallest media outlets. Taking into account your schedule, he should then attempt to book interviews at nearby facilities. Note: media outlets cluster. While no American city has quite the media concentration of London's Fleet Street, it is nonetheless true that in most places several media outlets will be proximate. So long as these are not directly competitive media, so long as you are not pursuing a directly competitive format, it makes superb good sense to attempt to maximize your time in one area by booking all the local media.

When the publicist calls these places, he should say where he is calling from and mention that you are now on the air being interviewed. This will conjure up a suitable image of yourself as a person of consequence, already media worthy. Media people have a pack mentality. They don't like to be left out. What your publicist is doing is giving them an opportunity to be part of a significant experience. This is yet another example of Assertive Courtesy.

Even if your publicist cannot be physically with you at your interviews (remaining behind in Boston, say, while you are in Chicago), this urgency can still be imparted. Remember: so long as you have time available, it is the responsibility of your publicist to fill it, whether he works near at hand or from a telephone in another city. Never forget this.

A Publicist Parable

Earlier this year I was the keynote speaker at a national trade association conference. This association had recently retained a publicist firm to handle promoting the organization, its convention, and the convention keynote speaker. On what basis the association reached its decision as to firm is mysterious; however the firm ended up with a nice monthly retainer fee of $1000 plus expenses.

Given my direct interest in the outcome of the firm's labors and my general interest in the field of promotion, I followed the firm's activities with close attention — and with mounting irritation, frustration, and disgust.

The association had not previously attempted to promote its very marketable activities nor did any of the trustees or the executive director have any background in public relations. The firm took full advantage of the association's luxurious naivete to weave the emperor's new clothes. Months passed. Nothing happened. The association, milked regularly for its fee, remained content. Admonitions from me were initially regarded as overzealous. But not for long.

Despite a very marketable commodity in the high tech field as their product, the publicist firm produced but two paltry radio interviews for their clients — both on stations of miniscule significance; one of those scheduled the executive director to do a live 10 minute interview across Chicago from the convention center, 45 minutes before he was scheduled to gavel his meeting into order.

No documents were sent to the association by the publicist firm, no media releases, no guidance was sought on how best to market the association, its convention or its eminent keynoter. No Media Activity Chart was produced or reviewed. None of my significant steps was followed.

The publicist consulting firm waxed fat and arrogant in its sloth; the client awoke one day with the uncomfortable realization that they had wasted a considerable sum of money and had nothing to show for it.

The publicist, of course, had the perfect answer for the nascent complaints: "We didn't have enough money to do a thorough job." They then had the audacity to request a raise.

Who was at fault in this situation?

In my opinion, both the publicist firm and the association bear their part in a very unhappy, unproductive relationship. The client approached the firm ill-prepared to demand in detail what they had every right to expect: expert technical assistance. The consulting firm, in turn, made no effort to meet the client's objectives and behaved throughout in a reprehensible, unprofessional manner. Theirs was the contemporary version of the "Slaughter Of The Innocents," and they played it very well.

Learn from this situation. Before retaining any professional publicist, review this chapter. If the publicist meets your reasonable objectives, well and good. If not — train your own.

Creating Your Own Publicists

I have, I'll admit, a suspicion about publicists and their firms, even though I have now formed one. I have heard too many reasonable complaints about them and, as you see from above, have only too recently been an inadvertent participant in a most unfortunate publicist-client relationship. I prefer another approach to retaining an outside publicist. I prefer to train my own.

I now have publicists in Boston, New York, Pittsburgh, Detroit, and Los Angeles. None was trained as a publicist; only one had promotional career aspirations. All do their jobs well, which is to say that each succeeds in getting me promoted in their cities. All began with me as their chief and indeed only client, although some now have other clients, too. For none of them is the work they do for me full time; all also have other jobs, other sources of income.

Finding And Training The Ingénue Publicist

Embryo publicists are everywhere. Believe me. I am related to one. I was introduced by a client to another, by a friend to a third. A university where I lecture assigned me a student who later became my fourth. My fifth I met in a taxi when he drove me to a media engagement. Yes, embryo publicists are everywhere.

You find them, too, in local collegiate journalism programs. Just ask. Too, certain states, like Massachusetts, maintain an Intern Program where college students who desire to learn a trade or skill can register and be assigned to a project. You can find out whether such a program exists by telephoning any career guidance office of any college. They should know.

I myself have not had good luck with such intern programs on the whole. Today's students, despite the careerist rhetoric bandied about, are often maddeningly capricious in their approach to the world of work. I prefer to work with adults, and through programs such as women's vocational re-entry programs I have no problem finding serious individuals interested in acquiring promotional skills. The question is: how to determine what they should do.

Just what the ingénue publicist can do for you is determined by what skills he has. You are now well aware of what a publicist might do:

- write well
- be familiar with media sources
- develop persuasive marketing materials
- pursue media targets
- maintain a Media Activity Chart

And all the rest.

Recruit an ingénue publicist who can supplement your own self-promotional efforts. In practice, the relationships you, the unabashed self-promoter, forge with the ingénue publicist will vary dramatically depending on their skill levels. Some, with poor writing skills, are best left to handle the less imaginative tasks of public relations: assembling packets, securing information on places to send them, monitoring their arrival, &c. Others, better prepared, can do more: drafting informational packets about you and selling you to media personnel.

Being a strong writer myself and having a clear sense of how I should be sold to the media, I rely on my publicists to help by staying up-to-date on the various media markets and by dogging the media, with letters and follow-up telephone calls, until I am booked.

It should go without saying, but doesn't, that where a publicist (whether experienced or not) does contact the media on your behalf, you must train that individual to get across your most salable points. This, of course, is an objective best achieved with practice. Never, never allow an unseasoned publicist to make any calls on your behalf until you have instructed him on the result you want to achieve and how this objective can best be met. And stay in the room while the first few telephone calls are made. Your image is at stake, your future relations with the media. A brusque, ill-prepared, superficial publicist (by no means confined to the ranks of amateurs, either) reflects badly on you. Remember: it takes time and practice to become a good representative for another.

The Partnership With Your Publicist

You now know what needs to be done in effectively making contact with the media. You know, too, what a full-pledged professional publicist ought to do. Inevitably when you work with the ingénue, you will decide who ought to do what task. Just make sure that every necessary step is assigned.

Working with the developing publicist in this fashion may bruise the hubris of those who regard the publicist less as a useful technician and more as an exotic status symbol. I don't worry about such things. I have promotional objectives to reach and my partnership with the developing publicist allows me to reach them. Here are the benefits of the relationship as far as I'm concerned:

- I get more attention. Developing publicists can focus on me in a way seasoned professionals cannot.
- I have more control over the promotional process. I know what needs to be done and can divide up the promotional tasks so that they can be accomplished expeditiously. If my part is to produce compelling documents, I can do so quickly and can keep a close watch — and substantial control — over what the new publicist does — in following up the mailing of these documents.
- It's cheap. As you see, professional publicists are not inexpensive, although the best are certainly worth the money. Nonetheless what they cost can be a significant expense for the ambitious though impecunious self-promoter. Ingénue publicists cost less. It is entirely possible to get good help from intelligent, thoughtful but not yet fully fledged publicists for $7-10 an hour.

The cost in part reflects the fact that they are still developing, in part the fact that they are learning from you. The more you have mastered the art of self-promotion, the more you can justify paying them less. Also, don't hesitate to keep their fee low if you are delivering media contacts to them which result in the promotion of their business and other interests. Through association with me, one of my publicists (who runs a consulting practice on the side), has received a string of promotional opportunities on radio, television and through print media which would otherwise not have come so easily.

While he makes some of his useful contacts on the telephone, of course, this individual also makes sure he drives me from place to place as I do my Boston media rounds. At each stop at the conclusion of my performance, he takes a couple of minutes to network, reintroduce himself, mention his other interests, leave materials, and to say that he'd like to be interviewed at a later date.

The timing of this approach is important; after my performance is a good time to strike, since the producer or host will feel, for a moment, relieved and accessible and my embryo publicist can derive maximum benefit from me when we are present, all blissful smiles and satisfactory result. So handled, this approach has paid handsome dividends for him.

So long as such an approach does not threaten your own promotional objectives, you can and should support it. After all, the fact that you help deliver such important benefits is a neat alternative to offering a higher wage. Let me assure you: there will always be someone competent enough who is eager to work with you because of this inducement. Always.

Even if the media attention you receive is not an unending panegyric.

CHAPTER 19

WHEN AND HOW TO USE NEGATIVE MEDIA

Most of the media you generate will be good, complimentary, often lavish in its superlatives, uncritical, sometimes fawning. This is of course the attention we want. But there are, sad to say!, times when we get something else. As cruel and unpredictable as the sea, the media can turn on its old favorites and, with positive gusto, assist in rending them limb from limb. Fortunately the unabashed self-promoter is by no means without resources in a situation where he is subjected to negative media. Indeed, depending on the circumstances, negative media, initially so distressing, can actually be a blessing in disguise, a wonderful opportunity for you to enhance your image and to exploit the media to your further advantage.

Here are the leading situations:

An Attack On An Individual, Organization Or Cause With Which You Are Not Associated

As previously discussed, the unabashed self-promoter is ever-alert for openings which he can exploit to enhance and reinforce his image before constituencies in which he is interested. An attack on an individual, organization or cause with which you are *not* associated can present a wonderful opportunity.

You will remember my story about the **Boston Globe**'s gratuitous attack on a local female radio commentator. I had no personal connection to the beleaguered victim, but that did not matter. I sensed an opening which could be exploited.

Like it or not, within every subset of society people share common opinions, prejudices and beliefs. When an individual holding these opinions, prejudices and beliefs is attacked, any outsider can stand tall as a hero by rushing to defend them.

The unabashed self-promoter becomes very good at discerning, in any given situation, just what the prevalent and shared beliefs are. He knows, for example, that despite the ravages of women's liberation, most men brought up to open a lady's car door, stand when she enters a room and light her cigarette (though we dislike the fact that she smokes) recoil with instinctive horror at the idea of attacks on women in the public press. Chivalry is not dead; it's just latent. This horror may seldom if ever be verbalized as such, but it is a very real thing, and of very real use to the unabashed self-promoter.

I myself am well aware of this horror and am equally well aware that such an attack enables me to rush to the defense of the victim in my heroic mode: bristling with moral indignation and cool outrage. My published defense of the lady in the **Boston Globe** enabled me to stand forth as an individual of heart, empathy, courage and zeal. Not so incidentally, it also helped me to a series of interviews on the major station with which the victim was affiliated.

And this is perhaps the point.

You should be most desirous of standing tall in the defense of an individual or cause when, through this defense, you can advance your self interest. The unabashed self-promoter is always looking for situations which he can exploit to leap frog over his competitors and clearly distinguish himself from the run of mankind.

Many individuals no doubt deplored the unreasonable attack on the radio commentator. But my defense was the only one published, the only one hung in the newsroom of her radio station.

An Attack On An Individual, Organization Or Cause With Which You Are Connected

Each morning I sit at my breakfast table with a pair of scissors and a mound of newspapers. I search these for many things, but one of my happier finds is an attack on an individual, organization or cause with which I am, however tenuously, associated. Having read and reread the attack, I clip it and conclude my breakfast with relish, knowing that I have just been handed yet another self-promotional possibility.

The example on page 353 demonstrate how the process works. The **Boston Globe** on May 3, 1982 ran a longish article attacking certain consulting firms for their recruiting tactics at major business schools. I was not mentioned in this article; mine is not a consulting firm of the kind criticized, nor have I ever recruited anyone at a business school. Nonetheless, I knew that this article created an excellent self-promotional opening for me.

The unabashed self-promoter must develop a proprietary interest towards all those movements, trends, institutions, events, and individuals with which he is somehow connected. Each time one of these is attacked in the media, the unabashed self-promoter has to realize that he has been given a perfect opportunity to respond. This is because of the media's Doctrine of Equity.

Under the Doctrine of Equity, the media feels obliged to publish or broadcast opinions which tend to produce a balanced assessment of a given topic. Tit for tat, ying for yang. Under the Doctrine of Equity, the media invites 'responsible' individuals to have their say on any given issue. Ordinarily the problem is there are not that many of these individuals readily at hand, and so the media will simply use the first seemingly-responsible individual who happens by.

That should be you.

I myself have a long string of proprietary interests including:

- nonprofit organizations
- Harvard
- the British monarchy
- home-based businesses
- entrepreneurship
- publishing companies
- continuing education programs
- consulting

Each time something negative — or wrong — appears in the media on any one of these — or several dozen other — topics, I give consideration to whether my interests are best served by rushing to the defense. Since something critical — or incorrect — is said about one of these topics every day in one media source or another, I find myself with far too many self-promotional possibilities to conceivably deal with all of them.

An Attack On A Group Of People, Including You — By Name

The game becomes more provoking — and infinitely more interesting — when you are attacked by name as part of a group being criticized. In this scenario, an organization or institution finds itself under attack and several people are specifically singled out for notice — one, unhappily, being you.

In this situation, if the individuals choose to respond at all (based on the criteria which follow), choose, that is, to invoke the Doctrine of Equity, they must do so in such a way that their collective weight completely crushes critic and charges.

I have used as an example of this situation, some silly and misinformed criticism made about three books on Harvard (one of them being mine) in a review by the university's chaplain. The collective result exposed their attacker as biased, ill-prepared, entirely unsatisfactory — and infinitely worse off then if he had simply declined the assignment. The experienced unabashed self-promoter usually has no difficulty in routing his opponent once he has made the decision that there is any point in trying to do so. (See samples, pages 351-352).

An Attack On You Alone

Most uncomfortable without question is the attack on you alone. Naked and exposed you awake to find yourself, your gaffes, errors of commission and omission, and sins venal and cardinal splashed on the front pages of newspapers everywhere and broadcast throughout the electronic media.

Now what?

Should You Respond?

Not every error the media makes about you calls for a response on your part. Nor does every criticism whether found in a media source or made directly by such a source.

All too often as an individual confronts some less than flattering fact about himself disseminated by the media, anger and frustration overwhelm reason. Not surprisingly, any action under such circumstances is often very, very unfortunate, often in fact worse than the original cause of provocation.

Ask yourself these questions:

- Have my material interests actually been damaged by what has been printed or broadcast? Or is it simply that my pride has been hurt and I want blind revenge?
- If I respond, can I afford to tell the whole truth, nothing but the truth?
- If I respond and tell a selective fraction of the truth, can the other side respond with further, more damaging information, allegations? Is there a way for the other side to get the full truth, I may not want publicized?
- Is the public really interested in this matter? Is the initial criticism, attack or complaint of compelling public interest? Can it be made to be? And is my response of any concern at all?
- If I respond will I give unnecessary circulation to the original criticism?
- Can I respond in such a way that my image and interests will not suffer. Will a victory be pyrrhic?
- Can I respond quickly enough to staunch the wound and get my point across, fully, finally?

Have I Been Damaged?

Most negative media doesn't leave a scratch, much less a scar. We live in a confrontational, argumentative society of pluralistic interests with often mutually exclusive antagonistic goals. Controversy and criticism are the lifeblood of this society. Everyone knows this, and most people are fully prepared to discount most of what they read and hear accordingly.

Moreover, attacks on you can actually be to your considerable advantage — depending on who makes them. An acquaintance of mine who is a union-busting consultant, specializing in keeping unions out of businesses and removing them once there, takes great and voluble pride in a massive clipping book stuffed with media articles abusing him. Is he anxious about them? Depressed? Worried? On the contrary. The attacks appear in union publications which universally detest him and his methods. They have, however, given him his credibility where he needs it — with the owners of companies who gage his desirability by the vengeful fury of his attackers, their opponents.

Calculating self-promoters may even wish to promote attacks on themselves for the advantages they bring in other quarters. John F. Kennedy's appearance in 1960 before a convention of conservative Southern ministers is a case in point. Had he been attacked in this forum because of his religion, he would have been well positioned to increase his share of support from middle class Roman Catholics everywhere, who were not as a group entirely supportive of his candidacy. As it was by coming to an unsympathetic forum and giving a ringing speech on behalf of the separation of church and state, he emerged as a statesman. I have often wondered, however, whether he wouldn't have preferred less open acceptance.

The only good reasons for responding to criticism appearing in the media are these:

- The facts as reported are entirely inaccurate. You are in a position to say so and can refute what is being publicized.
- Your material interests are substantially affected. By not taking action you will lose real dollars and social standing.
- You have spotted a self-promotional possibility which will leave you better off.
- You are not just seeking revenge.

Can I Afford To Tell The Whole Truth?

Think twice before you respond to criticism about you, accusations, innuendos and allegations, with half truths. Media people have seen and heard everything. Everything. Nothing phases them. Nothing that is except being lied to. That is like the scent of blood to a shark. It is the beginning of the end.

Media people, remember, regard themselves as the arbitors of truth. All other mortals are lesser creatures. Media people resemble the ancient gods. Like all gods in all cultures and in every age, these gods expect the rest of us to err. Good Calvinists all, media personnel are believers in the Total Depravity of Man. Sins are, therefore, entirely expected.

Our media gods are quite prepared to forgive us our sins, if we only have the good sense to acknowledge them — to the media. If we lesser creatures lie to the media, however, we have committed the Ultimate Sin and for this the media insists on maximum punishment. In this situation media people become vengeful furies and nothing, nothing will stop them until they have brought low the offender. In service to truth, they would regard themselves as culpable if they did anything less.

The key is that when admitting any unpleasant truth, you must give reasons which are acceptable and explicable to the general public. If you have indeed participated in something heinous, it is all the more important that the full extent of your involvement be acknowledged early and that your reasons be framed for maximum public acceptance.

Richard Nixon should have known as much and acted accordingly. The fact that he didn't has always made me question his much-vaunted intellect. He had, for instance, after the Watergate burglary only to go before the country via the media and say, "I have today given an official commendation to several patriotic and courageous men who last night burgled the offices of the Democratic Party in the Watergate. Many people will be shocked that I could even condone such an action much less commend it. The fact is if the Democrat party was to come to power now, a train of regrettable occurrances would inevitably follow. Thus in the national interest I acted to prevent this wholly tragic result.

Politics is a dirty business. I wish I could always behave in the Free World's premier leadership position with the manners which make people popular in a country club. But I cannot. I must make the hard choices and take the tough decisions. I have done so."

Who can doubt the enthusiastic reception of these remarks? Weakness, not leadership, did the man in.

What About A Selective Fraction Of The Truth?

What Nixon chose to do, of course, was doctor the facts and stonewall any further investigation. As the unabashed self-promoter well knows telling the whole truth makes sense from a utilitarian as well as ethical perspective in all these situations.

Where there is any way for the initial critic to get his hands on any more damaging material, as President Nixon soon learned, he could not control the sources of information. First, telltale rivulets, then a positive flood of damage followed. But the consistent thread was that the president had lied. Ultimately the lie itself became by far the most damaging issue.

Every unabashed self-promoter knows this, and he knows what the media will do to him if he is found out in a lie. Thus, unless you have complete control over all the relevant information, don't respond to attacks on you, criticism and abuse, with lies and half truths. You will be much worse off as our imperial president learned on the lonely beaches of San Clemente.

Does The Public Care?

Hard though it is for many healthy egos to accept, the public isn't at all interested in the seering criticism which appeared about you in the morning's newspaper. Unless this affects their vital concerns in a very direct, substantial and tangible way, whatever is published about you will engage their interest for only the most fleeting instant. While this is irritating to the unabashed self-promoter on most days, in this situation it is a blessing, and one which should not be forgotten.

Remember: Only sustained repetition of charges and criticisms will arouse the slumbering and apathetic public beast.

Think!

Do you really want this public to be prodded into paying closer attention to what you're doing? The unabashed self-promoter knows that under ordinary circumstances he can exploit the media virtually at will to his own advantage. As the public is aroused and as the media itself loses its own characteristic ill-organization and disinterest in content, the unabashed self-promoter will probably experience more difficulty in getting his unimpeded way.

Why risk it?

Will You Give Unnecessary Prominence To The Original Criticisms?

When you respond to any negative comment, you also, necessarily, give further and quite possible wider circulation to the original criticisms. Is this what you want?

It is only worth drawing the public's attention back to the original criticism if you can entirely dispel it. If you can in one fell swoop, explode the other point of view in such a way that your image is reinforced and so that no lingering questions remain.

Will A Pyrrhic Victory Be In Your Interest?

All too often those who respond to media criticism, even criticism which is totally false and malicious, find out they are, in the end, the unexpected losers. I am reminded in this regard of one of the volumes in John Galsworthy's **Forsyte Saga.** The hapless Soames Forsyte overhears Marjorie Ferrar, impecunious granddaughter of a marquis, call his daughter Fleur a "born little snob" in Fleur's own drawing room. Ever unimaginative, Soames takes out an action against Marjorie for damages. The result, while a technical victory, forces Fleur and her husband to leave London and its glittering society for an extended period abroad in less hospitable climes. In short, a pyrrhic victory.

With the media, as must by now be perfectly clear, perspective is everything. Technical winners can easily become actual losers. You may prove your point and the fallaciousness and error of the initial criticism, but you may in process besmirch your reputation and suffer irreparable loss. Is it worth it?

Can You Respond Quickly Enough?

The only response that's worth much is one that's delivered quickly. Are you prepared to respond? As will become very apparent as this chapter develops, speed, always a critical variable when dealing with the media, can become *the* crucial consideration when coping with negative media. Unless you are prepared to act with celerity, it may be better to do nothing.

Consult Your Advisors

In deciding whether or not to respond to criticism appearing in the media, it is ordinarily a wise idea to convene a group of trusted friends and associates who can help you consider. The greater the interests involved the more necessary for such a group. Into these discussions you should consider bringing your lawyer and someone familiar with the media.

Consult, too, one or two of your friends in the media. Do not do so in a group, however. Media people do not wish publicly to indicate a bias although they are perfectly happy to act as private advisors. Jimmy Carter learned this lesson the hard way during the 1976 presidential campaign when he called a group of media people together and asked for advice. They felt their objectivity was being compromised and said so very candidly. Nonetheless, never hesitate to ask one or two of your media friends for advice. That's part of what your Self-Promotion Network is for.

Responding

Once you have reviewed your situation and decided that a response is in your best interests, it is time to consider the available means of presenting your information.

Letter To The Editor

Perhaps the easiest and best-known response format is the ever-popular Letter To The Editor. There is scarcely a publication in the nation which does not maintain such a column. Readers love it because it gives them the opportunity to sound-off on any given issue; publications carry it because of the Doctrine of Equity. It is their way of indicating fairness and accessibility to print.

Sample letters to the editor appear on pages 352 and 353. Review them as models. Letters to the editor should be crisp, concise, pungent. A good length is 150 words, although your letter can be longer if you are an interested party, an authority, or where your points help clarify a complicated situation.

The tone of a letter to the editor should mirror your general image, although the best way of writing one is as the In-Command Authority.

From time to time in a letter, you will want to take a swipe at an individual. This is perfectly permissible, but you must not be heavy-handed about it. Note how I took on my critic in the letter on page 352, with a compliment first. The criticism you make against your target is more likely to stick if you present yourself as reasonable.

The letter to the editor should be sent as soon as possible to be a publicity source. It is usually quite sufficient to address the envelope in which it is mailed to:

Letters to the Editor
name of publication
address of publication

The letter should be typed on your stationery. To avoid any question, I type "For publication" at the top of the page and add this line at its conclusion, "Permission herewith given to edit for length so long as the sense is maintained."

The Response Article

Recently, I was keynote speaker at a convention in Chicago. One of the lunch speakers, editor of a trade newspaper, gave a rousing attack on consultants. I immediately went up and asked whether he was going to publish his remarks. He said no, and I urged him to reconsider. I said that I would like to respond to what he said — point by point — and that we could run what he said and my response as two columns. He concurred.

Whenever possible, go to the publication where criticism has appeared to ask for equal time. A point-by-point response article is a good way to proceed. This article, which may be published on the equivalent of an editorial page, enables you both to refute any criticism and to establish your own argument in some detail.

Again, speed is of the essence when considering such an article. Once the initial criticism has appeared, it is quite permissible to telephone the author of the article or his editor and suggest that you are unhappy with what has appeared and would like to propose a suitable follow-up.

As you know, I make it a point to telephone (or write, if time is of less concern) reporters who produce articles on the subject fields in which I am interested but in which I have not been featured. If their article is positive, I write to congratulate them on what they have written. I send them material about me, so that they know I am available as a source when future stories need to be written, and I suggest story topics.

If the article is not positive, I am not coy about saying so, and I am very clear about why I feel it was incomplete, inaccurate, distorted, &c. A good way to handle such a situation is:

- Compose a Letter to the Editor in response to the initial article.
- Call the reporter, indicate that you are an expert on the topic and that you are sending in a Letter to the Editor.
- Indicate that you are sending a copy of this letter to him along with supplementary materials.
- Suggest that a follow-up article be written which will enable your point of view to be covered.

Unless a reporter has a vested interest in a certain point of view, he will be most receptive to what you are doing. Please note you are not to criticize the reporter directly; you are instead simply to indicate that there is more to say, another important dimension to add.

You are likely to accomplish several things using this method:

- a published Letter to the Editor
- a follow-up article featuring you
- an addition to your Self-Promotion Network

The Op-Ed Piece

If you are an individual of local interest or if the criticism concerns an issue of general importance, consider responding in an Op-Ed piece. This format is so named because the article appears opposite the editorial page. I like to think of it, too, as an opinion-editorial piece because that's what it usually is.

These articles are run in most daily newspapers and many weeklies, too. They are usually 600-750 words in length and present the opinions of qualified writers. The Sentinel article on page 313 originally ran as an Op-Ed piece.

It is perfectly acceptable to use this format to deal with an attack made on you, if the issue is of general significance. Politicians, educational and business figures so use this format regularly.

Ordinarily you cannot get both a Letter to the Editor and an Op-Ed piece printed on the same subject. That is because they are both editorial features. However, it is perfectly permissible to have an Op-Ed piece and a follow-up article either about you or in which you are quoted, and the unabashed self-promoter, seeking to respond to criticism, attempts to so arrange matters.

The Principle of Multiple Use applies as well in responding to criticisms as it does elsewhere. Your job is to arrange matters so that, once you have decided to respond to criticism, to clarify a confused situation or to correct error, you get the widest possible exposure for your point of view.

N.B. Once you have so responded in print, of course, you can use your leave behinds as your introduction to electronic media as discussed in Chapter 13.

The Media Conference

For most of us in most situations the foregoing techniques will provide all that we need to know. There will be situations, however, when the criticism we wish to respond to is general and we must, therefore, hold a media (or press) conference to respond.

What Is It?

A media conference is an organized event whereby you or your organization attempt to gather at one time and in one place all the relevant media sources. Such an event, carefully managed by you, enables you to get your point across in a controlled situation and also enables the media to ask questions of the principals.

When To Organize A Media Conference

You can only, only organize a media conference when there is a hard news angle, that is when you have important, consequential information of wide general interest to the involved media and to their publics. Do not hold a media conference under other circumstances, or you run the very real risk that no one will cover it.

Organizing Your Media Conference

As in all other relations with the media in organizing your media conference you must know what you wish to accomplish. What is your goal. Do you wish to:

- refute criticism of you
- establish the culpability of another
- enhance your reputation
- rally a public

You need to decide in advance.

It is a good idea to write your goal(s) down and refer back to them in the planning process. Depending on how much time you have, this planning process might well be dangerously short. In such cases especially, it is of the utmost significance to write down the goals and abide by them religiously. One of the most famous — and disastrous — media conferences of all times would not have occurred if the principal had asked himself what he wished to accomplish at this conference. Richard Nixon's infamous media conference held in 1962 the morning after his defeat for the California governorship ("You won't have Nixon to kick around anymore.") is a glaring indication of how even those most accomplished in working with the media can lose sight of their objectives under stress. Remember this.

Prepare Your Materials

Your media conference can only be a success if you prepare all the necessary materials. Here is what you need:

Media Advisory

This document, sent in advance to the media sources you are inviting to cover the conference, tells them the:

- subject of the conference
- an indication of what will occur
- who will make presentations
- the date
- time
- place
- follow-up information

Backgrounder

It is ordinarily a good idea to accompany the media advisory with a page (250 words) of background information. This document contains the basic 5 w's of the case:

- who
- what
- where
- when
- why

Within the compass of 250 words you should be able to present all the salient background information about the case. This document should be both sent in advance to the media invited to cover the conference and should be made available at the time.

Response Sheet

If you are responding to charges, criticisms, &c., it is a good idea to draw up a Response Sheet. This sheet sets out:

- the charges, one by one
- your detailed responses
- citations about where media people can find supporting evidence for your claims.

You can offer this information in chart form.

Charge (including person making charge, date, place, &c)	Response	Confirmation of Response

Fact Or Biographical Sheet

It is helpful to the media people covering your conference if they have complete information about you (or your organization, &c). Give them this in a Fact or Biographical Sheet. If an institution or organization is involved give 100-250 words of background; there should be the same amount of material on you.

Media Release

A standard media release should be prepared for distribution at the time of the media conference. This will be the story (in up to 500 words) as *you* would like to have it.

Transcript Of Remarks

It is not only necessary but can be most helpful if you prepare, in addition to a standard media release, an exact transcript of your prepared remarks.

What Gets Sent In Advance?

Send the media advisory and backgrounder to the media sources in advance of the media conference. This may be supplemented by the fact or biographical information. All other materials should be available at the media conference. For ease of handling, arrange them in a manila folder with jacket pockets.

The Media Activity Chart

Draw up a Media Activity Chart of all the media you want to attend your media conference. Do not mail any materials until this chart is complete.

Specifics On Arranging The Media Conference

Your goal in arranging your media conference is ordinarily to do so for maximum exposure. Here are some hints for doing so:

- Place: Whenever possible choose a location convenient for the media, a downtown hotel, or city hall. The easier it is for the media to attend, the more likely they are to do so.
- Time: Tuesday, Wednesday or Thursday are your best days for prime news coverage. If your topic is not of first-class interest, however, consider a Friday media conference. Although Saturday newspaper readership drops at least 25%, the unabashed self-promoter will use a Friday for a topic because he knows the competition is less severe. Always, *always*, hold your media conference in the morning. 10 a.m.-11 a.m. is a very good time. Before you schedule your conference, check with the UPI or AP to see whether any other organization has one planned

for the same day. If you have a hot story, of course, the other organization will have to worry; if you don't, rearrange your schedule. The city desk or assignment editor of the local newspaper will also be able to assist you.

- Length: Plan your conference to last no more than 40 minutes, start to finish. This is quite enough.

Contacting The Media

First, send your media advisories. Note that you have done so on your Media Activity Chart.

Second, call each media source individually to ask whether they will be sending someone. These calls should be made 4 days before your event. Log this information. Place your call to the assignment editor of newspapers, radio and television stations.

Remember: You need to make these calls in sufficient time to allow for the difficulty of reaching these people and for sending them your background information in case it arrives. Do not hesitate, as the time approaches, to explain why you are calling. Ask them to write the information down.

Keep calling until all your media targets are accounted for.

Note: In a case where a media source is not interested, don't give up. Once a competitive outlet indicates they are coming, call the first back and say so. No media source likes to get scooped by a competitor. Under the Principle of Assertive Courtesy, it is your responsibility — and pleasure — to tell a media source that this catastrophe will occur unless they change their minds. They just might do so.

The day before the media conference, call everyone on your Media Activity Chart again. You are attempting to reconfirm all the promises to attend and are giving the old college try to persuade the hold-outs. If developments have taken place since your advisory was sent, don't hesitate to bring them to the attention of the assignment editor. You want a representative present; do whatever it takes to get one there.

The Tone Of The Media Conference: Some Do's And Don'ts

While getting the media people to attend your conference is certainly important (there cannot be one without them, after all), don't neglect planning the substance of what you are going to say or how you are going to say it. Here are some tips:

- Don't get angry.
- Don't get negative.
- Don't descend to the level of your attacker.

Don't Get Angry, Do Use Anger

People lose control of themselves when they are angry. They say too much and they say it in a regrettable way. Instead, deliver your facts coolly, reasonably, in control of them and of yourself. Use humor, not choler, to get your point across.

Remember: When you give a media conference, you are always in a position of risk as well as opportunity. Thus, you need to approach this situation with the utmost self-control. Real anger, vibrant and destructive, threatens this necessary control. On the other hand, feigned anger can be of the utmost assistance to the unabashed self-promoter who wishes to get his point across and has decided this kind of anger can help. Remember the famous incident involving Nikita Khrushchev at the United Nations, when he beat with his shoe on a desk in a presumed paroxysm of rage? In fact this incident, universally reported, was carefully staged. Khrushchev's own shoes never left his feet.

Don't Get Negative

Handle your presentation so that your image is confirmed as a reasonable individual attempting to bring out the whole truth and nothing but. Do not launch stinging attacks on individuals and drop acidulous comments, however warranted. Such comments belittle you. The most lethal approach, the most likely to be successful is to be sincere, suave, civilized, unflappably cool. Beware of an opponent who exhibits these traits. Emulate them.

I regard such an individual as far more dangerous than the zealous public servant, the outraged voice of reason, or the moralistic idealist, all of whom will quickly bore and tire the public. Remember the lesson of the incorruptible Robespierre, the civic-spirited master of the French Revolution. A man without a smile in his repertoir, *he* lost his head on the guillotine. Insouciance is your friend. So is the full panoply of feigned emotions.

By the same token, forebear from attacking the media itself as unfair, subjective, apathetic, or worse. You should know in advance that they are all these things — and more. However, it is extremely unwise of you to take this tack. First, the general public still perceives the media as the purveyors of truth. There will come a day when this will change, but it has not dawned yet. Thus, the public is disinclined to believe you when you attack the media for their subjectivity.

More importantly, it is your own fault, not the media's, if they have covered you and your causes in ways you do not like (or worse, ignored you). Provide the media with the material they need, in a form they can use, and they will use it. Provide the media with a compelling show, and they must report it.

As should by now be pellucidly clear, the media must dance to the unabashed self-promoter's tune —when we do things right. Criticizing them for their bias is not doing things right. Making that bias work on our behalf is.

Don't Descend To The Level Of Your Critics

You best approach a media conference as a peer of the media themselves; that is, as an olympian purveyor of truth. You are above the fray, above the common concerns of common men. You are interested only and solely in truth. As such, you cannot afford to descend to the level of your critics. The right tack to take with them is *de haute en bas*, as one of the illuminati to the sadly unenlightened. Be evidently sorry for them. Patronize them. Indicate how deeply unhappy you are to see so much potential for good be so hopelessly squandered.

Such tactics will produce fury in your critics and a smile from the public. The general public, the media, are all willing to forgive villains; there are numerous instances of this in very recent days. But they do not forgive bores and the self-righteous. A picture of an outraged individual, his face set in anger, shaking a fist, delivering words of fiery severity may leave an impression on the reader — but the reader does not wish to know this person.

The Last Bit Of Planning: Practice

Before your media conference takes place, practice it. Go to the location and:

- review the set up
- know where the electrical outlets are
- make sure you will not have a mirror as a backdrop or an open window
- confirm that tables for literature are available
- see who to contact during an emergency (a blown fuse, for instance) and make sure he'll be available during your conference.

Murphy's Law applies everywhere, but nowhere more so than at a media conference. The unabashed self-promoter has got to be an improviser and must learn to proceed calmly in situations which would unnerve the run of mankind. Practice will reduce the possibilities for the imp of confusion.

At The Conference

Arrive at your conference site at least thirty minutes before it's scheduled commencement. Set up a desk where you can check in all media people attending. Keep a complete list of their names and media affiliations. From these at least it is highly likely you will get coverage.

It is a good idea to have donuts and coffee on hand. People in the media are always hungry and in the morning crave their caffeine fix. If this will help put them in a good mood, well disposed to you, you shouldn't cavil at the expense. You do not, after all, stage a media conference very often.

Have someone present to approach each media representative and see whether they have all the relevant materials and to ask if there is anything special they need. Help them do their job, and they will help you. The easier you make it on them, the better. You will be needing media coverage again, and you might as well turn these people into your friends.

Start the media conference promptly. Do not wait for a late television crew or reporter. At that point, their being late is not your problem any more. You have given them plenty of advance warning.

If you want questions, allow 10-15 minutes for them. End promptly about 40 minutes after the start of the conference.

A Word On Props

Give consideration to what sort of props to bring to the conference. If you are charged with some particularly heinous crime, don't forget the wife and kids. They should look dewey-eyed and alluringly innocent. If you are throwing a last toss of the dice, remember a dog: Checkers went a long way to making Richard Nixon president.

Follow-Up To The Media Conference

Although the conference is over, your work continues. First, call all those who promised to attend but did not and offer them the chance for an interview. At the very least, offer an audio cassette of your media conference plus the media kit which you distributed. Call those who did not plan to attend and make the same offer.

Call local radio stations, too, and offer to give them a 1-2 minute quote summarizing your media conference.

For the 4-5 working hours after the media conference, you will very likely be on the telephone, mailing packets of material and having them sent by courier to important media sources. Plan for this. Plan, too, to schedule individual interviews with the electronic media. A media conference can launch a media wave. Take advantage of this opportunity.

Keep A File Of Results

Either hire a clipping service or delegate your friends to help you monitor the results. You need to know just what the media highlighted in your presentation. If you have planned properly you should not be surprised. But these matters are not always predictable. If a media source garbles your information or places the emphasis incorrectly, you may have to resort to a letter to the editor, op-ed piece or, in the worst case, yet another media conference. Thus, monitoring the result is of the utmost significance.

If You Emerge The Loser

If you have followed the suggestions of this chapter, you have emerged from a trying process triumphant. You have seized the opportunity of a risky situation and squeezed the advantage from it. Congratulations. You have reached an advanced stage of unabashed self-promotion. Please get in touch with me at once, since I need friends like you.

Perhaps, however, you have risked — and lost. The criticism has stuck, your reputation has been besmirched, your material interest adversely affected. What then?

First, lie low. The unabashed self-promoter, congenitally optimistic, knows he cannot win them all. There will come a day when he mishandles a situation, or when he plays against another unabashed self-promoter more expert than he is. This will happen, especially as more people use this book.

The best way to approach this situation is philosophically. Learn from it. Take whatever advantage is to be gained while you bide your time before trying again. For try again you will.

If you have been condemned by the media for some particularly shocking action, lie low and begin to adopt the trappings of the Redeemed Sinner. As I mentioned earlier, this image, connected to the deep evangelical strain of this country, is a powerful one and can be the unabashed self-promoter's trump card. "I sinned," you say. "I sinned badly, and I hurt people. But I am only human. I ask for your forgiveness. Please give it." Ah, this is so hard to deny. Keep the Redeemed Sinner image amongst your resources after a fall from grace. Move towards it at first slowly, cautiously, deliberately but as you gain acceptance stand forth boldly as the Unabashed Redeemed Sinner — and carry on.

Remember, too: If you have fallen, do not forget the noble phoenix of classical myth. This is a symbol of comfort to maimed and afflicted self-promoters. You will, I promise you, rise again. Review this book and keep alert for the exploitable promotional opportunities which come each day.

CHAPTER 20

A POTPOURRI OF PROMOTIONAL POSSIBILITIES

The unabashed self-promoter, treating the whole matter of generating publicity as a game with wondrous prizes, never tires of seeking creative, inventive ways to exploit the media and get his name and achievements before the widest possible public. He views everything that he does, everything that he has, every thought in his head in terms of their promotional possibilities. Needless to say the run of common men does not approach life in this fashion, and the result is that they remain in the deep shadow of obscurity, leading lives, as Thoreau might say, of "quiet desperation." It is, however, their own fault.

This chapter is intended to give you an idea of some — but by no means all — the promotional possibilities that are open to you. The range is necessarily unlimited. Indeed, if you properly condition yourself as an unabashed self-promoter, you will quickly discover that there are far too many possibilities to exploit given the maddeningly finite quantity of human time. In a strange way, however, I find this a comforting realization, knowing that at any given time, *any*, there is always a self-promotional possibility available, if only I choose to take it.

Getting Your Clients To Promote You

If you are an independent service provider, entrepreneur, consultant or the like, you probably work, as I do, with many individuals and organizations. No doubt if you are anything other than mediocre in the service you deliver, the people you work with give you periodic compliments. Nice, aren't they? Now imagine that these compliments are publicized so that they come to the attention of the widest possible audience. Your clients can do this for you. The sample on page 354 shows you how.

As an unabashed self-promoter, it is important that you be aware both what publications your clients maintain (in-house magazines and newsletters) and which ones they subscribe to and read. Both are important self-promotional vehicles for you. Keep a list of these publications and make an opportunity to peruse them so that you get an idea what kinds of articles they want.

As soon as you have done something good for a client, produced a beneficial result, saved some money, raised revenue, it is time to ask for a promotional favor.

- Ask the client if he feels it appropriate for you to be featured in the organization's publication. Perhaps there might be a feature piece on the work you're doing and why it's important. Perhaps a profile on you and your firm. Perhaps just a thank-you from the CEO for what you've already accomplished (see samples, page 354). You want to secure through publicity third party validation of your work so that you can bring it to the attention of other likely clients.
- Ask the client whether he would like to have his organization and your work featured in a trade publication. In this case, indicate what publication you have in mind and what kind of an article. The sample on page 354 is a good illustration of what you should be thinking of. It highlights both the work of the agency and my work as an expert in fund raising.

  Remember: Publications like success stories. If you have helped produce a success, consider who you wish to know about it. Every time I do something good, I want it brought to the attention of the widest possible public. You should too.

Note: Ideally the client will write the article either for submission to their own publication or to a national publication. However, if this seems unlikely, offer to do it yourself — as a draft. Submit your suggested copy to the appropriate officer for final checking and submission to the publication. Actually, I prefer to write such articles myself, because then I am sure of squeezing the utmost advantage from what I have done. And I'm not faced with the irritation of waiting for others, who are generally less publicity-minded, to get organized.

Write A Column Or Regular Article Series

Columns can be a marvelous source of self promotion. How do you get them?

The sample article on page 354 was published in the fall of 1982 in a publication of the U.S. Department of Health and Human Services called **Human Development News.** As soon as it appeared, I contacted the editor by telephone and asked whether she'd be interested in a regular series of articles on technical assistance for nonprofit organizations, her readers. She was. Now, in every other issue of the publication, there is a feature by me. I am not paid for it.

Not paid! Then why do it? Because there are many kinds of payment. In this case, the articles, based on the services of my consulting firm, are read by 40,000 nonprofit organizations around the country who can buy my technical assistance books, training workshops, and consulting services. In short, each article constitutes a free ad, packed with information of interest to the targeted population, promoting me and my services the while. It would be nice, of course, if I were paid, too, but it is not absolutely necessary.

Consider the following:

- If you provide a service of general interest to the public (something involving food, clothing, health, housing, investment, &c), consider writing a 650-word column every week or two. Mail this to the weekly newspapers within your marketing area. Do not initially ask for payment. Make sure, however, that your service or product is clearly identified at the foot of the article so people know how to get in touch with you. Build your column, as I did, out of your regular service. That way you are sure to know you can provide it when client prospects contact you. It is a good idea to accompany your column with a head shot of you. It will personalize your piece.

Is it necessary to query the publication in advance? Not necessarily. Just send along a cover letter and copies of your first three columns. Indicate in this letter:

- how often your articles will be published
- what lengths they will be
- whether you require payment.

Articles speak for themselves. If they are good and if the publication has no comparable feature (which you ought to know before mailing your copy), you have a superb chance of being the newest columnist on the block, with a continuing source of self-promotional possibilities.

After you have written your column for a time (say 4-6 months), open the question of payment. Remember: An editor will find it easier to pay you in ad space than in cash. One good way of handling this matter is to produce your column twice a month and have an ad run twice a month. If you do request cash payment, you should know that the rates for syndication under such circumstances are very low; you are very unlikely to get more than $10 per week per newspaper. (See samples, page 326).

Don't Forget Trade Publications

If your subject is not of general interest, or you wish to promote a technical angle of more concern to specialists, consider trade publications. Such publications are written by and for specialists. **Human Development News** is such a publication.

Again, as with general interest media, suggest either a regular column or a series of articles spread out over a year or two. If you are not to be paid, request payment in ad space. Do not diminish the impact of your ad by running in the same issue you have an article. Remember, the tag at the conclusion of your article should be written in such a way that it not only constitutes a free ad but also makes it very clear how readers may contact you. You will probably not be allowed to use your telephone number, so at least be sure to name your firm and its location.

Have A Day Declared In Your Honor

Have you ever wondered what it would be like to have a day declared in your city in your honor? Wonder no more! February 17, 1983 was "Dr. Jeffrey Lant Day" in Cambridge, Massachusetts and His Honor Mayor Alfred Vellucci arrived to declare it and give me a splendid proclamation. Even my friends, a fairly cynical bunch, were suitably impressed. How can you get one named after you?

- Have you had long service with a civic organization and are now retiring?
- Are you PTA president?
- Chairman of the local Kiwanis?
- Were you instrumental in the local art museum's fund drive?
- Have you been a foster parent?
- Have you made a public effort to keep your town clean and beautiful?
- Have you written a good book?
- Have you helped get a piece of legislation passed?
- Have you been an active church volunteer for several years?

Or have you done any one of a thousand other civic-spirited things. The answer is probably "Yes!"

Many branches of government produce citations, proclamations and other civic tributes. Here are some which do:

- your city council
- your mayor
- your state senate
- your state house of representatives
- your governor

Of course, the national legislature also does so and on up to the President of the United States himself.

How To Get A Citation Or Proclamation

On the whole, I prefer not to ask for these things myself. There is something unseemly about doing so and is *infra dig* for a mandarin figure. Instead have a suitable friend send a letter on your behalf. Of course, you can be of assistance by drafting it. Include information on:

- who you are
- what you have done, as specifically as possible
- the connection of the writer to you
- what award you would like
- what wording you want on the citation
- when and under what circumstance you want it presented
- who you would like to present it.

(See samples, page 346)

It will be easier for you to get such a citation or proclamation if you have thought through each of the items above and know exactly what you want. The more things you ask your contact to do, the more delay and confusion there will be.

Who Gets The Citation Request?

Who gets the request depends on who is being honored and why. If you are seeking a mayoral citation and the proclamation of a day in your honor, the request goes to the mayor of your home town. The best person to recommend you is someone who also lives in your home town, whether this person is known by the mayor or not. Indeed there is an erroneous belief that you have to know the mayor (or other presenter) personally to make this technique work. Nothing could be further from the truth. What you must have is a natural connection, such as being a resident of the town.

If you have been part of a project with statewide application, consider approaching either your state representative or state senator for a citation from his house of the legislature or even the governor.

Using The Citation, Proclamation As A Self-Promotional Vehicle

Receiving such a citation or proclamation is an event and should be treated as one. Make sure it is presented to you in a suitable place.

Citations and proclamations may either be presented at events such as conventions, annual dinners, board meetings, &c, or in the chambers of the offical making the presentation. Only arrange for the former if a suitably high functionary can be present to add importance to the occasion (see sample on page 319. Otherwise, go to the official.

In either case, arrange for a photographer to be present. If you are working with an elected official in his usual place of business, this will not be difficult; photographers are ordinarily available and simply need to be scheduled in advance. If the presentation is being made at your headquarters or event, you will have to arrange for the photographer.

Arrange for a good one. I saw one niggardly organization completely spoil a presentation event by entrusting the photographing to a young man who announced half way through that his camera batteries were dead. There should be a special circle of Dante's hell for such creatures.

An article and photograph about your award should be sent to:

- the local newspaper
- alumni publication(s)
- civic publications
- social/fraternal publications
- trade publications
- religious publications

And any other likely sources. If you merely get the award, frame it and hang it on your wall without deriving maximum publicity benefit from it, you have lost a wonderful self-promotional possibility.

Getting Citations And Proclamations Away From Home

Every governing body in this country has the means of honoring citizens. It seems to be our equivalent of the Order of the British Empire. Unlike this chivalric order, however, the unabashed self-promoter can succeed in getting hundreds if not thousands of citations and proclamations merely by approaching his objective with rationality, discipline, and thoroughness.

Each time you are a keynote speaker at an out-of-town convention, ask the organizers to get you an appropriate citation. They will probably have never had this request made of them and are sure not to know how to proceed. Help them:

- Decide which government body you would like to decorate you.
- Call the office and ask for the name, title, mailing address and telephone number of the individual handling such requests.
- Talk to the appointments secretary of the official you are pursuing. See what times correlate with scheduled convention activities.
- Present this information to relevant convention officials.
- Suggest what you would like the award for (ordinarily something connected to the work which has brought you to the attention of the convention.)
- Don't let the matter drop. Call the convention official back a week before the convention and ask how matters are going.

It is a very nice feeling to arrive in a strange city, fatigued, probably knowing no one, but to know that in a day or two, the mayor, the governor, or some other top official will trot over to recognize you. This is one of the many rewards of being an unabashed self-promoter, and you can justifiably savor it.

When else should you consider such an award when traveling?

- You are a long-time member of an association now retiring.
- You have published an article bearing on the city in question.
- You have been the chairman of the arrangements committee for a convention and want some recognition.

Use your imagination! Citations and proclamations make wonderful self-promotional vehicles. Keep mulling over what you are doing and how it can lead to having one.

Your Habits And Lifestyle As A Source For Self-Promotion

Everything is grist for the unabashed self-promoter's mill, everything. Think of the following as possibilities:

- your spouse
- your children
- your pets
- your hobbies
- your home
- your food
- your clothes
- your travels

Here are a few ideas based on these possibilities.

Your Spouse

Although you probably don't do so enough, from time to time, you probably compliment something your spouse does. This can now be turned into a source of self-promotion. Let's say it's your spouse's sinfully succulent chocolate chip cookies. An article about them in the food pages of the local newspaper, properly handled, would produce the following results:

- promotion of information on the cookies, to be sure
- increasing standing for spouse
- a nice plug for you, the unabashed self-promoter, your company, product or service, as part of the article.

Disseminating information on chocolate chip cookies may or may not be important; (it is, of course, if that is your business). What is important, however, is that as part of the presumably more significant article, the unabashed self-promoter gets a plug for that which really interests him: his product, service, message, company, or just himself.

You, the unabashed self-promoter, need to factor your spouse into your promotional plans. Take a good, long look at your spouse. Now do this:

- Write down all the promotional possibilities you discern.
- Consider what media sources, print and electronic, would be interested in knowing about them.
- Figure out how you can be promoted as part of the package.
- Write a query letter, draw up a standard media release or write an appropriate article, whichever seems to be the best alternative.
- Pursue the media source until your material is used.

You may have considered your spouse many things during the years you have been together, but I suspect you have not regarded this individual as a source for unabashed self-promotion. Now you know better.

Your Children

In the same way, consider your children. In virtually all articles about children, the parents are mentioned. Indeed, properly handled children can generate a significant amount of publicity for their parents and their parents' concerns. Indeed, I am firmly of the opinion that the promotional value of children begins even before they are conceived.

Right now in cities like Cambridge, thousands of two-career couples are grappling with whether they should have children or not. Career women my age, 36, are faced with a biological imperative, and they must act now or watch their opportunity to have children slip away, forever. The result has been a series of articles in which these professional couples air their concerns while in the process promoting themselves, their products and services in a seemingly incidental way.

Generally these articles feature 3 or 4 couples who have arrived at different decisions. This is a package. Don't overlook the usefulness of these packages as self-promotional vehicles. In a case where you are unlikely to be solely featured, approach a media source with the story idea and the names of others who can provide insight. (See samples, page 349).

Personally I was rather a latecomer to the world of self-promotion. I only started in organized fashion when I was 13, and then at my own inspiration. The wise parent, having read this book, will commence operations long before. Here are some possibilities:

- How are you handling your pregnancy? Are you still working? Are you taking special classes in diet, exercise, nutrition? This is a wonderful source for articles. So are the pregnancy clothes. Remember: The promotional possibilities of baby begin long before baby is born.
- What about the role of Dad? Is Daddy taking birthing and parenting classes? If so, don't overlook the promotional possibilities. A group of expectant fathers in a parenting class would make quite a suitable promotional package.
- How about the birth itself? If it is to be at home, why not invite media representatives to cover it? This could be a truly gripping story, entirely universal. Is there anything unusual about the method you employed? Did you use a midwife? Or videotape?
- Are you starting your baby off early on a career or hobby? Are you starting swimming lessons immediately, as some local parents did? Have you decorated your baby's room to suggest career possibilities? Think. All these are self-promotional possibilities for you, too.
- When your child is older, help him write to someone of consequence, a world leader, literary figure or another public figure. The best are those who are known to be difficult, enigmatic, reclusive. The letter should bear all the hallmarks of a child. It should be hand written on a yellow lined paper. It should be neat, but a misspelling or two doesn't hurt. Under no circumstances should it look as if mommy or daddy did it. Preferably it should ask a question which will be of general interest. Try having a five year old ask Commissar Andropov whether he wants a nuclear war with America. That sort of thing. This is the "Out-Of-The-Mouths-Of-Babes" category, and these letters get answers. And coverage.

  I know.

  I myself corresponded during my early adolescence with many of the great and renowned of the western world. In the process I amassed not only a valuable autograph and memorabilia collection but also an unending source for self-promotion. The cost, as should be noted, was minimal. The possibilities for publicity astronomical.

- As the children grow up, do not neglect their promotional possibilities. Commencements, degrees, citations, proclamations, publications, &c of the children should all be published in your local hometown newspaper with your own name. Children, gratefully, need not be physically present to be a fertile source of promotional possibilities, a fact which cannot fail to please most readers.

Your Pets

Americans are embarrassing about their pets. I may deplore the fact that we live amidst people who are foolish enough to evaluate others on the basis of good deeds to dogs, but I have no intention of not making good use of this curious situation. One woman I met on a radio talk show in New York now has a national reputation (and an apparently thriving business) because she makes dresses for parrots. Another man who was on the same show does historically accurate costumes for bull frogs. This is not the way I prefer to go down in history, but to each his own.

Pets produce publicity.

Here are some possibilities:

- Any unusual pet can provide a media hook. At my grammar school one of my pint-sized classmates had parents who had the good sense to get her a tiger cub. I wouldn't recommend it myself, but it did generate a lot of press.
- Any human-like activity favored by the pet generates media. Does your pet smoke? (Shame on you!) Drink? Chase women? If so, there is a prime candidate for the media. (Try **Playgirl** for openers.)
- Has your pet mastered any unusual tricks? In actual fact, they need not be so unusual; they should just not be commonplace in your neighborhood. That's a little easier to contemplate.
- How about any heroic actions carried out by the pet? If I were you, I'd forego the parlor tricks and work on training your dog (or your cat, for that matter) to pull waterlogged but still breathing humans from ponds. There is no surer way to front page coverage.

You get the idea.

Your Hobbies

Hobbies, as you will already have discerned from my stories about collecting campaign buttons and the epistles of statesmen, are a fruitful source of self-promotional possibilities. Indeed, a hobby really ought to be selected because of its self-promotional possibilities.

Whatever hobby you select must be consonant with your overall image, so that the publicity you generate doesn't jar the sensibilities of your potential clients and followers. I myself collect portraits in oil, which I shall tell you about in a bit. This seems to me a suitable avocation for a mandarin of refined taste, not to mention a dandy source for self-promotion.

Hobbies to be worthwhile as promotional possibilities must either be unusual or, if common, must be specialized. Stamp collecting per se is not terribly newsworthy, but stamps with war themes or what have you could be leveraged into media.

Once you have a hobby think of the different promotional possibilities it generates:

- Is your hobby unique?
- Is it the earliest of its kind?
- The most extensive of its kind?
- The only one of its kind in your area?
- Has it placed you in touch with unusual, notable people?
- What are the financial dimensions? Is it a good, unusual investment?
- Is there a news angle to your hobby?
- Is there a feature angle based on an assembly of others who have the same hobby?
- Can you get an award, recognition from a professonal association connected to your hobby?
- Who are the famous people who share your hobby?

These are the sorts of questions you need to ask yourself.

As I mentioned before, selected my hobby of collecting campaign buttons because I knew that at the time of an election I could get publicity as a sidebar piggybacking on the main event. Right now if I were inclined to start another hobby, I think I'd either do stamps with a theme ("Stop War") or the autographs of self-made millionaires. A little creativity here is most important.

Again, the key is to select a hobby with promotional possibilities, bring it to the attention of media sources, suggest the story angle, and be persistent until something desirable happens.

Your Home

I shall never forget a visit I made one day to a friend who was refurbishing an old turn-of-the-century townhouse in Boston's South End. Her bathroom had just been featured in the Home Section of the **Boston Globe** (along with a nice plug for her home-based business), and I wanted to see it for myself.

It was an old, rather dilapidated water closet transformed into something frilly, feminine — and botanical. Its chief feature was a bower of orchids in full bloom. I believe the article said something about a touch of colorful Polynesia in the Back Bay.

In point of fact, there was nothing very distinctive about this very common little room except for the orchids. They, however, were an inspiration, not least because they produced just the right hook for the story. Very clever, indeed.

We are consumed in this country with an unquenchable thirst for knowledge about the way other people live. All of us, of course, are aware of this national obsession as it pertains to established celebrities. However and wherever they live, we want to know. Most of us, however, are less aware that our own homes, be they ever so humble, can provide a rich source of promotional possibilities.

The Yard

Are your hedges neat, your marigolds magnificent, your yew trees cut into cunning patterns? Tell the local newspaper and have them send a photographer. Consider an article about how such miracles came to pass.

The Kitchen

As a culture, we are firmly fixated on the kitchen. Are your shelves unusual? Have you found a way of dealing with rodents and insects? Have you locked your refrigerator while dieting? Have you found a way to get your children to help with the dishes? Don't keep these things to yourself. Publish your secrets — and piggyback on them with mentions of your product, service, or company.

The Living Room

Do you live on the top floor of an apartment building? Have you found a convenient way of washing your outside windows? How did your yucca grow to such a height indoors? Have you a way of removing little evidences of your pets from the silk wallpaper? How have you managed to keep your chandelier so brilliant without taking it down? What a marvelous stereo unit. Did you build it yourself? Tell us the story of your living room — and promote yourself.

The Bath

Remember the orchids.

The Bedroom

Consider just how much you really do want to tell. Then contact the **National Enquirer.**

Your Food

Given the national obsession with food (which is arguably greater than that with sex), don't overlook its promotional possibilities. All major newspapers have food sections; many national magazines are totally devoted to food. You have merely to think of a catchy angle:

- unusual recipes
- seasonal food
- distinctive food designs and preparation

I confess that on the whole food bores me. Nonetheless, even I cannot remain entirely aloof. This year my birthday cake got a nice mention in a local newspaper (See samples, page 356), and I have a book contract to produce with a friend **The Great American Athlete's Cookbook.** This interesting idea links food and athletics, two of the things most Americans cannot get off their minds. The book ought to do quite well.

Your Clothes

I learned the promotional possibilities of clothes at an early age. I think I was 15 when I wore to some dance or other a candy striped jacket from the roaring twenties and a straw boater. This distinctive outfit was an instant sensation and promptly landed me in the school newspaper. It was a lesson I've never forgotten.

Women, of course, have traditionally been light years ahead of men in recognizing the promotional possibilities of clothes, but all too often they are interested simply in promoting the interest of one individual rather than bringing themselves to the widest possible public. In this regard both men and women have something to learn.

Here are few ideas:

- clothes in the workplace. Generate a story about fashion in the office in which you and your wardrobe are featured.
- chic maternity clothes. What is the well-dressed mother-to-be wearing these days?
- indestructible children's clothes. How to construct them.
- the clothes favored by entrepreneurs
- an advisory panel of college-aged men for a local department store. Why hasn't this happened before?
- what the well-dressed techie wears in the Silicon Valley.
- narrow ties or wide? Another angle on this pivotal debate.
- collegiate fashion. What the freshmen are wearing this fall.
- how much does the average man spend on clothes each year? Although as an unabashed self-promoter you are hardly average, this story starts with you.

Your Travels

Never, never, never go anywhere unless you have arranged with the local newspaper, at the very least, to file a story. More enterprising self-promoters will contact the nearest metropolitan newspaper or even a national magazine.

As you move into celebrity status it is expected that you will meet more and more persons of consequence on your travels. The further you are from Peoria the more likely this is to be true.

The unabashed self-promoter makes it a point when traveling abroad, for instance, to write in advance to:

- the American ambassador
- the cabinet minister who is closest to his professional field
- officers of appropriate clubs and associations
- religious leaders
- newspaper editors

Take note of this last. Just because you are no longer at home doesn't mean you don't want copy. Think of a story angle about you which is likely to interest the local media. Next time I go abroad I plan to use my authorship of this book as leverage. Just think how grateful the editor of the local newspaper in Majorca will be to interview an American authority on this important subject.

Note: Once you have arranged with editors for your stories to be reviewed, (you will rarely secure an out-an-out promise that they'll be published), it will be infinitely easier to get access to foreign notables. Also, don't forget that while these interviews raise promotional possibilities, they also allow you to deduct a percentage of your travel expenses as a business cost. Could anything be nicer?

More Suggestions

I am firmly convinced, as you see, that any human experience has promotional possibilities if handled properly. Take, for instance, the rather inconsequential fact that I do not own a television. Is there an angle here?.

Of course.

As you see from the sample on page 349, by grouping me with other non-watchers, an author develops a nice piece for the **Boston Globe.**

Another seemingly unlikely situation is when you move to a new town, as so many Americans do every year. Are you necessarily fated to arrive as an obscurity? By no means.

People always like to be wanted, and when we arrive in a new town, we are announcing in a very substantial way that we find desirable where they are and their characteristic lifestyle. Don't keep this happy intelligence to yourself. Enter a new town by distributing a standard media release with the theme, "Why I Chose Toledo." Develop your good reasons and be lavish with the praise. Local boosterism is very, very popular. Take advantage of it, and be the most famous newcomer in your new community.

The Birthday Party

Every yeár something like 225 million Americans celebrate birthdays. Very few of them outside the White House are considered newsworthy. This year I decided mine would be one of them.

Turning this very ordinary event into something worthy of media attention deserves thoughtful consideration. Having pondered the question, I decided to create an occasion of multiple attractions, multiple media hooks.

- First, I arranged matters so that the second edition of my book **Development Today** was ready for a February publication date.
- Second, I commissioned in the fall a portrait of myself so as to be completed by the time of the party.
- Third, I chose the theme "36, The Gateway To Middle Age" as one likely to produce comment from anyone even slightly older.

When matters had progressed so far, my friend Rodney Lister informed me that he had conposed and dedicated a piece of music for me. It occurred to us both that it would be quite delightful to arrange for its premier at the party.

What had originally begun as a mere birthday, now had been transformed to include a literary, artistic, and musical dimension. Suitably impressive invitations of unusual size and design were drawn up and sent to all guests. With this invitation went three descriptive enclosures resembling media releases: one for **Development Today,** another for the portrait by Pezzatti, a third about the music by Lister and its performers. (See samples, pages 355-356).

Given the distinctive nature of this packet, it wasn't long before the first mention of this party appeared in the press. (See samples, page 356). Other advance coverage followed.

At The Party Itself

As is always the case with parties I give, this one, despite foul weather, had many media people in attendance. It is my constant objective to transform these people into my friends, and I lose no opportunity of doing so. However, the star guest was the Mayor of Cambridge who came to declare "Dr. Jeffrey Lant Day" and to present a citation for "distinguished services to nonprofit organizations" and to deliver a very complimentary speech — all covered by the media.

After The Event

After the event I drew up a Media Activity Chart listing all the media personnel who had been invited to the party whether they attended or not. My assistant called each of them at regular intervals until suitable promotional opportunities had been created: articles by me, articles about me, television and radio interviews of various kinds. At least 15 such promotional possibilities were created, a complete wave.

It goes without saying that in creating your event, you should arrange it so that it offers the greatest interest to the greatest number; you should invite as many media personnel as possible, and you should relentlessly follow-up this invitation after the event until you have fashioned a series of suitable promotional opportunities.

The Promotional Possibilities Of Art

When the invitations to my birthday party were sent and people became aware that my portrait was to be unveiled, there was a good deal of curiosity. Why not? Such an event is, these days, unusual. Why, I was asked, had I spent a considerable sum of money on an item of no evident utility? Here's the answer, and it is one every unabashed self-promoter should ponder.

Primarily, of course, we are interested in promotion for what it can bring us today — celebrity standing, enhanced professional recognition, money. But there are other reasons which, as we get older, assume perhaps a greater importance.

To the unabashed self-promoter it matters not what happened as what was perceived to happen; not so much what he was as what people thought he was. The issue of perception is at the heart of what it means to be a successful self-promoter. We must take it into account at all times.

I commissioned a considerable portrait at age 36 in part because it was the realization of a childhood desire, in part because notwithstanding the advances in portrait photography, a photograph will never compete for depth of emotion and insight with oil and canvas. I also did it to indicate both to my contemporaries and to the run of posterity yet to come who I thought myself to be today, to fix an image against the immensity of time.

As I age, this image will remain: forever youthful, with a look of deep intelligence, perserverence, power and authority, a contemporary mandarin before the onslaught of old age.

I saw the value of such artistry once in London when I called upon Sir Harry Batterby. Then aged 100, the doughty but decrepit gentleman stood before a full length portrait as he had appeared as a young Member of Parliament in the 'twenties. I was struck not by what he had become as most people might have been but by the magnificence and vitality of what he then appeared to be, and I inwardly complimented the foresight which had occasioned such a work.

Long after I am gone, my message will remain to generate conversation, interest, even publicity. It was for such a reason that imperious kings installed painters at their courts. It is for us, unabashed self-promoters, to revive this tradition and to signal to our contemporaries that though we may be forced to leave this life the promotional apparatus we have launched will keep working, working down the long corridor of the unknown future.

CONCLUSION

THE UNABASHED SELF-PROMOTER AND THE JACKIE ONASSIS SYNDROME: YOUR EVERY LITTLE MOVE IS NEWS

I have lost it now, but the photograph was a classic. It showed a bedraggled Mrs. Aristotle Onassis in a babushka (of all things) sneezing. That's all.

Now millions of Americans have colds each year, but only Jackie O gets her sneezes covered by the wire services. This is the condition to which all unabashed self-promoters aspire, where our every little move is news.

With this book in hand, you, too, can succeed in promoting your message, product, or service — in becoming the elusive household name. But you must be willing to adopt the proper competitive attitude, prepare thoroughly, and implement persistently. This is the way to success.

I wish I could say that everyone who reads this book will be successful, but I sincerely doubt it. Some of you will prove unable to adopt the proper attitude; others will be technically incompetent. Still others will give up when confronted with the profound apathy and immobility of media personnel.

I want it very clearly understood, however, that your failure to succeed is your own problem. I guarantee the methods which appear in this book. I don't guarantee your ability to implement them.

For the rest of you, a luminous future beckons. In this future there is wealth, the thrill of having your ideas mouthed by others, the satisfaction of disseminating your product and service to the farthest possible extent, the joy of becoming a personage, the real comfort of self-realization. These are trophies which elude most people, but they come to us, unabashed self-promoters all, as a matter of course. They are the necessary and inevitable fruits of the system laid out in the pages of this book.

Take them, they belong to you. As a result of your work, your intelligence, your daring to risk, you deserve them.

As you ascend to your new eminence, however, hold onto one individual (that's quite enough) who remembers you from your inglorious days of insipid obscurity. With such a one on hand, you can measure your success not just by a swelling bank balance and the horde of new-found followers, but by that most delicious of emanations — envy. This gives a certain tangy zest to the mad elixir which you, the bounding, surgent, thoroughly unabashed self-promoter, have mixed and drunk. And enjoyed to the last oh-so-satisfying drop.

Appendix I: Feature Syndicates

Note: In writing this book the author contacted the country's leading feature syndicates. Few of those contacted responded which indicates the difficulty of breaking into this market.

1) Arkin Magazine Syndicate, Inc., 761 NE 180 Street, No. Miami Beach, FL., 33162
tel. (305) 651-3668

Contact: Joseph Arkin, Editorial Director

Arkin reports that it is best to query first with a topic unless it is an "ultra new idea." Last year they covered almost 200 different topics. They don't want to see "dog-eared scripts which author could not sell somewhere else. We are not a dumping ground for rejects." The format of the article should begin with a title at the top and a byline 3"-4" from top of page, space your article one and one-half. There should be no run over of sentences from page to page. Include a word count on a separate memo. Write on white pages on one side of the page only. The preferred length of features is 700-2200 words. It will accept single features but is not interested in columns. It does not buy all rights; it leaves book or reprint rights to the author. It is currently interested in "how to" articles for the small business owner applicable to several businesses not just one industry. It is not interested in personality pieces. Mr. Arkin offers as a tip reading trade and professional magazines carrying business (not technical) articles. A self-addressed stamped envelope (SASE) must accompany articles or they are thrown away. "If writing where expertise is required, submit bio to show why author has qualifications for subject."

2) Curious Facts Features, 6B Ridge Court, Lebanon, OH 45036
tel. (513) 932-1820

Contact: Dr. Donald Whiteacre, Editor

Curious Facts Features deals with 60 different outlets. It prefers articles to be submitted in typewritten format in 25 to 400 words. It accepts single pieces and buys all rights. It is looking for "all types of oddities, including oddities about laws, animals, people, &c." It wants "fresh items or prepared in a new way so historical items come out in a seemingly new way. No copyrighted material. All items must include 'sources'." "We will judge each item for its special 'glow'! That 'something' that makes it outstanding."

3) Interpress of London and New York, 400 Madison Avenue, New York, New York 10017
tel. (212) 832-2839

Contact: Jeffrey Blyth, Editor-in-Chief

Interpress has numerous outlets in both Europe and the U.S. Send manuscripts or tearsheets of between 1000-2000 words. It accepts single pieces and usually buys European rights. It is currently looking for "interesting offbeat stories and pictures that make people stop and read, a story that is likely to make readers say 'Gee Whizz!' "

4) Knowledge News & Features, Kenilworth, IL 60043
tel. contact by mail

Contact: Bureau Chief/Executive Editor

Prefers articles of 500 words plus, typed, double spaced, enclose SASE. It accepts single pieces and buys all rights. It is currently interested in business, motivational, creativity, communication, sales and public relations pieces. "Write clear, concise, cogent articles, very specific in nature."

5) The Register and Tribune Syndicate, Inc., 715 Locust Street, Des Moines, IA 50304
tel. (515) 284-8244

Contact: Dennis R. Allen, President

Deals with 1,700 daily dewspapers, weekly newspapers, and television stations nationwide. Wants "on-going column topics" of 300-750 words. It does not accept single pieces and does buy all rights. It wants "contemporary subject matter focusing on the current needs of the population." Mr. Allen advises that you "pick a topic area you know well, write in a chatty-folksy manner appealing to John Q. Public, and present the idea to the syndicate in a professional manner." Allow 3-4 weeks for a response from syndicate. If materials are to be returned provide SASE.

6) S.C.I. Singer Communications, Inc., 3164 Tyler Avenue, Anaheim, CA 92801
tel. (714) 527-5650

Contact: Marian B. Singer, Editor

Singer Communications deals with about 300 U.S. and overseas outlets. It wants articles typed, double spaced or ("even better") tearsheets of published features and books. It has no special requirement for length and will accept single pieces only if previously published. It does not buy all rights "but prefers licensing rights for worldwide syndication." It is particularly interested in massmarket features and is "wide open — women topics to computers, home repair to popular psychology." Tips for breaking in? "Interview celebrities, send published features and books." "All literary material should be of worldwide interest and not of a local nature." Add return postage.

7) United Feature Syndicate & Newspaper Enterprise Association, 200 Park Avenue, New York, New York 10166
tel. (212) 557-2333

Contact: Diana L. Drake, Managing Editor

"We sell to every daily and most weekly papers in the U.S. We don't buy single articles in most cases. We do buy columns and comic strips." United Feature Syndicate advises that columns vary in length from 400 to 1500 words. The average is 750 words. Single pieces are "rarely" accepted and the man to query on single pieces is Sidney Goldberg, Executive Editor. United Feature buys all rights. Tips? "Be professional. Know who we are and what syndicates are. Don't call us. Send a concise and professional query letter. We need six weeks to respond in most cases. You may call after six weeks if you haven't heard."

APPENDIX II: LECTURE AGENCIES

Note: In writing this book the author contacted the country's leading lecture agencies to request information about their services and the kinds of individuals they wanted to hear from. What follows are their exact words. If you have a lecture agency and are not included in this list, please send comparable information to the author for inclusion in the next edition.

1) American Program Bureau, 850 Boylston Street, Chestnut Hill, MA 02167
tel. (617) 731-0500

Contact: Andrea O'Brien, Speaker Development Coordinator

American Program Bureau is interested in hearing from new people by mail. "We are interested in nationally known speakers and topics of national interest." They deal in the College, Corporate and Civic/Trade/Professional markets and do not require an exclusive relationship. They usually market their speakers through a general mailing but will occasionally market one speaker individually.

In contacting American Program Bureau send: photographs, articles about yourself, articles by yourself, review copies of books, a résumé, biography, list of media exposure, and reference letters from prior sponsors.

"We are a celebrity agency representing nationally know speakers. Our clients expect us to provide them with well-known personalities."

2) The Associated Clubs, Inc., One Townsite Plaza, Suite 315, Topeka, KS 66603
tel. (913) 232-0892

Contact: Ben B. Franklin, Vice President

The Associated Clubs, Inc. are interested in hearing from new people "if experienced and qualified." They want programs in humor, entertainment, and world affairs. They are not interested in illustrated talks. "Over 95% of our business is with dinner clubs. We represent the clubs, not the speakers."

The Associated Clubs do not require an exclusive relationship. The intitial approach should be by letter with an audio cassette of a live speech. They do not want video cassettes. Also send: brochure, testimonial letters not only from clients but also from other professional speakers. "Pictures are not important unless we decide to use speaker. Speaking ability is paramount."

The Associated Clubs mail out lists of speakers, not just one. "Please realize that we don't represent the speakers; we represent the clubs which buy the speakers. We receive 1,000 applications each year and only about 2% can be used."

3) Royce Carlton, Inc, 866 United Nations Plaza, New York, New York 10017
tel. (212) 355-3210

Contact: Carlton S. Sedgeley, President

Royce Carlton, Inc. is interested in hearing from new people by mail. They want "high visibility" people and require an exclusive relationship. They deal in all major markets including college, corporate and civic/trade/professional. They do both group and individual mailings about speakers. In writing to Royce Carlton send all pertinent material about yourself including photographs, articles by and about you, and review copies of books.

4) The Contemporary Forum 2528A W. Jerome St., Chicago, IL 60645
tel. (312) 764-4383

Contact: Mrs. Beryl Zitch, Director/Artist's Representative

The Contemporary Forum wishes to hear from new people by letter. It is currently interested in topics dealing with politics, nuclear arms or "general topics." It does not require an exclusive relationship and markets principally to schools and associations. It also markets to the corporate sector. It mails information annually about its speakers and occasionally will do an individual mailing on one specific speaker.

In writing to The Contemporary Forum send brochures and background information including: photographs, articles about the speaker and by the speaker and a biography. If you have tapes, send them.

5) Dr. Gallatin Presents . . ., 80 E. 11 St., Suite 539, New York, New York 10003.
tel. (212) 228-2960

Contact: Dr. Gallatin, President

Dr. Gallatin Presents . . . is interested in hearing from new people by telephone or by letter. Right now, they are interested in topics in business, sales and motivation. They do not require an exclusive relationship and deal principally in the corporate and civic/trade/professional markets.

When writing send: articles by and about yourself, review copies of books, a list of the places where you've made presentations and letters of recommendation.

6) Hampton Communication Strategies, 4200 Wisconsin Avenue, N.W., Suite 106, Washington, D.C. 20016
tel. (202) 363-4941

Contact: Lou Hampton, President

Hampton Communication Strategies is interested in hearing from new people "only if they are already established speakers and are either humorists or specialists in communication." Humor and "how to" skills suitable for business and professional people are prime interests just now.

Contact Hampton Communications by mail. They do not require an exclusive relationship and deal principally with the corporate and civic/trade/professional markets "especially conventions coming to Washington, D.C." They mail both general lists of speakers and information about individual speakers. In writing, send photographs, articles by and about the speaker, a list of recent speeches and the name and telephone number of the individual at the organization sponsoring you.

7) Keynote Speakers, Incorporated, 460 Washington Avenue, Palo Alto, CA 94301
tel. (415) 325-8711

Contact: Barbara B. Foster, President.

Keynote Speakers, Incorporated is interested in hearing from new people "initially by telephone, then with background material." They are interested in "anything new that is also credible. Our interests are primarily academic rather than motivational or in the human potential movement field."

Keynote Speakers usually requires an exclusive relationship. It deals with the corporate and civic/trade/-professional markets. It does individual mailings about speakers but also does regular mailings to client prospects about all its speakers.

In writing send articles about the speaker, a résumé or some type of biographical data, a list of references and a tape of a recent talk. "Be as realistic as possible about your chances for success; determine just who your audience is and know if that audience is big enough to afford you. The agent makes the contact and introduces you to the potential audience, but after that it is really the speaker and the topic that make or break the deal."

Mrs. Foster also writes, "Our purpose is to fill a perceived need for informative speakers who are recognized experts in their fields, but whose names are not necessarily household words. We are meeting the growing demand for hard-core knowledge about the complicated and exciting world we live in."

8) Ida McGinniss' Speakers Bureau, Inc., The McGinniss Building, Suite 4, 6198 Butler Pike, Blue Bell, PA 19422
tel.: (215) 732-8158

Contact: Ida McGinniss, President

Ida McGinniss' Speakers Bureau is interested in hearing from new people. Make your initial contact by mail or telephone. Currently they are interested in motivation, business, economics and sports. They will not accept an exclusive relationship. They deal in all major markets and will do both individual mailings about a particular speaker and group mailings, too. In contacting them "send anything to convince our staff that the potential applicant is professional and qualified."

9) New Line Presentations, Inc., 575 Eighth Avenue, 16th floor, New York, New York 10018
tel. (212) 239-8880

Contact: Ms. Tish Martin, Associate Director

New Line Presentations, Inc. is interested in hearing from new people. It is currently most interested in politics and social topics. It requires an exclusive relationship and deals principally in the college market. It will do both individual and group mailings about speakers. In contacting them, send photographs, articles by and about yourself, reveiw copies of books and recommendation letters from other speaking engagements. "When information from a possible new client is received, the information is viewed and discussed by everyone in the agency, especially the sales agents. It is a 'democratic' decision to take on a new client (or not!)"

10) Quest Associates, Summit Park West, Danbury, CT 06810
tel. (203) 743-6292

Contact: Paul Bartz, President

Quest Associates is interested in hearing from new people first by letter. It is now interested in current events, entertainment and "how to" career opportunities. It does not require an exclusive relationship and deals in the college and civic/trade/professional markets. It will do both group and individual mailings about speakers. In writing send photographs, articles by and about yourself, an outline of your program, and an audio cassette. ("Video is required for later consideration.")

"Don't expect the moon, as they say. The market is tight and very competitive, and it often takes at least one year to establish the reputation of a speaker, especially if he is unknown outside his field."

11) Jackie Schorsch, 3488 Cornflower Trail, Northbrook, IL 60062
(312) 498-2058

Not in the market for new speakers. "If I were in the market for new speakers, I would want them to have some engagement in the near future so I could see, first hand, their performances. I have been 'burned' a few times by people I have recommended for certain performances without first seeing them myself; these have usually been recommendations from others 'in the know'."

12) Showcase Associates, Inc., Suite A-200, The Benson East, Jenkintown, PA 19046
(215) 884-6205

Contact: Claire Bonner, General Manager

Showcase Associates is interested in hearing from new people. Right now they are interested in motivation, space-oriented and entertainment topics. They do not require an exclusive relationship and deal in the college, corporate and civic/trade/professional markets. It does both individual mailings about speakers and group mailings. It wants to see reference letters in advance. "Please send us as complete information about yourself as possible. Contact us about three weeks after you send the material."

13) Universal Speakers, 235 Bear Hill Road, Waltham, MA 02154
tel. (617) 890-4211

Contact: David Rich, President

Universal Speakers wishes to hear from new speakers "if qualified." It is currently interested in topics in business, women's issues, and the media. It requires an exclusive relationship and promotes its speakers to the college, corporate and civic/trade/professional markets. It does both group and individual mailings. In writing, send photographs, articles by and about yourself, review copies of books, a résumé, an audio and video cassette, and letters of recommendation from past speaking engagements. "Have a clear sense of the level of interest of your program and a very real sense of whether people will pay to hear what you've got to say."

Note to readers: If you contact these agencies, please let the author know the results.

One final piece of helpful information. Consider joining the National Speakers Association, 5201 N. 7th St., Suite 200, Phoenix, AZ 85014. Tel. (602) 265-1001. The Association has 16 chapters across the nation and offers a wide variety of services to its members.

SAMPLE SECTION TABLE OF CONTENTS

SAMPLE MEDIA ADVISORY

Jeffrey Lant Associates, Inc.

MEDIA ADVISORY

For further information contact:

Jim Bacchi
(212) 533-7079

Dr Jeffrey Lant
(617) 547-6372

"Jeffrey Lant provides the ultimate advice on giving advice!"

Cleveland Press

CONSULTING EXPERT TO TELL NEW YORK HOW TO CREATE JOBS, HELP ECONOMY

Dr Jeffrey Lant, author of THE CONSULTANT'S KIT: ESTABLISHING AND OPERATING YOUR SUCCESSFUL CONSULTING BUSINESS, will be in New York on Thursday, September 23 to promote his new best-seller and to advise residents on how to cash in on one of America's growth fields -- consulting. On September 23 Lant will be available to the media for interviews. On Thursday, October 14 he will present his one-day intensive workshop "Establishing and Operating Your Successful Consulting Business" at the Doral Park Avenue Hotel, 70 Park Avenue, Manhattan.

Lant, who kicks off a seventeen state fall tour in September, is promoting his methods for creating lucrative part-time and full-time consulting jobs despite the flagging national economy. Lant will in part discuss:

- the reasons for the consulting boom
- the kinds of people who should consider the consulting option
- establishing yourself as an expert
- exploiting the media to promote yourself and your business
- getting a first assignment
- building a Supergroup of Independent Contractors
- expanding into related fields: creating a mini-conglomerate
- negotiating for success
- how and where to set up your office
- the legal form for your consulting business

(617) 547-6372
50 FOLLEN STREET, SUITE 507 • CAMBRIDGE, MASSACHUSETTS 02138

LANT IN NEW YORK, Page 2

Since January when THE CONSULTANT'S KIT was first published, Lant has been interviewed on average by at least one media outlet every day. He has been interviewed by NBC Radio, CBS Radio, the National Black Radio Network, Associated Press and by major media in: Boston, Pittsburgh, Detroit, Connecticut, Los Angeles, Cleveland, and other cities. Each time the listener and reader response has been extraordinary. In part this is because of Lant himself. "Lant's own style is fascinating," writes the Hartford Advocate; in part, it's because of the importance of the subject which, Lant feels, is indicative of a permanent change in the way Americans are working and living.

The 35-year-old Harvard-educated Lant is president of a Cambridge, Massachusetts consulting firm for nonprofit organizations. He is also the Editor of a newly-published (June) volume entitled OUR HARVARD: REFLECTIONS ON COLLEGE LIFE BY TWENTY-TWO DISTINGUISHED GRADUATES (Taplinger). It includes the original contributions of Buckminster Fuller, Erich Segal, Arthur Schlesinger, Robert Coles and other eminent Harvard men. Lant is also the author of DEVELOPMENT TODAY: A GUIDE FOR NONPROFIT ORGANIZATIONS and INSUBSTANTIAL PAGEANT: CEREMONY AND CONFUSION AT QUEEN VICTORIA'S COURT. His in-progress book is entitled THE UNABASHED SELF-PROMOTER'S GUIDE and will be published in Winter, 1983.

Lant is included in Who's Who in the East, Men & Women of Distinction, The Dictional of International Biography, The Book of Honor, and The International Who's Who of Intellectuals. In June Massachusetts Governor Edward King gave him an Official Citation for his work in promoting the interests of independent business people.

To arrange a convenient interview time, please call Jim Bacchi at (212) 533-7079 or Jeffrey Lant directly at (617) 547-6372. Photographs and review copies of THE CONSULTANT'S KIT are available upon request.

Available interview dates in New York for Dr Jeffrey Lant:

- afternoon and evening, Wednesday, September 22
- all day, Thursday, September 23
- evening, Wednesday, October 13
- evening, Thursday, October 14

(617) 547-6372
50 FOLLEN STREET, SUITE 507 • CAMBRIDGE, MASSACHUSETTS 02138

SAMPLE MEDIA RELEASE

For further information contact:
Roberta Leis, Program Director
MA Assoc of Community Health Agencies
617-473-5286, or

Dr. Jeffrey Lant (617) 547-6372

For Immediate Release
May 14,1983

National Fund Raising Expert To Address MACHA Conference

Waltham — Dr. Jeffrey Lant, president of a Cambridge consulting firm providing technical assistance to nonprofit organizations, will address the eighth annual meeting of the Massachusetts Association of Community Health Agencies on Wednesday, May 18 at 2:30 p.m. at the Sheraton Inn Conference Center in Boxborough, MA. Dr. Lant, author of DEVELOPMENT TODAY: A GUIDE FOR NONPROFIT ORGANIZATIONS, will be speaking on "Effective Fund Raising Techniques: The Art and Science of Development Today."

In an interview with (name of newspaper), Harvard-educated Lant said, "I have developed a complete step-by-step approach to raising funds economically and efficiently. I am glad to have been invited by the Massachussetts coalition to speak, so that I can share with its members my cost-effective techniques."

The 36-year-old Lant mentioned that he would pay particular attention to how an agency can organize an efficient fund raising planning process, how to create persuasive, compelling documents, the role of a board of Directors in both pleding and raising funds, how to assemble and guide dedicated community volunteers, and the role of professional fund raising consultants. "I think professional fund raising consultants are much misunderstood," Lant said with a smile. Lant is also the author of the national best-seller **THE CONSULTANT'S KIT: ESTABLISHING AND OPERATING YOUR SUCCESSFUL CONSULTING BUSINESS,** now in a sixth printing.

Lant, who in the last year has addressed organizations in 38 states, went on to say, "I want to share with the participating community health agencies my tested methods and show them how they can help themselves."

Lant, who was asked by (name of newspaper) to comment on the publication of President Ronald Reagan's tax returns and the president's charitable giving, said, "I wish the president would stop talking about the need for more voluntary contributions by private citizens if he intends to set the nation such a bad example." Lant said the president has "consistently gone on record as favoring tithing," (that is, donating 10% of an individual's income to charity), "but that his own level of charitable giving falls far short of this goal."

"It would be nice," Lant continued, "if I could point to the president as an example of the kind of active, committed citizen supporting nonprofit organizations as private citizens and on their Boards of Directors. But I can't." Lant said, however, he would give some suggestions to the groups in attendance "about how to find and cultivate such people."

Lant, who is also the Editor of a series of nonprofit technical assistance books published by JLA Publicatons, a division of his firm, has recently inaugurated a new Capital Campaign Fund Raising Process. "I am convinced that the only way most nonprofit organizations will get through the next decade is to build endowment funds and their overall capital position. I intend to deal with this subject as time allows."

Roberta Leis, MACHA Program Director for the Conference, said, "I'm delighted that Dr. Lant has consented to join us to set out the tested techniques of fund raising which he has written about. I am sure our members will profit from the experience."

— End —

SAMPLE BIOGRAPHICAL FEATURE STORY

Contact: Dr. Jeffrey Lant, president
Jeffrey Lant Associates, Inc.
50 Follen Street, Suite 507
Cambridge, MA 02138
All telephone calls to: (617) 547-6372

DR. JEFFREY LANT

As a corporate president, Dr. Jeffrey Lant is distinctly different. High above the historic Cambridge, Massachusetts Common, where George Washington took command of the Continental Army, steps away from Harvard University where he did his graduate work, Lant directs his "Mobile Mini-Conglomerate," Jeffrey Lant Associates, Inc. It has management consulting, publishing, educational training, advertising and public relations divisions — all bearing the distinctive Lant brand.

"I don't own a suit, a watch, or a clock, a car, or a word processor," Lant says expansively. Clad in khaki trousers, penny loafers, an Oxford button-down shirt, the boyish-looking Lant looks more like a candidate for a fraternity party than a seat on the Board of Directors. But looks are often deceiving.

"I'm listed in **Dun & Bradstreet, Who's Who In Business And Finance, The International Who's Who Of Intellectuals** and about a dozen other biographical directories," the 36-year-old Lant says. "I think people are fascinated by the fact that someone who deliberately thumbs his nose at the established patterns of business advancement can be such a success. I suspect it raises in them some disquieting — and creative — thoughts."

In 1982 Lant's unusual operating procedures not only gained him a healthy corporate profit but also a place in a book entitled **Maverick: Succeeding As A Free-Lance Entrepreneur** by Canadian author Geoffrey Bailey. Lant rises to express mock horror about this book. "What's the point of being a maverick," the Harvard-educated Lant proclaims, "if everybody else lines up to follow? Pretty soon I'll be in three-piece suits because every other CEO will be wearing designer tee-shirts to the office."

Lant was not trained as a businessman he's quick to point out. His Ph.D. is in Victorian English history. "I think this accounts for my success," he smiles. "A Harvard MBA would have ruined me, since I would have known the 'right' and 'wrong' ways to do things. As it was I just didn't know anything, so I was forced to do the things that worked."

Lant first established his management consulting firm, Jeffrey Lant Associates, Inc. in 1979 to assist nonprofit organizations. He added JLA Publications, which has published his own best-seller **The Consultant's Kit** (now in a sixth printng) in 1981, created The Mobile University a year later, and his New York advertising firm Promotion Results in 1983.

Is he over-extended?

Lant, with a grin that is nothing short of infectious, just laughs. "I'm the only person I know who can take afternoons off without feeling guilty. I guess it's just all in how you arrange matters."

Aside from his primary business ventures, Lant writes articles on a number of subjects in history, education and politics. He also found time in 1982 to edit **Our Harvard: Reflections On College Life By Twenty-Two Distinguished Graduates.** "It was fun working with Buckminster Fuller, Arthur Schlesinger, Erich Segal and my other contributors," he admits.

Jeffrey Lant is single and lives in Cambridge, Massachusetts inside what he calls his "International Headquarters." "I couldn't bear more than a 10-second commute each morning," he says.

— End —

Essentials Of The Fact Sheet, Chronology, Position Paper, Prepared Statement, And Backgrounder

These documents appear on the next pages. The following essentials apply to all:

- Type on your official letterhead.
- Double space on one side of the paper.
- All should be marked "For Immediate Release" with the date. If you wish the media to hold for future publication mark them "For release on (date)."
- You must include on at least the first page the name and telephone number of an individual handling follow-up telephone calls.
- On subsequent pages of a multi-page release, it is advisable to begin each page with a descriptive phrase about the matter being presented. You may also wish to include your telephone number on each page. If you put your releases on your office stationery this problem will be solved.

A note on the Chronology and Fact Sheet. If any of your facts is likely to be disputed, cite your source along with the information.

SAMPLE FACT SHEET

New England Electric's Coal-Fired Coal-Carrying Ship	For Immediate Release July 15, 1983
	For further information contact:
	Donald Greene, Director of Public Relations New England Electric System (617) 366-9011

ENERGY INDEPENDENCE

Why did New England Electric build this ship?	New England Electric commissioned the ENERGY INDEPENDENCE to help keep coal transportation costs down and to assure a reliable supply of fuel for its coal-fired generating units. New England Electric owns 51 percent of the ship.
When the ship is in operation what kind of transportation cost savings will there be?	When the ENERGY INDEPENDENCE is in operation, there will be an estimated savings of $2 million per year in coal transportation costs for New England Electric's one million customers.
Who will operate the ship?	Keystone Shipping Company of Philadelphia, a private shipping company which operates more than 800,000 tons of commercial shipping vessels, will operate the ship and owns 49 percent of it.
Where was the ship built?	The ship was built by General Dynamics Quincy Shipbuilding Division in Quincy, Massachusetts.
How long has it been since a coal-fired, coal-carrying ship was built in the United States?	ENERGY INDEPENDENCE is the first vessel of its type built in the United States in more than 50 years. The last U.S. coal-fired colliers were delivered in 1929 (Berwindglen and Berwindvale).
When will the ship begin operation?	The ship will begin operation in summer 1983.
What are the dimensions of the ship?	The ship is 665 feet long, 95 feet wide, and 56 feet deep. The ship has a draft of 32 feet.
How will the ship be propelled?	This coal-carrying ship will also be coal-fired. About 250 tons of coal will be burned each round trip. The ship is also equipped for oil-firing.
How fast will the ship travel?	The ship will travel at approximately 15 knots.
How many crew members will the ship have?	The ship has two alternating crews; each crew has 24 members.
How will the coal be discharged?	The ship is a completely self-discharging vessel. A 260-foot boom will swing from the center of the ship to discharge the coal as far as 215 feet from the side of the ship. The coal will then be discharged via a conveyor belt.
How long will it take to unload the vessel?	The conveyor belt will discharge 3,500 tons per hour, taking about 10 hours to unload the ship compared to about 40 hours with dockside unloading equipment for an equivalent cargo.
What is the cost of building the ship?	The cost of the ship is approximately $73 million.
How much will the ship carry per trip?	The ship will carry approximately 36,250 short tons per trip. One short ton = 2,000 lbs. One long ton = 2,240 lbs.
How much coal will the ship carry per year?	The ship will carry about 2.4 million tons of coal per year. This is about 2/3 of New England Electric's coal requirements.

SAMPLE CHRONOLOGY OF KEY EVENTS

Associated Press

WARSAW — Chronology of key events in the period of martial law in Poland:

1981

DEC. 13 — Following a threat by the independent labor union Solidarity to call a general strike, Gen. Wojciech Jaruzelski, the nation's leader, declares martial law, saying it is a necessary measure to save Poland from "the abyss." Thousands of Solidarity leaders, including Lech Walesa, are interned. Communications are restricted and intercity travel is banned. A nighttime curfew is imposed.

DEC. 16 — Violence flares at the Wujek coal mine in Katowice. Nine miners later are reported killed.

1982

FEB. 1 — Prices of food and fuel are increased 200 to 400 percent.

MARCH 20 — Authorities dissolve the pro-Solidarity Association of Polish Journalists.

APRIL 12 — "Radio Solidarity," the union's clandestine station, makes first successful eight-minute broadcast.

MAY 1-3 — Thousands of Solidarity supporters demonstrate in major Polish cities.

MAY 27 — Walesa is moved from internment near Warsaw to Arlamow, near the Soviet border.

JULY 21 — Jaruzelski orders the release of most internees, including all women, and says the authorities will ease travel and communication restrictions. Walesa remains in detention.

AUG. 31 — The second anniversary of the founding of Solidarity is marked by pro-union street demonstrations.

SEPT. 8 — Pope John Paul II calls on Poland's military government to respect the human rights of people interned and imprisoned under martial law.

OCT. 8 — Solidarity is formally banned by Parliament.

OCT. 11-13 — Rioting is reported in Gdansk, Nowa Huta and Wroclaw.

OCT. 29 — Tadeusz Grabski, a former Politburo member, warns of growing apathy among his comrades and says new "social conflict" will result if living conditions fail to improve rapidly.

NOV. 11 — Walesa is ordered released from detention.

DEC. 3 — A conference of Poland's 80 Roman Catholic bishops criticizes the outlawing of Solidarity.

DEC. 30 — Martial law is suspended but its major restrictions remain.

1983

JAN. 26 — Walesa is returned to the payroll of the Lenin shipyard in Gdansk.

FEB. 2 — Jozef Glemp is elevated to cardinal.

MARCH 9 — Jaruzelski and Glemp meet in Warsaw.

MARCH 14 — The government announces stiff price increases, with coffee, cigarettes and gasoline affected.

MARCH 28 — Walesa tells hundreds of cheering supporters "the time will come when we will win."

APRIL 9-11 — Walesa meets secretly with underground Solidarity leaders.

MAY 1-3 — Authorities use force to disperse powerful demonstrations in major Polish cities. One person is reported dead in Nowa Huta. A gang of men break into a Roman Catholic relief center inside a convent and beat six people.

MAY 19 — As many as 20,000 people attend the burial of Grzegorz Przemyk, whose mother claims was fatally beaten by police a week earlier.

MAY 27 — Walesa is questioned by police for two hours in an investigation of jailed Solidarity advisers.

JUNE 6 — After meeting with Glemp, Jaruzelski agrees to a church-sponsored agricultural fund for private farmers.

JUNE 16 — Pope John Paul II begins his second pilgrimage to his homeland. Tens of thousands march through Warsaw in giant protest against martial law.

JUNE 18 — The Pope hails Polish workers in a statement at Jasna Gora Monastery in Czestochowa.

JUNE 20 — In Katowice, the Pope calls for dialogue between workers and state.

JUNE 23 — Walesa meets the Pope in a private session. The papal visit ends.

JUNE 25 — A Vatican newspaper editor indicates in an article that the Pope asked Walesa to remove himself from Polish politics.

JUNE 26 — Walesa denies the Vatican newspaper speculation; the Vatican editor resigns, saying the article was based on his own speculation.

JULY 4 — Walesa begins an unauthorized vacation, risking dismissal from shipyard job.

JULY 5 — Jaruzelski is awarded the Order of Lenin by the Soviet Union, in move accompanied by endorsements from Poland's Communist allies. The award indicates Soviet approval of his handling of the Polish crisis since martial law.

JULY 9 — A policital front organized by the authorities appeals for the lifting martial law and amnesty for political prisoners.

JULY 13 — The Polish Politburo endorses the appeal.

JULY 14 — Parliament approves a new law on police, streamlining their power structure and strengthening their role.

JULY 18 — Walesa returns to his job in the Gdansk shipyards and gets official approval for the already taken vacation and for two more weeks.

JULY 18 — Poland's military council approves the lifting of martial law.

JULY 20 — Parliament approves a special emergency amendment for the constitution giving the government power to declare states of emergency.

JULY 21 — The military and Communist leadership announces that martial law will be lifted today.

SAMPLE POSITION PAPER

Hazardous Chemical
Right-To-Know Legislation

For Immediate Release August 3, 1983

For further information contact:
Jennie Paige, Director of Public Information
MA Hazardous Chemical Right-To-Know Committee
(617) 578-9034, or

Dr. David Kern, M.D., M.O.H.
(617) 587-0045

Testimony Provided to the Massachusetts Senate Committee on Commerce and Labor Senate Bill *98 Right-To-Know

My name is Dr. David Kern. I am a physician practicing in the areas of Internal Medicine and Occupational Health. Presently, I am on the full-time staff of Norfolk County Hospital where I see patients in the Occupational Health and Chronic Lung Disease Clinics. I would like to describe to you four recent clinical experiences I have had that illustrate the need for a RIGHT-TO-KNOW law in Massachusetts.

*CASE *1*

Two years ago, I was involved in a large study of Boston area plumbers who are regularly exposed to solvent-based glues used to connect plastic water pipes. Although this study was being carried out by the Harvard School of Public Health under the auspices of the National Institute for Occupational, Safety and Health, a federal agency, we were unable to obtain from the manufacturers a chemical analysis of the glues being used. Consequently, thousands of dollars of taxpayers' money was spent on laboratory testing in an effort to determine the chemical contents. Even then, probably all the chemicals were not identified. This waste of rare human and monitory resources would not have been necessary had there been a RIGHT-TO-KNOW law.

*CASE *2*

Last summer, I examined a 26-year-old warehouse manager who came to the clinic with a history of nine months of wheezing, cough, and shortness of breath. Previously, he had enjoyed excellent health and had been able to swim a mile daily. His problems had developed about a month after he began using a polyurethane foam generation process for packing materials at work. Initially, he noted improvement of his symptoms on the weekends when away from work. Because of this, he assumed that something in the foam process was responsible for his respiratory problems. He rearranged his work such that he was as far removed from the foam process as possible, but still noted persistent albeit diminished symptoms. This patient has a classical occupational disease, that of Toluene di-isocyanate induced asthma. A year later, this worker still suffers from respiratory symptoms and may well have asthma for the rest of his life. Had the foam liquid been appropriately labeled with a list of ingredients and had information on substance toxicity been readily accessible, this worker would have easily and early-on determined the cause of his respiratory symptoms at a time when his disease process may have been more reversible. Furthermore, he could have brought the available information to the first physicians he saw who unfortunately did not recognize the work relatedness of his symptoms.

*CASE *3*

Also, last summer, I saw a 21-year-old security guard who three weeks earlier had taken on a second job as a metal buffer at a plant employing 500 workers. After working there two weeks, he was asked to fill in as a degreaser operator that required him to dip metal parts into a tank filled with Trichloroethylene. Within a half hour of beginning work that first day, on a Friday, he noted nausea and a lack of alertness. He had difficulty eating lunch that day but felt better on leaving work. Early the next week, he again had the same experience and then suddenly fainted over the degreaser. He was treated at a local hospital and released. He continued to experience a wobbly sensation and nausea for several more days. This patient was experiencing the classical symptoms of acute and subacute Trichloroethylene toxicity on the central nervous system. Although he joked about the drunken-like feeling he had experienced, had he fallen over the degreaser, he might have died an anesthetic death. The worker was also unaware that Trichloroethylene has been found to be a cancer-producing agent in animals and has consequently come to be considered a potential human carcinogen by international agencies. Trichloroethylene should not be used as a degreaser solvent for there are many safer substitutes. Had the degreaser been clearly identified and had information on its acute and chronic toxicity, and easily available at the work place, then this episode and near tragedy may have been avoided.

*CASE *4*

This last case is a tragedy. A young man returned to his new job day after New Year's Eve. While performing a task that he had done once or twice before, a hose cupelling loosened and he was sprayed with hydrofluoric acid. Twelve hours later he was dead. It was reported that he was not wearing the required protective clothing at the time of the accident and that, consequently, he was at fault.

However, had the hydrofluoric acid been properly labeled and had information on its extreme toxicity been available, I feel certain that protective clothing would have been worn that day. Furthermore, if a RIGHT-TO-KNOW law had been in effect, I believe that the treating physicians would have been more familiar with industrial exposures and the potentially life-saving remedies available for workers receiving hydrofluoric acid burns. As it was, this young man died at one of our countries leading medical institutions.

In summary, it is clear to me that the RIGHT-TO-KNOW law is necessary in the State of Massachusetts. Such a law will inform workers as to the identity and toxicity of the chemicals they work with day in and day out. Such a law will allow for more efficient use of rare and costly technical and medical resources and will lead to a better informed medical community. Such a law will also go a long way toward preventing needless tragedy.

Note: This Position Paper has been delivered as a Prepared Statement. You may follow this format when delivering your remarks before the media, or, in this case, before a legislative committee and the media.

SAMPLE BACKGROUNDER

Hazardous Chemical
Right-To-Know Legislation

For Immediate Release August 3, 1983

For further information contact:
Jennie Paige, Director of Public Information
MA Hazardous Chemical Right-To-Know Committee
(617) 578-9034

WHY MASSACHUSETTS NEEDS
THE RIGHT-TO-KNOW
(SENATE BILL #98)

All over the country, people are recognizing thousands of heartbreaking cases of preventable disease — disease tied directly to exposure to work or exposure to chemicals that escape from a workplace. Here in Massachusetts, we, too, are part of the epidemic.

Cancer in Mass.

Massachusetts has the fifth highest cancer rate in the United States.
. . . Up to 40% of all cancer in the U.S. is related to workplace exposure.

For Massachusetts, this would mean:
. . . Up to 4800 deaths per year from job-related cancer.

A recent study showed a strong link between a number of types of cancer and occupational exposure in Massachusetts industries, including shipbuilding, construction, printing, shoe production, machining, and auto repair.

The list of substances used in this state that are known or suspected of causing cancer is very long — asbestos, benzene, chromium, coal tar, formaldehyde, trichlonethylene, and vinyl chloride are just a few.

Occupational disease in Mass.

Cancer, however, is just one of many diseases caused by working conditions. Lung and heart disease, kidney and liver damage head the list.
. . . 390,000 people are disabled and 100,000 people die each year from work-related disease in the U.S.
. . . 12,000 Massachusetts workers are disabled each year.

This figure contrasts markedly with the official state government figures (4000 work-related illnesses in 1979) which are based on reports submitted by employers. Statistics based on employer-supplied or workers' compensation records are gross underestimates of the true numbers, particularly in the case of occupational disease. One study showed that 90% of workers with occupational disease didn't file claims because they didn't know their disease was occupational or couldn't trace their disease to particular exposures. The official figure is also lower because when workers do file claims for illnesses, the claims are usually contested by the employer or its insurance carrier, and so are not counted.
The true cost of occupational disease is enormous. One 1979 estimate was that the annual cost of occupational cancer, alone, could exceed $11 billion.

Workplace chemicals — They don't stay in the workplace!

There are 200,000 chemicals currently in use.
. . . Over 100,000 of these chemicals are potentially dangerous.
. . . Most are know to those who use them only by trade names — not by their chemical name.
. . . 1000 new chemicals are produced each year — many of them untested for health effects.

This massive production of toxic chemicals has led to public concern over exposure to spills, leaks, fires, unsafe dumpsites, and the emission of toxic chemicals into the air, land, and water.
. . . 250,000-390,000 tons of hazardous waste are generated each year in Massachusetts according to a Mass. Department of Environmental Management estimate.
. . . One study found that 74% of companies generating more than 2200 pounds of hazardous waste each month do not report their emission as required.

Workers, themselves, can unknowingly harm their families, either by taking home toxic products like asbestos on their clothes, or by absorbing toxics that can cause damage to a fetus, or genetic damage to future children.
. . . 25% of brain tumors in children are caused by occupational exposure of the parents.

How Right-to-Know Will Help Massachusetts

Knowing what you are working with is the first step to taking the precautions necessary to making your job safe.

Time after time, people get sick or even die because they didn't know enough to take the right precautions.

How will the remainder of New England Electric's coal needs be handled?

New England Electric will continue to charter other vessels to supplement coal deliveries.

Where will the coal come from?

The coal will be supplied from fields in Pennsylvania, West Virginia and Virginia.

What will be the ship's route?

The ship will travel from ports in Philadelphia, Baltimore and Norfolk to Brayton Point Station in Somerset, Mass., and Salem Harbor Station in Salem, Mass.

How often will the ship make the trip?

The ship will make a round trip every five days.

How many trips per year will the ship make?

The ship will make about 63 round trips per year.

How much oil will be saved by burning coal at Brayton Point Station and Salem Harbor Station and what is the savings to customers?

Coal burning at Brayton Point Station and Salem Harbor Station means a saving of about 14 million barrels of oil per year and a saving of more than $60 million per year for customers.

What is New England Electric?

New England Electric System is a public utility holding company headquartered in Westborough, Massachusetts. Its three retail subsidiaries — Massachusetts Electric Company, Narragansett Electric Company in Rhode Island, and Granite State Electric Company in New Hampshire — supply electricity to more than one million customers. Other subsidiaries include a wholesale generating company, a fuels exploration and development company, a transmission company and a service company.

SAMPLE LIST OF CONTACTS

Subject: Special Needs Adoption

1. Robert G. Lewis, Executive Director
   Project IMPACT
   25 West Street
   Boston, MA 02111

   (617) 473-5286

Mr. Lewis is chief executive officer of a special needs adoption agency which coordinates 11 comparable statewide agencies.

2. Susan Klibanoff, writer
   c/o "Sunday's Child"
   Boston Globe
   Boston, MA 02107

   (617) 929-2000

Ms. Klibanoff writes a weekly feature focusing on special needs children up for adoption.

3. Jacqui LeBeau, Executive Director
   Extended Family Institute, Inc.
   25 West Street
   Boston, MA 02111

   (617) 475-2367

Ms. LeBeau is chief executive officer of a nonprofit organization specializing in the placement of black, hispanic, and other minority children.

4. George Collins
   53 Pond Road
   Cambridge, MA 02138

   (617) 367-9986

Mr. Collins is a special needs adoptive parent.

Note: Add yourself as one of the information contacts. Photocopy on your stationery with subject heading.

Essentials Of A Networking Follow-Up Letter To An Individual Just Met

- Letter may be typed or hand written. This is a personal note.

- Letter should be sent within 48 hours of meeting. Remember the old addage, "Out of sight, out of mind." Use networking information promptly.

- If you have both the contact's home and office addresses, use the office address. Your letter has a greater likelihood of being answered.

- Enclose appropriate leave behinds which contact can pass on to target.

- In paragraph 1, give your contact a specific compliment. People always pay attention to compliments about themselves.

- In paragraph 2, mention the name of the person you are seeking access to . Mention, too, what outcome you are seeking from this contact, e.g. a program on battered children.

- Tell contact when you will call (ten days after sending letter). Note this date on your calendar.

- Make the telephone call on the date you have promised to do so. Repeat your call until such time as your contact acts on your behalf.

- If contact fails to act within a reasonable time, send a letter directly to the desired target. Mention your contact's name in the first paragraph. Note on the bottom of this letter that you are sending a copy to your contact.

SAMPLE NETWORKING FOLLOW-UP LETTER TO AN INDIVIDUAL JUST MET

Dear Friend:

I was glad to have the opportunity of meeting you on our recent flight to Boston. So often the people one meets under such circumstances are scarcely inspirational, but I very much enjoyed what you had to say about educational policy.

I am grateful, too, for the information you gave me about your friend Ken Wendell of Detroit's "Morning Wake-up." I have, of course, often heard this program and have thought that my work with battered children would make an interesting and important show. I am enclosing some material about what I do and am glad to accept your kind offer to pass it on to Ken Wendell and his producer.

Why don't I call you in ten days to see whether you've received this letter, the material, and have had the opportunity to speak with Mr. Wendell?

Again, it was very pleasant meeting you. Thanks for your help.

Sincerely,

Unabashed Self-Promoter

Essentials Of A Letter To A Congressional Aide Requesting Information

- Call in advance to get name of correct legislative assistant, proper title, and address.

- If you are seeking information about a piece of legislation, have the bill number.

- Type letter on your stationery.

- In first paragraph, indicate your interest in the subject. Mention where you read about legislation, &c. Send copy of any article in which subject is mentioned. Source will want to have it for his files, particularly if your information source is not generally available.

- In second paragraph, advance your credentials.

- In third paragraph, indicate what you want to do: e.g. write an article.

- In fourth paragraph, indicate what you need including: fact sheet, congressional testimony, previous articles on the subject, list of local congressional supporters, and an indication of whether any local media have dealt with the issue.

- In fifth paragraph, indicate that you will send copies of all published articles. If article does not get published, send a typescript to indicate what work you have done. Indicate that you would appreciate being kept up-to-date on developments.

Note: Once article(s) have appeared, ask the congressman to insert them in **The Congressional Record.**

Remember: You may also use this procedure with trade associations, professional organizations, commissions, legislative committees, or any other organization regularly producing research data.

SAMPLE LETTER TO A CONGRESSIONAL AIDE REQUESTING INFORMATION

Mr. Larry Smith, Legislative Assistant
Office Of Representative Peter Atkins
House of Representatives
Washington, D.C. 20515

Dear Mr. Smith:

I am writing to you concerning H.R. 501 which would permit individuals using the short tax form (1040) to get credit for their charitable donations. I understand from the enclosed article from the **Cambridge Chronicle** that Representative Atkins is a prime sponsor of this legislation.

I am president of a Massachusetts-based consulting firm assisting nonprofit organizations. This legislation is of particular interest to our clients, and I would like to offer my assistance in promoting it, bringing it to the attention of the Massachusetts congressional delegation and local media.

Specifically I intend to submit to the **Boston Globe** an op-ed piece advocating the passage of this legislation. I shall also send a similar piece to the **Cambridge Chronicle** and to a newsletter for nonprofit organizations with which I have a connection.

I would be grateful to you if you would assist me in this work by:

- informing me whether you have on file anything published either in the **Globe** or other Massachusetts newspapers

- sending me basic information on the legislation including a background fact sheet, précis of congressional testimony, Massachusetts congressional supporters, reprints of articles from other states, and anything else which you feel might be of assistance.

I will keep you informed as my work progresses and send you any articles which may be published. I would be grateful if you would advise me on pending developments in Washington pertaining to this legislation.

Sincerely,

Unabashed Self-Promoter

SAMPLE PROBLEM-SOLVING PROCESS ARTICLE

Jeffrey L. Lant

All Cambridge is divided into two parts: those who are consultants and those who wish they were.

The high degree of interest in consulting among Cambridge residents is most obviously demonstrated by politicians' growing attention to the profession: Tommy O'Neill, for example, now proposes a tax on management consultants. Not that the new tax is likely to solve the problems of Prop 2½ since most would-be consultants will find themselves, five years hence, punching a time clock. The profession is, we have found, harder than it may seem. The following suggestions have been prepared, at the cost of labor lost, to help those who seek to avoid that modern golgotha: the traditional workplace.

MASTERING

The Consulting Game

$ $ $ $ $ $ $ $ $ $ $ $ $ $

$ $ $ $ $

Rule 1: Start Consulting Today.

Each practicing consultant knows that he is a good deal brighter than the run of humanity though convincing someone else to pay for this gift of nature will require more than a string of letters signifying various degrees of higher education following his name. The would-be consultant must come to realize that his own well-being rests on convincing the comparatively less well off that he is essential to the other's financial prosperity. Don't wait for the proper number of academic credentials to attract your propective clients. Look for your first consulting assignment today. While this first assigment may not be at the level of your dreams, at least you'll be getting paid while learning to be more proficient, and you will be gaining valuable references that will help later on.

Rule 2: Market Your References.

Understand that references from completed assignments give a consultant a legitimacy that no degree can ever provide. Having successfully completed an assignment, assiduously bring your achievement to the attention of other buyers of your service. Don't wait to be asked for the reference; force it to the attention of prospective buyers. Very often, in fact, they will be so impressed by your insistence that they will not trouble to look into the matter further. Don't press your luck, however.

Rule 3: Make Use of Your Competitors.

At first you will be troubled by the very idea of competitors. Don't be, for they are a veritable gold mine of useful information, used properly. Collect, for a start, every scrap of information on anyone doing anything remotely resembling what you would like to do. Find out: where they do it; how much they charge to do it; how many people do it; what people think of it once it's done; and what they'll be doing next. Much of this information is ridiculously easy to secure. For the rest, consider subscribing to the publications of competitors, taking their workshops, or even buying an hour's time to find out what you need to know. (Beginners, of course, need to be reminded to downplay the competitor angle.) By learning about their terrain, you may discover what is necessary to every consultant's success: an unfilled niche waiting for you.

Rule 4: Establish a Contact Bank.

If "no man is an island," consultants are the big city. We have inordinate needs which demand constant tending. Each consultant must have, therefore, at least three distinct networks of people. A fourth is optional.,

1. *The Mandarin Network.* The inspiration for this comes from those pre-Red aristocrats who grew their fingernails to indicate to a burdened world that they did no gainful toil. All successful consultants aspire to reestablish this congenial universe in their own lives. The Mandarin Network includes all those individuals who provide services that you need.

2. *Next Check Network.* Included in this network are all those individuals who can buy your services, now or in the future.

3. *Self-Promotion Network.* This is composed of individuals who are able to be helpful in keeping your name glowingly before a captivated public.

4. *The Astor Network.* (Optional). This network, more useful perhaps to roues and social climbers, is designed to insure that you will move in the right circles after 5.

How do you secure useful people for these networks? By doing an analysis of every conceivable need you have and by both staying alert to and creating opportunities for drafting people to fill these needs. By plugging people you meet and connive to meet into a Pyramid of Contacts, you will always know whether they are worth pursuing.

Rule 5: Build a Pyramid of Contacts.

People are worth pursuing if they fill a need or if they have access to someone who can do something for you. Do not pursue them for any other reason. Many consultants fail in their careers because they have an inadequate idea of who they need and of how to get access to those who can help. By keeping the Pyramid of Contacts in your mind at all times and mentally categorizing the peole you meet — beginners should write down all names — your own failure is inconceivable. Here's what a Pyramid should look like:

You want people who say:

1. I'll take care of it for you.
2. I'll call and set up the meeting with him, attend the meeting with you, and call later to move matters along.
3. I can't attend the meeting but I'll set it up and help you later.
4. I'll write a letter to him for you.
5. Call and use my name.
6. Even though I don't a contact, he'll have to see me. I have a Ph.D. from Harvard.

A quick analysis of the Pyramid of Contacts reveals that at its apex, the emphasis is on process: how to get you in touch with decision makers the right way, i.e. the way that insures the discussion will center on genteel niceties rather than your credentials which are, of course, taken for granted. At the foot of the Pyramid, the emphasis is on content: selling yourself, your credentials, trying to make a cogent case, all the things, in fact, which really don't work and which successful consultants strenuously avoid.

Rule 6: Form a Supergroup. Supergrouping is a key concept for the successful consultant. It operates rather like the solar system in which there is one sun (you) and other, minor revolving bodies (independent contractors). Supergrouping is born of the inevitable realization that no one makes money unless other people work for him, yet the inevitable problem that having other people work for you so crimps your style that any serious expansion might take years.

Use the Mandarin Network to recruit supergroupers: telephone answering services, secretarial help, printers, designers, contractors of every kind. Sign independent contractor contracts with those who might someday challenge you and make sure each one has a noncompetitive agreement included; that is, a clause which prevents supergroupers from offering the same service both to your current clients and within a certain time and in a certain place.

Rule 7: Become the Acknowledged or Perceived Expert in Your Field. Consultants succeed insofar as they are able to project themselves as the acknowledged or perceived experts in their fields. How they do so is not very mysterious: they exploit media to maximum effect. Successful consultants understand that the media needs them as much as they need the media, and that a tasteful symbiotic relationship necessarily ensues.

Print media is infinitely more valuable than electronic since print pieces can be placed on your letterhead and distributed as promotional literature. Successful consultants assume, after all, that no one will actually see the original piece, and they unhesitatingly brings it to the attention of people who really ought to see it.

If you do electronic media interviews and programs, of course, be sure to give your telephone number and address; many timorous souls feel odd doing so. No successful self-promoter twinges.

Your ability to establish yourself as the acknowledged or perceived expert has several obvious advantages: 1) clients come to you (which positions you nicely for subsequent negotiations); 2) you can charge more; and 3) you can quickly branch out into related fields such as workshops, seminars, and publications. (See below).

Rule 8: Choose the Right Image for Yourself. Too many consultants feel deprived unless dressed by J. Press and ensconced in chrome-plated aeries. This is a mistake. Many successful consultants, like I, have learned to emulate the old-time country practitioners who make house calls. Here, a solicitous informality should be the mode. Be careful, however. This informality works best when you are the acknowledged or perceived expert in the field; then your shirt-sleeves empathy is truly meaningful because what people expect from such an eminence is an austere, distant professional. The contrast will work strongly in your favor.

Rule 9: Expand Your Operations Into Logical Extensions of Your Work. Considered expansion is the key to wealth and ultimate leisure. No consultant who simply charges by the hour or day or even operates on healthy retainers will ever be rich, however substantial his annual income. Consultants, like other entrepreneurs, must extend their operations by degrees: 1) work alone until you get the hang of things (avoid partnerships); 2) take on associates who are paid by you as independent contractors; 3)

continued

January 30, 1982 The Cambridge Express

Consulting

extend your business into products which both promote you and project your expertise *and* make money, such as newsletters and books; and 4) take to the road via workshops and seminars which either promote you, make money, or help you gain associates in new areas, thereby expanding your empire.

Rule 10: Understand the Spectrum of Leadership Options. Every successful consultant must understand and use without hesitation every leadership option available to get people to do what he wants. This includes the full panoply of sticks and carrots. Women, as that wicked sprite Alexander Korda rightly points out, shouldn't hesitate to use sex when their guts tell them it's the right alternative (neither should men, of course); men on the other hand, shouldn't hesitate to use the lesser emotions and tears, if, again, they constitute the right move (neither, of course, should women.)

Identifying the available options and feeling both free and confident enough to draw them forth when needed is not, at first, easy. Most people who lunch at the Harvest have been rigidly socialized to repress rather than exploit the available options, foolishly believing the meritocratic cant about advancement via credentials. Like every other successful entrepreneur, I have learned better. I have, for instance, a printer who likes to be hugged in greeting. I was, however brought up in a typical WASP family where only the highest-rated Christian festivals (Christmas and the funerals of patriarchs) warranted hugs. Understanding the Spectrum of Leadership Options has enabled me, you should understand, to overcome this disability; I have learned, consequently, that hugs rather than my Ph.D. get me the cheapest printing in Harvard Square.

Jeffery L. Lant is a successful management consultant who lives and practices in Cambridge.

MASS HIGH TECH January 17, 1983

So you, too, want to be a consultant: Some practical advice on how to get started

By Jeffrey L. Lant

All high tech is divided into two parts: those who are consultants and those who wish they were.

So many local technologists have turned to consulting that it's beginning to interest the politicians. . . . .

SAMPLE SENTINEL ARTICLE

Jeffrey Lant Associates, Inc.

THE BOSTON GLOBE THURSDAY, MAY 14, 1981

Helping charity – and the taxpayer

JEFFREY L. LANT

America's more than 500,000 nonprofit organizations, particularly those in the human services where Reagan Administration budget cuts will be severely felt, have a fine opportunity to help themselves. But they'll have to act by the first week of June, when the House Ways and Means Committee finishes its tax work for the session.

Ways and Means is considering legislation allowing taxpayers to deduct charitable contributions regardless of whether they take the standard deduction. At present, taxpayers who use the short form or do not itemize deductions are not credited for their charitable contributions. Thus a gift of $100 to a nonprofit day-care center costs the full $100. The same gift by a taxpayer in the 40 percent tax bracket who itemizes his deductions costs $60.

There has, of course, always been this discrepancy, but the impact was less significant when fewer people used the short form. Since 1969 the Treasury has raised the standard deduction five times to simplify the tax system. As a result, less than 25 percent of all taxpayers itemize deductions.

The effect on charitable giving is hardly surprising. The more people using the short form, the fewer making charitable contributions and the smaller the contributions. A recent Gallup Poll shows that itemizers in the $10,000-$15,000 income bracket in 1978 contributed an average of $324 to charity, compared with only $249 for non-itemizers. When all income brackets are considered, the mean average contribution of itemizers was $652 compared to only $210 for non-itemizers.

In 1978 a movement arose in Congress to reverse that trend. The movement is currently spearheaded by Reps. Richard A. Gebhardt (D-Mo.) and Barber Conable (R-N.Y.) and Sens. Robert Packwood (R-Ore.) and Daniel P. Moynihan (D-N.Y.). Each year their bill (HR-501 and S-170) creeps a little closer to passage as the leading arguments against it have been dealt with.

The chief of those arguments has been its potential cost in lost federal revenue. Supporters of the legislation, using figures provided by Harvard economist Martin Feldstein, admit that it will cost the Treasury about $4.8 billion a year. However, they say that the benefit to public charities will be about $5.7 billion yearly, a figure that goes some of the way toward making up the $20 billion in Reagan-promoted federal budget cuts.

Increasing citizen support of civic organizations and broadening public participation is, of course, a hallmark of the Reagan philosophy. Thus it is no surprise to learn that both the President and the Republican platform endorse this legislation. Moreover, in the House and Senate the legislation has attracted broad bipartisan support: 108 House Democrats and 112 House Republicans are sponsors; 12 Senate Democrats and 12 Senate Republicans, too.

There seem to be two obstacles:

1) Liberal Democrats fear that the anticipated loss in federal revenue under this legislation might imperil favored social programs which the President's measures have already adversely affected. They have thus withheld their support. The Massachusetts congressional delegation, for instance, despite the wealth of nonprofit organizations in this state, has hung back.

Proponents counter the objections of the liberals by citing the incalculable advantages to be gained in encouraging more people to support public charities and nonprofit organizations, a benefit only a bill of this kind can provide.

2) Despite the high-blown Republican rhetoric in favor of this bill, there has not been a notable push from the White House for its passage.

At this juncture, nonprofit organizations can help themselves first by urging the recalcitrant members of the Massachusetts congressional delegation to support this legislation and, second, by urging House Speaker Thomas P. O'Neill and Rep. Daniel Rostenkowski (D-Ill.), chairman of Ways and Means, to do so. Unless they act, an important measure capable of mitigating the sting of the budget cuts on nonprofit organizations will be shelved until another Congress assembles.

Jeffrey L. Lant is president of a Cambridge-based firm assisting nonprofit organizations.

(617) 547-6372
50 FOLLEN STREET, SUITE 507 • CAMBRIDGE, MASSACHUSETTS 02138

SAMPLE WHITE KNIGHT ARTICLE (LOCAL NEWSPAPER)

Jeffrey Lant Associates, Inc.

Help for those troubled nonprofits

(Dr. Jeffrey Lant of Follen Street, is president of Jeffrey Lant Associates and the author of the newly-published. "Development Today: A Guide for Nonprofit Organizations." The views expressed in this column are Lant's and not necessarily those of the Chronicle)

1981 will be a year of uncertainty and difficulty for many nonprofit organizations both in Massachusetts and around the country. Many of them will reduce their budgets and cut back their programs. Others will simply go bankrupt. Here's why.

•The Reagan Administration. The new President is committed to reducing the federal budget (by $20 billion, he says), while at the same time increasing defense spending. The only way of attaining both goals is by significantly reducing the amount of money spent on human services, now fully ⅓ of the federal budget. Most of these services are provided by nonprofit organizations.

•Proposition 2½. This measure affects nonprofit organizations in two ways. First, it limits the ability of state and local government to contract for the kinds of services often provided by nonprofit organizations. The Boston Shakespeare Company has already found that local school districts no longer have the same discretionary money to hire its dramatic troupe.

Second, it has the affect of forcing private funding sources to direct money to (often public) projects they need not otherwise have considered. At its December 8 meeting, the Committee of the Permanent Charity Fund, Boston's bellweather foundation, allotted fully 40 per cent of its available funds to a housing project, which would otherwise have received public monies.

•Continuing inflation and high interest rates. Most foundations and charitable trusts invest in stocks and bonds, generally of the most conservative varieties. These conservative investments have been particularly affected by the weak health of the economy, with the result that 1) the capital assets of foundations have been undermined, and 2) whatever dollars are dispersed, buy less.

All of this is bad, very bad, news for nonprofit organizations, many of which have come to rely on federal, state, and foundation support.

Too often, these organizations emphasize their not-for-profit aspects, apparently forgetting that under the laws of the Commonwealth, they are also corporations. As such, not-for-profit organizations would be wise to ape the organizational and business practices of their for-profit relations. In so doing, the following organizational development and fundraising steps should be helpful:

•Establish your market. Too many nonprofit organizations don't know how they fit in their service area. Are you unique? Is all or part of what you do unparalleled elsewhere? How do you overlap with other organizations? Can you make a case that you are the only organization of your kind, the most efficient, the least duplicative? If you don't know the answers to these questions, you cannot make an effective case for public support.

•Know your needs. In embarking on any fundraising effort, too few nonprofit organizations have adequately assessed either the community's need for what they do, or what the organization itself will really need to be able to provide the service. Unless there is clear understanding on both counts, any fundraising effort will be handicapped from the start.

•Produce compelling documents. Too often, the documents and materials produced by nonprofit organizations have the look of internal memoranda, filled with jargon and office argot. They are not persuasive as marketing documents, don't adequately explain either who you are, what your place in the community is, or why you need the funds. All documents are public relations materials and ought to be modelled on newspaper feature stories, not technical, programmatic reports.

•Identify your contacts. More often than not, people fund people they know, rather than good programs per se. Most people suspect this basic fundraising fact of life, but organizations don't know how to go about establishing the necessary contact network to get access to funding sources.

Boards of Directors, volunteers, "friends," and agency staff have to be solicited for contacts. Even the most seemingly unconnected individual is in a position to give leads: to his bank, insurance company, and members of his family who work for corporations. Insofar as an organization can inspire these people to generate and connect with such contacts, it can produce money.

It should also be noted that the only potential bright spots for funding in the years ahead are the possibilities for corporate and individual contributions. Unfortunately both are directly related to who you know and thus necessitate the creation of an organizational contact network.

•Systematic follow-up. Nonprofit organizations are notoriously bad about following up the leads they have and supplying potential funding sources with whatever additional information they have requested. By adopting a corporate rather than a not-for-profit mentality, a more professional approach will result – and the dollars you need.

•Keep at it. Too many nonprofit personnel are willing to be put off. The slightest hint of a possible negative response is enough to make them queasy. This is fatal. Even negative responses come in varieties and must be sorted out. Properly handled, over time, many of them can be changed into the affirmative. The important thing [illegible] is that nonprofit representatives are not asking on behalf of themselves but on behalf of good causes, and often on behalf of the inarticulate and unrepresented, the elderly, handicapped children, lions in the zoo.

In the 80's, nonprofit organizations have to be more deliberate, better organised, more corporate about their programs, organizational development and fundraising. They will have to become more adept at program planning, marketing, and all aspects of public relations. Those that succeed in adopting such methods can mitigate the deleterious effects of the times – and emerge stronger than ever. Those that do not will suffer accordingly – with their service groups and causes suffering the worst effects.

CAMBRIDGE (MASS.) CHRONICLE THURSDAY, JANUARY 8, 1981

(617) 547-6372
50 FOLLEN STREET, SUITE 507 • CAMBRIDGE, MASSACHUSETTS 02138

Jeffrey Lant Associates, Inc.

Tough times ahead for non profits not ready to fight

By DR. JEFFREY L. LANT

Over the next decade, many of the nation's 500,000 nonprofit organizations will face very difficult times. Because all of us are in some way touched by the work of these groups — through hospitals, universities, religious institutions, museums, human service agencies — what is happening ought to be of widespread concern.

To begin with, certain external factors are adversely affecting nonprofit organizations:

● Inflation. The major concern of every citizen is also first on the list of problems for nonprofit groups. Whether a nonprofit organization has an endowment or not, inflation is the enemy. Organizations without endowments are finding it more and more difficult to do business, particularly if they are agencies dealing with the needy and have relied upon any kind of user fees.

On the other hand, agencies with endowments are also having problems. The return on their capital investments, largely in stocks and bonds, has not been good in recent years. More and more, I hear of such organizations dipping into their capital to make good the difference between what they must have to operate and what they receive in revenue. The long term implications of this situation are most alarming.

This same inflation, with the weakness it has brought to the stock and bond markets, is also wreaking havoc with the assets of foundations, which have traditionally supplied nonprofit organizations with grants. The Ford Foundation, the nation's premier grantsmaking foundation, provides a clear example of what is happening: its assets have been steadily shrinking over the last decade and thus its ability to make grants — at the very time inflation has soared and undercut the value of all those dollars still being given. Nearly every one of the nation's 28,000 private foundations finds itself in the same situation.

● Budget and Tax Cutting Initiatives. President Reagan says he will take $20 billion off the federal budget. He also says the defense establishment will be dramatically improved. These two presidential objectives spell trouble for nonprofit organizations, particularly those in the human services and education. The cutback in federal funds will have two important effects. Organizations relying on these dollars will face the likelihood of cutting back on the programs and personnel supported by these dollars. They will also lose that percentage of the grant termed "overhead," which goes to support their fixed operating expenses. In fact, these overhead monies have constituted a necessary source of unrestricted funds to many organizations.

Local tax cutting initiatives are adding to the problems of nonprofit organizations. Not only will local authorities be unable to contract out for as many of the services provided by nonprofit organizations (a fact which the Boston Shakespeare Company discovered the day after the election when one of its school contracts was cancelled); also, local foundations will feel pressured to support projects previously funded by state dollars.

The Committee of the Permanent Charity Fund, Boston's bellwether foundation, gave this excuse after its December meeting to dozens of local nonprofit organizations which had applied for funds. Many of these organizations are now in dire straits and several will close in the current year.

● Corporate Support. Many people in the nonprofit world took heart last year when for the first time in American history corporate philanthropy outpaced foundation giving. I was not among them. The monies that corporations give are almost always donated to very conservative, established projects such as art museums, opera companies, public television extravaganzas. They are safe, non-controversial and have immediate public relations benefits. Corporations have never been among the philanthropic pacesetters, and, in this conservative decade, they are not going to change their habits.

Adding to the problems of nonprofit organizations are certain internal difficulties. Unlike the external problems, these difficulties can be dealt with — and must be, if the organization stands any chance of surviving the years ahead.

● Marketing Problems. Nonprofit organizations do not, on the whole, understand marketing. Organizations are plagued by a lack of clarity about what they are in business to do, what it costs them to do it, and what their competition, both profit and not-for-profit, is doing.

Moreover, nonprofit organizations are too often unclear about the detailed needs of their service populations and now their proposed programs will solve community problems. Finally, organizations find it difficult to communicate this information to the public in a way which will be easily understood.

● Lack of Business Sense. Adding to the marketing difficulties, nonprofit organizations also suffer from a lack of business knowledge and from an inability to see that their services are amenable to business principles and are not at odds with them. Nearly all nonprofit organizations are also corporations under the law, not-for-profit corporations. Yet the executives of nonprofit organizations fail to see the connection between what they they do and what the executives of any other corporation must do to insure the success of their enterprise.

● Exclusively. Every nonprofit organization is begun by a dedicated group of people committed to some civic betterment. Yet, any organization succeeds only insofar as it brings others into the venture and enthuses them about the project. If the group remains exclusive, its chances of success are enormously reduced.

A commitment to broadening the base of the organization necessarily means building a strong, diverse board of directors. I have continually found that too many directors of nonprofit organizations are either ignorant of or unwilling to assume their obligations to govern.

Among their responsibilities perhaps the most misunderstood is a director's obligation either to give money or else work hard to find money for the organization. Unfortunately, executive directors are often unclear about how to motivate their boards to accept such responsibilities and how to attract worthy individuals to their organizations.

Serving on the board of a nonprofit organization should be regarded as a signal honor for any citizen — but it is a working honor, not a sinecure.

Sadly, thousands of nonprofit organizations around the country, dozens in Massachusetts, will go under in the next years. Many will take with them ideas which could have benefited all of us had their leaders done what was necessary to combat adverse circumstances and save their organizations. Fortunately, many other nonprofit organizations will make the necessary changes and will come through the difficult times ahead stronger than ever.

Jeffrey Lant is president of Jeffrey Lant Associates, Inc., a Cambridge firm supplying technical assistance to nonprofit organizations, and is the author of "Development Today: A Guide for Nonprofit Organizations."

Boston Herald American — Friday, February 6, 1981

(617) 547-6372
50 FOLLEN STREET, SUITE 507 • CAMBRIDGE, MASSACHUSETTS 02138

Jeffrey Lant Associates, Inc.

THE SUN, Sunday, November 15, 1981 Baltimore, MD

Digging harder for donations

By Jeffrey L. Lant

The nation's 500,000 nonprofit organizations have been subjected this year to a series of body blows that threaten the continued existence of a good many of their number: universities, museums, hospitals and the wide range of social-service and community-based programs.

The havoc began with the Reagan administration's federal budget cuts. The bulk of the $35.2 billion sliced from the national budget is being taken from educational and human-service programs, most created in the 1960s and almost all nonprofit. Many of these organizations now are forced to raise all or part of their budgets from private sources.

Next, the administration's tax cut is hurting the nation's nonprofit sector, a result its sponsors anticipated. As Norman Ture, undersecretary of the treasury for tax policy, said during the debate on the issue, "We're really going to put a lot of pressure on charitable institutions by cutting tax rates."

He was right. According to a study recently released by Independent Sector, a Washington-based coalition of 320 leading foundations, corporations and nonprofit organizations, $18 billion in donations will be lost to the nonprofit world between 1981 and 1984, the difference in donations projected under former tax laws and the new Tax Act.

As if this situation wasn't bad enough, the nonprofit safety net already had gaping holes.

Take grants-making foundations, for instance, traditional benefactors of the nonprofit community. A study released last summer by the Foundation Center in New York shows that foundation assets have decreased by 30 percent over the past seven years as a direct result of inflation. Foundations, the center concludes, are thus in no position to make up the dollar shortfall.

And corporations? Corporate philanthropy last year outpaced foundation giving for the first time in American history. Many rooted optimists have therefore concluded that salvation for nonprofit America lies with the nation's corporations. This is a doubtful position. No less an authority on the nation's business than the Secretary of the Treasury, Donald T. Regan, has said, "Corporate America isn't about to come to the rescue" of nonprofit organizations.

The best guess is that giving from corporations will rise moderately over the short term but will not keep pace with inflation and will not begin to make up the difference that nonprofit organizations will lose from other sources. Moreover, given the current political climate, it is unrealistic to hope that corporate giving will change from its well-established pattern of supporting only the most cautious (though occasionally flashy) projects.

There is, to be sure, some hope for nonprofit organizations as far as individuals are concerned. The Reagan tax package contains a provision under which individuals who do not itemize their deductions can now get credit for their charitable contributions. Next year these individuals will get a credit of $25 on the first $100 they give; by 1986 all charitable contributions will be counted. When this legislation is fully implemented, it is estimated that nonprofit organizations could gain by almost $6 billion.

Sadly, these sanguine expectations may not be entirely realized. Small contributors are less likely to take the trouble to itemize; even if they do, their contributions will go in far higher proportions (as they have historically) to religious organizations. The new law may not have much effect on the kinds of organizations being affected by the federal budget cuts.

In the face of this litany of bad news, many, perhaps most, nonprofit organizations can expect a sustained period of financial difficulty. If these organizations adopt a series of self-help suggestions, however, they should be able to improve situations that otherwise threaten to be dire.

In the long run, a broad-based, active board of directors offers an organization its best chance for healthy survival. Too many of the boards are both weak and exclusive, heavily weighted toward professionals in the subject field.

Instead, a board should be broad-based with individuals with corporate affiliations, a representative and two "technicians" (an accountant and a lawyer); only one or two members of a board should come from an agency's field of endeavor. Overall there should be at least 15 active board members, each of whom should be personally solicited once a year to make a pledge to the organization.

Next, an organization must develop its connections with potential funding sources. Too many nonprofit personnel assume that finding money is an objective process in which good programs automatically prosper. Fund-raising experts know but rarely say that virtually all foundation and corporate donations are given because somebody knows somebody. Therefore, organizations must hold regular workshop sessions with board members, staff and committed "friends" to find out who they know. At such meetings lists of local corporate and foundation executives should be circulated and annotated.

Board members must work in this networking process. No nonprofit organization can now afford the luxury of board members who consider fund-raising and networking beneath them.

Nonprofit organizations, too, often are run lackadaisically rather than as efficient, tight corporations. Each organization should have a strict reporting process in following up on linkages and developing potential funding sources.

Fund-raising is a long, time-consuming process that should take place year-round within the framework of a detailed plan. Money that an organization needs next year should be sought today.

Organizations that adopt such sensible self-help suggestions stand a better chance of remaining alive and healthy through what promises to be the extraordinarily difficult decade of the 1980s.

Mr. Lant is president of a Cambridge, Mass., consulting firm for nonprofit organizations and the author of "Development Today: A Guide for Nonprofit Organizations."

(617) 547-6372
50 FOLLEN STREET, SUITE 507 • CAMBRIDGE, MASSACHUSETTS 02138

SAMPLE ARTICLE FROM ADVANCE MEDIA RELEASE

Jeffrey Lant Associates, Inc.

Y annual meeting tonight at Bellevue

MELROSE — Dr. Jeffrey Lant, president of Jeffrey Lant Associates, a management consulting firm in Cambridge, tonight will address the 91st Annual Meeting of the Melrose YMCA, at Bellevue Gof Club at 6 p.m.

Dr. Lant, author of "Development Today: A Guide for Nonprofit Organizations," will speak on the need for citizen involvement in nonprofit organizations and will address his remarks specifically to the "Partners In Progress" capital campaign ofthe Melrose YMCA.

Dr. Lant, an expert in nonprofit organizations, told the Melrose Evening News that "the nation's 800,000 nonprofit organizations face today the most severe challenge of the century."

Dr. Lant cited as problems for non-profit groups, the federal government budget cutbacks, a drop in "real giving" by the nation's 25,000 private grantmaking foundations, and the "inability of America's corporations to make up the amount of dollars being lost from their budgets."

"The situation is as grave for the nation's nonprofit organizations as it has ever been," Lant said. "The inescapable conclusion is that private citizens must now come forward as never before to bolster and sustain organizations and causes in which they believe."

Lant told the Melrose Evening News that the ways in which private citizens can help will be the focus of his remarks, particularly how Melrosians can assist the YMCA's ongoing capital fund campaign.

The Harvard-educated Lant, who is author of the new best selling book, "The Consultant's Kit: Establishing and Opening Your Successful Consulting Business," is currently working as Development Counselor to the Melrose YMCA.

"As someone who has been working intimately with the YMCA for the last several months, I have come to appreciate the unique and important role of the YMCA in the Melrose community," Lant said.

"I will be doing everything possible in my remarks to drive home to the citizens of Melrose the wonderful asset they have in the YMCA and the absolute necessity of their continuing support for both the YMCA as an institution and its current capital campaign," he said.

When asked about the tenor of his remarks, Lant said, "At the conclusion of my speech, there will be neither a dry eye in the house nor an extra dollar in anyone's wallet. I want o make sure no one leaves without contributing!"

MELROSE (MASS.) EVENING NEWS
MONDAY, MARCH 8, 1982

(617) 547-6372
50 FOLLEN STREET, SUITE 507 • CAMBRIDGE, MASSACHUSETTS 02138

Jeffrey Lant Associates, Inc.

Hartford (CT) Advocate May 12, 1982

Packaging The Accessible Expert

Consultants are the social workers of the '80s

By Linda Blaker Hirsh

Harvard degree or natural sense of *chutzpah*? Both a patrician education and a brassy personality may have prompted Jeffrey Lant, a 19th-century-British-history major, to create Jeffrey Lant Associates, a Boston-based consultancy firm for non-profit groups. In Hartford last month he became a consultant for would-be consultants. In an intensive, one-day how-to workshop sponsored by the University of Connecticut's department of Extended and Continuing Education, Lant covered the consultant's world from identification to incorporation.

Collectively, this world represents a small-business renaissance, and these entrepreneurs of advice are giving this resurgence of free enterprise everything they've got. As a consultant's coach, Lant cheers them on, dangling the twin carrots of prosperity and freedom before the prospective experts-for-hire. Sitting in the Sonesta Hotel's Carleton C room, a windowless, woodpaneled Skinner box, some 14 conferees (who paid $195 for the seminar which included Lant's $30, 203-page, info-packed book, *The Consultant's Kit)* heard him promise, "I get better as the day goes on."

He did. As an inveterate people-watcher, I was amused to hear Lant's no-fail come-on and fascinated by his style, which combined a cultivated ethnic-on-the-rise kind of ambition with an inherited WASP-y charm. Lant's unique concept—and the perfect definition of himself as a consultant—is what he calls an "accessible expert" (imagine, if you will, a star surgeon who makes house calls like a country practitioner, and you'll get the idea.)

Lant was extremely accessible within the somewhat circumscribed limits of his workshop package. A bit flippantly, he described consultancy as a part- or full-time job which does not draw benefits—and therefore parallels coolie labor. But seriously folks, he went on to explain, a consultant is "Smarter than the people in the office, and acts that way." Consultants gain a broader perspective than usual from dealing with many organizations, become technical expects who can create up-to-date business literature during their thinking time, and develop an objectivity about inner-office politics. In addition, says Lant, "The consultant is the social worker of the '80s, a sophisticated handholder," providing solace to those who are lonely at the top.

To his almost-ready-to-begin conferees, Lant said, 'Start today. You are ready, because you have your brains (around his office Lant refers to himself as 'the product') and your specialty. Now take what you have and get your first client." This can be done by identifying a prospective client's problem and selling your skills in relation to that problem. In the process, a consultant may pick up more information to sell to others. For instance, Lant noted certain of his clients served coffee of "college cafeteria quality," and later referred them to a friend who did coffee service consultation, subsequently trading favors with him.

"I get better as the day goes on," says Jeffrey Lant.

This barter between contacts shows that such connections are the name of the consultant's game. Contacts may be quite incestuous. In fact, Lant urges prospective consultants to lean on family and not to neglect to tap friends, past and present job colleagues, and fellow members of organizations for contacts. Go to cocktail parties where you obtain introductions to whomever you want to meet, he says, even offering the formula for arranging a future meeting within the span of a one-minute introduction (complete with business card exchange).

Through this bag of tricks, says Lant, the consultant can build a service corps which he calls the Mandarin Network. Other contact webs, like the self-promotion (media) network, the client network, and even what he dubs the Astor network (from socially "right" circles) will take shape simultaneously. His initial contacts for these networks were then sorted into a pyramid of operability ranging from an "I'll-take-care-of-it-for-your" liaison at the apex to an "even-though-I-don't-have-a-contact-he'll-have-to-see-a-PhD-from-Harvard" self-reliance at the base. Lant gathered some of these contacts for a supergroup, "a solar system where the consultant is the sun and independent contractors who provide services such as printing, accounting, and secretarial are the minor revolving bodies."

Once the problem is identified and the client procured, Lant advises novices to feedback the problem, incorporating key phrases used by the client on the prospectus. When perceived as an expert, he says "you don't have to pander. I am belligerent."

Clearly, the meek do not inherit the consultant's turf. As for the weak, contacting seems to operate on the principle of the carnival strength test: The harder one hits, the higher one's pressure rises.

Consultants must have brains, degrees and expertise. By necessity, consultants must leave any accompanying sensitivities behind, trading them for a seething cleverness. This cleverness must be too big and too energetic to be contained within the nine-to-five world. Consultants are too '80s-creative for that world.

Except for the steps of setting up home offices with IBM Selectrics, stationery and the compulsory business cards, the conferees left knowing they could START TODAY to capitalize on their brains by starting at tonight's cocktail party to build a network for contacts. Crass as it may seem, Lant's means can be rationalized to justify his ends. After all, by solving problems, the consultant has the power to make life easier for the individual, the non-profit institution, or the corporation. And that, in 1982, is no mean service. □

Would-be consultants who missed Lant's Hartford workshop may want to consider attending his one-day seminar in Stamford on May 15. Call 486-3234 for cost and registration information.

(617) 547-6372
50 FOLLEN STREET, SUITE 507 • CAMBRIDGE, MASSACHUSETTS 02138

SAMPLE ARTICLE AND PHOTOGRAPH, EVENT CREATED BY YOU

Jeffrey Lant Associates, Inc.

Consulting Opportunities Journal

"America's Largest 'How-To' Marketing and Information Source for the Independent Consultant"

Volume 2, Number 3

FIRST ANNUAL BOSTON CONSULTING CONVENTION A SUCCESS

Michael J. DeVito, Executive Deputy Commission, Massachusetts Department of Commerce and Development, presents Dr. Jeffrey Lant and Maya Staver, joint sponsors of the first Boston Consultants Convention with a gubernatorial citation from Governor Edward King in recognition of their stimulating the consulting industry of the state.

Boston, Mass. - What was billed as the showcase for a tremendous array of talent actually did come off — almost to the letter. Maya Staver, the president of Creative Connections, a Boston-based networking organization had conceived the idea.

"Putting on this convention was a natural next step for me," said Staver who is also a meeting planning consultant. "Through Creative Connections I've been putting professionals together for years."

Dr. Jeffrey Lant, author of the newest book to hit the consulting scene, *The Consultant's Kit: Establishing and Operating Your Successful Consulting Business*, was the co-sponsor of Boston Consulting Convention (BCC). Said Lant, "My workshops on the essentials of consulting success have always drawn a diverse group. The success of *The Consultant's Kit* conclusively proved to my satisfaction that interest in the field is intense and growing. The convention allowed us to shape this interest in a new way," Lant told COJ.

Like any conference planners, Lant and Staver were faced with the problem of what aspect of the subject to tackle. "After consideration, we decided that consultants were most interested in job creation and marketing," Staver added. "So that's what we decided to concentrate on."

"Our first inspiration was a device we call the Premium Package," Lant told COJ. "We asked each participant to send us an ad offering one of his goods or services to other convention participants at a discount." The various ads, one each to a page, were printed and bound together in a neat little book.

"Frankly," says Staver, "we've gotten a lot of compliments on the Premium Package. I confess," she says with her deep infectious laugh, "that it *is* a good idea. But the point is we thought a sale would stimulate business." Lant and Staver have since wondered whether they may have held the first mass sale on consulting services in history. "If so," Lant says chauvinistically, "it's entirely appropriate that it took place in Massachusetts, where so many other firsts have occurred."

The same devotion to practical matters informed the creation of the workshop program. "Like every other professional," the 35-year-old Staver said, "I've been to too many boring seminars which weren't worth the money." "We want ours to be different — fact-filled, replete with immediately-usable advice and the kind of information you can only have through experience," chimed in Lant, who offers seminars around the country on both the essentials of consulting success and on fund raising for nonprofit organizations.

The program that resulted was both diverse and practical. Among the presented workshops were:

- Mary Bass, executive director, American Society of Professional Consultants, "National Trends in Consulting"
- J. Stephen Lanning, publisher, *Consulting Opportunities Journal*, "Creating Successful Newsletters"
- James Cameron, president, Brooklyn-based Cameron Communications, Inc., and creator of the NBC radio network "The Source," with Ed Golden, Boston bureau Associated Press, "Exploiting the Media for Consulting Success"
- Ralph Hoagland, creator of Store 24, a chain of all-day convenience stores based in Massachusetts, "Taking Entrepreneurial Risks in the 'Eighties"
- Miriam Uni, Boston-based consultant in human behavior and motivation, "Selling Your Potential"
- Dr. Michael Woodnick, president, Inter-act of Boston and Associate Professor of Speech Communications at Northeastern University, "Capitalizing on your Communications Style"
- William Van Loan, president, The Headquarters Companies, Boston, "The Office of the Future"

Lant himself spoke on "Things Your Mother Never Told You About Consulting." It was billed as "Ninety Free-wheeling Minutes" on the essentials of consulting success, and it so impressed Ed Golden of the Associated Press, who attended, that Golden promptly did an interview for the national AP wire.

"Lant is an amazing, spellbinding speaker," reported David Philcratz, a Cambridge wholistic health consultant who attended the workshop. "He has a knack for reducing complicated ideas to a single, pungent observation that leaves you wishing you'd said it first."

Workshops were scheduled in both the morning and afternoon so that the participants got to take two fact-filled programs.

Between workshops, abundant time was left for networking by the participants. Upon entering all were asked to give an indication of their interests and fields of expertise. These were then noted on a color-coded name tag to help consultants find the people they wanted to meet. "It's a device we use regularly at Creative Connections events," Staver observed. "It helps break the ice and expedites the process of finding the people you really want to meet." Throughout the day the staff of Creative Connections circulated throughout the hall also facilitating introductions. "We wanted no wall flowers," Lant noted.

Over a sit-down lunch, all the exhibitors (there were 15) were introduced and asked to say a few words about their exhibit and the services they provide. "I appreciated the consideration of being asked to speak," said Rusty McGowan, president of Star Associates of Boston, which both exhibited and handled the printing of the Premium Package. "All too often convention exhibitors are treated like second-class citizens. But not here!"

"I've been an exhibitor myself," Lant said, "and both Maya and I were adamant about doing all that we could do to facilitate the business prospects of those who displayed at the Consultants Convention. Besides, these people were offering an incredible array of services — from suites of downtown offices to investment counsel — and often at special convention prices."

Something else special occurred at the convention. Massachusetts Governor Edward King, who has made it a point of his administration to stimulate business through his "Make It In Massachusetts" campaign, sent Michael J. DeVito, Executive Deputy Commission, Department of Commerce and Development, to present Lant and Staver with gubernatorial citations for creating the innovative business forum for consultants. Staver's citation read: "In recognition of her contribution to stimulating a healthy business climate for entrepreneurs and independent contractors and for her continuing support for the role of the individual in generating new and increased opportunities for business."

It was an apt citation for the entire Boston Consultants Convention.

(617) 547-6372
50 FOLLEN STREET, SUITE 507 • CAMBRIDGE, MASSACHUSETTS 02138

SAMPLE ARTICLE ON EVENT CO-SPONSORED BY YOU OR FEATURING YOU

THE BOSTON GLOBE SATURDAY, JUNE 26, 1982

A guide to fundraising when funds are scarce

By Fred Biddle
Contributing Reporter

The recession has made the successful fundraiser not so much an ambitious cajoler as it has made him a realist, more than 60 boosters of nonprofit groups found out at a series of panels and seminars in Cambridge this week.

"Don't tell me you're going to reform the world for $10,000," said Jeffrey L. Lant, a consultant who has fashioned a career of telling charities, worthy causes and dreamers of the day how to grab big bucks at a time when they are simply not to be had. "To raise $20,000 of operating money when you've never raised a penny will be difficult."

Lant was addressing group representatives at Cambridge College yesterday in the final session of "Fund Raising for Non-Profit Organizations," a five-day how-to workshop in the business of fundraising that, at $300 a head, mainly attracted representatives of small, Boston groups that Lant says "didn't have access" to corporations and philanthropists.

But this week the groups gained that access, if only for a short time: In addition to hearing instructors such as Lant, who prescribed elaborate management setups for the groups as the most efficient (and successful) means of raising money, the groups faced off each day to hear such people as Elizabeth McCormack of Rockefeller Family Associates, and Davis Taylor, retired chairman of the board of Affiliated Publications.

Those panelists were "candid" in telling the group representatives what they looked for, said Cindy Kartch, a participant in the seminars and a student in the preparatory program for the master's degree in education at Cambridge.

"Young people with high ideals are a dime a dozen," she said, but being able to campaign in the financial world for those ideals is another matter. For that reason, this week's seminars would help lend skills "I feel I could add to my resume," she said.

MEDIA ACTIVITY CHART

NAME OF MEDIA SOURCE	CONTACT PERSON	TITLE	ADDRESS	TELEPHONE	SOMEONE I KNOW WHO KNOWS CONTACT	DATE OF FIRST CONTACT	TYPE	SUBSEQUENT CONTACT	RESULT

Essentials Of The Query Letter To An Editor About Forthcoming Anniversary, Commemoration, &c.

• Letter should be typed on your office stationery.

• In first paragraph, mention the reason you are writing, e.g. that an appropriate anniversary, &c. is forthcoming. Send this letter about 30 days in advance of the event. Enclose information about the forthcoming event if it is available.

• In paragraph 2, suggest what you'd like and also what your connection to the story will be. If you feel at all hesitant about suggesting an article solely about yourself, recommend a Package Article dealing with several individuals.

• In paragraph 3, suggest what aspect of your activities you would like covered. Enclose appropriate information about them, including brochures, leave behinds, articles by and about you, &c.

• In paragraph 4, advise the editor that you can make appropriate referrals to other individuals who are connected to the topic. Do not include their names and addresses in this initial letter; wait until the editor has expressed interest in the subject.

• Indicate how you will follow-up this letter. It is your responsibility to do so and to work with the editor to create an appropriate promotional vehicle.

Note: This same format can be used for any query to print media sources.

SAMPLE QUERY LETTER TO AN EDITOR ABOUT FORTHCOMING ANNIVERSARY, COMMEMORATION, &c.

Dear Editor:

Thursday, November 17 is American Enterprise Day. Established twenty-five years ago by the American Enterprise Foundation, this day is designed to draw attention to the role of the free enterprise system in American life, and, at the local level, provocative enterprises which are generating pivotal new ideas. I enclose background information from the American Enterprise Foundation.

I am writing to you today as president of a local small business to suggest an article on November 17 on several local enterprises which best epitomize the kinds of people and organizations helping create and maintain our free enterprise system. I would like to be included in this article.

Specifically, I would like to comment on my publishing house which publishes books of interest to small business owners. I enclose information on this work.

If it would be helpful to you, I am prepared to bring to your attention the names, addresses, and telephone numbers of several other local entrepreneurs who are making a real impact not just on this town but more generally.

I'd like to follow up this letter by telephoning you next week and discussing what kind of article might be of greatest interest to you.

I look forward to our conversation.

Sincerely,

Unabashed Self-Promoter

Essentials Of A Letter To A Journalist Not Returning Your Call, Answering Your Letter

• This letter follows an earlier letter introducing yourself and a series of telephone calls (usually three) designed to make direct contact with a journalist or other media source.

• Type letter on your stationery.

• Mention in first paragraph the background to the current situation, your subject area, the kind of article you are seeking, and date of first contact.

• In paragraph 2, mention the exact number of calls you have already made. Bring this number to the journalist's attention in such a way that he can say, if sufficiently brazen, that he hasn't received the messages.

• In paragraph 3, ask whether the journalist would like to telephone you. Include your number.

• In paragraph 4, bring to journalist's attention anything which has happened to you since first writing that would enhance your credibility and desirability. If this involves other, noncompetitive print media, enclose leave behinds. If other media are involved, advise journalist how materials can be made available.

• In final paragraph, indicate that you will call again if you have not heard from journalist in a reasonable period. It is your job to be persistent!

SAMPLE LETTER TO JOURNALIST NOT RETURNING YOUR CALL, ANSWERING YOUR LETTER

Dear Journalist:

As you may remember, I wrote to you three weeks ago concerning the possibility of an interview on my work with therapeutic massage. It seems to me that such an article might make an interesting part of your current series on health.

I have since attempted to call you on three separate occasions since writing to follow up my letter. Have you been receiving these messages?

Perhaps it would be more convenient if you telephoned me. If so, my work number is 678-9950. You may also reach me in the evenings at 548-9934.

I would also like to point out that since writing I gave a talk on therapeutic massage to the local Kiwanis club. This talk was enthusiastically received as you can see from the enclosed notice taken from their newsletter. I also have an audio cassette of this talk available in case you should be interested in hearing the presentation.

If I don't hear from you within a few days, I'll try again to contact you.

Sincerely,

Unabashed Self-Promoter

Essentials Of A Letter Offering A Syndicated Feature

- Call to get name, address of editor. This letter needs to be sent to a specific individual.

- Type on your stationery.

- In paragraph 1, mention the name of your feature. Indicate that you have done your homework by telling the editor you have reviewed his publicaton in advance of writing. It is as a result of this review that you you have decided to write.

- In paragraph 2, indicate whether there are others carrying your feature. If so, feel perfectly free to mention their names. *N.B.* Competing media will not carry the same features. Indicate in this paragraph the length of the proposed feature, how often you propose to do it, and when the publication can expect to receive it.

- In paragraph 3, state your payment terms. If you are willing to be paid in advertising space, say so. Ask for more space than the cash value of your column. Your ads, for maximum effect, should run alternately with your features.

- In paragraph 4, indicate that you are willng to start your relationship by offering to have the editor print, without fee, the articles you have sent. In this case, make sure you've written yourself a good free ad to conclude your article.

- Conclude by indicating how you will follow-up this letter.

SAMPLE LETTER OFFERING SYNDICATED FEATURE

Dear Editor:

Please find enclosed two of my recent columns entitled "Tax Planning for the Individual" and the typescript for my next column. I have reviewed your publication with interest but believe you carry nothing along the lines of the enclosed feature. I would, therefore, like to propose it to you as an ongoing feature.

Currently "Tax Planning for the Individual" runs in two other publications. The column runs twice each month and averages 650 words. I send them a week in advance of publication.

I offer these columns at $10 for each article published. Since some publications prefer to pay in ad space, I request $25 in ad space with the ads to run alternately to the columns.

To begin matters, I would be glad to have you run any of the enclosed columns compliments of me. If you wish to run a photograph along with this column, I will be happy to send a standard 5" x 7" head shot.

To see about your interest, I shall telephone you next week.

Sincerely,

Unabashed Self-Promoter

Essentials Of A Letter To A Newsletter Editor Asking Him To Reprint An Article By You

• This letter should be sent as soon as possible following publication of the original article and production of leave behinds.

• Letter should be offset print on your stationery. It is not necessary to personalize this letter.

• In first paragraph, mention the subject of the article, where it was first printed and when.

• In second paragraph, give the reasons why the newsletter readers will be interested in the topic. Indicate that as a result of this interest, you would like to offer the publication the opportunity of reprinting the piece.

• In third paragraph, make in known that if newsletter has a remuneration scale, you would like to be paid at the standard rate. *N.B.* Most newsletters do *not* pay for material. If there is not to be cash payment, propose to be paid in ad space. Also indicate that you would like complete follow-up information to be printed. This information should include:

- name of product
- cost
- your company name
- address
- telephone number
- your name
- biographical tag

• In fourth paragraph, indicate that if space limitations preclude publication of complete article, you give permission to edit so long as sense is maintained *and* complete follow-up information is published. Also indicate that if source is interested in subject but not in the article as it stands, you are happy to provide a commissioned piece.

• Finally, ask for a copy of the issue in which your article appears.

SAMPLE LETTER TO A NEWSLETTER EDITOR ASKING HIM TO REPRINT AN ARTICLE BY YOU

Dear Newsletter Editor:

Please find enclosed a copy of a recent article of mine concerning unabashed self-promotion. This article lists helpful public relations information for anyone with a message they want America to hear, anyone with a product they want America to buy. It appears in the current issue of the Independent Computer Consultants Association Magazine.

It occurs to me that your readers, too, will be interested in how to secure free publicity from the media. Hence, I would like to offer you the possibility of reprinting this piece to which I hold all rights.

If you have a standard rate of remuneration, I would be grateful if, upon publication, you would remit it. If not, I am happy to give you the opportunity to publish this piece, if:

- You would remunerate me in ad space;
- You would run the box at the conclusion of the article. This box has complete follow-up information for your readers.

If space limitations preclude publishing the entire article, I hereby grant permission for you to edit so long as the sense of the piece is maintained and complete follow-up information is included. If you find the current form of this article somehow inappropriate for your publication but are interested in the subject, I would be happy to write something exclusively for you. Please let me know.

If you do use some or all of this article, please be good enough to send me, upon publication, a copy of the issue in which it appears.

Many thanks for your consideration.

Sincerely,

Unabashed Self-Promoter

Essentials Of A Letter To A Newsletter Editor Offering Cooperative Marketing Agreement

- This letter follows the publication of one of your articles in which a *product* was featured.

- It should be typewritten on your stationery and sent about 30 days after publication. You must allow time for reader response.

- In the first paragraph, thank the editor for publishing your article. Add a specific compliment concerning the lay-out, type face, printing, &c. to set the tone of the letter.

- In the second paragraph, mention the brisk response you have had to the article. I tend not to mention the exact number of those responding; do so if the number is impressive.

- In paragraph 3, mention that you would like to enter into a Cooperative Marketing Agreement. If you have such agreements with other organizations, &c it is perfectly appropriate to mention them by name.

- In paragraph 4, discuss the specifics of the Cooperative Marketing Agreement, exactly what the publishing source does and exactly what you do.

- In paragraph 5, discuss how the responses will be handled. Also state the specific percentages which will accrue to the publisher for sales he generates.

- In paragraph 6, state what you will do to follow-up this letter.

N.B. JLA maintains *many* cooperative marketing agreements. Readers interested in discussing one with us are encouraged to get in touch.

SAMPLE LETTER TO A NEWSLETTER EDITOR OFFERING COOPERATIVE MARKETING AGREEMENT

Dear Newsletter Editor:

Thank you for publishing my article on unabashed self-promotion in your current issue. I am especially taken with the lay-out which is most distinctive.

Since the article appeared, we have had a very brisk response from your readers for both our public relations services and **The Unabashed Self-Promoter's Guide**, so brisk in fact that I have a proposal for you.

As you may know, we maintain cooperative marketing agreements with many publications, and individuals who distribute our products in return for a percentage of the sale. I think both our organizations would benefit from such an agreement.

Under our standard Cooperative Marketing Agreement, you provide advertising space on a regular basis to promote our products. I'm sure **The Unabashed Self-Promoter's Guide** would be one of particular interest. We provide the ad copy.

Responses to the ad may either be returned to you (whereupon you deduct your percentage and send the remainder with fulfillment information to us) or directly to us. In the latter case, we will remit an appropriate percentage to you along with a regular monthly accounting. In the case of our books, you receive 30% of the sale price if we fulfill orders; 40% if you fulfill orders yourself.

To discuss this arrangement, I shall call your office in ten business days. I look forward to further productive dealings.

Sincerely,

Unabashed Self-Promoter

Essentials Of A Query Letter To An Electronic Media Source

Note: This letter can be adapted as the standard query letter to any media source. The difference is that a print media source will probably not be interested in an audio cassette.

- Address this letter to a specific individual. Be sure to include his proper title.

- Type on your letterhead.

- In first paragraph, indicate the general subject on which you wish to speak and where you would like to make your presentation. (Producers, for instance, often handle several programs.)

- In paragraph 2, present more detailed information about your topic. What is it? What issues does it involve? Why would people be interested? Why is this topic appropriate for this show?

- In paragraph 3, indicate what materials you have enclosed which throw further light on both your background, the subject you propose to address, and its importance to the audience. If you have additional leave behinds from media sources, be sure to enclose them. They give you both third-party validation and legitimacy. If you have an audio cassette available, whatever the source, so indicate.

- In paragraph 4, indicate whether you have flexibility in scheduling your interview or not. Indicate as much flexibility as you possibily can.

- Conclude with an indication of how you intend to follow-up this letter. Remember: Once you have written this letter, it is your responsibility to pursue the source until you have had a final "Yes!" or "No!"

SAMPLE QUERY LETTER TO AN ELECTRONIC MEDIA SOURCE

Dear Producer:

Please find enclosed information about my work as a marriage counselor. I think this would make an interesting segment on the "Max Williams Show."

As you see from the enclosed materials, my work as a marriage counselor touches on many facets of life today. Common issues in my work include: communication, empathy, sex, and children. I deal with those who have been married for many years. I also deal with those in common law marriages, those in open relationships, and those whose views on marriage have shifted over time. Given the demographics of your audience, I think that many would be interested in these common marriage issues.

I would very much like to come on the "Max Williams Show" and take calls from the audience on their problems. To aid you in making your decision I am enclosing:

- biographical information on me

- background information about my business including general information on marriage counseling.

I am also enclosing a copy of an article about me based on a speech I recently gave to the local Rotary Club. This speech is available on an audio cassette in case you would like to hear it.

As I am based locally, I have considerable flexibility about when I would appear. I shall be happy to arrange a time at your convenience.

I shall follow-up this letter with a telephone call in ten days.

Sincerely,

Unabashed Self-Promoter

Essentials Of The Letter To An Organization's President Or Program Chairman From A Contact Seeking To Have You Invited To Speak

N.B. It is up to you, the unabashed self-promoter, to request that the person with the contact activate it on your behalf. As soon as you have decided the organization is appropriate for you, do so.

- This letter may go either on the writer's personal or official stationery.

- If possible, in first paragraph it should refer to the fact that the organization's officer to whom sender is writing has requested speaker suggestions.

- In second paragraph, bring forward connections of writer to suggested speaker. This paragraph begins to establish the potential speaker as an individual of consequence, the kind of individual the organizaton ought to have as a speaker.

- The third paragraph gives further information about the recommended speaker, mentioning subject to be addressed. If there is any question about whether this topic would be of interest to the membership, address it here.

- In the fourth paragraph, the writer indicates what follow-up to this letter he has suggested. Will he call the decision maker, or has he suggested that the potential speaker, you, call? This paragraph should also introduce the subject of publicity, framing it in such a way that your public relations skills are seen as a decided benefit to the organization. If you have leave behinds which confirm your promotional expertise make sure these are made available to person recommending you so that they may be sent to decision maker.

- This letter needs to be followed up within ten business days.

SAMPLE LETTER TO AN ORGANIZATION'S PRESIDENT OR PROGRAM CHAIRMAN FROM A CONTACT SEEKING TO HAVE YOU INVITED TO SPEAK

Dear Organization President:

You have several times asked members of our group to suggest speakers of interest. I have found one who I am most enthusiastic about and who I want to bring to your attention: Mary Smith.

I have known Mary for many years. During that time she and I have often discused her absorbing interest in micro-computers, a field in which she is very well versed.

More recently Mary has established a consulting service which, among other things, offers training programs to new computer users. With this in mind, I think Mary could give us a most interesting program on "When You Need A Computer, How To Use It Once You've Got It."

I've asked Mary to call and discuss with you directly the possibility of speaking to our organization. In case you wish to call her first, however, her office number is 548-8765. One real plus in her working with us, beyond her grasp of an important subject and good communications skills, is her knowledge about the publicity process. I think as a result of her talk, we could get some badly needed press. As you can see from the enclosed materials, her recent talk to the Weston Country Club helped them!

In any event, you should be hearing from Mary soon. I'm sure you'll enjoy meeting her.

Sincerely,

Friend of Unabashed Self-Promoter

Essentials Of The Letter To Your Professional Association Requesting That You Be Invited To Make A Presentation

- Call ahead to get the name, address, and telephone number of the program chairman.

- Type the letter on your stationery.

- In the first paragraph, mention that you are a member of the association. If you have been a member for any length of time, say so. Also state the purpose of your letter, e.g. to speak on a given topic. Name that topic.

- In paragraph 2, mention other recent speaking engagements particularly if they concern the same topic. Were they well received? Say so! Enclose appropriate leave behinds on your presentations.

- In paragraph 3, state your preferred presentation format. Also, go into greater detail about what you will talk about. Mention that you will work with the organization to make your engagement a mutually rewarding public relations opportunity. Say that you are willing to draft an appropriate media release, &c. Also indicate that you have a photograph available for the newsletter.

- Indicate how you will follow-up this letter.

SAMPLE LETTER TO YOUR PROFESSIONAL ASSOCIATION REQUESTING THAT YOU BE INVITED TO MAKE A PRESENTATION

Dear Program Chairman:

I have been a member of the Advertising Club for 6 years and have often attended many interesting and informative programs. Now I think I have something of equal value which I would like to share with the members, namely a lecture on "How To Get On Radio."

As you will notice from the enclosed materials, I have recently made presentations to two local organizations on this topic, the Library Association and the Chamber of Commerce. Both, as you will note, were very well received. Now I would like to make some of my information available to our professional group.

What I propose is a one-hour presentation, 45 minutes of lecture, 15 minutes of questions on the ways members can get on the radio and use this appearance as a source of free advertising. I will work with the organization to insure that there is adequate information about the event; if you are interested, I can draft an appropriate media release. I would also appreciate an item being run in our newsletter. I have a photograph which can accompany this piece.

I shall call you next week and discuss my appearance, arrange an appropriate date, and begin discussing the publicity.

I feel sure that my fellow members will feel the topic and my presentation not only useful but enjoyable.

Sincerely,

Unabashed Self-Promoter

Essentials Of The Letter To An Organization Where You Have Spoken Asking To Do The Program Again At The Next Available Meeting

Note: If the current program chairman is not handling the next program, send the current chairman a thank-you note. Get the name, address, and telephone number of the next chairman and address this letter to him. Send a copy of this letter to the current chairman along with your thank-you note.

- This letter may either be typed or hand written. It is, after all, ostensibly a thank-you note.

- In the first paragraph, begin by thanking the program chairman for his help and for the opportunity he afforded you. Tell him what kind of reaction you have had. Share a particularly enthusiastic letter about your presentation.

- In the second paragraph, broach the subject of the *next* meeting. Indicate that you are available. If you want to present another topic (either solely or in addition to the one you have just done), say so.

- In the third paragraph, indicate when you will be back in touch.

- End with yet another expression of your gratitude.

SAMPLE LETTER TO AN ORGANIZATION WHERE YOU HAVE SPOKEN ASKING TO DO THE PROGRAM AGAIN AT THE NEXT AVAILABLE MEETING

Dear Program Chairman:

I am happy to have the opportunity to write and thank you for permitting me to speak before the regional meeting of the New England Visiting Nursing Association. I have had several telephone calls already and many kind remarks. I am also enclosing a copy of one of the letters I've received. This made me feel quite good. It is always a pleasant feeling to be so lavishly complimented!

It seems to me that given this kind of response, it is worth thinking about repeating the presentation next year at the next regional meeting. Since I understand that you are again arranging this meeting, I hope you will keep me in mind.

Since you asked me to participate in this year's meeting about two months before it occurred, I'd like to be in touch with you at the same time next year to discuss how we can make this year's program even better. I'll call you, therefore, March 15.

Again, many thanks.

Sincerely,

Unabashed Self-Promoter

Essentials Of The Letter Of Recommendation From An Organization Where You Have Made A Presentation

- Request this letter as soon after your presentation as possible. Before you leave the lecture site, intimate that you would like such a letter.

- The letter should be placed on the organization's letterhead.

- In the first paragraph, the writer should mention your name, the date of your speech, the name of the organization addressed, the kind of meeting, and the topic of your presentation.

- In paragraph 2, the writer should begin to show how worthwhile the presentation was.

- In paragraph 3, the writer should indicate how professional you were to work with particularly with regard to public relations. It is important that some mention of your public relations skills be in a letter of recommendation because your desire to have further publicity will then seem perfectly nature to subsequent organizations. As it should be. Writer should mention what kind of publicity resulted from your assistance.

- In paragraph 4, the writer deals with your speaking skills. If there was an evaluation, the writer may quote from it. If a review was published, writer should mention it.

- In paragraph 5, mention should be made of the materials you distributed to the audience and how you handled the important question period.

- The writer should conclude by mentioning the amount of your fee, if any, the value of your presentation to the audience, and whether you will be invited back.

Note: Feel perfectly free to give a copy of this sample letter and list of essentials to the program chairman of the first organization where you speak. It'll give him the idea of what kind of recommendation letter you'd like.

SAMPLE LETTER OF RECOMMENDATION FROM AN ORGANIZATION WHERE YOU HAVE MADE A PRESENTATION

To Whom It May Concern:

I am writing on behalf of Curtis Smith, who on April 13, 1983 addressed a monthly meeting of the Boston Computer Society. His topic was "Making Computers User Friendly."

Although I had not before this meeting had the pleasure of meeting Curt, his reputation preceeded him. It proved, if anything, understated.

First, I would like to say that it was a real pleasure working with a pro like Curt in advance of the meeting. He worked closely with us to get outside publicity, and he provided us with excellent copy (and a photograph) for our in-house publication. As a result of working with him, we received considerable advance publicity including a radio interview. The speech itself was, therefore, well attended.

Those who came had, I'm sure, a superb evening. Curt is a rousing speaker, engaging, informative, humorous. An evaluation form we distributed after his presentation confirmed this as did a review which was published in a follow-up issue of our newsletter.

Curt also made available many materials for the audience, which numbered 100, and was willing to take questions — which he fielded admirably.

In conclusion, I would like to say that I feel Curt's fee of $250 was well worth it and that we will have him back in the future.

Sincerely,

Program Chairman

Essentials Of The Adult Education Marketing Letter

- Call to get correct name, title, address.

- Type letter on your stationery.

- In first paragraph, state why you are writing and the name of your proposed course. If you have not yet thought up a catchy title, at least mention the subject.

- In paragraph 2, state what format you are recommending and the topics which the course will cover.

- In paragraph 3, give an indication of what materials the course will utilize. Whenever possible use your own. After all you're the expert!

- In paragraph 4, give some of your credentials. If it is not clear why these have prepared you to teach the course, say why you are. You need not submit a résumé at this time, just an indication that you are in fact qualified to be the instructor.

- In paragraph 5, indicate when you will be in touch to schedule an appointment where all the remaining particulars can be discussed.

SAMPLE ADULT EDUCATION MARKETING LETTER

Dear Dean of Continuing Education:

I am writing today with a proposed workshop entitled "Establishing And Operating Your Successful Consulting Business." Having perused your current catalog, I find you have no comparable course, and I hope, therefore, you would consider mine.

This course is a one-day, intensive workshop. It covers the following topics:

- the world of the consultant
- pro's and con's for the new consultant to consider
- how to find your consulting niche
- the essentials of marketing your consultancy
- how to use the media to become *the* recognized expert in your field
- how to create *ad hoc* and standardized proposals
- the essentials of consulting contracts
- the consultant on the job: structuring your consultancy for success
- where to locate your office, how to run it
- incorporation? partnership? sole proprietorship?

The course materials will include Dr. Jeffrey Lant's well-known book on consulting. Entitled **The Consultant's Kit,** this book is now in a sixth printing. In addition I shall supplement this book with materials based on my own consulting practice.

I am the president of a local management consulting company (information enclosed). I have five years of on-the-job experience in addition to a B.A. in economics and an M.B.A. from the University of Wisconsin.

I think this class would best be offered as a noncredit workshop, although I am open to other suggestions. I have prepared other materials concerning this course which I shall be happy to send once you have expressed an initial interest. To see about this interest and to schedule an appointment at which we can discuss all the specific matters pertaining to this course, I shall telephone you next week.

Sincerely,

Unabashed Self-Promoter

Essentials Of An Introductory Letter To A Lecture Agent

Essentials Of An Introductory Letter To A Lecture Agent

- Call ahead to make sure you are sending the letter to the right person: the individual who reviews new talent.

- In the first paragraph, indicate that you have experience, e.g. that you have addressed important organizations (by name) and that you have been paid.

- In paragraph 2, give the names of your regular presentations or fields in which you are competent to speak. Enclose information which gives further details about your areas of expertise. If your fields are in any way obscure or technical, explain why they are particularly salable just now.

- In paragraph 3, indicate what else you have available that proves you are a good speaker, e.g. technically competent, and, if you're smart, capable of making money for the lecture agent.

- In the next paragraph, indicate that you have letters of recommendation available and say whether you have been invited back.

- Conclude by telling the agent how you intend to follow-up this letter. Also, ask for basic information about the agent, if you don't already have it.

SAMPLE INTRODUCTORY LETTER TO A LECTURE AGENT

Dear Lecture Agent:

I should like to explore with you the possibility of my securing representation from your firm.

As you will notice from the enclosed materials, I have already had a good deal of experience addressing principally professional associations. In the last year alone I have made 15 presentations before such organizations as the American Fibre Board Association, the Lumberman's Association, and the New England regional meeting of the Cranberry Growers Association. I have been paid for most of these presentations.

Ordinarily I speak on one of three topics. These include:

- "Interest Rates: Up Or Down?"
- "James Watt: Friend Or Foe?"
- "The Long-Term Consequences of Trade With The Soviets"

I have enclosed articles which provide further information on each of these topics.

I should like you to know that in addition to the enclosed materials, I also have audio cassettes from each of my presentations and from the three radio programs which I have appeared on in the last 5 months. I can make these available at your convenience.

As you will see from the enclosed letters of recommendation written after my presentations, audience reaction has always been particularly strong. I have already returned to two of the organizations at their request to make follow-up presentations.

I shall telephone your office in the near future to schedule a meeting at which we can discuss representation. In the meantime, I should be grateful if you would send me basic information about your firm and its services.

Sincerely,

Unabashed Self-Promoter

Essentials Of A Letter Requesting A Day In Your Honor

- Get a friend to send this letter.

- Tell him who you want to contact on your behalf. If necessary, get him that individual's name, title, address, and telephone number.

- The letter should be typed on your friend's stationery.

- The first paragraph should deal with the achievements which merit recognition and why this is the time to honor them (e.g. upon retirement from post).

- Paragraph 2 deals with the honoring vehicle. This paragraph should make it clear when the date of honor is to be, what kind of honor you are suggesting, and that you want the individual being addressed to attend to make a presentation.

- Paragraph 3 may add additional information testifying to the worth of the individual being honored, specifically his connection to the writer.

- The final paragraph suggests how the follow-up will be handled.

SAMPLE LETTER REQUESTING A DAY IN YOUR HONOR

Dear Mayor:

Next month Don Smith retires from his post as PTA president. For the last three years Don has served as president and has given unstintingly of his time and resources. His presidency has been marked by many notable achievements not least by the inception of the high school scholarship fund.

Upon his retirement the town's school committee and the administration of both the junior and senior high schools is having a dinner in his honor. It is our hope that you will attend this dinner and will be willing to bring a proclamation making June 13 "Don Smith Day" in our town.

I have known Don Smith many years both as friend and colleague. More recently I have worked with him as treasurer of the PTA. I am therefore most enthusiastic about the forthcoming event.

I'll call you next week to ascertain your interest and to schedule an appointment where we can work out the details.

I look forward to speaking with you.

Sincerely,

Colleague of Unabashed Self-Promoter

SAMPLE PIGGYBACK ARTICLE, RELEASE BY YOU, AND THE RESULTING ARTICLE

THE BOSTON GLOBE
APRIL 6, 1983

King gets job as consultant

By Chris Black
Globe Staff

Former governor Edward J. King, who has been seeking a full-time job since leaving office in January, took a part-time post yesterday with an exclusive group of senior consultants at Hill and Knowlton, an international public relations firm.

King will become part of a group made up of leaders in various fields who work with the company's top corporate clients as consultants, the company said in its announcement.

"They want to establish a presence here in the Northeast. My initial efforts will be directed to that end," said King at the Commonwealth avenue office he has established.

Hill and Knowlton, the world's largest public relations and public affairs counseling firm, opened a Boston office six weeks ago and is making a marketing push to win clients from the region's high technology industries. As governor, King was strongly supported by large segments of the industry.

James A. Baar, senior vice president and manager of the company's new northeastern regional office in Boston, described King as "a major addition" to the senior consultants' group. Other members

■ KING
Continued from Page 1

of the group include Douglas MacArthur II, former ambassador to Japan and Iran; Najeeb E. Halaby, former head of Pan American World Airways; and Liz Carpenter, Lady Bird Johnson's press secretary during former President Johnson's White House years.

"His [King's] background is really excellent for this," said Baar in a telephone interview. "Not only was he governor of Massachusetts, but for 15 years he was treasurer, comptroller and executive director of Massport and head of the New England Council. He was very much involved with the business world and is a very knowledgeable fellow."

He said the company approached King several weeks ago.

King is the first senior consultant hired to work out of the new Boston office, Baar said. Neither he nor King would disclose King's salary.

Baar said the position is a part-time job and King will continue to serve on four corporate boards of directors in addition to working with Hill and Knowlton clients. King serves on the boards of the Baird Corp., the Nautilus Fund, Cambridge Plating Co. and E. C. Hilliard.

King was defeated by Gov. Michael S. Dukakis in the Democratic primary election last September. Since leaving office in January, he has been looking for a job and has expressed an interest in finding a full-time position as a chief executive officer for a private company.

Yesterday the former governor said he is still looking for a full-time position but added that the new part-time job may keep him busy enough.

"Chief executive officer positions just don't happen because I lost an election," he said.

As time passes, he said, his prospects of joining the administration of President Ronald Reagan have dwindled. "The opportunity has faded and that is fine. There really is no rush" to take a full-time job, he said.

Asked if he is considering another run for governor, he said, "It depends upon what I am doing." If he makes a commitment to accept a demanding full-time job, he said, another campaign is less likely than if he continues to work on a number of part- time projects.

"It depends on how the state is going, whether there are significant tax increases, how the state economy is, how the political climate seems to be for a moderate," he added.

He said he still had many political supporters. "We got a lot of votes. Of course, the present governor got more. We understand that," he said.

Lant On King As Consultant

Cambridge. Dr. Jeffrey Lant, author of the national best-seller **THE CONSULTANT'S KIT: ESTABLISHING AND OPERATING YOUR SUCCESSFUL CONSULTING BUSINESS,** today welcomed former Massachusetts Governor Edward King to the consulting profession and congratulated him on his appointment as Senior Consultant to the public relations firm of Hill and Knowlton.

Lant, 36-year-old president of a Cambridge consulting firm providing technical assistance to nonprofit organizations, called King "a superlative addition to the ranks of America's consultants." Lant cited King's track record both as former Executive Director of MassPort and as governor and said, "His clients will be very lucky to get him."

Lant, featured last November in the new book **MAVERICK: SUCCEEDING AS A FREE-LANCE ENTREPRENEUR,** said King would be "one of the select few consultants to begin as a Mandarin consultant not just a technical assistant." Lant said Mandarin consultants are those who give advice but do not implement it, while technical assistants have to implement their own recommendations.

Lant said, however, that there were probably a few tricks of the trade which King still probably didn't know. The Harvard-educated Lant said these tricks are included in his best-selling book. "Has King read the book yet?," Lant was asked. "I'm not sure," the engaging young entrepreneur said, "so I sent him a copy with my compliments." Lant also announced that he has invited King to be his guest at his next all-day training session for consultants. It will take place May 7 at the Boston Park Plaza Hotel.

THE BOSTON GLOBE MONDAY, APRIL 11, 1983

PEOPLE & PLACES

BY MARGO MILLER

Edward J. King got his first lesson in horning in on someone else's publicity, not from his new firm, Hill & Knowlton, but from a publicist who shall remain nameless. This publicist, who has a business consulting firm in Cambridge, took the occasion of King's new job to issue a press release "welcoming" the former governor of Massachusetts to the profession and "congratulating" him on his appointment as a senior consultant at Hill & Knowlton. King "is a superlative addition to the ranks of America's consultants," said the publicist. The press release goes on to ask a question (whether King has read the publicist's book on consulting) and gives the publicist's own answer: "I'm not sure, so I sent him a copy with my compliments." The publicist also announced that he has invited King to be his guest at his next all-day training session for consultants.

Adjusting to life without television

By Leah Rosch
Special to The Globe

I guess you could say that I'm a bona fide card-carrying member of a minority. Whether it's a religious minority or a political one or one as traumatizing as the she-didn't-attend-her-senior-prom minority, I am counted among the ranks of the few. Yet, no minority to date has left me feeling so much of an alien and produced as many lifestyle adjustments as the one I recently joined.

According to the A.C. Nielsen Company, there are 1,460,000 of us. That's a mere .6 percent of the American population who don't own a television set. I am not in the low-income bracket – or so says the IRS – so it isn't that I can't afford one. I am hardly a highbrow who believes that watching TV is one of the basest of pastimes. Nor is my schedule too busy to allow me the time to sit down in front of the television. I am merely a creature of circumstance, and when, two months ago, the picture tube of my 10-year-old Sears' black and white blew, I just never got around to replacing the empty space left on my bookshelf.

As a member of the first generation to grow up on the video medium, I thought a TV set as essential as hot and cold running water. When I went to college, I took a part-time job in a bookstore and used my first paycheck as a deposit on my very own television set. And I had had it ever since.

Television inspired the cheap-date syndrome in college. There was never a need to venture out on a Saturday night, not with the "All in the Family-M*A*S*H-Mary Tyler Moore-Bob Newhart-Carol Burnett Show" lineup. We would situate ourselves in front of the set at 8 and stay glued to it until 11.

Once I became part of the working world, television determined my workday schedule. I diligently plugged away at the typewriter all morning, knowing that if I reached some level of accomplishment by 1, I could reward myself with an hour soap break. I would sit mesmerized by the perils of the "All My Children" gang. If I missed that intermission, I made sure to catch the afternoon talk show continuum. I could always count on Mike and Merv to give me more trivial information in their combined three hours than I could ever have hoped to gain on my own. In fact, precious hours were wasted each morning as I pored over the TV Guide, trying to determine which TV-break would prove more profitable for that day.

My nighttime viewing selections offered a bit more in the way of intellectual stimulation. I have a passion for old movies. Thus, any feature film from the '40s or musical from the '50s being aired on television received my attention, regardless of the hour. "60 Minutes" became a Sunday evening tradition. And I was hooked on Masterpiece Theatre productions, particularly "Upstairs, Downstairs." There were times when I was more up to date with the goings-on in the Bellamy household than my own.

Old habits are hard to break, they say. My addiction to television ended cold turkey and did cause me to go through various phases of withdrawal. I am coping, but not without some interesting side effects.

I now find that I am not only talking to myself – something, I admit, I have always done – but I am talking *back* to myself, in lieu of having a TV to talk back to. I am also talking to my plants, carrying on long-winded discussions about Reagan's budget cuts and my views on nuclear proliferation. I think it's killing them. My cats seem to be suffering from distemper of late, as they, too, are privy to my monologues; I'm sure that's why I find them cowering in the corner the moment I set foot in the apartment.

The worst part has been feeling like an outsider with friends. I am forced to sit silent, listening to their TV-oriented conversations. "You didn't know Mrs. Pynchon (of "Lou Grant" fame) had a stroke?" a colleague asked me incredulously. I sheepishly confessed that I didn't, remembering how sad I had felt when Hazel of "Upstairs, Downstairs" died of Spanish influenza five years ago.

I now realize why some friends beg off from invitations to visit and why others come burdened down with a variety of table games.

But the news isn't all bad. I am no longer a hard-core insomniac, as I once believed. Because I work better late at night, I had myself convinced that it was impossible for me to fall asleep before the wee hours of the morning. Thus, "The Mary Tyler Moore Show" reruns in New York and I signed off simultaneously each night at 3 a.m. Now when I finish working, I can crawl into bed with a book and drift off with little trouble as early as midnight. That virtually puts me on schedule with the rest of the world.

I am also reading again. Not just the classics laden with dust from disuse on my bookshelves, but new and noteworthy volumes procured from the library. I have come to understand my 4th grade teacher's motto: "Your library card is your best friend."

My eating habits have changed, too. I no longer have evenings of marathon snacking, consisting of runs to the refrigerator with each commercial interval.

CONTENTED, Page 36

■ **CONTENTED**

Continued from Page 35

Dinner is suddenly an enjoyable venture. Before, I had 30 minutes to throw it together between the end of the nightly news and the start of prime time viewing. Now I actually think about what I'm going to wolf down.

Believe it or not, others in the non-TV minority, "normal" in every additional respect, are also surviving quiet well.

Quincy Cotten, assistant to the president of Autumn Press Publishers, is a deliberate non-television person. "I would never get one. I would lobby not to get one even if I were to live with someone who really wanted one," she said. Growing up in London, Cotten said that her parents didn't believe in TV. But she remembers that among her friends, more had televisions than telephones. "I don't know when I would have time to watch," Cotten pondered. "I leave work at the end of the day, go home, get myself a drink, put my feet up and read a newspaper or magazine and then get around to thinking about dinner. TV would interrupt my ability to do that. I guess that's why you have TV dinners," she concluded.

Peter and Jackie Gordon have been without their 17-inch Sony color television set since last August when it was stolen. They didn't replace the set immediately because they didn't want to spend the money, and eventually it was because "we got out of the habit," explained Dr. Gordon, a radiologist. "We used to do something that was fairly destructive," he said. "We would watch TV while eating dinner." "Now we may read the paper during dinner," chimed in Jackie, a projects manager at a testing company, "but at least we can talk to each other."

Ralph Long, an engineer, gave his set away eight years ago. "None of it is high quality. Even educational television, or what they call educational, is too low quality to learn anything from,' he said, adding, "I couldn't tolerate the commercials. I watched 'Shogun' last year, and only because we turned down the sound during commercial breaks was I able to get through it." Long contends that he communicates with people a lot better now. "You can't communicate with anybody or anything sitting in front of that box."

Greg Check, an accountant, parte with his 12-inch Sony two months ag and has every intention of continuing t live without it. "I feel better without it. was too easy to just sit down in front o the television and not think," h explained, continuing, "There really isn anything on TV worth watching. It's cheap escape."

"It's boring," said Jeffrey Lant, a consultant and author, when I asked why h didn't have a television. "I spend my tim more productively. I write a lot. And read. saw a survey that said the average perso reads four books a year; I read that man in a week." Lant does feel the need to a least appear to be part of the mainstream however. "I read the TV column in Th Globe so I can keep up on the shows an make the same inane comments as every one else." Would he ever consider buyin one? "Every year for the last 15 years, have said I would buy a television. Ther are times when one wishes to be brainles and bombarded by idiotic thoughts. But haven't bought one yet."

While our reasons for not owning a se may differ, we all agree that it is possibl to belong to the non-television faction an still lead a contented existence. Even in culture pervaded by television.

The only problem I have yet to lick i how to fill that empty space on m bookshelf.

SAMPLE PHOTOGRAPHIC RECEIVING LINE PICTURE

JUN 28 1983

NEWS-TRIBUNE
WALTHAM, MA
D. 14,047

Attend conference

Shown at a recent conference concerning how to raise funds for corporations and foundations held at Cambridge College, are, left to right: Dr. Jeffrey Lant, author of "Development ~~Today~~: A Guide for Non-Profit Organizations, Israel Jimenez of Waltham, John Neely of Waltham, Javier O. Caban of Waltham, Eileen Brown, president, Cambridge College.

HARVARD
Magazine

September-October 1982 *Volume 85, Number 1* *University edition*

Harvard on Harvard

Peter J. Gomes

Toby Marotta '67, Ph.D. '78, *Sons of Harvard: Gay Men from the Class of 1967*, William Morrow, $13.50

Jeffrey L. Lant, Ph.D. '77, editor, *Our Harvard*, Taplinger, $19.95

Diana Dubois, editor, *My Harvard, My Yale*, Random House, $15

Jeffrey L. Lant and Diana Dubois are no innovators, and their books are derived from earlier and more successful ones. Dubois's *My Harvard, My Yale* is an American spin-off of the English *My Oxford, My Cambridge*, and Lant's *Our Harvard: Reflections on College Life by Twenty-two Distinguished Graduates* is the cousin, if not the son, of Brooks Atkinson's *College in a Yard: Minutes by Thirty-nine Harvard Men*, published in 1957 (and currently being revised). Both Lant and Dubois are outsiders to the Harvard College experiences they have collected, although she has lived in Cambridge, and he, who took his Ph.D. from Harvard in 1977, was a resident tutor in Dudley House and energetic in undergraduate affairs. As a result, one senses that their search for the Harvard experience is not unlike that of Evelyn Waugh's Charles Ryder, in *Brideshead Revisited*, who seeks at Oxford "the low door in the garden wall." Lant says as much in his "Introductory Essay," an apostrophe to the Harvard College he never experienced—and that possibly never existed except in the annotated memories of some of his contributors. His Harvard is "a place where gifted young men are free to explore, free to fail without fear of repercussion, where casual brilliance is valued, where style is important, where there remain time and resources abundant enough to waste without remorse, where the focus is on a valued past and an exciting present, where undergraduates are not prematurely burdened shoring up security against an uncertain future." The present age is "this malign careerist trend," and he looks forward to the day when it will end: "Someday, guiltless undergraduates will again be free to indulge their untrammeled animal spirits and their exuberant, if unformed, intelligence." And when that next "golden age" of Harvard College dawns, says our redactor, "I plan to be here to savor it." Lant tends to be more optimistic about Harvard's past and its future than his contributors, nearly all of whom seem rather melancholy and dutiful. Only the truly angry and the truly sentimental have anything to say; the others are too sophisticated to be sentimental or too indifferent to be angry. The essays in both collections group themselves either around mentors or movements, with the older generation defining its Harvard in terms of memorable professors: Charles Townsend Copeland, Roger Bigelow ("Frisky") Merriman, Crane Brinton, and Perry Miller. Graduates of the last 25 years or so tend to define themselves in terms of the movements of which they were or were not a part, including remnants of the hateful McCarthyism, the civil-rights and anti-war movements, and the feminist and countercultural movements of the late Sixties and early Seventies. Lant's book does not acknowledge the existence of Radcliffe women at all, but Dubois has included several among her essayists: Marian Cannon Schlesinger '34, who liked Harvard; Alison Lurie '47, who did not; Faye Levine '65, famous for her Crimson article on "The Three Flavors of Radcliffe"; and Beth Gutcheon '67, who apparently is unaware that horsemeat can still be eaten at the Faculty Club.

Both collections contain some memorable moments. Buckminster Fuller '17, writing in *Our Harvard*, describes himself as possibly "the oldest living undergraduate." David McCord '21, in the same collection, concludes his characteristically deft essay on an uncharacteristically pessimistic note. Of his generation, he writes, "We never dreamed the world's smoke signals were in code. The code is now broken, and we read the dreadful summary: use freedom to kill freedom." Robert Coles '50 is the only person included in both collections, and the only current member of the College faculty in either. In *Our Harvard* he praises the exemplary humanity of his two greatest teachers, Perry Miller and Werner Jaeger, and the new life they gave, one to Puritan New England, and the other to ancient Greece: "I write, then, to acknowledge a privilege of my youth. . . . I am anxious to salute two guides, and, yes, to salute the place where they worked and worked."

HARVARD
Magazine

November-December 1982 *Volume 85, Number 2* *University edition*

Gomes on Harvard on Harvard

I can thank Peter Gomes, who is a scholarly professor of moral philosophy as well as the minister of Memorial Church, for noting the limits of my articulateness in trying to explain gay liberation ("Harvard on Harvard," September-October, page 8). What I object to in his review of my *Sons of Harvard* is his characterization of the gay classmates who help me there as "dreary." These individuals are among the boldest, most high-minded, most truly liberated and liberating Harvard men I've encountered during my nearly twenty years of involvement with the University. How many others would speak the truth about their most intimate feelings and experiences? How many others see that this, too, is in the Harvard tradition?

The only ones I've encountered lately are the good souls who tenderly and humorously recall their Harvard pasts in Jeffrey Lant's *Our Harvard*. Gomes's review dismisses all the contributors to this volume as "melancholy and dutiful. Only the truly angry and the truly sentimental have anything to say; the others are too sophisticated to be sentimental or too indifferent to be angry."

We gay Sons of Harvard may not be literate enough to meet Gomes's standards at every turn, but we are idealistic enough to be truly sentimental and angry when we see an important University official being inappropriately snobbish and condescending. We want Harvard to be concerned with promoting empathy, understanding, and compassion as well as with grading intelligence, articulateness, and style. And we want the Reverend Peter Gomes to live up to that title by seeing beyond the superficial when assessing fellow Harvards on Harvard.

TOBY MAROTTA '67

San Francisco

I know Peter Gomes and I like him (as who does not?). He is even favorably mentioned in my book *Our Harvard: Reflections on College Life by Twenty-two Distinguished Graduates*; John Adler, the youngest contributor, has him to the life. Perhaps because he is so favorably mentioned, he was fearful of overpraising the book. If this is the case, however, he has surely overcompensated. His review of my book bears little resemblance to the text. If I were the standard author of a standard volume, I might think twice about protesting the treatment, but as the editor of a flock of 22 eminent contributors it is, I think, my duty to complain.

The charges and errors, as is common in these cases, run from the picayune to the cosmic. Since they are interspersed in the review, I shall handle them similarly here.

Item: Our Harvard is derivative from a "more successful" volume, *College In A Yard*, published in 1957. It is true that both are collections of essays on Harvard College by Harvard men; nothing else is very similar. *College In A Yard* is an authorized book compiled by a dedicated partisan of the College; it has the strengths and all the weaknesses of authorized volumes. Its list of contributors is impressive (so is mine), but what they have to say is often thin. Indeed it is precisely because I was unhappy with this book that I ventured to propose another book handled in a different, more expansive fashion.

Item: Gomes criticizes my historical sense of the College and suggests that what he sees as my romanticized view of the Harvard past is due to the fact that I myself did not attend it and that the memories of my contributors have been "annotated." Perhaps it's just as well that he doesn't say from whence I have taken my view of Harvard (Gomes neglects to mention all but three of my contributors). My sense of Harvard's past is in this instance based on the considered opinions of these contributors: Buckminster Fuller, David McCord, John Finley, Thomas Boylston Adams, Robert Stuart Fitzgerald *et al*. Under the circumstances I find his opinion startling to say the least. Just where he gets his impression of the College in other days he doesn't say; he didn't go there either.

Item: "Lant's book does not acknowledge the existence of Radcliffe women at all." I need hardly remind Peter Gomes that no women have attended Harvard College. It would therefore have been impossible to include them as contributors in a book about the College. That my contributors chose not to concentrate on Radcliffe in their essays on their undergraduate careers is, I think, telling, but its precise significance I leave to sociologists who conjecture on such matters.

Item: Wrong selection of contributors. There is a lengthy passage in the Gomes piece on the categories of contributors I neglected to include. I anticipated this criticism and long ago found it beside the point. My book was never intended to be representative of everyone's Harvard College experience; indeed any such exercise strikes me as both fatuous and doomed to failure. Any editor assembling a volume on the College would necessarily get a rather different book. What I would have liked to see instead of a list of who was left out was a sense from the reviewer of who was included—and what he said. This is sadly lacking.

Item: "These new collections do not presume to be very much and hence are not." I leave it to the editor of *My Harvard, My Yale* to defend *her* book, but I say this of mine: I resent this statement and reject it. The objective of *Our Harvard* was to collect a body of distinguished, thoughtful individuals of polished style and give them the opportunity to reflect on the significance of their college days. Gomes may say that this is not much; I profoundly disagree. Age, when it brings considered perspective, is surely worth attending to even when one disagrees. Why else do we have colleges at all? Arthur Schlesinger, Thornton Bradshaw, John Simon, Anton Myrer, Robert Coles, Peter Prescott, Erich Segal, John Spooner, Jonathan Larsen, and the rest of my contributors have this perspective and their words—often hauntingly beautiful—are very much worth having.

Item: My class year. I received my Ph.D. in '75 not '77. This is a small matter but perhaps (as is it repeated incorrectly twice in the piece) a telltale indication of how *Our Harvard* as a whole was read.

JEFFREY LANT

Cambridge

SAMPLE NEGATIVE MEDIA ON SUBJECT OF INTEREST TO YOU AND THE RESPONSE

THE BOSTON GLOBE MONDAY, MAY 2, 1983

When stalking MBAs, firms play hardball

By Steve Curwood
Globe Staff

"Call me tomorrow if you're interested in working at Bain," the Harvard business student was told recently at the end of a summer job interview, and so began a storm of controversy.

Giving a student less than 24 hours to respond befits the reputation of Bain and Co. as an occasional spitballer in the hardball game of MBA recruitment. But instead of quickly landing the recruit, Bain found itself being investigated by the student government council.

Last month the council asked Bain to stop the high-pressured tactic. The management consulting firm denied any wrongdoing but agreed to reopen all offers anyway.

Aggressive recruiting of masters of business administration – especially by financial service companies such as investment banks and consultants – has become a serious problem for the nation's top business schools. Faculty find the recruiters disruptive. And students, already under the pressure of a rigorous curriculum, must deal with the lure of high-paying jobs as early as the second semester of their first year.

Moreover, there is a fear that some business schools are evolving into mere finishing schools for the consulting and investment banking professions. That concern strikes at the heart of what some faculty say is wrong with American business, as students seek short-term success in the marketplace of jobs instead of developing management careers.

The deep skepticism held by some professors about the value of consulting doesn't help.

"In what cases do you find that when the men in suits have gone through there are bodies

■ MBA
Continued from Page 1

all over the place? Hit men and consultants," says Jeffrey Pfeffer who teaches organizational behavior at Stanford.

"[Consultants] don't produce anything, they don't make anything. They argue that they are of value to the executives that hire them, but does that increase the value of the company?"

Management consulting firms are hired by corporations to do specific work such as strategic planning and marketing.

Partly as a result of Pfeffer's attitude, most top-flight business schools have now developed recruiting guidelines.

One person with strong opinions about those guidelines is, Bruce Henderson, chairman of the Boston Consulting Group. "I don't think it's the school's business to tell students who they can talk to and when they can talk to someone," says Henderson. "Are they age 3 or 4? My assumption is they are adults, so why should the schools care who they talk to?"

Henderson is still smarting from an incident in 1981, when his firm was kicked off the Stanford campus for a brief period for violating guidelines on recruiting first-year students.

That same year, Bain was under fire at Harvard when it was reprimanded by the administration for making "exploding offers" – offers that shrank in value the longer it took a student to say yes.

The annual rite begins each February. Interviews – and not classes – take center stage. First-year students are interviewed for lucrative summer jobs that pay as much as $1000 a week. Graduating MBAs encounter lofty offers of $50,000 and more for a year. Harvard reports a 1981 graduate took a job with an investment banking firm for $85,750.

Because of that kind of money, consultants have increased their desirability – so much so at the top business schools that they have become the most popular career choice. In 1980 more than a third of Stanford's MBAs signed up with consultants, and the hires were generally regarded as the cream of the class.

JEFFREY PFEFFER
Skeptical about consultants

"Do I want to go into consulting?" Michael Taylor, a first-year Stanford MBA student, looked surprised by the question, and then quickly nodded. "If I can go to work at a major consulting firm like Bain or McKinsey I'll meet and work with the top executives right away."

But professors say the cost to young careers is too high. While an entry-level job to middle management lacks the glamour and excitement of consulting, it's a much surer path to those top executive jobs, they say.

"Of the top 3500 executive jobs in America . . . only 30 or 40 came from consulting," said Bill Lear, who was chairman of the F&M Schaefer Brewing Company before he began career counseling for MBA students at Columbia University.

"The rest, more than 3000 people, came up through the ranks of line management," he said. "I have nothing against consulting or investment banking, if that's what someone wants to do for a whole career. But it's not a good stepping-stone.

"The trouble is you never learn a trade (other than consulting), and by the time you try to get out you may be too highly paid, and too spoiled to go down into a profit center and roll up your sleeves to learn about management."

Another concerned professor is Steven C. Wheelwright, who teaches manufacturing policy at Stanford Business School, and has also taught at Harvard.

"Here you have those who should be the best potential professional managers 10-15-20 years down the road doing the short-term stuff.

"[My students] tell me, 'The reason I'm taking a consulting job is I don't know what I want to do and make commitment for long haul, so I would rather make the quick money and then I can have some time, just as an outside observer.' That's the worst of the short-term management view."

And Tom Peters, best-selling author and lecturer at Stanford, puts it this way:

"Stanford goes on with this bull that we train general managers. That's an out-and-out lie. We don't."

Peters, who along with Robert Waterman wrote the successful book, "In Search of Excellence: Lessons From America's Best-Run Companies," is a management consultant himself, and a veteran of the top-level consulting firm, McKinsey & Co. But he's not blind to the effects of his own business.

"One of my students said last year: Stanford should not be called the graduate school of business – it ought to be called the graduate school of business analysis."

Which is just what the consultants and investment bankers want. The skills needed to get a honors grade in a business school case study are exactly those needed to analyze strategy for clients or to assess the value of a company for a merger, acquisition or stock offering for an investment banking house.

And while the spectacular starting salaries for consulting and investment banking reflect the bidding wars that go on in recruiting, they only partially explain why students choose these careers over hands-on line management.

Part of it is school culture. An offer from Bain, Boston Consulting Group, McKinsey, Morgan Stanley, First Boston or Goldman Sachs automatically certifies an MBA as among the very best. It's the ultimate high grade for whole *raison d'etre* of coming to business school: employment.

In fact some students seek these offers even if they have no intention of working the long hours or enduring the punishing travel that is often encountered by fledgling consultants and investment bankers.

"It's just good to get offers," said one second-year Harvard MBA.

Consultant to Stanford Prof: 'You space cadet'

The Globe's story May 2 on the hardball recruiting tactics purportedly used by some management consulting firms at significant business schools struck me as unfortunate.

The heart of the article comes in some entirely silly comments by one Professor Jeffrey Pfeffer of Stanford Business School who argues, "Consultants don't produce anything. They argue that they are of value to the executives that hire them, but does that increase the value of the company?" It's nice to know that California since Jerry Brown continues to produce space cadets.

Consultants are retained by firms for many reasons. Here are some of them:

- The recommendations we produce lead to enhanced efficiency, cost savings and improved sales – far in excess of our fees.
- We have the luxury of being candid, honest and objective. We tell it to executives like it is – bluntly and to the point. No one has ever argued that these traits are prominent in corporate settings.
- We have perspective on problems and solutions. Consultants with a national practice see more situations developing than regular employees. This is one of our chief values. We don't suffer from the corporate myopia which is such a distinctive feature of the current American business scene.
- We are cheap. When the problem is finished, we move on. Study after study shows that the American corporation is top-heavy with overpaid, purposeless executives. The same cannot be said of consultants.

The thrust of the article is that there is a dichotomy in business schools (and hence in business) between whiz-kid consultants and good solid managers. Rubbish! As the Globe's own recent spotlight investigation of the management of Big Steel showed, there is almost a criminal absence of managerial talent in our chief national industries.

I say it's too bad that these guys, and their facile apologists – and not consultants – are running the show.

People like me are out to change matters.

JEFFREY L. LANT
Jeffrey Lant Associates

Cambridge

This worked for us

Planning Partnership For The Elderly

by John Paul Marosy
and William Sen

IN 1982, Minuteman Home Care Corporation of Lexington, MA, made 136 new friends who contributed over $50,000 in support of our work to aid the elderly and handicapped. These new friends include 13 corporations, nine foundations and 114 individuals. We learned that a private fund drive, while unable to entirely replace state and federal funding, can provide benefits which go far beyond the dollars raised.

As the Area Agency on Aging for a 16-town area west of Boston (including the town of Lexington, where the Minuteman statue stands), our nonprofit agency has started creative home care, health, housing and legal programs to help elders continue to live in the dignity and independence of their own homes.

Early this year, the board of members voted unanimously to seek private funds to assure the start-up of a new service, Project Share-a-Ride (a coordinated transportation program involving 12 agencies), and to continue the existing levels of two others, Protective Services (aid to victims of elder abuse) and Home Delivered Meals. Future federal funding looked uncertain and we were determined to continue the development of needed cost-effective services. We selected as our most likely new supporters the growing high technology companies with plants in our service area, as well as several Boston-based foundations.

John Paul Marosy (right) and corporation and government officials greet the first wheelchair van for Project Share-a-Ride.

Active participation by the president of the board, Barbara K. Smith, was essential to the campaign's success. She and three staff members attended a workshop offered by Dr. Jeffrey Lant of Jeffrey Lant Associates, Inc., Cambridge. Using the procedures outlined in his book, *Development Today**, the board and staff began to recruit new supporters. Each of the board members contributed to the campaign, which helped in our approach to other groups.

The process used has four essential steps:

- Research the names of decision-makers in targeted organizations;
- Develop personal contacts with them;
- Send personalized letters to the contacts, with telephone follow-up;
- Coordinate public recognition with the development of services.

A few hours in the public library scanning the Standard and Poors Directory and the Foundation Directory for Massachusetts provided the names of officers and directors of the area's 20 largest companies and foundations. Board members reviewed these lists to identify personal and professional associates. Most of our board members are elders and long-time residents of the area and they knew a surprisingly large number of decision-makers.

A unique aspect of our fundraising effort was the receipt, early in the campaign, of a donation of $500 worth of word processing services in lieu of cash.

This gave us the ability to make each request for funds unique. Sample letters were typed and stored in the word processor memory. It was then possible to send a worksheet stating the name and address of the targeted potential donor, the paragraphs applicable to the request and the amount being requested.

Within a few weeks of the initial mailing, the Digital Equipment Company expressed its interest in helping. We launched the campaign at a press conference to publicly acknowledge the company's $5,000 gift.

A series of special events and press releases kept the campaign in the public eye until its conclusion at our September annual meeting. We found that the key to success is thorough and persistent follow-up. Contributions were received from one out of five of the companies and foundations we contacted.

Successful fundraising by a medium-size, nonprofit agency like ours is feasible if its goals are clear and its board members take an active part. Private funding gives flexibility and options for innovations not normally available with government categorical funds.

In 1983, we hope to involve our new partners in a search for adequate office space and in mapping out a service marketing strategy as part of our 3-year area plan on aging. In the process, we are helping them to see that their private dollars and expertise can complement the conscientious use of essential federal and state funding for basic services. ■

John Paul Marosy is executive director and William Sen a board member of Minuteman Home Care Corporation, 20 Pelham Rd., Lexington, MA 02173.

**"Development Today" is published by JLA, 50 Follen St., Suite 507, Cambridge, MA 02138.*

$24.95 + $1.50
postage and handling

Human Development News, November-December 1982

50 FOLLEN STREET, SUITE 507 • CAMBRIDGE, MASSACHUSETTS 02138
(617) 547-6372

Jeffrey Lant Associates, Inc.

WINTER
1981-2

CVNA The Independent

CAMBRIDGE VISITING NURSING ASSOCIATION

76, Going on 176

Committee of Permanent Charity, Cambridge Trust, Hyams Trust, Old Colony Charitable Foundation, Cambridge Foundation, Prudential Insurance, A.C. Ratshesky Foundation, Arthur D. Little Foundation, one anonymous foundation, and scores of individuals - thank you, one and all. Your generous contributions - totalling over **$70,000** - put CVNA well on its way toward its capital fund drive goal of $100,000. And, thank you, Dr. Lant, our very effective fund raising consultant. CVNA has been in the same building at 35 Bigelow Street for 76 years. Now, through the help of these foundations and individuals, we begin the next 76 years - and more - able to effectively, efficiently reach more people in Cambridge with caring, professional assistance.

SAMPLE BIRTHDAY PARTY INVITATION

Dr. Jeffrey Lant

requests the pleasure of your company

at a party celebrating:

- *The Publication of "Development Today: A Guide For Nonprofit Organizations"*
- *The Completion of his Portrait by Pietro Pezzati*
- *The Preview Performance of a New Musical Work dedicated to him by Rodney Lister, and*
- *His 36th Birthday – The Gateway to Middle Age*

Thursday, February 17, 1983

Cocktails 6pm - 9pm

The Signet Society
46 Dunster Street
Cambridge, Mass.

R.S.V.P. - (617) 547-6372

SAMPLE BIRTHDAY PARTY MEDIA RELEASE

LANT PORTRAIT BY PEZZATI TO BE UNVEILED FEBRUARY 17TH

On Thursday, February 17 at an afternoon party at The Signet Society, Harvard, Pietro Pezzati, the well-known Boston painter, will unveil his newly-finished portrait of Jeffrey Lant. Lant commissioned octogenarian Pezzati to do his portrait last fall, and the work, 40" by 48" (exclusive of frame), was completed in December, 1982. The forthcoming occasion will be its first showing.

"I'm thrilled by the result," Lant said. "Mr Pezzati has not merely captured a likeness, he has done something infinitely more difficult -- he has caught a glimpse of my soul." Lant declined to give further details of the portrait until its unveiling.

Pietro Pezzati (known familiarly as "Peter") was born in Boston in September, 1902. He attended Boston schools, including the Child-Walker School of Art where he first became acquainted with the noted Boston painter Charles Hopkinson, well known for his boldly innovative art. This introduction was the turning point of his life, for Hopkinson first undertook to give Pezzati further study in his distinctive techniques and later invited him to share his studio at the then newly-constructed Fenway Studios.

Eminent American after eminent American came to this studio to be painted, including President Calvin Coolidge. "He wasn't nearly as taciturn as people usually think" Pezzati said. "And Mrs Coolidge -- Grace was her name -- was positively engaging -- and quite chatty." Pezzati still works in the same studio.

Pezzati has specialized throughout his long, distinguished career in creating portraits in oil, particularly official portraits. His work is represented in the Fogg Museum at Harvard, Harvard Business School, Harvard Medical School, The Harvard Club of Boston, Phillips Academy, Yale Medical School, Massachusetts General Hospital, the law offices of Hale & Dorr and Goodwin, Proctor and Hoar, the Clowes Collection of the Indianapolis Museum of Art, Boston City Hospital and in dozens of other institutions around the country. His portrait of former Navy Secretary Charles Francis Adams hangs in the wardroom of the missile destroyer of the same name.

His work has also been exhibited at the Vose, Child and Brown Galleries and, nationally, at the Corcoran Biennial in Washington, D.C., the Pennsylvania Academy Annual and the New York World's Fair as well as through many groups and one-man shows.

How many commissions from private individuals has Pezzati undertaken? "Oh, my," he said. "I can't remember any more, but there have been dozens and dozens."

Pezzati said of his newest portrait, "I am delighted that Dr Lant has chosen an unconventional pose for his picture. It is unusual enough nowadays for a man of his young age to be painted -- though common enough earlier in the century when Sargent, say, was working -- but this portrait is striking both because of its dramatic combination of monochromatic elements and rich, alluring color and its striking air of artful artlessness." Like Lant, Pezzati declined to give further details of his portrait beyond saying, "I think it's one of my best!"

SAMPLE BIRTHDAY PARTY MEDIA RELEASE

SOMERVILLE COMPOSER TO PREVIEW WORK IN HONOR OF AUTHOR LANT'S BIRTHDAY

The young and rising Somerville composer Rodney Lister has composed an unusual birthday present for his friend Jeffrey Lant which will be previewed on February 17th on the occasion of Dr Lant's 36th birthday -- a song entitled "From The Sea and The Mirror: The Botswain and the Mate."

Based on a selection from a poem of the well-known poet W.H. Auden, Lister has composed a lively three-minute work which brilliantly evokes traditional sailors' songs. The poem itself is a parody of a song sung by the Botswain and his Mate in Shakespeare's play "The Tempest." "The Tempest" is the source of the title of Dr Lant's first book INSUBSTANTIAL PAGEANT (subtitled CEREMONY AND CONFUSION AT QUEEN VICTORIA'S COURT.) "The link was an excellent inspiration," the 31 year old Lister said. "This composition is a wonderful mélange of some of the most fertile minds of history -- Shakespeare, Auden, Lant, and me!"

Lister, the former Leonard Bernstein Fellow, has had his music performed both in the United States and abroad. Educated at the New England Conservatory and Brandeis University, Lister has studied with the well-known composers Virgil Thomson, Donald Martino, and Peter Maxwell Davies. Davies has called him "a composer of enormous promise and individuality" and commissioned him to do a piece -- "A Little Cowboy Music Too" -- for his ensemble, The Fires of London. Lister is collaborating with Davies and Peter Sellers, the audacious wunderkind director, in the American premier of Davies' work "The Yellow Cake Review" on February 25 and 27 under the auspices of the newly-formed Music Production Co.

Assisting the composer on February 17th will be mezzo-soprano Mary Kendrick Sego, violinist Joel Smirnoff of the Boston Symphony, and clarinetist Ian Greitzer. Mr Lister will be at the piano.

The first performance of "The Botswain and the Mate" will take place on February 25 at 8 p.m. and will be repeated on February 27 at Emmanuel Church, 15 Newbury Street, Boston. Tickets are available at the door for $6 and $4. "It's alot cheaper to hear the piece at Jeffrey's party," Lister acknowledged, "but it's harder to get invited."

The Boston Herald
January 26, 1983

Immodest

JACK-O-LANT: No one could ever accuse author **Jeffrey Lant** of hiding his light under a bushel. The never-modest Cambridge consultant is throwing himself a 36th birthday party, has commissioned a portrait by **Pietro Pezzati** ("he has caught my soul"!), will preview a performance of a new musical work dedicated to him by Somerville composer **Rodney Lister** (. . . inspired "by some of the most fertile minds of history —Shakespeare, Auden, Lant and me!" lisped Lister) to certify he's 36.

"The gateway to middle age," moaned Lant.

Not one to waste postage, Lant thoughtfully tucked a press release on his latest book, "Development Today," in with his birthday invitation.

"Written by a master," burbled the book blurb written by the same master: Jeffrey Lant. So much for not hiding one's light under a Lant-ern.

The Cambridge Express March 5, 1983

One of **T.S. Eliot's** (Harvard, class of 1910) old haunts, The Signet Club was the site of another celebration—this one a birthday—for **Dr. Jeffrey Lant**, author of *Development Today! A Guide for Non-Profit Organizations.* Calling his birthday "the gateway to middle age," Lant enlisted as a celebrant none other than **Mayor Alfred Vellucci**. Hizzoner, having proclaimed Feb. 17 "Jeffrey Lant Day," then waxed sentimental about Cambridge, calling it "the Florence of the Western Hemisphere."

.... To further the Italian connection, another Pietro Pietro Pezzati, the famous portrait artist, was also in attendance for the unveiling of his portrait of Dr. Lant, lending credibility to the Mayor's claim . . . and we always thought we lived in the Athens of America. Oh well, it's nice to be here anyhow. We might add that Lant's birthday cake read "Jeffrey-Bright Star Over Cambridge" . . . and that's the kind of night it was.

ABOUT THE AUTHOR

Jeffrey L. Lant is President of Jeffrey Lant Associates, Inc., a management and development firm for nonprofit organizations, based in Cambridge, Massachusetts. He received his B.A. degree *summa cum laude* from the University of California, Santa Barbara; a Certificate of Advanced Graduate Studies in Higher Education Administration from Northeastern University, Boston; and M.A. and Ph.D. degrees from Harvard University, where he was Woodrow Wilson Fellow, Harvard Prize Fellow, and winner of Harvard College's Master's Award. Before forming JLA, Dr. Lant taught and/or administered at Harvard, Boston College and Northeastern University. Dr. Lant is included in *Who's Who in the East, The Dictionary of International Biography, The International Who's Who of Intellectuals, Men and Women of Distinction, The Book of Honor, Contemporary Authors, Who's Who in Finance and Industry,* and other biographical guides. He is also the author of *The Consultant's Kit: Establishing and Operating Your Successful Consulting Business* and *Insubstantial Pageant: Ceremony and Confusion at Queen Victoria's Court.* He is both the Editor of *Our Harvard: Reflection On College Life By Twenty-Two Distinguished Graduates* (Taplinger, 1982) and General Editor of the JLA Nonprofit Technical Assistance Series. In June, 1982, the Governor of Massachusetts awarded him an Official Citation in recognition of his "services to independent business people." He has also been honored by the Boston City Council, the Massachusetts House of Representatives, and the City of Cambridge. The Associated Press has called him "one of the top consultants in the country." He is associated with over 20 American colleges and universities through the Mobile University of which he is president.

OTHER JLA PUBLICATIONS, SERVICES AND PRODUCTS

AN INTRODUCTION TO PLANNED GIVING: FUND RAISING THROUGH BEQUESTS, CHARITABLE REMAINDER TRUSTS, GIFT ANNUITIES AND LIFE INSURANCE

Edited by Daniel W. Vecchitto

Nonprofit Technical Assistance Series
Volume II

This new book with contributions by eight development experts comes in the nick of time for nonprofit America. Heres's information on:

- Starting a planned giving program
- Bequests
- Charitable remainder unitrusts
- Pooled income funds
- Gift annuities
- Life insurance
- Marketing a planned giving program
- Selling investment objectives to donors

AN INTRODUCTION TO PLANNED GIVING has two purposes: to assist the more than 80% of Americans who die without adequate estate plans, thereby leaving billions of dollars for the probate courts to distribute. These Americans could save taxes, enhance their families' finncial security, and help their favorite charities with a planned gift. This book is also a vital tool enabling nonprofit organizations to find the extra resources they need during an extended period of financial adversity.

AN INTRODUCTION TO PLANNED GIVING offers immediately-usable information on:

- Avoiding unnecessary taxes on income, capital gains and estates
- Charitable gifts that pay donors income for life
- Proven techniques for building productive relationships between donors and charities

"Excellent!" *Grantsmanship Center News*

Excerpted in *Foundation News*

THE CONSULTANT'S KIT: ESTABLISHING AND OPERATING YOUR SUCCESSFUL CONSULTING BUSINESS

By Dr. Jeffrey L. Lant

"Jeffrey Lant provides the ultimate advice on giving advice."

Cleveland Press

Jeffrey Lant, president of a Cambridge, Massachusetts management and development firm for nonprofit organizations, is also nationally recognized as "the consultant's consultant." Now he has written the book that contains the essentials of part-time or full-time consulting success in your own field of interest and expertise. In **THE CONSULTANT'S KIT** you'll find critical information about:

- Determining your optimal consulting skills
- Learning to make other people's needs your opportunities
- Networking for success
- Effective marketing techniques
- Becoming *the* recognized expert in your field
- Negotiating for success
- Developing the right contract for you and your client
- Independent contractors: using and controlling them
- Creating an efficient office with the right image
- The legal form of your business
- Increasing your income through workshops and publications

"**THE CONSULTANT'S KIT** is info-packed . . . Lant's own style is fascinating."

Hartford Advocate

"Brimming with key market techniques . . . Opens new vistas in this fascinating occupation. Worth every penny!" *Best Sellers Magazine*

"Jeffrey Lant is a consulting pioneer!" *Boston Herald American*

"One of the Best Business Books of 1982" *Boston Globe*

"Jeffrey Lant is one of the top consultants in the country." *The Associated Press*

"Jeffrey Lant, that happy, indominable self-help hormone let loose in the consulting arteries of America." *Boston Magazine*

DEVELOPMENT TODAY: A GUIDE FOR NONPROFIT ORGANIZATIONS

by Dr. Jeffrey Lant

"Jeffrey Lant has fashioned a career of telling charities, worthy causes, and dreamers of the day how to grab big bucks at a time when they are simply not be had."

Boston Globe

If you run a nonprofit organization, serve on the board of a a nonprofit organization, are employed by a nonprofit organization, benefit from a nonprofit organization, or care about the distinctive contributions of nonprofit organizations to American life — this book is for you.

DEVELOPMENT TODAY Is Needed

Reaganomics, shrinking resources, a muddled economy are all threatening both the work and even the existence of America's nonprofit organizations — schools, colleges, hospitals, arts groups, civic betterment societies of every kind. These threatening circumstances have caused many such organizations to go out of business; many more have had to reduce their programs — with as yet incalculable effects on our society. If there was ever a moment in the history of the nonprofit idea for tested, economical fund raising methods, that moment is *now*. **DEVELOPMENT TODAY** fulfills this pressing need.

DEVELOPMENT TODAY Is Complete

Here, at last, is single book containing all the essential information needed by a nonprofit organization for successful fund raising from individuals, corporations and foundations. In it you'll find practical, useful information on:

- organizing an agency fund raising planning process
- producing inexpensive, compelling fund raising documents
- who to involve in the fund raising process and what they should do
- getting leads to corporate and foundation funding sources
- organizing and coordinating your fund raising effort
- training volunteer solicitors
- ensuring a successful capital fund drive
- arranging popular, lucrative special events
- how to make direct mail work for your organization
- the best way to apply for federal grants

and much, much more.

DEVELOPMENT TODAY Is Unique

DEVELOPMENT TODAY is not theoretical. It is designed to be a working tool for nonprofit organizations needing money. Part of its usefulness is its extensive samples section — over 70 pages of materials which can be put to work right now to help you raise money: successful fund raising documents, letters to funding sources, training materials for volunteer solicitors, pledge cards, log forms, contracts questionnaires, to name only a few — all the pattern documents an agency needs and which are often so difficult to create. No other book on the market offers such an array of practical materials.

DEVELOPMENT TODAY Is Written By A Master

Dr. Jeffrey Lant is well known to nonprofit organizations for his innovative work solving their problems. **DEVELOPMENT TODAY** sets out — in the author's characteristically trenchant style — information gleened from years of effort and experience with dozens of organizations nationwide.

GUIDELINES FOR EFFECTIVE WRITING: QUALITIES AND FORMATS

By Professors Walter Lubars and Albert Sullivan

Without good writing skills, an organization will always have severe problems with its public relations, document development, and all internal communications. Here's the book to help you forestall such unnecessary, expensive problems and enhance all your written communications. Find out through **GUIDELINES FOR EFFECTIVE WRITING** about:

- Crispness: how to eliminate the redundant, banal, diffuse and vague
- Flow: the use of transitions to increase smoothness
- Organization: tips on research, planning, organizing your notes
- Readability: practical rules to keep your reader reading all the way
- Clarity: how to communicate what you really mean
- Color: tips on how to add "style" to your style
- Dynamic punctuation: a new look at how marks move the reader and arouse his interest
- Revising and polishing: eight tips on how to edit and revise your drafts to make them crisp, flowing, properly organized, readable, clear, colorful, vivid and mechanically correct.

JLA WORKSHOPS

For Nonprofit Organizations

Development Training Workshop: This program, originated by Dr. Jeffrey Lant, has been offered in more than 40 cities around the country. Based on **Development Today** and using Dr. Lant's latest research about fund raising, this program deals with raising money from individuals, corporations and foundations. It may be offered either as a one-day intensive program or crafted as a longer or shorter program as needed by your organization. It can also be offered as part of an organization's state, regional or national convention. Discounts are available on texts for programs of over 20 participants. Here's what some participants have said of the program:

> "Informal, lively, exciting . . . Dr. Jeffrey Lant will be so sought after it's going to be hard to get into his classes."
>
> Larry Roberts, President
> Northeastern Christian Junior College
> Villanova, PA

> "The Development Training Workshop has got to be one of the best workshops in the field today. I was amazed at the voluminous amount of information and the practicality of it all!"
>
> Kevin Frederick
> The King's Daughter's School
> Columbia, Tennessee

> "Gave me a lot of practical advice . . . addressed the concerns of my organization . . . and with humor!"
>
> Mary Ann Larkin, Chairperson of Development
> The Watershed Foundation
> Washington, D.C.

Introduction to Planned Giving Workshop: This program is designed to clear up the confusion about a much-misunderstood field and tap new sources of support for hard-pressed organizations. Like the Development Training Workshop, this program can either be a one-day intensive session or may be used in connection with your state, regional or national convention. The following critical topics are covered:

- Why the Economic Recovery Act of 1981 makes planned giving increasingly popular with donors.
- Why it is now more important than ever for charitable organizations to develop viable planning giving programs.
- Making different donor assets work both for the donor and the institution. What to do with real estate, jewelry, art, antiques, as well as cash and securities.
- Charitable bequests: types and tax benefits
- Charitable remainder unitrust and annuity trusts: definitions, examples, and tax implications.
- The planned giving program in a general development effort: how to get it successfully off the ground.

- Specific attention is also given to:

  — pooled income funds
  — charitable lead trusts
  — gifts of life insurance
  — retained life estates

Each workshop participant is given as part of the tuition a copy of JLA's unique publication *An Introduction To Planned Giving* which has been excerpted in both *Foundation News* and the *Journal* of the National Society of Fund Raising Executive.

For Individuals Interested in Part-Time Or Full-Time Consulting

Establishing And Operating Your Successful Consulting Business Workshop: This popular program, already offered in 30 states, provided both established and aspiring consultants the information they need to launch successful part-time or full-time consulting practices. It includes information on:

- determining optimal consulting skills
- selecting a specialty
- getting a first assignment
- how much to charge
- how to avoid giving away free advice
- marketing
- exploiting the media to become *the* recognized expert in your field
- building a Supergroup of independent contractors
- expanding into related fields
- when to subcontract
- noncompetitive agreements
- writing successful proposals
- standardized contracts
- cooperative marketing plans
- setting up an office

In addition to the regular workshop schedule, JLA can book this program into your organization's meetings and conventions as a special feature.

For specific times and places of forthcoming workshops, write JLA for information or call (617) 547-6372.

For Individuals And Organizations Interested in Publicity And Public Relations

The Unabashed Self-Promoter's Workshop is Dr. Jeffrey Lant's newest program. Based on the book of the same name, this workshop is now being offered around the country through The Mobile University, JLA's noncredit continuing education program.

This is the course no one can afford to miss who has a message they want America to hear, a product or service they want America to buy. It includes information about:

- prerequisites for promotional success
- fashioning a Quintessential American Success Image
- information sources
- how to create a Standard Media Kit
- the three basic article formats by you
- how to get articles by you published
- arranging and handling the print media interview
- piggybacking and multiple use
- electronic media options
- arranging your media wave
- and much, much more.

Dr. Jeffrey Lant is widely regarded as one of the top workshop and platform speakers in the country as participants in his programs consistently affirm. In this program you can learn the methods which have made him continually sought after by the media.

Products And Services Recommended By Dr. Jeffrey Lant

For Publicity-Seekers

THE PUBLICITY MANUAL by Kate Kelly. One of the best-known volumes in public relations. This is a book you'll want to have in your publicity library.

For Consultants, Independent Service Providers, And Entrepreneurs

THE CONSULTING OPPORTUNITIES JOURNAL. *The* essential publication for consultants and entrepreneurs of every description. Order through JLA and receive — free! — the report on "Marketing Your Consultancy: How To Establish Yourself As The Expert."

For Individuals And Organizations Needing Equipment Of Any Kind

U.S. GOVERNMENT SURPLUS: A COMPLETE BUYER'S MANUAL BY J. Senay. Information on how individuals and organizations can acquire at a fraction of its value government surplus.

For Individuals Interested In Multi-Level Marketing Opportunities

If you are interested in breaking into Multi-Level Marketing, one of the fastest ways to escape the time trap and build a national sales force, JLA maintains a list of recommended companies. If approved, you will work with Dr. Jeffrey Lant in the development of your sales force.

ORDER FORM

1. **THE CONSULTANT'S KIT: ESTABLISHING AND OPERATING YOUR SUCCESSFUL CONSULTING BUSINESS** by Dr. Jeffrey Lant (ISBN 0-94037-00-5) $30.00 .... ________

2. **DEVELOPMENT TODAY: A GUIDE FOR NONPROFIT ORGANIZATIONS** by Dr. Jeffrey Lant (ISBN 0-940374-01-3) $24.95 .... ________

3. **AN INTRODUCTION TO PLANNED GIVING: FUND RAISING THROUGH BEQUESTS, CHARITABLE REMAINDER TRUSTS, GIFT ANNUITIES, AND LIFE INSURANCE** Edited by Daniel Vecchitto (ISBN 0-940374-02-01) $24.95 .... ________

4. **GUIDELINES FOR EFFECTIVE WRITING: QUALITIES AND FORMATS** by Professors Walter Lubars and Albert Sullivan $10.00 .... ________

5. **THE UNABASHED SELF-PROMOTER'S GUIDE: WHAT EVERY MAN, WOMAN, CHILD, AND ORGANIZATION IN AMERICA NEEDS TO KNOW ABOUT GETTING AHEAD BY EXPLOITING THE MEDIA** by Dr. Jeffrey Lant (ISBN 0-94034-06-4) $30.00 .... ________

6. **PROFESSIONAL'S GUIDE TO PUBLIC RELATIONS SERVICES** by Richard Weiner. 4th edition (ISBN 091-3046-108) $60.00 .... ________

7. **PROFESSIONAL'S GUIDE TO PUBLICITY** by Richard Weiner. 3rd edition (ISBN 0-913046-07-8) $9.50 .... ________

8. **THE PUBLICITY MANUAL** by Kate Kelly (ISBN 0-9603740-1-9) $29.95 .... ________

9. **OXBRIDGE DIRECTORY OF NEWSLETTERS** (ISBN 0-917460-11-1) $60 .... ________

10. **U.S. GOVERNMENT SURPLUS: A COMPLETE BUYER'S MANUAL** by J. Senay $7.95 .... ________

11. **CONSULTING OPPORTUNITIES JOURNAL** $24.00 one year
$39.00 two years .... ________

TOTAL ________

Please make your check payable to JEFFREY LANT ASSOCIATES, INC. When ordering items 1-10 above please add $1.50 postage and handling for any one, $2.50 for any two, and $3 for any three or more. Massachusetts residents add 5% sales tax.

INFORMATION

I would like additional information about the items listed above: (please specify) ____________

Please send information about:

1. Publicity services offered by JLA and Dr. Jeffrey Lant ________
2. JLA Nonprofit Technical Assistance ________
3. Unabashed Self-Promoter's Workshop ________
4. Establishing and Operating your Successful Consulting Business Workshop ________
5. Development Training Workshop ________
6. Planned Giving Workshop ________
7. Multi-Level marketing opportunities recommended by JLA ________
8. I belong to an organization which may be interested in having Dr. Jeffrey Lant as a guest speaker. Please contact me. ________

Name ____

Address ____

City/Town ________ State ________ Zip ________

Telephone (area code) ____________________ (number) ____________________